THE RESTORATION OF CREATION
IN CHRIST

The Restoration of Creation in Christ

Essays in Honor of Dean O. Wenthe

Edited by
Arthur A. Just Jr. and Paul J. Grime

CONCORDIA PUBLISHING HOUSE · SAINT LOUIS

© 2014 Concordia Publishing House
3558 S. Jefferson Ave.
St. Louis, MO 63118-3968
1-800-325-3040 • www.cph.org

Unless otherwise indicated, all Scripture quotations are from The ESV Bible® (The Holy Bible, English Standard Version®), copyright © 2001 by Crossway Bibles, a publishing ministry of Good News Publishers. Used by permission. All rights reserved.

Scripture quotations taken from the New American Standard Bible®, Copyright © 1960, 1962, 1963, 1968, 1971, 1972, 1973, 1975, 1977, 1995 by The Lockman Foundation. Used by permission (www.Lockman.org).

Unless otherwise noted, the quotations from the Lutheran Confessions in this publication are from *The Book of Concord: The Confessions of the Evangelical Lutheran Church*, edited by Theodore G. Tappert, published in 1959 by Fortress Press.

Pages xxvi–xxvii: Composite mosaic photos: Steve Blakey, BB Design, Inc., Fort Wayne, Indiana.

Pages 26–32: Translation based on Sources Chrétiennes, vol. 187. Copyright ©1972 Les Éditions du CERF. Used with permission.

Page 230: Copyright © 2003 John Webster. Reprinted with the permission of Cambridge University Press.

Page 231, note 12: Copyright © Bernd Wannenwetsch, ed. 2009, *Who Am I? Bonhoeffer's Theology through His Poetry*. T&T Clark, by permission of Bloomsbury Publishing Plc.

Pages 244–45: Brian Wren, *Piece Together Praise: A Theological Journey—Poems and Hymns Thematically Arranged* . London: Stainer and Bell Ltd., 1996; co-published with Hope Publishing Company.

A version of the final essay, "Jesus: The Second and Greater Adam" (pp. 307–16), previously appeared in *Modern Reformation* 22, no. 6 (November/December 2013): 40–45 (http://www. modernreformation.org). The editors express their thanks for permission to include this expanded article here.

This work uses the SBL Hebrew Unicode font developed by the Font Foundation under the leadership of the Society of Biblical Literature. For further information on this font or on becoming a Font Foundation member, see http://www.sbl-site.org/educational/biblicalfonts.aspx

Manufactured in the United States of America

1 2 3 4 5 6 7 8 9 10   23 22 21 20 19 18 17 16 15 14

CONTENTS

ABBREVIATIONS

AC — Augsburg Confession

AE — Luther, Martin. *Luther's Works.* American Edition. Vols. 1–30: Edited by Jaroslav Pelikan. St. Louis: Concordia, 1955–76. Vols. 31–55: Edited by Helmut Lehmann. Philadelphia: Muhlenberg/Fortress, 1957–86.

ANF — *The Ante-Nicene Fathers.* Edited by A. Robert and J. Donaldson. 10 vols. Buffalo: The Christina Literature Publishing Company, 1885–96. Reprint, Peabody, MA: Hendrickson, 1994.

Ap — Apology of the Augsburg Confession

CSSB — *Concordia Self-Study Bible.* General editor, Robert G. Hoeber. St. Louis: Concordia, 1986.

CSEL — *Corpus scriptorum ecclesiasticorum Latinorum.* Vienna: Verlag der Österreichischen Akademie der Wissenschaften, 1866–.

CTS — Concordia Theological Seminary, Fort Wayne

DBW — Dietrich Bonhoeffer Works. 16 vols. General editor Wayne W. Floyd. Minneapolis: Fortress Press, 1998–2013.

Ep — Epitome of the Formula of Concord

FC — Formula of Concord

LCMS — The Lutheran Church—Missouri Synod

NPNF[1] — *A Select Library of the Christian Church: Nicene and Post-Nicene Fathers.* Series 1. Edited by P. Schaff. 14 vols. New York, 1886–89. Reprint, Peabody, MA: Hendrickson, 1994.

NPNF²   *A Select Library of the Christian Church: Nicene and Post-Nicene Fathers*. Series 2. Edited by P. Schaff and H. Wace. 14 vols. New York, 1890–1900. Reprint, Peabody, MA: Hendrickson, 1994.

PG   *Patrologia Graeca*. Edited by J.-P. Migne. 161 vols. Paris, 1857–66.

PL   *Patrologia Latina*. Edited by J.-P. Migne. 217 vols. Paris, 1844–55.

SA   Smalcald Articles

SC   *Sources Chrétiennes*. Edited by the Institut des Sources Chrétiennes. 563 vols. Paris: Éditions du CERF, 1942–.

SD   Solid Declaration of the Formula of Concord

TLSB   *The Lutheran Study Bible*. General editor, Edward A. Engelbrecht. St. Louis: Concordia, 2009.

WA   *D. Martin Luthers Werke: Kritische Gesamtausgabe*. 73 vols. in 85. Wiemar: Hermann Böhlau, 1883–.

CONTRIBUTORS

Dean Wenthe's life has been defined by his tenure as professor and president of Concordia Theological Seminary in Fort Wayne, Indiana. Of the nineteen contributors to his festschrift, seventeen of them are also defined by their relationship to him through CTS: nine contributors were called to be professors during his presidency, most of whom were previously his students (Bushur, Gieschen, Grime, Pless, Quill, Rast, Roethemeyer, P. Scaer, Ziegler), four other essayists are also former students (Gard, Harrison, Just, Murray), two have been his colleagues since the early years when the seminary was in Springfield, Illinois (D. Scaer, Weinrich), and two received their honorary doctorates during his presidency (Kleinig, Obare). The other two contributors' relationships to Dean Wenthe are through editorial work on Concordia Commentary with Concordia Publishing House (Mitchell), and as a colleague from Concordia Seminary, St. Louis, who also happens to be a shirt-tail relative (Egger).

James G. Bushur serves on the faculty of CTS as Assistant Professor of Historical Theology and Director of Deaconess Studies. He served as pastor of two congregations in Indiana (1994–2006). He received his M.Div. (1993) and S.T.M. (1998) at CTS and his Ph.D. at the University of Durham, UK (2010). Dr. Bushur specializes in patristics studies and is a member of the North American Patristics Society. He was called to the faculty of CTS in 2006.

Thomas J. Egger has served on the faculty of Concordia Seminary, St. Louis, Missouri, as assistant professor of exegetical theology since 2005. He served as pastor at Zion Lutheran Church in Storm Lake, Iowa (2000–2005). He received his M.Div. from Concordia Seminary in 1997. He was a guest instructor at Concordia Lutheran Seminary, Edmonton, Alberta, Canada, in 1999. He has served as academic advisor to first-year seminary students since 2010. Professor Egger's sister is married to Dean Wenthe's son, Matthew.

Daniel L. Gard serves on the faculty of CTS as Professor of Exegetical Theology. He served as pastor of St. Paul Lutheran Church, Woodland, Indiana. He is a 1984 graduate of CTS and holds a Ph.D. in Hebrew Bible/Judaica with minors in New Testament and Liturgics from the University of Notre Dame (1992), where he was a colleague of Dr. Wenthe. Dr. Gard is a Rear Admiral in the U.S. Naval Reserves and serves as the seminary's Dean of Military Chaplaincy Programs.

Charles A. Gieschen serves on the faculty of CTS as Professor of Exegetical Theology and Academic Dean. Before coming to the seminary, he was Associate and then Senior Pastor of Trinity Lutheran Church in Traverse City, Michigan (1985–96). He received his M.Div. from CTS (1984), his Th.M. at Princeton Theological Seminary (1985), and his Ph.D. from the Department of Near Eastern Studies at the University of Michigan (1995). Dr. Gieschen serves on the American Editorial Board of the journal *HENOCH: Studies in Judaism and Christianity from Second Temple to Late Antiquity*. He is a member of the Society of Biblical Literature and the International Enoch Seminar. He was called to the faculty of CTS in 1996 at the beginning of the presidency of Dean Wenthe.

Paul J. Grime serves on the faculty of CTS as Dean of the Chapel and teaches in the Pastoral Ministry and Missions department. He has a Bachelor of Music degree in organ performance and church music from Valparaiso University, a Master of Music in organ performance from the College-Conservatory of Music at the University of Cincinnati, his M.Div. (1986) and S.T.M. (1987) from CTS, and a Ph.D. in Religious Studies from Marquette University (1994). He served as pastor of St. Paul's Lutheran Church in West Allis, Wisconsin from 1987 to 1996. Dr. Grime served as Executive Director for the LCMS Commission on Worship in St. Louis. During his tenure he served as project director, first for the development of *Hymnal Supplement 98* and then for *Lutheran Service Book*, the Synod's new hymnal, and for all of its companion volumes, which were published in 2006 and 2007. He was called to the faculty of CTS in 2007.

Matthew C. Harrison serves as the thirteen president of The Lutheran Church—Missouri Synod. He served as a pastor at St. Peter's Lutheran Church in Westgate, Iowa (1991–95), and Zion Lutheran Church in Fort Wayne, Indiana (1995–2001). He joined the staff at the LCMS International Center in St. Louis in 2001 as the Executive Director of the Synod's former World Relief and Human Care ministry. President Harrison received his M.Div. degree from CTS in 1989 and his S.T.M. in 1991. In 2011, he received two honorary doctorates: a Doctor of Laws from Concordia University, Ann Arbor, Michigan, and a Doctor of Divinity from CTS. He is a prolific writer whose books include *A Little Book on Joy* and *Christ Have Mercy: How to Put Your Faith in Action*. He compiled and translated *At Home in the House of My Fathers*, a collection of sermons, essays, addresses, and letters by the first five presidents of the LCMS, and edited *The Lonely Way: Selected Essays and Letters* by Hermann Sasse. President Harrison was a student of Dean Wenthe.

Arthur A. Just Jr. serves on the faculty of CTS as Professor and Chairman of Exegetical Theology, and Co-Director of the Good Shepherd Institute of Pastoral Theology and Sacred Music. Prior to being called to CTS in 1984, he served as pastor of Grace Lutheran Church in Middletown, Connecticut from 1980 to 1984. He received his M.Div. from CTS in 1980, his S.T.M. from Yale Divinity School in 1984, and his Ph.D. from the University of Durham in England in 1990 in the New Testament. Dr. Just served as Dean of the Chapel (2000–2007) and Director of Deaconess Studies (2003–11) at CTS. He published a two-volume commentary on the Gospel of Luke for the *Concordia Commentary* series (1996, 1997) and the Lukan volume for the *Ancient Christian Commentary on Scripture.*

John W. Kleinig served as a lecturer at the Australian Lutheran College, formerly Luther Seminary, beginning in 1982. He retired from full-time teaching at the end of 2009 and is now engaged in writing a commentary on Hebrews. He was one of the seventeen students in Luther Seminary's first graduating class in 1968. After his ordination in 1969 he was called to serve as chaplain at Luther College, Melbourne (1969–72), and later at St. Peter's College, Brisbane (1973–79). He received an M.Phil. (1982) and a Ph.D. (1990) from the University of

Cambridge. In addition to his commentary on Leviticus for the *Concordia Commentary* series (2003), he published *Grace Upon Grace: Spirituality for Today* (2008) on the nature and practice of evangelical piety. Dr. Kleinig received a Doctor of Divinity degree from CTS in 1998 during the presidency of Dean Wenthe.

Christopher W. Mitchell serves at Concordia Publishing House, St. Louis, Missouri, as editor of the Concordia Commentary series. He studied at the University of Wisconsin—Madison (B.S., M.A., Ph.D. in Hebrew and Semitic studies) and Concordia Seminary, St. Louis, Missouri (M.Div.). He published a commentary on the Song of Songs for the *Concordia Commentary* series (2003) and has served alongside Dean Wenthe as in-house editor of the Concordia Commentary series from its inception in the 1990s.

Scott R. Murray has served as Senior Pastor at Memorial Lutheran Church and School, Houston, Texas, since 1996, following pastorates in Cobourg, Ontario, Canada, and New Orleans, Louisiana. He received his B.A. from Concordia College, Ann Arbor; the M.Div. from CTS, an M.A. from Loyola University, New Orleans; and the Ph.D. from New Orleans Baptist Seminary, New Orleans. He writes the "Memorial Moment," a daily devotion based on the church fathers, which is distributed to an international list of more than 1400 subscribers. Presently, he is the Chair of the Luther Academy Board of Directors. He is the author of numerous journal articles as well as several books: *Law, Life, and the Living God* (Concordia, 2002) and *A Year with the Church Fathers* (Concordia, 2011). He is Fourth Vice-President of The Lutheran Church—Missouri Synod (2010–present).

Walter Obare Omwanza is presiding archbishop of the Evangelical Lutheran Church in Kenya. He studied at Matongo Lutheran Theological College (MLTC) and graduated with a General Certificate in Theology in 1978. He was ordained as a pastor in 1982, after which he served as a parish pastor in nine congregations simultaneously. In 1991 he again studied at MLTC, where he received a Higher Diploma in Theology (1993) and began a teaching career at MLTC. After receiving an M.A. from Concordia Seminary, St Louis, he returned to Kenya and continued at MLTC until August 2002, when he was called into the office of the Presiding Bishop of the ELCK. He was consecrated a bishop on the November 24, 2002. In 2005, he consecrated a Swedish pastor as bishop of the Mission Province, a group within the Church of Sweden that opposes the ordination of women; his action prompted the Lutheran World Federation to terminate his leadership position in that organization. He was awarded a Doctor of Divinity degree by CTS in 2006 during the presidency of Dean Wenthe.

John T. Pless serves as Assistant Professor of Pastoral Ministry and Missions at CTS, where he also serves as Director of Field Education. He served for seventeen years as campus pastor at University Lutheran Chapel at the University of Minnesota in Minneapolis. He received his M.Div. from Trinity Lutheran Seminary, Columbus, Ohio. He entered LCMS by colloquy at CTS in 1983. Prof. Pless is the author of many books, including *Handling the Word of Truth: Law and Gospel in the Church Today; A Small Catechism on Human Life; and most recently Martin Luther: Preacher of the Cross.* With LCMS President Matthew Harrison he is editor of *Women Pastors? The Ordination of Women in Biblical Lutheran Perspective.* He is book review editor for *Logia: A Journal of Lutheran Theology,* a member of the editorial council of *Lutheran Quarterly, and* co-president of the International Loehe Society. He was called to the CTS faculty in 2000.

Timothy C. J. Quill serves as Associate Professor of Pastoral Ministry on the faculty of CTS. He served as a parish pastor for fifteen years in parishes in Connecticut and Missouri. He received his M.Div. (1980) and S.T.M. (1993) from Concordia Seminary, St. Louis, and his Ph.D. from Drew University (2002). Called to the faculty of CTS in 1998, he developed the seminary's Russian Project, which brought more than forty students from Russia and the former nations of the Soviet Union for study on the seminary campus. He also assisted in the establishment of Lutheran Theological Seminary in Novosibirsk, Siberia, and other theological seminaries in Russia, Kazakhstan, Kyrgyzstan, Ukraine, Moldova, Belarus, and Lithuania. Since 2002, he has served as Dean of International Studies, and currently serves as Director of Theological Education for the LCMS.

Lawrence R. Rast Jr. is the President at CTS and Professor of American Christianity and American Lutheranism. He served as pastor of Ascension Lutheran Church, Madison, Tennessee (1992–96). He received his M.Div. (1990) and S.T.M. (1995) from CTS. In 2003, he earned his Ph.D. from Vanderbilt University, Nashville, Tennessee. Dr. Rast is a member of the Board of Directors for the journal *Lutheran Quarterly*; he is also on the editorial committee of the *Concordia Historical Institute Quarterly*. He is a faculty representative on the LCMS's Commission on Theology and Church Relations (2006–present) and has been Chairman of that commission since 2010. He was called to the faculty of CTS in 1996 at the beginning of Dean Wenthe's presidency.

Robert V. Roethemeyer serves on the faculty of CTS, combining his role as Director of Library and Information Services with the newly created portfolio of Director of Institutional Assessment and Planning. Among his many contributions to CTS has been the shepherding of the expansion project of Walther Library. He received his M.Div. from Concordia Seminary at St. Louis in 1986, and his M.A.L.S. studies in Library and Information Science at the University of Missouri in Columbia in 1993. Professor Roethemeyer previously served as Public Services Librarian and Art Curator at Concordia Seminary in St. Louis (1988–97) and as pastoral assistant at Blessed Savior Lutheran Church in Florissant, Missouri from 1989–95. He was called to the faculty of CTS in 1997 near the beginning of Dean Wenthe's presidency.

David P. Scaer is a professor of Systematic Theology and New Testament and holder of the David P. Scaer Chair of Biblical and Systematic Theology at CTS. At the seminary since 1966, he serves as Editor of the *Concordia Theological Quarterly* (1969–94; 1999–present) and was Academic Dean (1984–89). He has served as the organizer of the annual CTS Symposium on the Lutheran Confessions since 1978. He is a member of the Society of Biblical Literature, the Institute for Biblical Research, the Alliance of Confessional Evangelicals, and the Christianity Today Institute, for which periodical he also serves as a research scholar. A third-generation Missouri Synod Lutheran clergy-man, Professor Scaer was brought up in Brooklyn, New York, where his father, the late Reverend Paul H. Scaer, served his lifetime ministry at Trinity Lutheran Church of Flatbush. Dr. Scaer has been a colleague of Dean Wenthe since the latter joined the faculty in 1971 while the seminary was in still in Springfield, Illinois.

Peter J. Scaer serves on the faculty of CTS as a professor of New Testament. From 1996 to 2000 he served as pastor of Emanuel Lutheran Church in Arcadia, Indiana. He did his undergraduate work in the Classics at Indiana University Bloomington, graduating in 1988. From there he went on to CTS (M.Div., 1992), and to Notre Dame, where he earned his M.A. (1995), and completed his dissertation on the Lukan Passion narrative (Ph.D., 2001). A member of the Exegetical Department, he was called to the faculty of CTS in 2000.

William C. Weinrich is Professor of Early Church History and Patristic Studies. He is a graduate of the University of Oklahoma, Concordia Seminary, St. Louis (1972), and received his Doctor of Theology degree from the University of Basel, Switzerland (1977). He joined the seminary faculty in 1975. Dr. Weinrich served the Synod in numerous capacities: Commission on Theology and Church Relations (1992–2001); Doctrinal Review Commission (1992–98); Third and Fourth Vice-President of the LCMS (1998–2001; 2001–2004, respectively). Dr. Weinrich served thirty years in the Indiana Air National Guard, retiring as a Lieutenant Colonel in 2002. During the first decade of Dean Wenthe's presidency, Dr. Weinrich served at his side as Academic Dean.

Roland F. Ziegler serves as Associate Professor of Systematic Theology at CTS. Born in the state of Baden-Württemberg, Germany, he studied at the Universities of Tübingen and Erlangen, and at the Lutheran Theological Seminary in Oberursel. He received his Dr.Theol. from the Eberhard-Karls-Universität Tübingen in 2011. He is the co-editor of *Hermann Sasse: In Statu Confessionis, vol. 3* (Göttingen: Edition Ruprecht, 2011), and is the author of *Das Eucharistiegebet in Theologie und Liturgie der lutherischen Kirchen seit der Reformation: Die Deutung des Herrenmahles zwischen Promissio und Eucharistie* (Göttingen: Edition Ruprecht, 2013). He was called to the faculty of CTS in 2000.

In addition to the contributors to this festschrift, several CTS graduate assistants are gratefully acknowledged for their contributions toward the completion of this project: proofreading (Christopher Gerdes, John Henry III, and Robert Paul), inputting Greek and Hebrew fonts (Roger Peters), organizing requests for copyright permissions

(Andrew Preus), and checking Latin translations (Christian Preus, M.Div. student). And lastly, gratitude is extended to the Rev. Robert Smith, electronic resources librarian at Walther Library, for his invaluable help in navigating the copyright permissions waters.

The festschrift begins with articles that locate Dean Wenthe's career in his architectural legacy with the new library (Roethemeyer) as well as his place among the presidents of Concordia Theological Seminary (Rast). Then his good colleague, William Weinrich, shows how important primary texts are to Dean's scholarship, as well as the significance of liturgy and the pascha in Dean's teaching. Then come the Biblical essays, Old Testament first (Mitchell, Kleinig, and Gard), followed by the New Testament (P. Scaer, Gieschen, Just). The bishops then weigh in (Obare and Harrison), the festschrift concluding with essays by colleagues at this seminary, in the church, and at our sister seminary (D. Scaer, Grime, Pless, Quill, Bushur, Murray, Egger).

Each essay accents some aspect of the theme of this festschrift—*The Restoration of Creation in Christ*—as well as many of the accents of Dean Wenthe's teaching throughout his career at Concordia Theological Seminary.

DEAN O. WENTHE

A BIOGRAPHICAL APPRECIATION

Dean Orrin Wenthe was born in the modest central Illinois town of Effingham just before the twentieth century reached its halfway point. Located today at the intersection of Interstates 57 and 70, Effingham has always been a "crossroads." At the time of Dr. Wenthe's birth, the Pennsylvania and Illinois Central railroads crossed paths in Effingham. Today, Effingham is best known for the "Cross at the Crossroads," a 198-foot tall cross that dominates the short stretch of road where the two interstates join together.[1] Dean Wenthe has always maintained "the Christological crossing" as the center of the biblical witness and heart of the Christian faith. As professor, pastor, and president, Christ has always been at the center of Dean Wenthe's confession and practice.

Whether he would pursue pastoral service as his life's vocation, however, was not a certainty. As he approached graduation from Effingham High School in 1962, Dr. Wenthe explored the possibility of studying physics at the University of Illinois.[2] Instead, Christ led him toward the pastoral ministry. He prepared for the Office of the Ministry

---

[1] http://www.crossusa.org/index.html (accessed October 14, 2013).

[2] Dell Ford, "Concordia's Wenthe Prepares His Students to Be Shepherds," *Journal Gazette* (September 2, 1997).

at Concordia College, Milwaukee (Associate of Arts, 1965), Concordia
Senior College, Fort Wayne (Bachelor of Arts, 1967), and Concordia
Seminary, St. Louis (Master of Divinity, 1971). He received his Master
of Theology (Th.M.) at Princeton Theological Seminary (1975), and a
Master of Arts (M.A. 1985) and Doctor of Philosophy (Ph.D. 1991)
from the University of Notre Dame.

Just prior to his vicarage, on July 26, 1969, Dr. Wenthe married
Linda Arnholt. They have been blessed with four sons, Timothy,
Matthew, Joel, and Joshua, three daughters-in-law, and eight grand-
children.

After his seminary graduation, Dr. Wenthe was called to Concordia
Theological Seminary in Springfield, Illinois, first as Instructor (1971–
1973) and then as Assistant Professor (1973–1977). While in Springfield
he served as a chaplain in the Air Force Reserves. In 1977 he accepted a
call to Zion Lutheran Church in Atlantic, Iowa, where he served as
pastor for three years. He returned to the seminary (now in Fort
Wayne) as Associate Professor of Old Testament in 1980, and in 1992
he was elevated in rank to Full Professor. While teaching at the
seminary, he served pastoral vacancies at Emmanuel Lutheran Church
in Wayne Trace (Soest), Indiana, and Zion Lutheran Church in Garrett,
Indiana. From 1989 to 1996 he was pastoral assistant at Emanuel
Lutheran Church in New Haven, Indiana.

For Dr. Wenthe, the transition between professorial and parish life
was largely seamless. Dean loved parish life; he also loved seminary life.
After returning to the seminary in 1980, he noted "how great it is to be
back. The three years of parish experience have deepened our
appreciation for the strategic work that the sem is called upon by the
church to perform."[3]

His service to the church-at-large has been rich and varied. He has
served for various lengths of time on the Exegetical Subcommittee of
the Church Literature Commission (1972–1978), the Commission on
Ministerial Growth and Support, and the Commission on the Sanctity
of Life; as an advisory member of the Commission on Theology and
Church Relations (1996–2010), the Board for Mission Services (1996–

---

[3] Dean O. Wenthe to Robert D. Preus, September 3, 1980.

2010), and the Boards for Higher and Pastoral Education (1996–2010); as a guest instructor at Concordia Seminary, St. Louis in 1974, 1978, 1979, and 1992; and as an LCMS representative to the Lutheran/Catholic dialogues. He has delivered papers at numerous conferences and written articles for a variety of theological journals. He served as an associate editor of the *Concordia Self-Study Bible* and is currently the General Editor of Concordia Commentary: A Theological Exposition of Sacred Scripture, published by Concordia Publishing House, for which he is also writing the commentary on Jeremiah. In 2009 he edited the volume on *Jeremiah/Lamentations* in the Ancient Christian Commentary on Scripture (InterVarsity Press).

Dean Wenthe was called as the fifteenth president of Concordia Theological Seminary on February 17, 1996. As he accepted the call to the presidency, he reflected on the Synod's tradition of pastoral formation and the role he had played in it:

> The Lord has blessed the Lutheran Church—Missouri Synod with a dual tradition of academic excellence and compassionate pastoral care in theological education. As a professor at Concordia Theological Seminary, it has been a privilege to place theological reflection and confession in the service of the Church's work of nurture and outreach.

Convinced that the call to the presidency was from God, he, typically with great humility, thought of the institution first.

> As our culture places new challenges before the church, a marriage of clarity of mind, integrity of confession, and charity of heart will hold the Gospel before our age in all its brilliance. The seminary, under God's grace, can form pastors who will integrate an unswerving commitment to the Triune God with sterling care for God's people.[4]

His installation as president was on April 28, 1996.

President Wenthe's accomplishments in office are too lengthy to list at this point. He admits that his "pet peeve" is "disorganization, messiness. To have things not in their proper place," yet the result was a series of remarkable accomplishments during his tenure as president of

---

[4] Dean O. Wenthe to Raymond A. Mueller, chairman of the Board of Regents, February 23, 1996.

the seminary.[5] Included among them, but not exhaustive by any means, are:

1. He guided the seminary to its first ever ten-year accreditation from both the Association of Theological Schools and the Higher Learning Commission of the North Central Association, the highest level of accreditation achievable.

2. His commitment to mission led CTS to be known the world over for its international work, particularly through his support of the "Russian Project."

3. His compassion found concrete expression in the establishment of the Deaconess Program in 2003.

4. Finally, under Dr. Wenthe's leadership, the seminary, after more than thirty years of on again/off again planning, successfully began expansion of its library facilities, creating a structure that can only be described as world class.

Dr. Wenthe retired from the presidency on June 5, 2011. However, that has not stifled his creative and energetic service. In addition to returning to the classroom and continuing work on his Jeremiah commentary, he was most recently named interim president of the Concordia University System, which oversees the ten colleges and universities operating under the auspices of the LCMS.

One thing that has always characterized Dr. Wenthe is his engaging, encouraging personality. From the time I was a student at this seminary, agonizing over sermon preparation, to discussing "future possibilities" with him following his election to the presidency of CTS in the spring of 1996, to serving with him in seminary administration, he has consistently held forth a gracious, Christ-centered vision for this institution and encouraged his colleagues in the same. His clarity of thought and charity of heart has encouraged and inspired parishioners and, especially, students entering the pastoral ministry in coming to a deeper understanding of their Lord Christ.

Our primary calling as theologians is to interpret reality for ourselves and for our people. In our day, we behold the tragic paradox of secular

[5] Dell Ford, "Concordia's Wenthe Prepares His Students to Be Shepherds," *Journal Gazette* (September 2, 1997).

man seeking something more solid than the phony, penultimate, pleasure trips, of either the gross or more refined variety, that are constantly held before us as the only route worth traveling . . . and, in their seeking, find no one to speak to them of that which is solid and real. The saints whom you serve will at times overwhelm you with their support and love. The sinners whom you serve will at times send you scampering to the throne of grace for more patience and wisdom than your flesh can muster. And yet, on this latter point, I can forthrightly say that for all their frailties you will find your flock a joy to serve.

I was simply not prepared for that closeness which is forged between Pastor and people as they seek to live a real life in the midst of a phony world.

Frankly, IT'S GREAT!!! And if these tasks do not plant the seeds of joy and happiness in our service, then we have ourselves drifted from that which is real.

For his more than forty years of service to this seminary, fifteen of which were spent as president of Concordia Theological Seminary, we can only give thanks to God, especially for Dr. Wenthe's collegiality and the way in which he has embodied the CTS mission to form servants in Jesus Christ who teach the faithful, reach the lost, and care for all.

Lawrence R. Rast Jr.

A Select Bibliography

Books

Concordia Self-Study Bible: New International Version. Edited by Robert Hoerber, Horace D. Hummel, Walter R. Roehrs, and Dean O. Wenthe. St. Louis: Concordia, 1986.

Genesis 1:1—25:11 (with Timothy Huber). St. Louis: Concordia, 1990.

Genesis 25:12—50:26. St. Louis: Concordia, 1990.

All Theology Is Christology: Essays in Honor of David P. Scaer. Edited by Dean O. Wenthe. Fort Wayne: Concordia Theological Seminary Press, 2000.

Concordia Commentary Series. Dean O. Wenthe, general editor. 22 volumes to date. St. Louis: Concordia, 1990–present.

Ancient Christian Commentary. Editor of Jeremiah, Lamentations. Downers Grove, IL: InterVarsity Press, 2009.

Articles

"Theological Significance of the Passing through the Sea at the Exodus for Old Testament Theology." Springfielder 36 (June 1972): 54–58.

"Historical-critical Interpretation of the Baptism of Jesus from the Perspective of Traditional Lutheran Exegesis." Springfielder 37 (March 1974): 231–40.

"Exegetical Study of 1 Corinthians 5:7b." Springfielder 38 (Summer 1974): 134–40.

"Parable of the Ten Bridesmaids: Matt 25:1–13." Springfielder 40 (June 1976): 9–16.

"The Parable of the Ten Bridesmaids." In Parable Interpretations: A Modern Anthology. Edited by John W. Sider. Westmont College, 1981.

"Prophet, Priest, King, and Teacher? The Old Testament, Inter-testamental, and Hellenistic Antecedents for Jesus' Role as Rabbi and Teacher." In *A Lively Legacy: Essays in Honor of Robert Preus*, 182–211. Fort Wayne: Concordia Theological Seminary Press, 1985.

"The Flesh and Blood Spirit." *Lutheran Witness* (March 1986).

"Creation." In *Wings of Faith: The Doctrine of the Lutheran Church for Teens*, 36–39, edited by Terry K. Dittmer. St. Louis: Board for Youth Services, The Lutheran Church—Missouri Synod, 1988.

"Sanctification." In *Wings of Faith: The Doctrine of the Lutheran Church for Teens,* 26–28, edited by Terry K. Dittmer. St. Louis: Board for Youth Services, The Lutheran Church—Missouri Synod, 1988.

"God as Communicator: The Old Testament Model." In God's Communicators in Mission: A Booklet of Essays Delivered at the Third Annual Missions Congress, Concordia Theological Seminary, Fort Wayne, Indiana, September 30—October 2, 1987. Fort Wayne: Great Commission Resource Library, 1988.

"Neo-Donatism or Neo-Docetism?" With William C. Weinrich. *Concordia Theological Quarterly 54* (April/July 1990): 209–12.

"Concordia Theological Seminary: Reflections on Its One-Hundred-and-Fiftieth Anniversary at the Threshold of the Third Millennium." *Concordia Theological Quarterly 60* (January/April 1996): 7–16.

"A Strikingly Theological Hermeneutics." *Concordia Theological Quarterly 62* (October 1998): 183–86.

"God's Character and the Calling of God's People: Contextual Relations." In Church and Ministry: The Collected Papers of the 150th Anniversary Theological Convocation of The Lutheran Church—Missouri Synod, 25–58. St. Louis: Office of the President, The Lutheran Church—Missouri Synod, 1998.

"From Death to Life—The Christological Crossing: A Homily for Heino O. Kadai." *Concordia Theological Quarterly 63* (July 1999): 165–168.

"A Tribute to Kurt Marquart" In *Mysteria Dei: Essays in Honor of Kurt Marquart,* 29–32. Fort Wayne: Concordia Theological Seminary Press, 1999).

"Post-Modernism and Sacred Scripture." In Let Christ be Christ: Theology, Ethics & World Religions in the Two Kingdoms: Essays in Honor of the Sixty-fifth Birthday of Charles L. Manske, edited by Daniel N. Harmelink. Huntington Beach, CA: Tentatio Press 1999.

"More than Leader, Administrator, and Therapist: The Scriptural Substance of the Pastoral Office." In *All Theology is Christology: Essays in Honor of David P. Scaer*, 199–213. Fort Wayne: Concordia Theological Seminary Press, 2000.

"Introduction: The Ten Commandments, The Creeds, The Our Father, Baptism, The Keys, Communion." In *We Believe: Essays on the Catechism*. Fort Wayne: Concordia Theological Seminary Press, 2000.

"What Will It Mean to be Lutheran in the Twenty-first Century?" In *What Does It Mean to Be a Lutheran?*, edited by John and Jennifer Maxfield. St. Louis: Concordia Historical Institute; Crestwood, MO: The Luther Academy, 2001.

"Redeeming Time: Deuteronomy 8:11–18." *Concordia Theological Quarterly* 65 (April 2001): 157–59.

"Amos 9:11–15: The Blood of Jesus in the Booth of David." In *Hear the Word of Yahweh*, 23–44. Saint Louis: Concordia Academic Press, 2002.

"The Biblical Trinitarian Narrative: Reflections on Retrieval." *Concordia Theological Quarterly* 67 (July–October 2003): 347–59.

"The Social Configuration of the Rabbi-Disciple Relationship: Evidence and Implications for First Century Palestine." In *Studies in the Hebrew Bible, Qumran, and the Septuagint Presented to Eugene Ulrich*, 143–74. Boston: Brill, 2006.

"Looking at the Moral Vision of the New Testament with Richard Hayes." *Concordia Theological Quarterly* 70 (January 2006): 33–42.

"The Rich Monotheism of Isaiah as Christological Resource." *Concordia Theological Quarterly* 71 (January 2007): 57–70.

"From Creation to Consummation: The Inclusive Identity of Israel's God as Challenge to Ancient and Contemporary Pluralisms." *Lutheran Theological Journal* 43 (August 2009): 132–39.

"The Sacred Character of Human Life." *Concordia Theological Quarterly* 75 (July–October 2011): 370–71.

"The Psalms as Homiletical Resource." *Concordia Pulpit Resources* 22 (November 27, 2011–February 19, 2012): 3–4.

EVERLASTING SON OF THE FATHER

During Dean O. Wenthe's tenure as president of Concordia Theological Seminary, the three-decade dream of expanding the library on the Saarinen-designed campus became a reality. Careful and painstaking work with architects and contractors who were sensitive to the seminary's desire to maintain the integrity of the original design of the campus resulted in an expansion of the existing library into a world-class facility that will serve the seminary for years to come.

The architectural beauty of the CTS campus is matched by an artistic plan unified under the theme of the ancient church's hymn of praise, the *Te Deum*. Wood, metal, fabric, and stone are joined in various works of art around the campus, inviting all who step on the campus to rejoice in the beauty of God's creation as it points to his saving work in Christ.

Among those original works of art is a combination of  bas-relief and mosaic on the south wall of the Dining Hall.

By carving into the white-washed rectangular bricks, Saint Louis artist William Severson was able to create a captivating image of the saints gathered together, singing their praises to God. A pattern of colored plastic, enameled copper, and stained glass chips in the center of the image takes the shape of a loaf of bread.

In the final design of the library expansion, two brick towers of white-washed brick were erected next to the grand staircase that connects the first of two "lantern" buildings with the main collection in the lower level. These towers serve as the canvas for a new work of art created by Fort Wayne artist William Lupkin.

In form, this new work of art was inspired by the carved relief in the Dining Hall. In theme, this work builds upon Christ, "the everlasting Son of the Father," represented in the existing library mosaic by the incarnate Christ holding the Bible with the Greek letters Alpha and Omega inscribed upon its open pages.

The new work begins at the bottom of the staircase with Christ and continues with images depicting the foundation of the law and the prophets, as well as the apostolic witness, on the first column (facing page). The second column (above) begins with Luther, nailing the Ninety-five Theses, and Chemnitz, holding a Book of Concord. This Biblical and confessional identity is handed on to our seminary founders, Loehe, Craemer, Sihler, and Wyneken, who in turn hand it on to our students, diaconal, international, and pastoral. In its wholeness, the work captures the transmission of the Word through the ages, providing a fitting image of the role of a theological library and a seminary faculty.

Robert V. Roethemeyer

A color version of this artwork may be viewed at http://www.ctsfw.edu/librarymosaic.

FOUNDING A SEMINARY IN THE WILDERNESS

CONCORDIA THEOLOGICAL SEMINARY THEN AND NOW

Lawrence R. Rast Jr.

1

As President of Concordia Theological Seminary (1996–2011), Dean Wenthe always reminded us to be alert to the beauty that is all around us. Whether it was lovely weather, a superb golf shot, or, most often, the exquisite architecture of Eero Saarinen featured on the seminary campus, Dean was sensitive, and sensitized others, to the beauty that enfolds us.

In this, Dr. Wenthe has been strikingly consistent. In an article published in the *Lutheran Witness* in 1986, Professor Wenthe pointed us to the beautiful practices of the historic Church. Noting that it is a matter of "Christian freedom" to adopt practices that are neither commanded nor forbidden in the Scripture, he urged us, nevertheless, to "fashion our whole life around the Resurrection reality" using "practices that have served to make concrete spiritual matters in light of Easter's truth for generations of Christians." Included in his list of eight such practices is, not surprisingly, the following: "Use art, whether traditional crucifixes and mosaics, or the most adventuresome of contemporary expressions to focus your devotion and reflections."[1]

---

[1] Dean O. Wenthe, "The Flesh and Blood Spirit," *The Lutheran Witness* (March 1986): 14–15.

Preparing years ago for my first trip to the Eastern Sierra and knowing that Dr. Wenthe has been most everywhere, I sought his advice on what to see. Upon his advice, I entered the area by way of the Tehachapi Pass, then traveled up the Owens River Valley, and finally visited Mammoth Lakes, Mono Lake, and Yosemite Park. What were particularly striking along this route were the contrasts. From the peak of Mount Whitney—the highest point in the contiguous United States—to Death Valley—its lowest point—is only some one hundred miles as the crow flies. And yet, the contrast between the two settings is striking. The verdant alpine pastures quickly give way to the valley of death.

In other words, as beautiful as the wilderness is, it can also be a dangerous place.

Human experience bears this out. In April 1992, Chris McCandless hitchhiked to the Stampede Trail in Alaska. Outfitted with a mere ten pounds of rice, a .22 caliber rifle with a small supply of ammunition, and a camera, he entered the wilderness. He survived a little more than three months. The following September, a group of hunters discovered his body.

The Church's experience mirrors this reality, too. In the summer of 1619, a group of Danish Lutherans, led by their Captain, Jens Munck, and accompanied by Pastor Rasmus Jensen, made their way into Hudson Bay as they sought a Northwest Passage. Munck and his sixty-four comrades were the first Europeans to attempt to winter in the area of what is today Churchill, Manitoba, Canada. Unprepared for the bitter cold and beset by unforeseen challenges, by Easter of 1620, sixty-two of the original crew had perished, including Pastor Jensen. Munck and two others struggled back to Denmark in the frigate *Unicorn*. [2]

God's beautiful and good creation has become a dangerous wilderness. The reason is clearly revealed in the account of the Fall into sin (Genesis 3). The creation, where God and man should have dwelt together in peace, has been fundamentally disrupted by human sin. [3]

---

[2] Captain Munck's (also spelled Munk) account of the journey was translated and published in English as *The Journal of Jens Munk,* ed. W. A. Kenyon (Toronto: Royal Ontario Museum, 1980).

[3] See Romans 8:19–22.

And because human beings are no longer naturally in relationship with God, relationships between human beings and the creation, as well as between one another, are also disordered.

The First Adam fell and thereby transformed his paradise into a dangerous wilderness. In contrast, the Second Adam "was led up by the Spirit into the wilderness to be tempted by the devil," overcame him, and regained paradise for us (Matthew 4:1–11). This was the ministry of Jesus—to restore that which man had destroyed.

The evangelist St. John writes in his Prologue: "He came to his own, and his own people did not receive him" (John 1:11). Israel rejected its promised Messiah. Beyond that, his own creation struggled against him. He had no place to lay his head; his life was one of emptiness and solitude (Matthew 8:20).

This resistance of both humankind and creation to its Lord frames the narrative of the early chapters of Matthew. There is a mountaintop to valley-of-death rhythm to the account. After presenting the genealogy of Jesus in chapter one, Matthew takes us to the mountaintop as he tells us of the promise of the Savior's birth and its fulfillment. Immediately after Jesus' birth, however, the violence of human sin threatens to destroy Jesus as Herod brutally sends all of the boy children in and around Bethlehem into the valley of death.

The account in Matthew 4 of the temptation of Jesus features the most extended interchange between Jesus and the devil. It is a dangerous moment, humanly speaking, for here the devil tries to repeat his victory over the First Adam in the Garden. But where the First Adam failed, the Second Adam triumphed. The temptations are extreme, as the text recalls the wilderness in which Israel wandered for forty years. But all Israel was rebellious, and the law only functioned to show just how sinful they were. Now Jesus is here in the wilderness to fulfill that law for us—to keep its every point perfectly. And he is here to suffer the punishment for all human sin, all so that the sins of every person—past, present, and future—would be forgiven. This is his work, the great mercy and grace that God has for us, that we might "be his own and live under him in his kingdom."

Just as our Lord fought the devil and his temptations, Christians throughout the ages have struggled with the reality of life in the Church

Militant. The Church Militant, said Gerhard, "is still fighting, under the banner of Christ, against Satan, the world, and the flesh."[4] At times, that struggle is more pronounced than others—but it is always there.

2

Under Dean Wenthe's patient, capable, and charitable leadership, Concordia Theological Seminary reestablished itself as a strong institution and continues forward in its mission to form servants in Jesus Christ who teach the faithful, reach the lost, and care for all. In his owns words, Wenthe points us back to the real things that strengthen us as we journey through a sometimes beautiful, sometimes challenging, wilderness.

> Luther, Bach, and all who with the disciples have beheld the Spirit wailing and talking know that this Spirit is for real! Thus, the real presence in the Lord's Supper is not a surprise for us—but what we would expect from our living, resurrected Lord. Similarly, the simple washing of Holy Baptism is not an empty rite, but a full expression of Jesus' promise in the real world.

> Far from fleeing to the unreal, ephemeral, and empty world of the "spiritual," Easter Christians rush to the reality of Word and Sacrament.[5]

Dean Wenthe served faithfully and well for fifteen years as sixteenth president of Concordia Theological Seminary.[6] One of the great testimonies to his presidential leadership is that he led the seminary out of a period of significant challenge and left the institution in a significantly stronger position at his retirement.[7]

---

[4] Quoted in Heinrich Schmid, *The Doctrinal Theology of the Evangelical Lutheran Church,* 3rd ed., trans. Charles Hay and Henry E. Jacobs (Minneapolis: Augsburg, 1899), 587.

[5] Wenthe, "The Flesh and Blood Spirit," 1.

[6] Only August Crämer (1878–1891, serving unofficially in that capacity from 1875) and Robert Preus (1974–1993) served longer than Dean Wenthe; his tenure was matched by that of founding president Wilhelm Sihler (1846–1861).

[7] Heather Schultz, "15 Years of Service at Seminary: His Legacy Includes Stable Finances, Expanded Library," News Sentinel (January 19, 2011), online at http://www.news-sentinel.com/apps/pbcs.dll/article?AID=/20110119/NEWS01/101190 312/1001/NEWS (accessed October 31, 2011).

Such leadership has rich precedent in the history of Concordia Theological Seminary.[8] Indeed, the founding of the institution is a testimony to the vision and guidance of remarkable and gifted servants of God. Concordia Theological Seminary has been served by sixteen presidents over the course of its history.

1. Wilhelm Sihler (1846–1861)

2. C. F. W. Walther (1861–1875)

3. August Crämer (1878–1891)

4. Reinhold Pieper (1892–1914)

5. R. Biedermann (1915–1921)

6. H. A. Klein (1922–1935)

7. H. B. Hemmeter (1935–1945)

8. G. Christian Barth (1945–1952)

9. Walter Baepler (1953–1958)

10. George Beto (1959–1962)

11. J. A. O. Preus (1962–1969)

12. Richard J. Schultz (1970–1974)

13. Robert D. Preus (1974–1993)

14. David Schmiel (1993–1995)

15. Dean O. Wenthe (1996–2011)

16. Lawrence R. Rast Jr. (2011–present)

Never a president of the seminary, but first among those servant leaders, was Friedrich Wyneken (1810–1876).[9] Born May 13, 1810,

---

[8] The standard history is Heintzen's *Prairie School of the Prophets: The Anatomy of a Seminary, 1846–1976* (St. Louis: Concordia, 1989). However, see also Otto F. Stalhke, "Concordia Comes to Springfield: 100 Years—1874–1974," *Springfielder* 38 (April 1974): 102–105. Available online at http://www.ctsfw.net/media/pdfs/stahlke concordia100years.pdf (accessed October 14, 2013).

[9] Norman J. Threinen, "F. C. D. Wyneken: Motivator for the Mission," *Concordia Theological Quarterly* 60 (January-April 1996): 19–45; Johann Christoph Wilhelm Lindemann, Friedrich Konrad Dietrich Wyneken: *An Evangelist among the Lutherans of North America*, trans. Sieghart Rein (Fort Wayne: Concordia Theological Seminary, 2010); online at http://www.ctsfw.net/media/pdfs/wynekenbiography.pdf (accessed October 14, 2013). Robert E. Smith, "Wyneken as Missionary: Mission in the Life &

Wyneken came to the United States at the age of twenty-eight.[10] The circumstances were difficult. The economy had just collapsed in the "panic" of 1837. Additionally, however, the church in America was in crisis. Lutherans were struggling with the question of confessional identity and some, perhaps most, had lost the heart of the Lutheran confession.[11] Although Wyneken was described as "a fiery zealot against all narrow churchliness" early in his ministry, in time he became one of the leading advocates of a robust confessional Lutheranism in the United States.[12]

The situation, as Wyneken quickly came to understand, was dire. His *Notruf,* or "emergency call," captured the difficulties perfectly.

> Oh, truly, dear brethren, it breaks the heart of a preacher, who himself has been forced to see souls go to their ruin without being able to help, who himself has wandered about brokenheartedly, as among the ruins of Jerusalem, and has seen the destruction growing ever more rapidly. It grieves him deeply when his appeals to God and his cries for help to the brethren in the blessed Fatherland go unheeded. "Zion stretches out her hands, but there is no one to comfort her." Therefore I have set out for the beloved homeland to ascertain whether the hearts of our brethren are completely hardened to the misery, and, behold, I found hearts which had been opened by the Lord to the misery and lamentation and were willing to help. In this reawakened hope I am again presenting to the church, with a prayer to God who desires to

---

Ministry of Friedrich Conrad Dietrich Wyneken," in *Let Christ Be Christ: Theology, Ethics & World Religions in the Two Kingdoms*, 321–40, ed. Daniel N. Harmelink (Huntington Beach, CA: Tentatio Press, 1999).

[10] Lawrence R. Rast Jr., "The More Things Change: Capturing Wyneken's Vision for Today," *For the Life of the World* 14, no. 1 (March 2010): 4.

[11] See Lawrence R. Rast Jr., "The Doctrine of Justification in American Lutheranism," in *A Justification Odyssey*, Papers Presented at the Congress on the Lutheran Confessions, Bloomingdale, Illinois, April 19–21, 2001, Association of Confessional Lutherans Free Conference, no. 12, and Luther Academy Lecture Series, no. 8, ed. John A. Maxfield (St. Louis: Luther Academy, 2002): 38–61.

[12] Letter of L. A. Petri to Pastor Luehr, around May 25, 1842, partly quoted in E. Petri, *Ludwig Adolf Petri: Ein Lebensbild* (Hanover: Verlag von Heinr[ich] Feesche, 1888), 260–62; cited in Threinen, "F. C. D. Wyneken: Motivator for the Mission," 21.

help, the need and once more calling out in the name of Jesus: "Help! Help quickly! Help with Christian generosity!"[13]

One of the most pressing needs was that of pastors. At first he pleaded with his fellow Germans to send pastors. However, he quickly shifted his strategy toward that of preparing pastors in the United States itself. The call was heard by the Rev. Wilhelm Löhe of Neuendettelsau, Germany, who responded with great vigor. By 1844 Löhe had trained and sent men to the United States; Wyneken, who was convinced that training needed to occur in America itself, had two students at his parsonage in Fort Wayne. In 1845, when Wyneken moved to Baltimore, a key moment occurred. Both Löhe and Wyneken knew that Fort Wayne was a strategic location for the future of confessional Lutheranism in America. They needed a man with particular gifts to start seminary training on the frontier. They found the right man to lead the effort in Wilhelm Sihler.[14] Sihler had come late to the faith after serving in the Prussian military. A man of considerable intellect, he pursued graduate studies in Berlin and received a Doctorate from the University of Jena. He abandoned the academy for the parish, however, after becoming convinced of the biblical character of the Lutheran confession. Following his immigration and a brief pastorate in Pomeroy, Ohio, Dr. Sihler was called to be the third pastor of Saint Paul Evangelical Lutheran Church in Fort Wayne in 1845.[15]

By October 1846, Concordia Theological Seminary was ready to begin operations under Sihler's able leadership. Erich Heintzen, pro-

---

[13] F. C. D. Wyneken, *The Distress of the German Lutherans in North America,* trans. S. Edgar Schmidt, ed. R. Rehmer (Fort Wayne: Concordia Theological Seminary Press, 1982), 19–20.

[14] James L. Schaaf, "Father from Afar: Wilhelm Loehe and Concordia Theological Seminary in Fort Wayne," *Concordia Theological Quarterly* 60 (January-April 1996): 47–73; John T. Pless, "Wilhelm Loehe and the Missouri Synod: Forgotten Paternity or Living Legacy?" A paper delivered at the International Loehe Society, Wartburg Theological Seminary, Dubuque, Iowa, July 12, 2005. Available at http://www.ctsfw.edu/document.doc?id=284 (accessed October 20, 2013).

[15] Lewis W. Spitz Jr., "Professor Wilhelm Sihler: Founding Father of Lutheranism in America and First President of Concordia Theological Seminary," *Concordia Theological Quarterly* 63 (April 1999): 83–96; Lewis W. Spitz Jr., *Life in Two Worlds: Biography of William Sihler* (St. Louis: Concordia, 1968).

fessor of historical theology and historian of this seminary, opened his
account of the *Prairie School of the Prophets* with the following picture:

> On a late Indiana summer's day in 1846, a band of 11 youths, fledgling
> students of theology, accompanied by their tutor, appeared on the
> streets of Fort Wayne on the banks of the Maumee. A strange site they
> were, with all the earmarks of fresh arrivals from the "old country."
> From Bavaria, from Schleswig, from Mecklenburg, from Wuertem-
> berg, from Hannover they had come—the "12 apostles" sent by
> Wilhelm Löhe of Bavaria, a small-town pastor with a big heart and a
> worldwide vision. [16]

By the time Wyneken and Loehe established CTS, there were
already several Lutheran seminaries in the United States. Its future
sister, Concordia Seminary, then in Altenburg, Missouri, and later in
Saint Louis, had been founded in 1839.[17] But there were seminaries that
served other synods as well. The Lutheran Theological Seminary at
Gettysburg was established in 1826.[18] Lutheran Southern Seminary,
today in Columbia, South Carolina, was founded in Pomaria, South
Carolina in 1830.[19] The Ohio Synod opened a seminary in 1830 in
Canton, Ohio, though it soon moved to Columbus. Roughly contem-
porary with the Fort Wayne seminary was the theological department at
Wittenberg College, which traced its roots to 1845.[20] It was at this last

---

[16] Erich H. Heintzen, *Prairie School of the Prophets*, 17.

[17] For the history of Concordia Seminary, St. Louis, from which President Wenthe
graduated in 1971, see Carl S. Meyer, *From Log Cabin to Luther Tower: Concordia
Seminary During One Hundred and Twenty-five Years toward a More Excellent Ministry,
1839-1964* (St. Louis: Concordia, 1965).

[18] Abdel Ross Wentz, *History of the Gettysburg Theological Seminary of the General
Synod of the Evangelical Lutheran Church in the United States and of the United
Lutheran Church in America, Gettysburg, Pennsylvania, 1826-1926* (Philadelphia:
Printed for the seminary by the United Lutheran Publication House, 1927); Frederick K.
Wentz, et al., *Witness at the Crossroads: Gettysburg Lutheran Seminary Servants in the
Public Life* (Gettysburg: Lutheran Theological Seminary at Gettysburg, 2001).

[19] H. George Anderson and Robert M. Calhoon, *A Truly Efficient School of Theology:
The Lutheran Theological Southern Seminary in Historical Context, 1830-1980*
(Columbia: Lutheran Theological Southern Seminary, 1981).

[20] See Donald L. Huber, *Educating Lutheran Pastors in Ohio, 1830-1980: A History of
Trinity Lutheran Seminary and Its Predecessors* (Lewiston, New York: Edwin Mellen
Press, 1989); Willard D. Allbeck, *Theology at Wittenberg, 1845-1945* (Springfield, OH:
Wittenberg Press, 1945).

seminary that matters of confessional perspective clashed most seriously with that of the soon-to-be-opened seminary in Fort Wayne.

Wittenberg College owed much to its first president, Ezra Keller. A General Synod pastor, he migrated from Maryland to Ohio after doing exploratory mission work on behalf of the national body. A chance meeting with a confessional Lutheran pastor left Keller utterly perplexed—he simply lacked the categories to understand the man, his position, and his practice:

> He is an accomplished gentleman, and an ardent Christian, but a fanatical dogmatist . . . . He is quite antiquated in his views of Christian doctrine and church polity. He considers subscription to the unaltered Augsburg Confession, without note or comment, as indispensable to constitute a man a Lutheran. The Lutheran Church, based on the Augsburg Confession he considers the Apostolical Catholic Church. He believes in baptismal regeneration, and the real presence of the *body* and the *blood* of Christ in the Lord's Supper. He recommends private confession and absolution; makes the sign of the cross in the administration of the ordinance of baptism, and conforms to the various forms of the symbolists.[21]

Others shared Keller's concerns. In an article titled "Seminaries and Colleges in the West," "An Eastern Man" outlined the incredible opportunity for "inner mission" by noting that there were some 10,000–15,000 members of the Lutheran Church in the west who had no access to the means of grace. As such, he believed it was imperative that the church establish institutions of higher education, including theological seminaries, in the west. But not just any institution would suffice. Noting the existence of the seminary at Columbus, the author opined that its so-called "friends" had actually derailed its mission. Its problem? An insistence on the use of formal German and, worse, its increasing commitment to the Lutheran Confessions. As a result, "An Eastern Man" concluded that "It is nothing." That is, because its theology was old and European, it simply could not speak to the modern, informed man of the nineteenth century. As a result, another institution, an

---

[21] M. Diehl, *Biography of Rev. Ezra Keller, D.D., Founder and First President of Wittenberg College* (Springfield, OH: Ruralist Publishing Company, 1859), 261; emphasis original. See also "State of Religion in the West," *Lutheran Observer* (November 6, 1846).

"institution of the West," "well adapted to the wants of the church" was desperately needed.[22]

That institution was, of course, Wittenberg College. And what made Wittenberg the future of Lutheranism in the minds of "An Eastern Man" and Keller was its willingness to depart from Lutheranism's confessional past. As Keller himself put it:

> I am every day becoming more convinced of the necessity of raising up an American ministry to spiritualize the millions of Germans who are seeking a home in our happy land. Those who are educated in Germany are not qualified for the work, and cannot be persuaded to lay aside their foreign prejudices, and modes of thought and action.[23]

One cannot underestimate the antagonism between the two groups of Lutherans.

> The whole difference resolves into this, that [the Old Lutherans] base their views and practices on the symbolical books of the church—[the New Lutherans], on the Bible alone. We stand on the same ground where the Reformers stood—the Word of God; they stand on a platform with Romanist and Puseyites—the opinions of men, called the sense of the Church. Our form of doctrine is the rock of ages; theirs is the shifting sand. We contend for a religion internal, spiritual; they for a religion external, formal.[24]

The problem with such European preachers was that they were hopelessly bound by subscription to a useless theological past. Thus, in order for the Church to grow and flourish, it was imperative that an indigenous ministry be raised up, lest the delusions and darkness of the past continue to lead people into superstition and error. In the end, "if the foreigners among us prefer [the old doctrines and practices], let them go back to the land of kings and established churches."[25]

Wyneken and his colleagues founded Concordia Theological Seminary specifically because they were convinced that the old doc-

[22] An Eastern Man, "Seminaries and Colleges in the West," *Lutheran Observer* (October 30, 1846).

[23] Diehl, *Biography of Rev. Ezra Keller*, 261.

[24] Diehl, *Biography of Rev. Ezra Keller*, 232; emphasis original.

[25] An American Lutheran, "The New Theological Seminary in Philadelphia," *Lutheran Observer* (November 20, 1846).

trines and their attendant practices were truly in line with what the Scriptures teach. And so they were determined to establish a seminary that was committed both to historic, confessional Lutheranism and to the formation of pastors for service on American soil.

First president Sihler thus carried a heavy burden as he sought to establish the fledgling institution in the challenging context of the American frontier. There were the "American Lutherans," noted above. There were also more exotic figures in the Fort Wayne area, such as John Chapman, or, as he is better known, Johnny Appleseed (1774–1845).[26]

Still, by 1846 Wilhelm Sihler was ready to begin training students in Fort Wayne. He sought men who met the following eight qualifications:

1. they must "cling to the saving doctrine and remain in what has been entrusted to them, just as the right church—called Lutheran—from the beginning accepts God's word, confesses and teaches it";

2. they must not be "associated with this anti-scriptural 'church-merging' and false 'unionism' of our times," which characterizes the American Lutherans;

3. they must have a "healthy and thorough knowledge of the truth, and if God will, have personally experienced this truth";

4. they must desire to "teach this truth to others," "know how to connect Law and Gospel," and work to "thwart the rabble rousers and false religious enthusiasts";

5. they must "humbly and sincerely love their church";

6. they must be "willing to bear all sorts of internal and external troubles and tribulations for the sake of the one faith";

7. they must "take care of themselves and the flock which might be entrusted to their care by the Arch-shepherd, who will faithfully tend to them with Word and Sacrament, both individually and as

---

[26] http://www.britannica.com/EBchecked/topic/106148/John-Chapman (accessed October 17, 2013). Chapman had tenuous ties (at best) to the Lutheran tradition via the reformer Emanuel Swedenborg and his "new" interpretation of the Christian faith. http://www.swedenborg.org/FamousSwedenborgians/JohnChapman.aspx (accessed October 17, 2013).

a group, and by their lives and conduct will bear the fruit of the spirit and be an example to them"; and finally,

8. they must "take care to be of one mind in the spirit and in peace with one another, always conscious that not only have they been created by the same Father . . . redeemed by the same Son and sanctified by the same Spirit, but that in this most holy matter—the building of His holy church—they are God's co-workers."[27]

A faithful seminary had been established in the wilderness. It continues to operate—purely by God's grace—even today.

Heintzen remarks concerning the entering class of 1846: "The arrival of this unprepossessing contingent marked the formal beginning of what is now Concordia Theological Seminary. The beginning was like a little cloud, no bigger than a man's hand. But through the years it grew and refreshed the land by sending out several thousand bearers of the water of life."[28]

From its beginning in 1846 in the transitioning town of Fort Wayne—transitioning from frontier to settled region (1846–1861)—through its brief sojourn in Saint Louis (1861–1875), to its long and fruitful residence in Springfield, Illinois (1875–1976), and finally with its return to its roots here in Fort Wayne (1976, though on a different campus than before), this seminary has always recalled the principles upon which it was founded. It continues to do so today.

3

The world continues to be a dangerous place. We recognize that we will be "led up by the Spirit into the wilderness" and we will "be tempted by the devil." The world, however, is also a transformed place because of Christ. And his greater promise is that he will never leave us or forsake us (Hebrews 13:5).

---

[27] Wilhelm Sihler, "The Lutheran Seminary at Fort Wayne," trans. Erika Bullmann Flores, *Der Lutheraner* 3, no. 5 (October 31, 1846): 29–30. Available online at http://www.projectwittenberg.org/etext/cts/ctsborn.txt (accessed October 14, 2013). Because of its historical significance, Sihler's entire article is reprinted in translation at the end of this essay.

[28] Heintzen, *Prairie School of the Prophets*, 17.

As we make our pilgrimage through this life as the people of God, Dean Wenthe has consistently reminded us to appreciate the beauty that is all around us. Years ago, he participated in archeological digs at the biblical city of Capernaum and shared his reflections on his experience with readers of the *Lutheran Witness*. His words then apply today, for while he positions us in the context of the biblical narrative, even more importantly, he points us constantly to Christ. For wherever Christ is, there is our home.

> In making his home at Capernaum, Jesus came to your home and to mine. Like the ordinary residents of Capernaum, we, too, welcome the Incarnate Son of God, for He has chosen to dwell at your address and mine, as surely as in a small house in Capernaum. And His presence through baptism, the Lord's Supper and the Gospel, is as real now as it was then.
>
> Rejoice, traveler, for in departing for Capernaum you will discover that another Traveler has come to be with you! He is not only the One who remains in our homes and by our sides throughout life's pilgrimage, but also the One who is now our safe dwelling—the One toward whom we travel in faith and hope. Pleasant sojourning, Christian pilgrim![29]

---

[29] Dean O. Wenthe, "Rediscovering Jesus' Hometown," *The Lutheran Witness* (March 1987): 23.

BIRTH ANNOUNCEMENT
OF CONCORDIA THEOLOGICAL SEMINARY

"The Lutheran Seminary at Fort Wayne."
by Wilhelm Sihler, 1801–1885
Translated by Erika Bullmann Flores
Der Lutheraner
Vol. 3, No. 5, pp. 29–30.
October 31, 1846

It has pleased the almighty and all gracious God to revive our precious Lutheran Church on both sides of the Atlantic, despite the false influences of the "unionists" of our times, therefore faithful members of the church in the German fatherland lovingly worked for their brothers-in-faith here in America. Through their efforts, during the past four years nineteen faithful and loyal men have joined us from abroad in order to serve the Lutheran church as preachers and teachers after having been carefully prepared and instructed at home. Recently the love of these devoted men for their American brothers has excelled. Because of the current need, and in anticipation of increased future need, they have decided to establish a seminary in Fort Wayne, so that faithful, qualified young men can receive the necessary training to take over the holy office of the preacher in the Lutheran church. To this end they have not only made money available already for the building project, they have also sent a Professor of Theology as well as eleven young men which have been trained by notable Lutheran pastors.

These have already arrived here last month, and another Professor of Theology will soon join them. After the most basic arrangements have been made—work on the proposed seminary will not commence until next spring—classes are expected to start already this month, with the help of the almighty God.

At this time we are not releasing details concerning these classes. For now we only want to call the attention of the reader and the faithful, Lutheran congregations to two particulars: one is a short explanation of the purpose of the seminary, and the other is a request to all faithful members of the Lutheran church who do not yet have to support such an institution, that they will help take care of this little seedling, that they will help tend it with their assistance and prayers. Referring to the purpose of the seminary, we freely admit that it is our heartfelt desire and will to prepare servants for our church, under the mercy and with the blessing of the triune God,

1. those who cling to the saving doctrine and remain in what has been entrusted to them, just as the right church—called Lutheran—from the beginning accepts God's word, confesses and teaches it;

2. those who do not wish to become associated with this anti-scriptural "church-merging" and false "unionism" of our times. Regretfully, many of the so-called Lutheran synods are embroiled in this matter in either word or deed,[1] but those who fight for the faith which had once been given to the saints, who wish no other union, nor join it, than that of the same faith, confession and doctrine in all matters as given to us through God's Word of truth, leading to salvation;

3. those who have a healthy and thorough knowledge of the truth, and if God will, have personally experienced this truth;

4. those who diligently teach this truth to others, who share the Word of God, know how to connect Law and Gospel, and thus thwart the rabble rousers and false religious enthusiasts;

5. those who humbly and sincerely love their church, in whose clear conscience is embedded the secret of faith;

6. those who are willing to bear all sorts of internal and external troubles and tribulations for the sake of the one faith;

7. those who take care of themselves and the flock which might be entrusted to their care by the Arch-shepherd, who will faithfully tend to them with Word and Sacrament, both individually and as a group, and by their lives and conduct will bear the fruit of the spirit and be an example to them;

---

[1] It is a well-known fact that the so-called Lutheran General Synod, for instance, teaches the Reformed view of the holy sacraments, and in their worship services follow the Methodist model; also, members of the Lutheran synods of Ohio and Michigan serve mixed congregations, which means that, for instance, during Holy Communion, Reformed and Lutherans are together.

8. those who take care to be of one mind in the spirit and in peace
    with one another, always conscious that not only have they been
    created by the same Father, were redeemed by the same Son and
    sanctified by the same Spirit, but that in this most holy matter—
    the building of His holy church—they are God's co-workers.

It is our intent, with the help of the Holy Spirit, to produce such servants for the church, sooner or later, depending on their age and talents. To reach this goal, to make this possible—and this is another reason for my brotherly address—prayer and help is needed not only from those precious brothers-in-the-faith in Germany, but also here in America, for whom this institution is being established.

How many of those here are building houses and barns and are planting orchards, with their children in mind; they carefully tend to these buildings and plantations so that their children and children's children can enjoy the benefits of them. Should they not also help groom this spiritual plantation and tend to it with their faithful prayers and assistance, from which they and their children will, with God's blessing, reap the heavenly reward? Would they willingly watch their friends work their fields and build their houses, while they themselves are fit and strong enough to at least help?

Therefore, I am hopeful that I am not asking the faithful sons of our beloved church in vain—though because of her current decay and distortion there may not be many—to help the German brothers and brothers-in-faith with prayerful hearts and open hands. Are not our feet willing to carry the entire body in whatever direction the head guides it, in return the eyes and hands, yea the entire body bends down to the feet and cares for them, whenever ill has befallen them. Should then we, who are the spiritual body in Christ, be shamed by our physical body, and not tend to one another and together do works of love?

Should we, to whom the precious treasure of the true faith and the unaltered sacraments have been given by the Lord to perpetuate and propagate, remain cold, mistrustful and idle? Should our fervor for the preservation of the pure, saving truth be surpassed by the fervor of the papists and religious dreamers for the preservation of their false doctrine? Therefore, beloved brothers and brothers-in-faith on this side of the Atlantic, you who still love your church as the pillar and foundation of the truth, who are concerned with the preservation thereof among the thousands of emigrating brothers-in-faith who come every year, give a hand here! Together let us—as Nehemiah and his followers of old—with the one hand fight the papists and religious fanatics, the false brothers with their anti-scriptural union, and with the other hand, however, let us—build!

Now the faithful Lord and God who lets the sincere succeed, will make these lovely words of promise come true with us. In His mercy. Amen.

Dr. W. Sihler
Luth. Preacher at Fort Wayne, Indiana
Currently Director of Seminary
Fort Wayne, October 24, 1846

ON THE HOLY PASCHA

BY THE BLESSED HESYCHIUS, PRESBYTER OF JERUSALEM

William C. Weinrich

The contribution of Dean O. Wenthe to the Church and to Concordia Theological Seminary has been substantial and will prove enduring. From many conversations I know his conviction, which I share, that theological study is best pursued on the basis of texts. His own engagement with the Old Testament is a model of theological reflection, for in his hands the Scriptures are interpreted not as mere historical artifact but as the living voice of the Church's faith. Nowhere is that voice more evident than in the Church's preaching by which the prophetic and apostolic proclamation finds its echo in the hearts and minds of the people of God. The Scriptures exist to be preached. Ancient Christian paschal homilies are excellent examples of extending the history of Israel into the reality of the Church's own sojourn toward the holy land of the final beatific vision. In honor of my long-time friend and colleague, therefore, a translation with interpretive comments on a paschal homily from fifth-century Jerusalem may be welcome.

WHO WAS HESYCHIUS OF JERUSALEM?

Unfortunately, little is known of the man who may well have been the most productive and honored Christian writer of the church at Jerusalem in the first half of the fifth century.[1] An early biographical

[1] For summaries of the life and work of Hesychius of Jerusalem, see especially Jean Kirchmeyer, "Hésychius de Jérusalem (saint)," in *Dictionnaire de spiritualité ascétique et mystique, doctrine et histoire* (Paris: G. Beauchesne, 1968), 7:399–408; K. Jüssen,

mention of Hesychius from ancient sources occurs as an entry for March 28 in the *Menologion* of Emperor Basil II (AD 976–1025):

> Our holy father, Hesychius, was both born and nurtured in Jerusalem. Having studied the whole of Scripture with the greatest acumen, he became rich in knowledge toward God. For this reason he withdrew [from the city] and becoming a monk he lived in the desert. Visiting the holy fathers who were there, he gathered from each one the blossoms of virtue, as though he were an industrious bee. Since he was unable to hide such virtue, the chief priest of Jerusalem at that time prevailed upon him and he was ordained presbyter. Remaining near to the sepulcher of the Lord and to other places where our Lord Jesus Christ endured the holy sufferings for us, he plumbed the depths of the fountains of knowledge and wisdom. From there he interpreted the whole of Scripture and explained them clearly and made them profitable for many. For that reason he became to all celebrated and famous. And having served God in every way, he hurried up to him with rejoicing.[2]

From this description we acquire the barest of outlines of Hesychius' life: a native of Jerusalem, he became a monk in the Judean desert but was recalled by the Bishop of Jerusalem and ordained presbyter. In that capacity he became a celebrated teacher and a commentator of the entire Scripture.[3] There is also mention of the significance of Christ's sufferings in the interpretive work of Hesychius.[4] Nothing in this description, however, assists us in determining the chronology of Hesychius' life. Our first fixed date is AD 412. According

---

"Hesychios v. Jerusalem," in *Lexikon für Theologie und Kirche* (Freiburg: Verlag Herder, 1960), 5:308–309; Johannes Quasten, *Patrology* (Utrecht: Spectrum Publishers; Westminster, MD: The Newman Press, 1960), 3:487–96; A. Wenger, "Hésychius de Jérusalem," *Revue des Études Augustiniennes* 2 (1956): 457–70.

[2] *Menologii Graecorum* for 28 March (*PG* 117:373–76); translation mine. A *menologium* is a book in which the days of commemoration of saints are noted with short biographical information. The *Menologium* of Basil II is regarded as the foremost example of medieval Byzantine manuscript illumination.

[3] That Hesychius was born and grew up in Jerusalem seems to be the sense of the Greek (ὑπῆρχε μὲν τῶν Ἰεροσολύμων καὶ γέννημα καὶ θρέμμα).

[4] The words καὶ προσμένων τῷ τοῦ κυρίου τάφῳ καὶ τοῖς ἄλλοις τόποις ... ἤντλει πηγὰς γνώσεως καὶ σοφίας, which I have translated "remaining near to the sepulcher ... ," may well suggest that Hesychius was in the habit of lecturing in the basilica near the site of Christ's burial place.

to the *Chronicle* of Theophanes the Confessor (d. AD 818), in the same year that Cyril of Alexandria was ordained Bishop of Alexandria, Hesychius was already in full bloom as teacher in the church of Jerusalem.[5] If this dating is accepted, then we may with some certainty assume that Hesychius was ordained presbyter under Bishop John of Jerusalem (386–417).[6]

The rank and reputation of Hesychius is clearly evident from the report of the events on May 7, 428, when he accompanied Juvenal, Bishop of Jerusalem, to the laura of St. Euthymius for the dedication of its monastic church.[7] The scene is described by Cyril of Scythopolis in his *Life of Saint Euthymius*:

> Archbishop Juvenal came down to the laura, accompanied by the sainted Passarion, then rural bishop and archimandrite of the monks, and by the inspired Hesychius, priest and teacher of the church, and he consecrated the church of the laura on 7 May of the eleventh indiction in the fifty-second year of the life of the great Euthymius. When the laura had been consecrated and had as priests John and Cyrion, the archbishop ordained Domitian and Domnus deacons. The great Euthymius rejoiced in spirit, especially at seeing together with

---

[5] τῷ δ᾽ αὐτῷ ἔτει ἤνθει ταῖς διδασκαλίαις Ἡσύχιος πρεσβύτερος Ἱεροσολύμων; *PG* 108:228. The *Chronicle* gives the year as *anno mundi* 5907 (= AD 414/415). There seems to be no compelling reason to doubt this claim of Theophanes. However, commentators do provide a caution, since shortly afterward in the *Chronicle* Theophanes asserts that the time of Hesychius' death is roughly contemporaneous with the year that Valentinian III married Eudoxia (AD 436/437) and the year in which Melania the Younger died (AD 439) (*PG* 108:241–44). That dating is, however, almost certainly mistaken, as other evidence suggests. For an English translation of Theophanes' *Chronicle*, see *The Chronicle of Theophanes Confessor: Byzantine and Near Eastern History AD 284–813*, trans. Cyril Mango and Roger Scott (Oxford: Clarendon Press, 1997), here p. 129.

[6] John II, Bishop of Jerusalem, succeeded his more famous predecessor, Cyril of Jerusalem. His episcopacy was riddled with controversy. Perhaps influenced by Epiphanius of Salamis, Jerome attacked John as a committed Origenist, a reputation reinforced by his hospitality to Origenistic monks exiled from Egypt by Patriarch Theophilus. Later Jerome, allied with Paulus Orosius, a friend of Augustine, criticized John as too receptive of Pelagius. John presided over the Synod of Diospolis (AD 415) which, in fact, did not explicitly condemn Pelagius. Some scholars claim that John, not Cyril of Jerusalem, was responsible for the *Mystagogical Lectures*.

[7] The year of the dedication was either AD 428 or 429. Michel Aubineau prefers AD 429 (*SC* 187:38). For AD 428 see Y. Hirschfeld, "Euthymius and his Monastery in the Judean Wilderness," *Liber Annuus* 43 (1993): 344.

the patriarch the Abraham-like Passarion and the divine Heyschius, who were celebrated luminaries, resplendent in the whole world.[8]

Little, if any, biographical information exists of the life of Hesychius after this event. However, there is an interesting story told by John Rufus, a strong "monophysite" and opponent of the Council of Chalcedon, that connects the Empress Eudocia, herself sympathetic to the "monophysite" cause, and Hesychius. The story implies that Hesychius was himself favorable to the "monophysite" cause or, at least, skeptical of the results of Chalcedon:

> At the moment when that irregular council was about to take place, the sky became altogether obscure and filled with darkness and gloomy clouds. And in the holy city of Jerusalem and the towns surrounding it and in many locales within Palestine there was a rainstorm of stones. Concerning their form, they are altogether similar and resembled those precious stones that are made. There was upon them various and strange markings, so that many of the people gathered them up. When, however, certain persons made use of them without discernment, they became blind. It is said that Hesychius, the preacher of Jerusalem, gathered up many of them, showed them to the Empress Eudocia and sent some of them to Constantinople as a demonstration of that prodigy that announced the blindness that would seize the world in the wake of the apostasy of the bishops.[9]

---

[8] Cyril of Scythopolis, *Life of Saint Euthymius* 16, in *Lives of the Monks of Palestine by Cyril of Scythopolis*, trans. R. M. Price with introduction and notes by John Binns (Kalamazoo, MI: Cistercian Publications, 1991), 22. For the Greek, see *PG* 114:629. A laura (λαύρα) was originally a cluster of cells or caves for hermits, along with a church and a refectory. Later these hermits might be organized as by St. Euthymius (AD 377–473). Passarion was an important figure of early Palestinian monasticism. Here he is said to be "rural bishop" (χωρεπίσκοπος), an assistant to a bishop of a large city or diocese, especially tasked to oversee areas distant from the city. Passarion is called "Abraham-like" because of his reputation for support of the poor and hospitality to the stranger (cf. Genesis 18:1–8). Passarion built a house for the poor outside the eastern gates of Jerusalem. Cyril reports that Passarion died seven months after the consecration of the monastic church.

[9] John Rufus, *Plerophoriae* 10 (*Patrologia Orientalis* 8:22). This is my translation of the French of Aubineau (*SC* 187:38–39). See also Siméon Vailhé, "Notes de literature ecclésiastique," *Echos d'Orient* 9 (1906): 219–20. John Rufus was ordained priest by Peter the Fuller, the anti-Chalcedon bishop of Antioch (c. AD 475). He became bishop of Maiuma and was a leader of the "monophysite" movement after Chalcedon. He wrote the *Plerophoriae* c. AD 515, most likely during the patriarchate of Severus of Antioch.

The story indicates that Hesychius was still alive at the time of the Council of Chalcedon (AD 451), and it is the common opinion that Hesychius died shortly thereafter. While one cannot be certain, it seems most likely that Hesychius lent his support to the early anti-Chalcedon "monophysite" response in Palestine. From his writings it is evident that Hesychius was faithful to the "Alexandrian" approach to the interpretation of the Scriptures, and his Christological statements, although simple and non-technical, are decidedly Cyrillian and strongly anti-Nestorian. His preferred Christological confession was "the Word incarnated" (ὁ λόγος σαρκωθείς), a phrase that occurs in this homily and in many other places within his writings.[10]

The Cyrillian "one nature" Christology was characteristic of most Palestinian monasticism. Passarion, mentioned above, exerted great influence upon Peter the Iberian who was a major figure in the resistance to Chalcedon.[11] Hesychius' association with Bishop Juvenal of Jerusalem (AD 422–458) is also suggestive of Hesychius' Alexandrian leanings. Juvenal was one of the staunchest supporters of Cyril of Alexandria at the Council of Ephesus (AD 431) and had even supported Dioscorus and Eutyches at the Second Synod of Ephesus (AD 449), that synod so famously called "the Robber Synod" by Leo I, Bishop of Rome. At the Council of Chalcedon, however, Juvenal was eventually persuaded to affirm the "Tome" of Leo and the orthodoxy of Flavian. For this, Juvenal was denounced in Palestine as a Judas, and when he returned home he was confronted by a hostile mob of monks and forced to flee. Later, with imperial assistance Juvenal was able to

---

See Cornelia B. Horn, *Asceticism and Christological Controversy in Fifth-Century Palestine: The Career of Peter the Iberian*, Oxford Early Christian Studies (Oxford: University Press, 2006), 12–44. For Empress Eudocia (= Athenäis), see E. D. Hunt, *Holy Land Pilgrimage in the Later Roman Empire AD 312–460* (Oxford: Clarendon Press, 1982), 221–48.

[10] See Homily 5 below: ὁ Λόγος ὁ σαρκωθεὶς καὶ ξύλῳ προσηλωθεὶς καὶ ἐκ νεκρῶν ἀναστὰς καὶ εἰς οὐρανοὺς ὑψωθείς (*SC* 187:66). Aubineau gives a helpful summary of the various forms this confession took in the writings of Hesychius (*SC* 187:94–95).

[11] Peter came to Jerusalem c. AD 437 and built a monastery close to the so-called Tower of David. It was Passarion's care for the poor, strangers, and orphans that especially appealed to Peter. See Horn, *Asceticism and Christological Controversy*, 150–52, 280–84.

return.[12] Was Hesychius involved in these contentious events? Later, Pope Pelagius II (AD 555–561) would accuse Hesychius of precisely that: "It is certain (*constat*) that he freely received Eutyches himself in Jerusalem and that he wrote books against the holy synod of Chalcedon and against the letter of Leo, of blessed memory, which was given to Flavian, Bishop of Constantinople."[13] A chapter against Theodore of Mopsuestia, taken from Hesychius' *Church History*, was read at the Fifth Ecumenical Council. Hesychius writes of Theodore: "He wrote that [Christ] is not the incarnate Word, as we have been taught in the Gospels, but a man who through the advance of life and the perfection of sufferings was conjoined to God the Word."[14] It is reasonable to suspect that Hesychius was sympathetic to the initial opposition to Chalcedon. But, however that may be, Hesychius apparently did not live to experience its development and aftermath. Perhaps that is why Cyril of Scythopolis, a strongly pro-Chalcedon advocate, could call Hesychius a "luminary, resplendent in all the world."[15]

The Greeks commemorate Hesychius on March 28. Around AD 570 the pilgrim from Piacenza notes that outside the gates of Jerusalem, east of the pool of Bethesda, there was a tomb of "St. Isicius" at which bread was distributed to the poor and needy. As Cornelia Horn notes, "Under the date of 22 September, the *Georgian Lectionary* attests to the building and the tomb of a priest 'St Eusychius.' "[16]

---

[12] For this anti-Chalcedon uprising in Palestine, see Aloys Grillmeier, *Christ in Christian Tradition*, vol. 2, part 1: *From Chalcedon to Justinian I* (Atlanta: John Knox Press, 1987), 98–105.

[13] The quote comes from Pelagius, *In defensione trium capitulorum* II. The Latin is given by Aubineau (*SC* 187:39). For the full text, see R. Devreesse, ed., *Studi e Testi* 57 (Rome: 1932). The "Three Chapters" were three famous Antiochene theologians (Theodore of Mopsuestia, Ibas of Edessa, Theodoret of Chyrrus) condemned at the Fifth Ecumenical Council (553).

[14] See Mansi, *Conciliorum Omnium Amplissima Collectio*, 9:248–49; Eduard Schwartz, *Acta Conciliorum Oecumenicorum*, 4/1: *Concilium Universale Constantinopolitanum sub Iustiniano Habitum*, ed. Johannes Straub (Berlin: Walter de Gruyter, 1971), 90–91.

[15] On the basis of Cyril's positive affirmations concerning Hesychius, Kirchmeyer expresses doubts about the truthfulness of Pelagius' claim that Hesychius wrote against Chalcedon ("Hésychius de Jérusalem," 403).

[16] Horn, *Asceticism and Christological Controversy*, 282; by permission of Oxford University Press. The "building" refers to the "house for the poor outside the eastern

Although Hesychius commented upon the entire Scripture, many of his works have been lost or perhaps subsumed into various *florilegia*.[17] However, among his extant works are a *Commentary on Leviticus*, a *Commentary on Job*, glosses on the Psalms, on the twelve Minor Prophets, on Isaiah, and on the Canticles, a *Great Commentary on the Psalms*, and various homilies.[18] Hesychius is said also to have written a history of the Council of Chalcedon in four books and a *Church History*. Unfortunately, these are lost, except for one chapter of the *Church History* that was read at the Fifth Ecumenical Council (AD 553). Ironically, Hesychius found a greater echo in the West than he did in his native East. He is quoted by Amalaric of Metz (d. c. AD 850) and receives abundant quotation by Rhabanus Maurus (d. AD 856) in his own commentary on Leviticus.[19] In the Middle Ages Hesychius is regarded as an authority in questions relating to sacramental theology. In this context Hesychius is quoted by Alexander of Hales (d. c. AD 1245), by Bonaventure (d. c. AD 1274) and by Thomas Aquinas (d. c. AD 1274).[20]

The following translation is on the basis of the Greek text provided by Michel Aubineau in the series *Sources chrétiennes*, volume 187 (Paris: Les Éditions du CERF, 1972). Aubineau also provides a helpful intro-

---

gates of the city" built by Passarion. According to the Palestinian-Georgian Calendar (codex Sinaiticus 34), Hesychius is remembered on 22 September.

[17] For discussion of Hesychius' works, see Quasten, *Patrology*, 3:490–96, and Kirchmeyer, "Hésychius de Jérusalem," 399–403.

[18] The *Commentary on Leviticus* exists only in a sixth-century Latin translation (*PG* 93:787–1180). Since its Biblical citations are from the Vulgate, it was earlier thought to be inauthentic. However, a Greek fragment (Leviticus 14:4–7) has allowed scholars to demonstrate the originality of the commentary, although the translator used the Vulgate for quotation and revised Hesychius' Christological statements to conform to the Definition of Chalcedon. For the Greek fragment, see A. Wenger, "Hésychius de Jérusalem. Le fragment grec du commentaire 'In Leviticum,'" *Revue des études augustiniennes* 2 (1956): 464–70. The *Commentary on Job* (chapters 1–20) in twenty-four homilies exists only in an Armenian version. The *Great Commentary on the Psalms* is printed under Hesychius' own name (*PG* 93:1179–1340) and under the name of John Chrysostom (*PG* 55:711–84). Psalm 37 is edited by R. Devreesse, "La chaîne sur les psaumes de Daniele Barbaro II: Hésychius de Jérusalem," *Revue Biblique* 33 (1924): 512–21.

[19] For example, Rhabanus Maurus, *In Leviticum*, prologue (*PL* 108:247).

[20] See Kirchmeyer, "Hésychius de Jérusalem," 407.

duction and commentary notes. The reader will be instructed when these have been used.

HOMILY ON THE PASCHA

1. Bright is the heaven, made resplendent by the dance of the stars.[21] Yet brighter still is the world when the morning star is rising. But the circumstance of this present night is illumined not so much by the stars as it is by its present gladness since our God and Savior has won the victory. For he says, "Take courage! I have overcome the world!"[22] For since God has conquered the invisible foe, we also shall certainly gain for ourselves the victory against the demons.[23] Let us, therefore, remain close-by the saving cross so that we might carry away the first fruits of the gifts of Jesus. Let us keep the feast of this sacred night with sacred torches, raising up a holy melody and singing out a heavenly hymn: "The Sun of righteousness, our Lord Jesus Christ, has illumined this day throughout the whole orb of the world of men. He rose through the cross. He has saved the faithful."[24]

2. Therefore, let no one disbelieve the symbols of the cross, but let him worship the blessed and thrice-blessed wood of the cross. Let him not disbelieve the symbols of the cross that has opened the doors of heaven to us. No longer shall "they light a lamp and place it under a bushel"—by bushel I speak of the Law—but they place it upon the

---

[21] "Dance of the stars" translates τῇ τῶν ἄστρων χορείᾳ. The term χορεία refers to a circular dance with music perhaps sung by those dancing. The word for "bright" (δαιδρός) can also mean "joyful." Given the celebrative nature of the paschal victory, these associations should be kept in mind. In their own way, even the celestial bodies partake in a victory dance.

[22] John 16:33.

[23] The verb "gain for ourselves" is ἀποισόμεθα (future middle ἀποφέρειν) and suggests the taking of a prize. Given the context of victory over an enemy, our translation wishes to suggest the taking of booty, the despoiling of an enemy's goods. That something like this is intended is supported by the following sentence. The Christians, too, "carry away the first fruits." The victory of Christ does not benefit himself alone. All united to him in his victory are themselves victors and share the spoils.

[24] Although not demanded by the text, I have interpreted the words in quotation marks to be the "heavenly hymn" to which Hesychius refers. Reference to the "Sun of righteousness" comes from Malachi 3:20, a text frequently adduced to give image to the rising of the Son of God. Thus, in baptismal imagery east was regarded as the direction of new life; west, from whence comes the dark, was a figure of the realm of Satan.

lampstand—by lamp I mean the Word. The Word was present in the Law, but to the unfaithful it was hidden within the Law as though under a bushel. But when the Word came upon the cross, that is, when he was placed upon the lampstand,[25] then he illumined the whole orb of the world of men.

3. My beloved, behold Rome which rules by the symbols of the cross that is honored in the center of the Forum.[26] My beloved, behold Paul who puts into writing his immortal letters and has designated himself as a slave of the cross.[27] He was not ashamed of the cross, that scandal for the Jews, that foolishness to the Greeks! He has displayed [the cross] as a phylactery of wisdom.[28] By the wood of the cross he has aroused the churches of the whole world of men. The staff of Moses, by

---

[25] As is clear, the lampstand is the cross upon which the lamp (the Word) is placed. The Word is light of the world *from the cross*. The image of the lamp and of the lampstand was variously used by the fathers. For some the lampstand was the Virgin Mary. More frequently the lampstand was the Church. For a brief summary of the sources, see Aubineau (*SC* 187:76–78). However, the image of the cross as the lampstand is not unique to Hesychius.

[26] The second mention of the "symbols of the cross" (σταυροῦ συμβόλοις). Mention of Rome may be a reference to Constantinople, the "New Rome." Aubineau notes that in the forum at Constantinople there was a porphery column at the top of which stood a statue of Constantine in whose right hand was a terrestrial orb surmounted by a cross (*SC* 187:80). For description he cites Nicephorus Callistus, *Ecclesiastical History* 8.49 (*PG* 145:1325); Socrates, *Ecclesiastical History* 1.17 (*PG* 67:120; *NPNF*² 2:21). Aubineau, however, is inclined to favor Jerusalem itself as the reference. Jerome writes: "From the time of Hadrian to the reign of Constantine—a period of about one hundred and eighty years—the spot which had witnessed the resurrection was occupied by a figure of Jupiter; while on the rock where the cross had stood, a marble statue of Venus was set up by the heathen and became an object of worship" (*Letter* 58:3 [*CSEL* 54:531; *NPNF*² 6:120])." The cross erected in the Basilica of the Holy Sepulchre would have looked over the forum built by Hadrian. Aubineau writes: "The cross erected on Calvary and overlooking the Forum could therefore have appeared to Hesychius and his hearers as revenge for the humiliation described by Jerome" (*SC* 187:81; my translation).

[27] Perhaps Hesychius has in mind Romans 1:1; Philippians 1:1; and Titus 1:1 where Paul speaks of himself as δοῦλος Χριστοῦ Ἰησοῦ (Titus 1:1: θεοῦ). If so, Hesychius believes that in naming Christ Jesus, Paul is thinking of the crucified.

[28] Hesychius is using 1 Corinthians 1:23–25. What Hesychius has in mind by speaking of the "phylactery of the cross" is unclear. Certainly the image suggests that the cross was regarded as that which guards and protects against demonic forces. Aubineau cites Ps-Chrysostom, *In Pascha sermo* 6.51: (*SC* 27:177; *PG* 59:743). Does the phrase also suggest a practice, such as wearing the cross?

itself, drove away the scourges of the Egyptians,[29] but, by virtue of its relation to the wood of the cross, the staff put an end to the transgressions of men. There Pharaoh, pursuing Israel, is drowned in the sea. Here the devil is brought to naught, but those who worship the Savior are saved. There, by stretching out his hands Adam drew death upon us. But by the stretching out of his hands, our Master has saved all things.

4. But, O wood, more magnificent than the heaven, surpassing the vaults of heaven![30]

O wood, thrice-blessed, which transports our souls to heaven!

O wood, which has procured for the world its salvation and has chased away the diabolic army!

O wood, which has hurled the thief into paradise and made him to dance with Christ![31]

"Truly, truly, I say unto you, today you shall be with me in paradise."[32]

Let us imitate the good intention[33] of this murderer.[34] No, rather, because of his faith afterward let us imitate the man inspired by the

---

[29] Aubineau makes note of the strange language that the rod of Moses "drove away the scourges" (μάστιγας ἀπήλασεν) of the Egyptians when, in fact, Moses threatened and brought on the scourges (SC 187:82–83). He wonders whether there was not a confusion between ἀπήλασέ and ἐπάγειν (ἐπάγειν appears frequently in the Exodus story [Exodus 10:4, 13; 11:1; 15:19, 26]). However, the language of Hesychius is determined by the following sentence. The rod of Moses caused the sea to cover Pharaoh and his army, thus putting an end to the tyranny of the Egyptians and thus the sufferings of Israel (Exodus 14:16, 21, 26).

[30] The preacher four times addresses the wood of the cross directly. The rhetorical effect of this can be felt if one speaks the four-fold address with increasing vocal intensity. The rhetorical nature of the passage can also be seen in the chiastic structure of the adjectives in this first direct address: μεγαλοπρεπέστερον οὐρανοῦ καὶ τὰς οὐρανίους ἀψῖδας ὑπερβάλλον.

[31] The image is that of throwing a javelin or shooting an arrow (ἀκοντίσαν).

[32] See Luke 23:43. The image of the dance echoes the first line of the homily (see note 12).

[33] Translating τὴν ἀγαθὴν γνώμην. Aubineau translates "les bonnes dispositions" (SC 187:65).

[34] The Gospels speak of "malefactors" (Luke 23:39: κακούργοι) or of "robbers" (Mark 15:27; Matthew 27:38: λῃσταί). Whether Hesychius is following an apocryphal tradition or is engaging in a rhetorical comparison (he who took life now receives life) cannot be determined. Aubineau mentions *Narratio Iosephi* 2 as a possible parallel (SC 187:88).

Spirit.[35] For what indeed does he say? "Remember me, Lord, in your kingdom."[36] And by a single assent of faith[37] he inhabits paradise and walks about the heavens! "For truly, I say to you," it says, "today you shall be with me in paradise." Let us remain, we as well,[38] near the cross of the Savior, saying those very same words, "Lord, remember me in your kingdom," so that also we[39] might become partakers of paradise and enjoy the kingdom of the heavens.

5. The present festival, brothers, is a celebration of victory,[40] the victory celebration of the universal King, Son of God. For today the devil has been defeated by him who was crucified. But our race is made joyful by him who is raised up.[41] For the day which is today[42] cries out for my resurrection and says: "In my course I have seen a new spectacle.

There it is said of the bad thief, Gestas, that "he killed wayfarers with the death of the sword."

[35] The contrast is between ἀνδροφόνος and πνευματοφόρος, "bearer of the Spirit."

[36] Luke 23:42.

[37] Translating ἐν μιᾷ καταθέσει πίστεως. Aubineau translates "après un seul acte de foi" (SC 187:65). The phrase refers to the immediately preceding words of the robber, "Remember me, Lord, in your kingdom." That may be an "act" of faith, but the word καταθέσις indicates that the act of faith was an assent to what Jesus had just said, "Today you will be with me in paradise." Hesychius echoes a homiletic use of the good robber's faith present also elsewhere (Ps-Chrysostom, In Adoration of the Venerable Cross [PG 62:747]; Chrysostom, Sermon on Genesis 7.4 [PG 54:613]). Our interpretation is supported by a comment from Ps.-Chrysostom: "The robber inhabits paradise by his faith and also by his word (ἐν πίστει τε καὶ λόγῳ).

[38] The "we" of the exhortation is given emphasis: παραμείνωμεν καὶ ἡμεῖς.

[39] The emphasis on "we" is repeated: ἵνα καὶ ἡμεῖς . . . γενώμεθα.

[40] The Greek is νικητήριον ἡ παροῦσα πανήγυρις. Usually the singular (τὸ νικητήριον) indicates a prize of victory, while the plural (τὰ νικητήρια) refers to the victory celebration (= οἱ γάμοι [Matthew 27:2, 3, 4]). However, in the context of a "festal assembly" (πανήγυρις) the singular here clearly refers to the festive celebrations in the aftermath of a victory. The term πανήγυρις (πᾶς + ἄγυρις = ἀγορά) refers to a general or national assembly, usually festive. Perhaps in the present context the festive assembly is implied to be that of the Church.

[41] Hesychius mentions first "him who was crucified" (διὰ τὸν σταυρωθέντα), then of "him who is raised up" (διὰ τὸν ἀναστάντα). It is characteristic of paschal homilies to hold closely together the death and the resurrection of Christ. Taken alone, neither has meaning in itself. The festive celebration of the cross cries out for "my resurrection." The work of resurrection is, at this point, not focused on a past event but on the present power of the resurrection even now to raise up the dead to faith.

[42] Translating ἡ σήμερον ἡμέρα. The "today" which cries out for "my resurrection," that is, the day of my victory through the cross is the day of my baptism.

A tomb is opened and a man is being raised and bones are rejoicing[43] and souls are made glad and men are being formed[44] and heavens are rent asunder and powers are crying out, 'Lift up your gates, you princes [and be lifted up you everlasting doors and the King of Glory shall enter in].'[45] Today I have seen the heavenly King, girded around with light, ascending beyond the lightning and rays, beyond the sun and the fountains of the waters, beyond the clouds, both spirit of power and life eternal." For he was at first hidden in the womb of the flesh, then afterward hidden in the womb of the earth. In the first womb he was sanctifying those who are born through conception, in the second womb making alive through the resurrection those who are dead.[46] "For sorrow and pain and groaning have fled away."[47] "For who has known the mind of God, or who has been his counselor"[48] if not the Word who was made flesh and was nailed to the tree and has risen from the dead and has been exalted to the heavens?[49]

6. This very day is the announcement of joy.[50] For on this day the Lord arose again, raising up with him the company of Adam.[51] For he

---

[43] See Psalm 51:8 [50:8 LXX]: "You will cause me to hear rejoicing and gladness; the bones which have been afflicted shall rejoice" (ἀγαλλιάσονται ὀστᾶ τεταπεινωμένα).

[44] Translating ἀνθρώπους πλασσομένους. The verb πλάσσειν is used for the creation of man (Genesis 2:7: καὶ ἔπλασεν ὁ θεὸς τὸν ἄνθρωπον). The victory of the cross is the event of a new creation.

[45] Psalm 23:7 (LXX). Hesychius does not quote the entire verse but writes "and that which follows" (καὶ τὰ ἐξῆς). I have placed what follows in brackets. The reference to "men are being formed" is to a new creation (see Genesis 2:7). For "heavens are rent asunder" (οὐρανοὺς σχιζομένους) Aubineau suggests Mark 1:10. However, although the phraseology occurs in Mark 1:10, the context suggests that here Acts 1:9–11 is in mind. Certainly the words from Psalm 23:7 were interpreted as foretelling the ascension. See Aubineau, SC 187:89–91.

[46] Hesychius makes this contrast with the construction ὅπου μέν . . . ὅπου δέ, "in the one place . . . in the other place." For translation I have made the references explicit: "in the first womb . . . in the second womb."

[47] Isaiah 35:10.

[48] Isaiah 40:13; Romans 11:34.

[49] The "who" of the prophet Isaiah's rhetorical question is answered through this semi-creedal summary. Aubineau writes: "One can discern here an echo of the symbols in use" (SC 187:95; my translation), and he refers to the creeds of Nicaea and Constantinople.

[50] Translating χαρᾶς εὐαγγελισμός.

was born for the sake of man and he rose again with man.[52] Today, through him who rises again, paradise is laid open and Adam is given life and Eve is consoled and the invitation is extended[53] and a kingdom is prepared and man is saved and Christ is worshiped. For having trampled death under foot[54] and having taken the tyrant captive and having despoiled Hades, as a victorious King, as a glorious commander, as an invincible charioteer, he ascended into heaven and said to his Father, "Behold, O God, here am I and the children you have given to me"[55] and what follows. And from his Father he heard, "Sit at my right hand until I place your enemies as a footstool under your feet."[56] To him be glory, now and unto the ages of ages. Amen.

---

[51] Translating συνεγείρας τὴν τοῦ Ἀδὰμ ἀγέλην. The word ἡ ἀγέλη refers to a herd of horses or oxen, or to any herd or group. It comes from the verb ἄγω and so suggests a group that is led or guided. Here Adam is representative of the whole of humanity. As Adam goes, so go we all.

[52] Translating ἐγεννήθη γὰρ διὰ τὸν ἄνθρωπον καὶ ἀνέστη ἐν τῷ ἀνθρώπῳ. Aubineau notes the difficulty in translating this last phrase. Hesychius represented an "Alexandrian" emphasis in his Christology and so rejected any idea of an "indwelling" of the Word in man. We have translated as does Aubineau, "he rose again with man." However, when Aubineau interprets this translation as an "accompaniment" (*accompagnement*) and in his note translates "he is arisen with all men" (il est ressuscité *avec* tous les hommes), we must register a certain caution. It is true, as Aubineau notes, that the present phrase restates the earlier συνεγείρας τὴν τοῦ Ἀδὰμ ἀγέλην. We should, however, note the singular (ἐν τῷ ἀνθρώπῳ). Hesychius is trying to express the mystery that in the flesh of Christ all of humanity is included. For Aubineau's note, *SC* 187:96.

[53] Translating καὶ κλῆσις πληθύνεται. The noun ἡ κλῆσις can refer to a legal summons to a court. But here it assumes the meaning of invitation to a feast. The invitation is to all nations (Adam!).

[54] Perhaps reflecting 1 Corinthians 15:25–27. Aubineau refers to other texts that speak of Christ placing or trampling death under his feet (Melito of Sardis, *Fragment* 13 [*SC* 123:238]; Athanasius, *On the Incarnation* 27 [*SC* 18:261]; Romanos the Melodist, *Hymns* 43; 44; 45 [*SC* 128:532, 552, 584]). Often it is the devil who is placed under Christ's feet. But the meaning is the same. Death is but the devil present in his work. For other texts, see Aubineau, *SC* 187:97–98.

[55] Isaiah 8:18; Hebrews 2:13. Hesychius has changed the declarative statement of Isaiah into an address to God. The LXX reads ἰδοὺ ἐγὼ καὶ τὰ παιδία ἅ μοι ἔδωκεν ὁ θεός. The last clause in Hesychius reads ἅ μοι δέδωκας, ὦ θεός. After the words quoted Hesychius adds "and that which follows" (καὶ τὰ ἑξῆς). This suggests that he has Isaiah 8:18 in mind. It is unclear, however, how the remainder of Isaiah 8:18 would be relevant to Hesychius' point. For this reason I have not included the rest of Isaiah 8:18 in brackets. Hebrews 2:13 has only the words (with the change noted above) which Hesychius quotes explicitly.

[56] Psalm 110:1 (109:1 LXX); Acts 2:34.

[A homily] of the blessed Hesychius, priest of Jerusalem, for the day
of the Pascha.

THE MEANING OF THE CROSS
IN HESYCHIUS' PASCHAL HOMILY

The destruction of Jerusalem by the Romans under Hadrian (AD 135)
was disastrous not only for Jewish holy places but also for Christian
holy places. Jerome writes: "From the time of Hadrian to the reign of
Constantine—a period of about one hundred and eighty years—the spot
which had witnessed the resurrection was occupied by a figure of
Jupiter; while on the rock where the cross had stood, a marble statue of
Venus was set up by the heathen and became an object of worship."[57]
That changed with the rise of the Christian emperor, Constantine. We
are informed by Socrates that Constantine's mother, Helena, had the
statue of Venus thrown down and discovered the remains of the true
cross. "The emperor's mother erected over the place of the sepulcher a
magnificent church, and named it *New Jerusalem*."[58] It was in this new
church, the Church of the Holy Sepulchre, that Hesychius taught and
preached.[59]

Most likely Hesychius preached this homily in the Martyrium, close
by the relics of the true cross, during the first liturgy of the paschal vigil
around midnight. At the beginning of his homily Hesychius exhorts his
listeners, "Let us remain close-by the saving cross" (Homily 1). As the
worshipers would move throughout the night toward the Anastasis
where a third liturgy would be held around daybreak, the focus of this
first liturgy was the adoration of the cross: "Let no one disbelieve the

---

[57] Jerome, *Letter* 58.2 (*NPNF*[2] 6:120; *CSEL* 54:531). Jerome continues: "The original
persecutors, indeed, supposed that by polluting our holy places they would deprive us of
our faith in the passion and in the resurrection."

[58] Socrates, *Ecclesiastical History* 1.17 (*NPNF*[2] 2:21).

[59] Good depictions of the plan of the Basilica of the Holy Sepulchre are given by
Aubineau (*SC* 187: between 56 and 57). One might distinguish four parts of the basilica:
1) first atrium, entry to the church; 2) Martyrium, the great five-aisled nave of the
church; 3) interior atrium, between the Martyrium; and the 4) Anastasis, the traditional
site of Jesus' burial and resurrection. At the northwest corner of the interior atrium was
"Calvary." Here stood a large cross. The paschal homily of Hesychius probably took
place in the Martyrium but in close proximity to "Calvary."

symbols of the cross, but let him worship the blessed and thrice-blessed wood of the cross" (Homily 2). Indeed, in Homily 4 Hesychius addresses the cross directly, as though it were the personification of Christ. There is no thought here of suffering and death. The cross has become the chief sign of Christ's victory, a victory that has cosmic consequences because the death of *this* man was the death of the divine Word, whose death defeats death and the invisible army of the devil. Jesus is God the Word. His death and resurrection, therefore, were not mere events in time, geographically located and isolated. They had universal effect, for *where* the Word is, *there* occurs that which the Word effects: "The Sun of righteousness, our Lord Jesus Christ, has illumined this day throughout the whole orb of the world of men. He rose through the cross. He has saved the faithful" (Homily 1). Indeed, the present power of the cross is but the instrument of Christ who now sits at the right hand of the Father. For Hesychius, the cross, the resurrection, the ascension and the session of Christ at God's right hand are not discreet, sequential events. The cross is that in which the others are implicit. The event of the cross bears within itself the life of man and the heavenly glory of Christ who has brought with him to the Father "the children" whom the Father has given to him (Homily 6).[60] The term "children" makes it clear that Hesychius is referring to the baptized, perhaps those who have earlier in the evening been baptized. The victory of Christ is not remembered as a past act of greatness, but as a present experience of the Church: "For today the devil has been defeated by him who was crucified" (Homily 5).

The cross is variously depicted according to its redemptive significance. A summary of some of the most important may be helpful:

1)   The cross effected victory over Satan. "For since God has conquered the invisible foe, we also shall certainly gain for ourselves the victory against the demons" (Homily 1). The whole first chapter depicts the church's paschal liturgy as a victory celebration of a conquering army.

---

[60] See Job Getcha, "The Unity of the Mystery of Salvation according to the Festal Homilies of Hesychius of Jerusalem," *Studia Patristica* 37 (Berlin: Akademie-Verlag, 2001), 472–76.

2) The cross is called a "phylactery of wisdom" (Homily 3). Although rare in Christian usage, the term φυλακτήριον occurs elsewhere. In *On the Holy Pascha* of Hippolytus the term is twice used of the blood on the door-posts of the Jews in Egypt, and Cyril of Jerusalem calls the sign of the cross "a great protection" (μέγα φυλακτήτιον), a "sign of the faithful and fear of demons" (σημεῖον πιστῶν καὶ φόβος δαιμόνων).[61] Thus, apparently, the cross is protection against death and the demons.

3) The cross corresponds to the staff of Moses (Homily 3). This typology was frequent in early Christian literature and a favorite also of the anti-Chalcedonian monks of Palestine.[62] In our homily the image refers to Moses stretching his staff over the waters of the Red Sea, allowing Israel to be saved, while destroying Pharaoh and putting an end to his wickedness. In the same way, sinful men are drowned in the font of baptism and arise as saved Israel. The transgressions of sinful men are put to an end.

4) The cross effects a new creation of a new humanity (Homily 6). Putting death to death, the resurrection of Christ is the raising up of man. The day of resurrection sees a new spectacle: "A tomb is opened and a man is being raised and bones are rejoicing and souls are made glad and men are being formed" (Homily 5). Significantly this statement is followed by a quote from Psalm 23:7 commonly interpreted in early Christian texts to refer to the exaltation of Christ, and with him the exaltation of man. Therefore, Hesychius concludes his homily with a conversation between Christ and the Father. As a victorious king Christ comes to the throne room of the Father and announces himself: "Behold, O God, here am I and the children you have given to me." To this the Father replies, "Sit at my right hand until I place your enemies

---

[61] Hippolytus, *On the Holy Pascha* 2.2; 15.2; also 51.6 (*SC* 27:119, 143, 177); Cyril of Jerusalem, *Catechetical Lectures* 13.36 (*PG* 33:816). See G. Q Reijners, *The Terminology of the Holy Cross in Early Christian Literature as Based upon Old Testament Typology*, Graecitas Christianorum Primaeva, vol. 2 (Nijmegen: Dekker & van de Vegt, 1965), 203–205.

[62] See Reijners, *Terminology of the Holy Cross*, 107–18; Horn, *Asceticism and Christological Controversy*, 366–69.

as a footstool under your feet."[63] The victory of Christ is the exaltation of man.

5) The event of the cross was the occasion of the despoiling of hades (Homily 6). This was a common theme of Holy Saturday.

6) By way of baptism the dialogue of Jesus with the good thief becomes a dialogue of Jesus with every sinner: "Let us remain, we as well, near the cross of the Savior, saying those very same words, 'Lord, remember me in your kingdom,' so that also we might become partakers of paradise and enjoy the kingdom of the heavens" (Homily 4).[64]

7) The cross was a lampstand upon which the Light of the world was placed (Homily 2). The image allows Hesychius to make the common early Christian assertion that the cross of Christ rendered what was hidden in the Law to become light to the darkness of humankind. In the cross man's mind is illumined to Truth and his heart is made clear of the darkness of sinful passions.[65]

As one who has dedicated his life to the study of the Law, Dean Wenthe is also aware of the Light upon the lampstand of the cross. Thus, he, and we his colleagues, join with Hesychius in saying, "To this Light be glory, now and unto the ages of ages. Amen!" (Homily 6).

---

[63] See notes 55 and 56.

[64] Use of the dialogue between Jesus and the thief was frequent in paschal sermons. See Aubineau and the sources cited there (*SC* 187:87).

[65] See note 25.

(HOW) SHOULD LUTHERANS READ THE OLD TESTAMENT?

A TEST CASE: THE SAVING CROSS IN EZEKIEL 9

Christopher W. Mitchell

Over the past twenty-one years, I have had the extraordinary privilege of serving with Dean O. Wenthe on the Editorial Board of the Concordia Commentary series,[1] an international effort, with authors recruited from confessional Lutheran church bodies around the world, to publish distinctively Lutheran volumes of exegetical theology covering all the books of sacred Scripture.[2] Although I never sat at the feet of Dr. Wenthe in the classroom, he is an exemplar of Lutheran exegesis and a mentor who has exerted a profound and enduring influence on me.[3] I have learned much from his evangelical churchmanship, his perpetually humble Christian demeanor, and most of all our exegetical conversations, particularly about the subject at hand: (how) should Lutherans read the Old Testament? Since Luther himself extensively read from the Old Testament, as did the apostles, yea, our

---

[1] In addition to his editorial role, Dr. Wenthe is also writing on Jeremiah for this series. For updated information, visit http://www.cph.org/commentaries.

[2] It was Dr. Wenthe who thought up, and insisted upon, the subtitle of the Concordia Commentary: "A Theological Exposition of Sacred Scripture." As I recall, his choice of wording was intended to accent our connection to the historic "great tradition" of the church catholic.

[3] I well remember Dr. Wenthe's initial response (c. 1993) to my first prospectus for writing the Concordia Commentary on the Song of Songs (published ten years later in 2003): "As we embark on this exegetical journey, God will open our eyes to new vistas of hermeneutical richness," a characteristically gracious way for him to say, "Chris, you have a lot to learn!" He was right.

Lord Jesus Christ himself (Luke 4:16–20; cf. Luke 24:25–27, 44–45), I am confident that Dr. Wenthe would agree that we must dispense with the provocative parentheses around "how"; yes indeed, Lutherans *should* read the Old Testament. The remaining question on the table is, then, "how?"

As Dr. Wenthe and I (together with our other editorial colleagues) have interacted with, and read manuscripts from, various scholars around the world, we have gained new appreciation for both the unity and the diversity among confessional Lutheran exegetes, even as we have endeavored to preserve and shape the legacy of Lutheran exegesis in the volumes to be bequeathed to future generations of the Church's pastors and scholars. On the one hand, there is widespread agreement about the nuts and bolts of philological and exegetical procedure, and also about the theological/doctrinal/confessional boundaries within which we (must and do) conduct our exegesis. On the other hand, there remains a certain amount of divergence, even disagreement, about some hermeneutical aspects of what constitutes genuine and faithful Lutheran exegetical theology. A long shadow, from which it is difficult to completely escape, has been cast by the Enlightenment, rationalism, and the historical-critical method.[4]

In contradistinction to critical methodology, conservative Lutherans have championed the historical-grammatical method. That method is certainly the place to begin—with painstakingly careful philological analysis of the original language of the text and consideration of all aspects of its historical context (affirming its historicity). In the Concordia Commentary series, which covers each pericope in three sections, the fruit of that method is on display in the first two sections: (1) each author's original English translation of the text and (2) the textual notes on the Hebrew, Aramaic, or Greek.

But what should go in the third section, the theological exposition or commentary proper? We practitioners of the historical-grammatical method, even if we might (but seldom do) agree wholeheartedly about all the grammatical details of the text and about all facets of biblical history, may have divergent views about the destination of the theo-

---

[4] See Horace D. Hummel, *Ezekiel 1–20*, Concordia Commentary (St. Louis: Concordia, 2005), 4.

logical exposition and the hermeneutical vehicle(s) by which to arrive there. Among the contested topics that have surfaced are these:

1. Can allegory, if defined and practiced circumspectly, ever be a legitimate hermeneutic for the exegete (as it seems to have been for some biblical authors)? Many interpreters today are paranoid of getting the scarlet letter "A" (for "allegorist") branded on their forehead,[5] even though the apostle Paul, for example, regarded at least some contours of the Old Testament as ἀλληγορούμενα (Galatians 4:24; see also, e.g., Ezekiel 16 and 23 for lengthy passages that are clearly intended to be allegories).

2. What exactly is the distinction between allegory and typology, and what are the limits of biblical typology?[6] One author, at least in an initial draft, renounced typology per se as a pagan, Platonic method. Others have struggled with the admissibility or reliability of typology vis-à-vis what they consider to be the most (or only) trustworthy way in which the Old Testament testifies to Christ, namely, verbal (rectilinear) prophecy.

3. How should an exegete categorize and capitalize on the many other different ways in which the Old Testament adumbrates, prefigures, anticipates, points to, and is to be integrated with the New Testament? In my opinion, this is the most interesting question because I believe there is a plethora of different hermeneutics at work in the Scriptures themselves, and the exegete needs to be sensitive to all of them.

Those who follow in the train of Martin Luther concur with the dictum that interpreters of the Old Testament should seek *was Christum treibet*, "what proclaims Christ," in each passage.[7] But how

---

[5] Hummel, *Ezekiel 1–20*, 4, describes his own "hermeneutical posture" as " 'spiritual' or 'pneumatic' exegesis" (citing 1 Corinthians 2:13–15) as practiced in the Early Church, though now "critics tend to pillory" spiritual exegesis as " 'allegorical,' which they allege is the antipode of 'historical' interpretation."

[6] Cf. τύπος, "type," and related vocabulary in Acts 7:44; Romans 5:14; 1 Corinthians 10:6, 11; Hebrews 8:5; 9:24; 1 Peter 3:21.

[7] See, for example, these remarks of Luther in their hermeneutical contexts: "All the genuine sacred books agree in this, that all of them preach and inculcate [*treiben*] Christ" (AE 35:396; WA Deutsche Bibel 7:384–85). "All the stories of Holy Writ, if viewed aright, point to Christ" (AE 22:339; WA 47:66).

exactly is this to be done in all the different genres of literature enshrined in the canon? All agree that Scripture interprets Scripture, so any particular text must be expounded in light of its immediate and larger context. But in what proportion and to what extent? To what degree should the New Testament color our interpretation of the Old Testament? Matters of controversy, particularly for Old Testament exegetes, include whether—or how—exegesis should be trinitarian, Christological, spiritual, incarnational, sacramental, ecclesiological, doctrinal, evangelical/missional, and kerygmatic/homiletical. One manuscript frequently employed "Trinity" and "trinitarian," but the author bristled at the editorial suggestion that these (at least on occasion) be clarified—in an Old Testament commentary—as referring to "Father, Son, and Holy Spirit" (is there any other Trinity?). In what manner are Old Testament texts to be connected with Christ? One commentator argues (with some persuasiveness) that "Christocentric" and "Christological" are inferior to "Christotelic," for Christ is the "goal/fulfillment" (τέλος in Romans 10:4).[8] At a pastors' conference, when the present author presented his interpretation of the Song of Songs, one influential pastor vociferously objected to considering any part of the Old Testament (especially a Wisdom book!) as incarnational.[9] And Old Testament authors who advocate sacramental exegesis can define the method quite differently and arrive at conflicting conclusions (more on this below regarding Ezekiel 9).

Though it is probably futile and fruitless to attempt a definitive answer to these hermeneutical questions in the abstract, I do want to suggest that these are issues that we exegetes need to contemplate and engage. What matters most is the actual employment of biblical hermeneutics in the process of expounding the specific texts of Scripture, both for the benefit of the Church and as testimony to the world. As an editor, I encourage each author to maximize and run with his own particular hermeneutical strengths. I do draw the line if an author wants

---

[8] John R. Wilch, *Ruth*, Concordia Commentary (St. Louis: Concordia, 2006), 60–64.

[9] For a broad discussion of the hermeneutics of Old Testament interpretation, including those that are Christological, analogical, figuration, typology, allegory, historical, eschatological, ecclesiological, sacramental, soteriological, and prophetic, see Christopher W. Mitchell, *The Song of Songs*, Concordia Commentary (St. Louis: Concordia, 2003), 1–97; for incarnational in particular, see 471–73.

to "excommunicate" in print other authors who practice hermeneutics that can find support in the sundry ways in which Scripture interprets Scripture within the canon as a whole.

I also would like to suggest that as we wrestle with these issues we all would benefit from a fuller consideration of the catholic history of interpretation. In recent decades it has become increasingly accepted (even expected) by many publishers that, after the author carries out his exegesis (by whatever method), he may, even should, include a sprinkling of early church interpretation.[10] But then typically the Lutheran exegete leapfrogs ahead a thousand years and cites a bit of Luther's own exegesis (though if it smacks of allegorizing, it is often dismissed by alleging that poor Luther was still afflicted with the hermeneutics instilled in him during his Roman years). Next, the conservative expositor skips another three hundred years (if he stops briefly for Keil and Delitzsch, c. 1860–1890) or four hundred years (if he does not) and spends the majority of his space discussing works from recent years.

That usual process completely bypasses medieval interpretation (which, by the way, is not all worthless allegory). It also ignores most of the history of Lutheran interpretation, including the age of Lutheran orthodoxy. Experts on that period are rare, and I certainly am not one of them. But as I have dabbled in the interpreters after Luther and before Keil and Delitzsch (roughly three hundred years, 1550–1850), I have been impressed with their clarity and rigor. Granted, much of that literature is, strictly speaking, systematic theology, sermonic, or devotional, but within and underlying it is exegesis that, in my opinion, is sometimes richer in theological content than anything written previously or subsequently.

The orthodox Lutherans operated with broad and well-honed hermeneutics, and their philological expertise often was not that far behind what is available today. A major reason for our neglect of them is, no doubt, that most remain in Latin or German. Fortunately, a few translation efforts are underway. For example, Concordia Publishing House has embarked on a multi-year effort to publish English translations of the volumes of Johann Gerhard's *Loci Theologici* (1610–1622), a dog-

---

[10] Two newer series that are wholly devoted to this endeavor are the Ancient Christian Commentary on Scripture (InterVarsity Press) and The Church's Bible (Eerdmans).

matics work chock full of profound exegesis. A desideratum is an English translation of Salomon Glassius' *Philologia Sacra* (1623), which was the standard Lutheran hermeneutics textbook for over two hundred years. (I recall that twenty years ago Dr. Wenthe was already calling for its translation.) Under the rubric of what we would call the text's *sensus plenior*, "fuller sense," Glassius discerns a multiplicity of "senses" that scriptural texts may have, resulting in rich and fulsome exegesis: *sensus literalis*, "the literal sense"; *sensus mysticus*, "the mystical sense"; *sensus allegoricus*, "the allegorical sense"; *sensus typicus*, "the typological sense"; and *sensus parabolicus*, "the parabolic sense." Many Lutheran interpreters today, in their theory and/or praxis, shy away from some of those senses (perhaps to avoid the charge that their method strays outside the confines of what the academy sanctions). That narrowness may result in a poverty of exegesis.

I believe that if we were more familiar with the broad scope of methods employed in the history of interpretation, particularly Lutheran orthodoxy, there would be greater concord about hermeneutics and what does (and what does not) constitute genuine Lutheran exegetical theology. We are all heirs of the dogmatics from that era, and via dogmatics we have also inherited much exegesis of key texts. The Lutheran doctrine that we have received from Luther, the Book of Concord, and later Lutheran dogmaticians is the result of Lutheran exegesis. While we remain well-versed in that doctrine, we are much less conversant with the exegesis that produced it. Most of us, including myself, would be better exegetes if we knew more of it.

Turning to Ezekiel, I must cite the two Concordia Commentary volumes by Dr. Horace D. Hummel, one of my formative professors and a longtime mutually respected colleague of Dr. Wenthe. In the summary of his method of interpretation,[11] Dr. Hummel contends that "even the famous *quadriga* ... of classical allegorism can be affirmed" within the "one, unified *fourfold* sense of Scripture":

1. The historical meaning of the biblical passage remains factual and foundational.

2. Creedal and doctrinal conclusions follow, based on the text.

---

[11] Hummel, *Ezekiel 1–20*, 1–6.

3. "Tropological" or moral implications are part of the message.

4. And, finally, the "anagogical" or eschatological scope of the passage must be considered: all of history and life should be viewed *sub specie aeternitatis* ["under the aspect of eternity"] as part of God's eternal plan.

Specific applications of what I have summarized must be applied to each pericope in its particularity.[12]

Dr. Hummel's exposition of Ezekiel is thoroughly Christological. He views the divine Glory, who is prominent throughout the book, as the preincarnate Christ; indeed, he interprets "*Christ as the divine speaker throughout the book.*"[13] At the same time, Dr. Hummel stresses that our interpretation needs to be trinitarian, so that we do not end up with a kind of "unitarian 'Yahweh,' " for *opera ad extra indivisa sunt* ("God's external works are indivisible," i.e., all three persons of the Godhead are at work in them).[14] He also emphasizes a "sacramental" view of history: " 'Prophecy-fulfillment' and 'typology' are the usual shorthand terms for what I like to call that 'sacramental' view of history, in which the saving Christ truly is present 'in, with, and under' the original word and historical event recorded in Scripture—in the Old Testament as well as the New Testament."[15] Dr. Hummel thus operates with a broader meaning of "sacramental" that is not restricted to texts that specifically involve the New Testament Sacraments, Baptism and the Lord's Supper (although he does refer to them often): "I know of no better umbrella term to suggest the underlying unity of the peculiar means of salvation chosen by God in both Testaments than 'sacramental.' "[16]

I now turn specifically to Ezekiel 9, which provides a test case illustrating many of the issues discussed above. In a vision Ezekiel hears

---

[12] Hummel, *Ezekiel 1–20*, 5.

[13] Hummel, *Ezekiel 1–20*, 1; emphasis original.

[14] Hummel, *Ezekiel 1–20*, 66. See his commentary on Ezekiel 1:25–28 (pp. 64–68), including his quotations of the unsurpassed work of the sixteenth-century Lutheran reformer Martin Chemnitz, *The Two Natures in Christ*, trans. J. A. O. Preus (St. Louis: Concordia, 1971). See also Hummel's first textual note on Ezekiel 9:4 (p. 268).

[15] Hummel, *Ezekiel 1–20*, 5.

[16] Hummel, *Ezekiel 1–20*, 2.

God summon six angelic executioners and also a (seventh) "man," who applies a saving "cross" to the penitent. The text (Ezekiel 9:1–6) may be translated literally thus:[17]

> [1]Then he [Yahweh] called out in my ears in a loud voice, "Bring near the executioners of the city, each with his implement of destruction in his hand." [2]And look, six men are coming from the direction of the upper gate that is faced north, each with his implement of shattering in his hand. But there was one man in their midst vested in white linen, with a scribe's writing kit at his waist. They entered and stood beside the bronze altar. [3]Now, the Glory of the God of Israel is ascending from on the cherub, on which it had been, to the threshold of the temple. He called out to the man vested in the white linen with a scribe's writing kit at his waist. [4]Yahweh said to him: "Pass through the midst of the city, the midst of Jerusalem, *and you shall cross a cross* (וְהִתְוִיתָ תָּו) on the foreheads of those who moan and groan over all the abominations being committed in her midst." [5]And to these [six others] he said in my ears, "Pass through in the city after him and slaughter. Do not let your eye pity, and do not have compassion. [6]Old man and young man, girl and little children, even women you shall kill to destruction. But do not go near any person who has the cross on him. And from my sanctuary you shall begin."

Two key questions arise in the interpretation of this passage. The first is whether the linen-clad man who applies the cross is a Christ figure or an angel. Angels, who are directly engaged in divine service, are often depicted as wearing white linen (see Revelation 15:6; 19:14; cf. the bride of Christ in Revelation 19:8). Yet Christ may appear in angelic form,[18] especially in visionary contexts, as seems to be the case with the brilliant figure depicted in the same terms, "one man vested in white linen" (אִישׁ־אֶחָד לָבוּשׁ בַּדִּים), seen by Daniel in 10:5–6, and likewise Daniel perceives "a man vested in white linen" (אִישׁ לְבוּשׁ הַבַּדִּים) in Daniel 12:6–7 (see also Revelation 10, where the mighty "angel" may be

---

[17] All Scripture translations are the author's.

[18] See Charles A. Gieschen, *Angelomorphic Christology: Antecedents and Early Evidence* Arbeiten zur Geschichte des antiken Judentums und des Urchristentums, vol. 42 (Leiden: Brill, 1998).

Christ himself).[19] Many interpreters regard the man in Ezekiel 9:2–3 (who reappears in Ezekiel 9:11; 10:2, 6–7) "vested in white linen" (לְבֻשׁ בַּדִּים), as a figure depicted with the vesture of a priest, perhaps the high priest.[20] Linen (שֵׁשׁ) was used in the tabernacle curtains (e.g., Exodus 26:1, 31) and in the high priest's ephod and other vestments (e.g., Exodus 28:4–6, 8, 15, 39). "White linen" (בַּד in Leviticus 16:4, 23, 32) is (to be) the fabric of the high priest's vesture when he presents the sin-offering on the annual Day of Atonement.[21] All the priests were to wear undergarments of "white linen" (בַּד) while ministering or they would die (Exodus 28:42–43; cf. Leviticus 6:3 [ET 6:10]; 1 Samuel 2:18; 22:18; Ezekiel 44:17–18; 2 Chronicles 5:12). An ecclesiological application of this text is that such vesture worn by Christ and his ministers (angels and priests) in the Old Testament informs the liturgical practice of the Church, particularly the vestments worn by the pastor as he stands *in loco Christi* between the people and their God.

A second key question is how to interpret the saving cross imposed on the penitent by the liturgically vested man. The construction with the verb and cognate accusative וְהִתְוִיתָ תָּו (Ezekiel 9:4) is, literally, "you shall *taw* a *taw*." In the paleo-Hebrew script, used in preexilic times and probably still by exiled Ezekiel, the letter *taw* had the shape of two crossing lines, so at the very least it may be called a "cross" in that general sense.[22] Numerous northwest Semitic inscriptions, seals, and

---

[19] Modern commentators typically dismiss the possibility of a Christological interpretation of the figures in Ezekiel 9, Daniel 10, Daniel 12, and Revelation 10. In the Early and Medieval Church it was not so.

[20] Priestly and liturgical imagery abounds in the book of Ezekiel, himself both a prophet and a priest (Ezekiel 1:3).

[21] While C. F. Keil, *Biblical Commentary on the Prophecies of Ezekiel*, 2 vols., trans. James Martin (Edinburgh: T&T Clark, 1876), 1:126–27, notes this and other connections between the garb of the seventh "man" and that of Christ (Revelation 1:13–15; cf. Daniel 10:5–6; 12:6–7), he declines to identify this man as Christ or a Christ figure in contradistinction to the six angels in Ezekiel 9. Most modern commentators give even less consideration to the possible Christology.

[22] Commentators who translate it "cross" include C. F. Keil, *Ezekiel*, 1:129, and Leslie C. Allen, *Ezekiel 1–19*, Word Biblical Commentary, vol. 28 (Dallas: Thomas Nelson, 1994), 116, who, however, disavows its Christian significance (p. 148). Cf. Moshe Greenberg, *Ezekiel 1–20*, Anchor Bible Commentary, vol. 22 (New York: Doubleday, 1983), 177.

coins attest the various shapes of *taw* in the first millennium BC: Ҳ Ҳ
𝗍 𝗍 +.[23] While the paleo-Hebrew script generally was replaced by the
Aramaic ("square") script in postexilic times, some use of the old script
persisted, as attested by various Jewish coins, the Qumran scrolls in
which it is used for the Tetragrammaton (the divine name YHWH), and
the derivative alphabet of the Samaritan Pentateuch.

Given the Early Church and Reformation-era interpretations (some
of which are cited below) that associate the *taw* in Ezekiel 9 with the
cross, one can ask whether those Christian interpreters were aware of
the cross-like shapes of the *taw* in paleo-Hebrew. An early affirmative
answer is provided by Origen (c. AD 184–254), who solicited from Jews
of his day their traditional understanding of the meaning of this *taw*.
One Jew, "one of those who believe in Christ, said the form of the Taw
in the old [Hebrew] script resembles the cross [τοῦ σταυροῦ], and that
it predicts the mark which is to be placed on the foreheads of the
Christians."[24]

---

[23] For a simple chart, see the bottom line in the insert in the hardcover editions of
Gesenius' Hebrew Grammar, GKC (Oxford: Clarendon, 1910), x. See the more extensive
charts for extrabiblical Hebrew and Moabite in John C. L. Gibson, *Textbook of Syrian
Semitic Inscriptions*, vol. 1: *Hebrew and Moabite Inscriptions* (Oxford: Oxford University
Press, 1971), 1:117–18, and for Phoenician inscriptions in John C. L. Gibson, *Textbook
of Syrian Semitic Inscriptions*, vol. 3: *Phoenecian Inscriptions* (Oxford: Oxford University
Press, 1982), 3:180. See also the chart "Development of the Semitic Alphabet" in *Sign,
Symbol, Script: An Exhibition on the Origins of Writing and the Alphabet* (Madison:
Department of Hebrew and Semitic Studies, University of Wisconsin—Madison, 1984),
33. One can find many "Paleo-Hebrew alphabet charts" by searching the Internet for
those words.

[24] Origen, *Selecta in Ezechielem* (*PG* 13:800d), as translated in Saul Lieberman, *Greek in
Jewish Palestine* (New York: Jewish Theological Seminary of America, 1942), 187–88,
quoted in Daniel I. Block, *The Book of Ezekiel: Chapters 1–24*, New International
Commentary on the Old Testament (Grand Rapids: Eerdmans, 1997), 312. A century
and a half after Origen, Jerome (c. AD 400) echoed Origen's remarks: "In the ancient
Hebrew alphabet, which the Samaritans use to this day," the *taw* resembled a cross and
was a prophetic symbol of the sign imprinted on the foreheads of Christians; quoted in
G. A. Cooke, *A Critical and Exegetical Commentary on the Book of Ezekiel*, International
Critical Commentary 21 (Edinburgh: T&T Clark, 193)], 106–107. Block's commentary
is one of the best on Ezekiel. His excursus, "The Afterlife of the Taw on the Forehead"
(pp. 310–14), surveys early Jewish and Christian interpretations. He notes that "early
Jewish commentators on Ezekiel 9 quite naturally referred to the blood of the paschal
lamb as a mark of salvation. However, when the church fathers began to link the mark
of Ezekiel and the blood of the Passover lamb [cf. 1 Corinthians 5:7] to the cross and

The mainstream LXX has "put a sign" (δὸς τὸ σημεῖον, Ezekiel 9:4), but more precise is the rendition of Aquila and Theodotion, σημειώσεις τὸ θαῦ, and the Vulgate's *signa thau*, "mark a *tau*," which relate to the Greek *tau*, τ or T. Dr. Hummel points out that T is the shape of a "tau cross," one of the many forms in which a cross appears in ancient times as well as modern, while X is a "St. Andrew's cross," since ancient tradition holds that that apostle was crucified on a cross of that shape.[25] Nevertheless, most English translations avoid calling it a "cross" and prefer the bland and generic "mark" (e.g., KJV, RSV, NRSV, NASB, NIV, ESV).

Our exegesis deepens and broadens as we consider closer and more distant parallels in the Old Testament. Besides Ezekiel 9:4, 6, the noun תָּו occurs elsewhere only in Job 31:35, where it denotes Job's written signature. (A cross or X can still be used today by the illiterate in lieu of a signature.) The *taw* in Ezekiel 9:4–6 probably is best interpreted as Yahweh's signature of ownership, marking those individuals within the larger body of apostate Israel who truly belong to him through faith; they alone are the ones exhibiting repentance as they "moan and groan" (Ezekiel 9:4) over Israel's abominable sins. See also Isaiah 44:5, where, after the eschatological outpouring of Yahweh's Spirit (in baptismal terms, Isaiah 44:3), members of the true Israel will write לַיהוה, "belonging to Yahweh," on their hand.

The *taw* in Ezekiel 9 marked the faithful as those to be spared in the destruction of the apostates. Ancient and modern interpreters have compared it with other saving signs in the Old Testament: the "sign" (אוֹת) God put on Cain so that he would not be killed (Genesis 4:15); the blood of the Passover lamb applied by the Israelites to their lintels and doorposts (the method of application prescribed in Exodus 12:22 is cruciform!) with the promise that their firstborn would not be killed by the destroyer (Exodus 12); the gold plate on the high priest's forehead engraved with קֹדֶשׁ לַיהוָה, "holy to Yahweh" ("Yahweh's holiness") to mediate grace to Israel through sacrificial atonement (Exodus 28:36–

---

blood of Christ, the Jews reversed their position" (p. 312). Block himself, however, does not capitalize on the theological continuity between Ezekiel 9 and Revelation 7; neither does he perceive a connection to Christian Baptism.

[25] Hummel, *Ezekiel 1–20*, 275.

38); the phylacteries (תּוֹטָפֹת) worn on the hand and forehead (Exodus
13:16; Deuteronomy 6:8; 11:18; cf. Matthew 23:5); and the scarlet cord
in Rahab's window that saved her and her family in the destruction of
Jericho (Joshua 2:18–21; 6:22–25).[26]

If we are to employ the kind of Lutheran hermeneutics advocated
above (trinitarian, Christological, spiritual, sacramental, ecclesiological,
inter alia) we must trace the language and themes identified in the Old
Testament into the New Testament and consider their eschatological
trajectory. The view that the saving cross serves as a kind of signature of
God's name finds support in Revelation, which abounds in allusions to
Ezekiel.[27] Revelation 7:1–8 and 9:4 unmistakably allude to Ezekiel 9:4–6:

> Four angels are ready to unleash destructive winds, but another angel
> comes and tells them not to do so until he puts a seal on the foreheads
> (as in Ezek 9:4) of the servants of God. A total of 144,000 faithful from
> the twelve tribes of Israel are sealed—a symbolic number representing
> the entire church militant on earth, since God's Israel consists of all
> Jewish and Gentile believers in Christ (Romans 9–11; Gal 6:16). The
> sealed believers in Christ are then spared when the demonic forces
> arise from hell to torment humanity (Rev 9:4). The mark put on their
> foreheads is "the seal of the living God" (Rev 7:2), which would be a
> stamp having God's name or signature. In Rev 14:1 the 144,000 are
> about to join the church triumphant, and there they are described as
> having "his [the Lamb's] name and the name of his Father written on
> their foreheads."[28]

Invoking other New Testament passages, Dr. Louis Brighton interprets the seal and divine name in Revelation as spiritual marks con-
ferred through Christian Baptism and faith in the Word of the Gospel.[29]
Dr. Hummel concurs:

---

[26] If one surveys the commentaries, one will find these and many more proposed biblical
parallels.

[27] For example, the vision of Yahweh's throne with four supporting creatures in Ezekiel
1 and 10 is analogous to that in Revelation 4, and Ezekiel's eschatological vision (Ezekiel
40–48) is the main Old Testament precedent for the imagery in John's eschatological
vision in Revelation 21–22.

[28] Hummel, *Ezekiel 1–20*, 276–77.

[29] Louis Brighton, *Revelation*, Concordia Commentary (St. Louis: Concordia, 1999), 180,
183–93, 364–75.

In New Testament theology, the divine sealing and the imposition of the name of God are accomplished in the Sacrament of Holy Baptism. Christian Baptism takes place in the triune name (Mt 28:19). Those baptized into Christ are adopted as sons of God and so become descendants of Abraham (and hence true Israelites) and heirs of all God's promises (e.g., Gal 3:26–29). The book of Acts records the outpouring of the Holy Spirit in conjunction with Baptism (e.g., Acts 2:38–39; 9:17–18; 10:47; 11:16), and so the New Testament speaks of Christians as being "sealed" with the Holy Spirit (e.g., 2 Cor 1:22; Eph 1:13; 4:30). Receiving the Spirit of sonship enables the Christian to name God as his Father (Rom 8:15). That Baptism marks a Christian as belonging to Christ (and him alone) is the background of 1 Cor 1:10–17, where St. Paul must argue against the schismatic view that Christians belong to separate parties apparently based on who baptized them (cf. also Eph 4:4–6).[30]

Turning from Scripture to the history of interpretation, early church fathers clearly were following such lines of thought as they connected the *taw* in Ezekiel 9:4–6 to the cross of Jesus Christ, the Gospel, and the Sacraments of the Church. Tertullian (c. AD 160–c. AD 225) did so in broad strokes:

> Now the Greek letter *Tau* and our own letter T [are] the very form of the cross, which He predicted would be the sign on our foreheads in the true Catholic Jerusalem. . . . Now, inasmuch as all these things are also found amongst you, and the sign upon the forehead, and the sacraments of the church, and the offerings of the pure sacrifice, you ought now to burst forth, and declare that the Spirit of the Creator prophesied of your Christ.[31]

Cyprian (c. AD 200–258) related the cross specifically to the Passover and the blood of Christ (as will Gerhard, quoted below):

---

[30] Hummel, *Ezekiel 1–20*, 277–78.

[31] Tertullian, *Against Marcion*, 3.22 (*ANF* 3:340–41; see also n. 14 on p. 340), cited in Hummel, *Ezekiel 1–20*, 277. Hummel recommends that the reader "see also *An Answer to the Jews*, 11 (*ANF* 3:167–68), where Tertullian asserts that temporal and eternal ruin shall come to all except 'he who shall have been frontally sealed with the passion of the Christ,' then quotes Ezek 8:12–9:6 and declares Christ himself to be the sign promised in the Old Testament."

That the sign pertains to the passion and blood of Christ, and that
whoever is found in this sign is kept safe and unharmed, is also proved
by God's testimony [in Ex 12:13 about the blood of the Passover
lamb]. . . . What previously preceded by a figure [type] in the slain
lamb is fulfilled in Christ, the truth which followed afterwards. . . .
When the world shall begin to be desolated and smitten, whoever is
found in the blood and the sign of Christ alone shall escape.[32]

Augustine cited Ezekiel 9:4–6 to expound the doctrine of the
Church (as will Luther, quoted below): the Church consists of repentant
believers who mourn the sins of those around them. They appear to be
mixed in with the rest of reprobate humanity, but by their repentance
they separate themselves in God's sight. They are marked invisibly on
their foreheads, meaning in their consciences. The sign is "the mark of
Christ."[33]

Luther, too, relates Ezekiel 9 to the doctrine of the Church and the
Christian life as one of repentance:

Therefore, whoever wants to have fellowship with Christians and does
not want to be an outright child of the world, let him be on the list of
those who are willing to sigh and mourn, so that he may be com-
forted, as this promise [Mt 5:4] says. We have an instance of this in
Ezekiel 9 [which he then recaps]. . . . This is the Christians' advantage.
In the world they have to see nothing but sorrow and trouble. Yet
when the world is at its smuggest and is riding along on sheer joy,
suddenly the wheel turns, and a misfortune comes upon them in
which they have to stay and perish. But the Christians are rescued and
saved, the way dear Lot was saved in Sodom. . . . Though you have to
mourn and be sorrowful and daily see your heart troubled, take it in
stride and hold fast to this saying.[34]

The seventeenth-century Lutheran Johann Gerhard connects
Ezekiel 9 directly to Baptism, and so his interpretation is rightly called
"sacramental" in that specific sense. In his locus on Baptism he explains

---

[32] Cyprian, *Address to Demetrianus*, 22 (*ANF* 5:464), cited in Hummel, *Ezekiel 1–20*,
277. Hummel adds: "In *Three Books of Testimonies against the Jews*, 2:22 (*ANF* 5:525),
Cyprian asserts that 'in this sign of the Cross is salvation for all people who are marked
on their foreheads,' and immediately cites Ezek 9:4–6 as his first proof text."
[33] Augustine, Sermon 57, 7 (*NPNF*[1] 6:438).
[34] Luther, "The Sermon on the Mount," AE 21:21.

that the sign of the cross is made on the forehead and chest to indicate that the baptizand receives grace and regeneration unto eternal life solely by the merits of Christ crucified. The cross also indicates that the baptizand believes in Christ crucified, receives Christ's name, and is sent to serve in the Church Militant under the banner of Christ. As biblical support, Gerhard cites Ezekiel 9:4 as well as Genesis 48:14 and Revelation 7:3.[35]

The last example I will cite also comes from the era of Lutheran orthodoxy, specifically, the introduction to Ezekiel 9 by Franz Vierling (late sixteenth century) in the *Altenburger Bibelwerk*, a study Bible with the translation and prefaces of Martin Luther.[36] It is notable because it identifies the priestly figure as Christ himself and the sign he administers as a cross—the cross on which Christ shed his blood. Note also Vierling's affirmation that Christ works salvation "through the Holy Spirit in the Word and Sacraments," which has become typical phraseology in The Lutheran Church—Missouri Synod today:

> Beloved Christian, today the holy prophet Ezekiel teaches beautifully and comfortingly that those men who have been signed on the forehead by the man in white clothing or linen will be preserved through all misfortune in life and death. This man is our dear Lord and Savior Jesus Christ, who has the linen robe of his innocence and makes righteous all who believe in him and who sigh and jammer about their own sins and about all the cruelty that happens contrary to God. For the sign is a cross, that is, the bloody offering of Christ on the trunk of the cross, with which he, the Lord Christ, through the Holy Spirit in the Word and Sacraments, marks all believers and makes them secure through the costly merit of his life and death. Who now has the sign of faith and is sprinkled with the blood of Christ, he will be preserved to

---

[35] "De sacro baptismo," §260, *Loci Theologici* (ed. Eduard Preuss; Berlin: Gustav Schlawitz, 1866), 4:392. (The summary of Gerhard's view is based on this author's own translation; at the time of writing, that locus of Gerhard has not yet been published in English.) Similar are Gerhard's comments about Ezekiel 9:4 in *A Comprehensive Explanation of Holy Baptism and the Lord's Supper (1610)* (Malone, TX: Repristination Press, 2000), 200–201.

[36] *Biblia: Das ist die ganze Heilige Schrift des Alten und Neuen Testaments, verdeutschet durch Dr. Martin Luther, mit dessen Vorreden und Randglossen, sowie mit den Summarien M. Viti Dieterichs, nebst den Vorreden und Schlußgebeten Francisci Vierlings* (Altenburg, 1676), also known as the *Altenburger Bibelwerk*.

eternity, and also in this life will often be saved out of great woe and danger and be defended from all conflict. That we consider also in the context of the ninth chapter.[37]

These Lutheran hermeneutics can rightly be called ecclesiological, evangelical/missional, and kerygmatic. The theology of such passages supports the Church's traditional practice of the pastor making the sign of the cross upon the baptizand, and of the congregation members crossing themselves at the Invocation and other parts of the service in remembrance of their Baptism. Then, "for the last time, the sign of the cross is made upon the body of the baptized Christian in the funeral and interment in anticipation" of the bodily resurrection on the Last Day—the final deliverance from judgment and destruction.[38]

In conclusion, I hope this essay has highlighted the kinds of hermeneutical issues Lutherans do (and should) engage while expounding the Scriptures. This holds not only for the Lutheran scholar who is writing a Bible commentary, but also for the parish pastor in the course of his ministry of congregational worship, preaching, teaching, and administering the Sacraments. Furthermore, I hope the example of Ezekiel 9 shows that we can glean much of value from the history of interpretation, including what seems to be the most neglected period of exegesis, Lutheran orthodoxy. Such historic exegesis informs our own understanding of what constitutes genuine Lutheran scholarship and also provides exegetical theology that is eminently beneficial for the Church today.

---

[37] Translated by this author from the *Biblia* [*Altenburger Bibelwerk*] (repr., St. Louis: Concordia, 1890), 2:414.

[38] Hummel, *Ezekiel 1–20*, 278.

THE MYSTERY OF CHRIST AND COSMIC RESTORATION

John W. Kleinig

In Ephesians 1:9–10 Paul speaks about the mystery of cosmic restoration, the reunion of heaven and earth under Christ. He pictures this as the restoration of a once-disjointed body that is brought together with each part in its proper place under its head.

All too often Christians confuse mysteries with secrets.[1] So, when they explain the Christian faith and commend it to others, they, knowingly or unknowingly, explain it away. They seem to assume that the mystery of Christ is a cognitive matter, something that is unknown for want of information about him or understanding of him. But a mystery is not the same thing as a secret. Even though both have to do with something that is hidden and unknown, a mystery differs from a secret in one important respect. A secret remains a secret only as long as it is still unknown. Once it is revealed, it ceases to be a secret, because a secret exists only as long as information is withheld or the facts are unknown. But a mystery remains a mystery even when it is revealed, because it needs to be experienced to be known. In fact, the more you know about it, the more mysterious it becomes.[2] Think of the mystery of

---

[1] See the frequent translation of mystery as "secret" in the NIV (Matthew 13:11; Mark 4:11; Luke 8:10; 1 Corinthians 2:7; 4:1; 2 Thessalonians 2:7). The New Testament does not use this term for things that have been deliberately kept secret or for what is experienced by higher states of human consciousness, but for the unseen presence and work of the invisible God in the world.

[2] Mystery is commonly defined as that which goes beyond normal human comprehension, like the perception of ultra-violet light to human eyesight. The implication is that if humans were more perceptive and intelligent, they would be able to discern it

life or of love! You may be able to explain a mystery, but you can never explain it away. It remains a mystery no matter how much you know about it or how fully you experience it.[3]

In the ancient world the caretakers of a holy place, a site or the shrine that was dedicated to a god or goddess, were sometimes called mystagogues. They were the stewards of a god's house. Their task was to show the devotees of that deity around the holy place. As they did so they told the stories of the local god, the myths that were associated with the place. Those stories explained the nature of the deity that was present there and the rituals that were associated with the service of that deity. In this way they initiated people into the mystery of that god. They revealed what was hidden from human sight but experienced by those who were involved in the cult of that god. A mystagogue who had been initiated into the mystery "led" (ἄγω) others together with himself into that mystery. In classical Greek, "mystagogy" was the term for the initiation of people into the experience of a mystery.[4]

My basic contention is that all pastors, all teachers of the Christian faith, are mystagogues.[5] Their task is to initiate people into a wonderful

---

clearly and understand it fully. In contrast to this view, the writers of the New Testament do not just use this term for that which is beyond normal human understanding, but for that which is hidden from all human perception and knowledge, no matter how acute and refined, like the real presence of Christ's body and blood in the Eucharist. It deals with what is unseen because it is not temporal but eternal (2 Corinthians 4:18). The mystery of the Christian faith has to do with what Luther calls the theology of the cross, God hidden and revealed in what is contrary to him, the human nature, weakness, suffering, and folly of the incarnate, crucified and yet exalted Son of God ("Heidelberg Disputation," AE 31:52–54).

[3] The Greek word μυστήριον is derived from the verb μύω, which means to walk about with shut eyes. Mystery therefore has to do with the experience of unseen, non-empirical realities.

[4] In the ancient world the term mystagogy was also used in a much more specialized way for initiation into the so-called mystery cults, such as the cult of Demeter at Eleusis, the cult of Isis in Egypt, and the oriental cult of Mithras which spread out over the Roman empire. In my opinion, the best account of these cults is given by Walter Burkert in *Ancient Mystery Cults* (Cambridge, MA: Harvard University Press, 1987).

[5] For a discussion of pastors as stewards of divine mysteries, see Jonathan F. Grothe, "The Mysteries and the Ministry," and Charles R. Hogg Jr., "The Mystery of Pastoral Existence," in *Mysteria Dei: Essays in Honor of Kurt Marquart*, 55–65 and 101–13, ed. Paul T. McCain and John R. Stephenson (Fort Wayne: Concordia Theological Seminary Press, 2000).

mystery that seems too good to be true, a mystery that evades human grasp and amazes the imagination. Our faith deals with invisible realities (Hebrews 11:1; cf. 2 Corinthians 4:18), things that are hidden from human sight, gifts from God that no eye has ever seen, no ear has ever heard, and no human mind has ever conceived (1 Corinthians 2:9). The core of that mystery is the *presence* of the crucified and risen Lord Jesus in the Church and the Church's access to the heavenly realm through him in the Divine Service.

Yet the mystery of Christ goes beyond what happens in the Divine Service, for it embraces the whole history of the world and the whole of our physical lives as we journey with Christ from earth to heaven. It, in fact, embraces the whole creation. What Jesus has accomplished for us and given to us will remain a mystery until his visible reappearance on the Last Day. Only then will all that is now hidden be disclosed for all to see. Then the full spiritual depth and entire cosmic extent of that mystery will be revealed.

Some years ago, the Australian social researcher Hugh Mackay wrote an article for the newspaper *The Australian* in which he summarized the results of the research that he had done on the attitudes of the so-called Generation Y. He noted that it is the most intensely tribal group of young people in living memory. For me, the most interesting finding from his research was his claim that this generation was fascinated by three things—community, imagination, and mystery. If that is so, the Church should be well placed to commend the Christian faith to them. That, at least, is my contention. Yet, sadly, it seems that to meet the challenge of the modern world the Lutheran Church may have, all too often, inadvertently misrepresented the faith by rationalizing it and explaining it away. I maintain that Christian preachers and teachers should, instead, treat the faith as a mystery and seek to be good mystagogues in the way that they commend it to others, not as a private esoteric experience, like an hallucinogenic trip with drugs, but as a communal, liturgical manifestation.[6]

---

[6] There is much that can be learned from the early Christian practice of mystagogy in preparing candidates for baptism and their initiation into the Divine Service through liturgical catechesis as explored by Edward Yarnold in *The Awe-Inspiring Rites of Initiation: The Origins of the R.C.I.A.* (Edinburgh: T&T Clark, 1994). In this book he

Those people who have been steeped in the tenets of post-modernism have an inbuilt suspicion of abstract thought and universal theories. They reject general explanations in favor of subjective experience and their own interpretation of it. Yet at the same time many of them hanker after some assurance that their experiences are grounded in reality, unlike a drug-induced hallucination, and are therefore able to be shared with others in common discourse. The Church may therefore be able to use the concept and reality of mystery to commend the Christian faith to them.

Mystery is a term that is well-suited to describe the common personal experience of the spiritual realm that surrounds and pervades the sensible material realm, like a fifth dimension. It assumes that there is more to human life on earth than is evident to the five senses, something beyond normal sense experience that integrates it and helps to make sense of it. The mystery of the Christian faith has to do with the hidden presence of Christ with us here on earth and our restoration by his restoration of all creation. It is a commonly shared experience of faith in him. It does not supply a theory that is able to explain everything, but provides a vision of life that helps people appreciate their unique location in God's creation, a vision of reality that is both subjective and objective, inward and outward, mental and physical, heavenly and earthly, devotional and liturgical, personal and cosmic, the vision of the incarnate Christ in whom the fullness of the godhead dwells bodily and in whom we, too, are fulfilled (Colossians 2:9).

In this essay I aim to summarize the teaching of the New Testament on the mystery of Christ and our participation in that mystery. I will not deal with the matter systematically[7] or comprehensively;[8] rather, I only

---

outlines the stages of initiation and then publishes four sets of mystagogical homilies from the fourth century.

[7] The most significant Lutheran theological treatment of this theme in English comes from Wilhelm Stählin in *The Mystery of God: The Presence of God with Men*, which was published in German by Johannes Stauda: Kassel-Wilhelmshohe in 1936, translated by R. Bird Hoyle for publication by SCM: London in 1937, and republished by Concordia Publishing House: St. Louis in 1964. Stählin (1883–1975), the bishop of Oldenburg and then professor of theology at the University of Münster, was a leader in the influential high-church Berneuchen liturgical movement between the wars. He uses Luther's formula "in, with, and under" for the presence of Christ's body and blood in the Sacrament to reflect systematically on God's presence in the Divine Service. While there

intend to examine what can be ascertained about it by an analysis of the use of the term μυστήριον[9] in the gospels[10] and in the Pauline epistles.[11] This study is presented as a tribute to my dear friend and fellow Old Testament scholar Dean Wenthe, whom I first met when I was expounding the mystery of the Divine Service in a Bible study on Hebrews. It is just a small token of gratitude to him for his generous hospitality and warm encouragement of me as a scholar, gratitude, too, for his immense contribution to the worldwide cause of confessional Lutheranism as the president of Concordia Theological Seminary and as a passionate teacher of Christ's incarnate presence in the Divine Service.

THE MYSTERY OF GOD'S KINGDOM

While the theme of Christ's teaching as the revelation of a mystery is implicit in all the Gospels, Christ himself uses this term only once in his explanation of the parable of the sower (Mark 4:11; cf. Matthew 13:11; Luke 8:10). After Jesus had taught this parable to the crowd, the twelve

---

is still much that is good in this work, it suffers from poor translation, its cursory treatment of the scriptural foundations for its assertions, its neglect of dogma as normative for liturgy, and its lack of emphasis on the role of the written Word of God in the liturgical disclosure of the divine mystery.

[8] Note the use of this term in the Revelation to St. John for the seven lamps as seven churches with the risen Lord Jesus as the lampstand (1:20), the fulfillment of prophecy by the reign of Jesus as the Messiah (10:7), and the identity of Mother Babylon (17:5, 7). For an analysis of this usage, see Louis A. Brighton, *Revelation*, Concordia Commentary Series (St. Louis: Concordia, 1999), 269–70, 443–44.

[9] Until the second half of the twentieth century, it was fashionable to assume that Paul and the evangelists borrowed this term from the pagan Hellenistic mystery religions. In his careful study of "μυστήριον, μυέω" G. Bornkamm has argued that this is most unlikely. See *Theological Dictionary of the New Testament*, 10 vols., ed. G. Kittel, trans. G. Bromiley (Grand Rapids: Eerdmans, 1967), 802–28. He shows that it was first used in the LXX to translate the Aramaic term *râz* in Daniel 2:18, 19, 27, 28, 29, 30, 47. There it refers to "an eschatological mystery, a concealed intimation of divinely ordained future events whose disclosure and interpretation is reserved for God alone and for those inspired by His Spirit" (4:814–15). It was then used in a similar sense in Jewish apocalyptic and Rabbinic literature. His findings have been confirmed by Raymond E. Brown in *The Semitic Background of the Term "Mystery" in the New Testament*, Facet Books, Biblical Series, vol. 21 (Philadelphia: Fortress Press, 1968).

[10] Mark 4:11; Matthew 13:11; Luke 8:10.

[11] See Romans 11:25; 16:25; 1 Corinthians 2:1(?),7; 4:1; 13:2; 14:2; 15:51; Ephesians 1:9; 3:3, 4, 9; 5:32; 6:19; Colossians 1:26, 27; 2:2; 4:3; 2 Thessalonians 2:7; 1 Timothy 3:9, 16.

apostles and his other disciples asked him about his use of parables. Before he explained the parable of the sower, Jesus remarked that the mystery of God's kingdom had been given only to them; it was inaccessible to those who are outside his circle of disciples, even though they saw him and heard what he said. Jesus' parables were utterly opaque to them because they were still outside God's kingdom.

In Mark's Gospel, Jesus has six main things to say about the mystery of God's kingdom, his eventual rule over the whole of his creation. First, God's good and gracious rule on earth is concealed from human sight and yet revealed in Jesus the Messiah. The man Jesus embodies the mystery of God's kingdom. He ushers in God's kingdom, mysteriously, by his incarnation, teaching, and sacrificial death. Like his identity as God's Son, the Messiah, his kingdom is not apparent to human perception. Paradoxically, that mystery is concealed in his humanity in order to be revealed in a hidden way by his teaching in parables (4:11–12). The parables reveal what is otherwise hidden (4:22).

Second, God himself reveals the mystery of his kingdom through his Word, the Word that Jesus preaches and teaches. The use of the theological passive formula "it has been given" indicates that God the Father gives the disciples access to it (4:11). Jesus is the sower of the seed, the Word of God that produces repentance and speaks forgiveness to those who receive it.[12]

Third, only his disciples have access to this mystery. They alone are in on it (4:11). This is rather surprising, for the word that reveals this mystery is preached to all. Yet Jesus explains the word only to his disciples who have faith in him (4:1, 10–13, 33–34). He initiates them into the mystery of God's kingdom. They alone have ears to hear the mystery (4:9, 23), because the mystery is always a divine gift that can only be had as it is received through hearing God's Word. It comes to the disciples of Jesus through hearing his Word rather than their observation of him.

Fourth, the word that reveals the mystery is like a lamp that lights up a one-roomed ancient Palestinian house at night (4:21–23).[13] The preaching of the Gospel is a theophany, the Father's self-disclosure to

---

[12] The term "the word" appears eight times in the explanation of the parable.

[13] The parable of the lamp in 4:21–25 has, most likely, been added there to explain the nature of the harvest that is mentioned in 4:20.

his royal sons, a divine self-manifestation that illumines and enlightens the disciples of Jesus. It produces the harvest of light in them.

Fifth, by his preaching Jesus discloses the hidden mysteries of God's kingdom verbally rather than visually. Its manifestation is like the theophanies in the Old Testament. Unlike pagan theophanies in which deities showed their faces visibly to their devotees for replication in the idols that gave ongoing access to them, the Lord "appeared" to the Israelites at Sinai by speaking to them and by his name that was spoken upon them with the Aaronic benediction in the Divine Service. So too, in this age, Jesus discloses God's hidden presence by what he says to his disciples.

Sixth, the power of the Kingdom resides mysteriously in the Word, the seed that produces the harvest without human assistance (4:26–29), the tiny seed that grows the kingdom and becomes the largest plant in the garden. Only at the end, on the Last Day, will God's Son and everything else that is now hidden be visibly manifest (4:22). What is now heard will then be seen. So in Mark, Jesus conceals the mystery of God's kingdom in his humanity in order to reveal it to his disciples through his teaching of God's Word.

Matthew and Luke interpret the mystery in a slightly different way. In Mark's account, Jesus speaks about *the mystery* (singular) of God's kingdom, because Mark wants to emphasize its embodiment in Jesus; in Matthew and Luke he speaks about *the knowledge of its mysteries* (plural). Their focus is on their human appropriation of God's manifold gifts by the reception of Christ and his teachings.

Matthew puts the emphasis on *knowing the Word* (13:13, 14, 15, 19, 23).[14] He omits the parable of the lamp, apart from its interpretative sentences about the abundance of gifts for those who are enlightened. This is added to the words of Jesus to his disciples about God's gift of knowledge to them (13:12), the knowledge that leads to repentance and divine healing (13:15). He also adds the words of congratulation by Jesus to his disciples for seeing and hearing what all the prophets had

---

[14] Matthew picks up the verb συνίημι (Hebrew בִּין) from Isaiah 6:9, 10. See also a possible echo of this in Paul's σύνεσις in Colossians 1:9; 2:2; Ephesians 3:4.

longed for so ardently (13:16–17).[15] So, in Matthew the people who understand the Word of the kingdom produce the varied harvest of spiritual health according to their level of understanding. Theophany comes through spiritual understanding, that is, insight into the mysteries of God's hidden rule through his Son Jesus, the Messianic King.

Like Matthew, Luke puts the emphasis on the knowledge of the mysteries of God's kingdom that comes from hearing the Word. On the one hand, he stresses the role of the Church as the place for divine theophany by adding the clause: "so those who come in can see the light" (Luke 8:16). He seems to envisage the house churches where the Gospel was preached in his day. The enlightening Word lights up each congregation and shines out from it into the world of darkness. The proclamation of the Gospel therefore draws those who are outside the Church into it and into the light of Christ.[16] On the other hand, instead of focusing on *what* is heard, as in Mark and Matthew, Jesus speaks in Luke about *how* the Word of God is heard (8:18). It needs to be *retained* for it to produce saving faith (8:12) and the harvest of enlightenment (8:16–18).[17] Only those who keep on hearing the Word with a good and honest heart and retain it there through meditation on it receive the gift of knowledge, the knowledge of God's mysteries, for the Word alone gives continual access to them. So, in Luke the Word of God initiates the disciples into the mysteries of God's kingdom by giving the knowl-

---

[15] Luke places this unit in 10:23, 24 after his prayer of thanksgiving to the Father for his revelation of himself to the disciples through him as the Son.

[16] Arthur Just gives this fine summary: "The Lukan hearer will connect the light to Christ and his Gospel. The one who places the Gospel on the Lampstand is Christ, working in the Christian community through those who have been catechized and baptized. After having heard and believed the Word, the baptized are not to hide Christ's Gospel. The illuminating Word that is in them should light up the house Church and shine from it, like a beacon, to others journeying toward it. And when the others come after a long journey, the baptized will illuminate the house Church for them when they enter it. This illumination would involve the interpretation of the Word of God within the community of the baptized. . . . The light of Christ's presence in the faithful community shines out from the house Church so that those who leave the world and enter the Church may learn how to hear the Gospel by observing the faithful community at worship." *Luke 1:1—9:50*, Concordia Commentary, 2 vols. (St. Louis: Concordia, 1996), 1:352–53.

[17] Luke reworks the sentence to put all the emphasis on the retention of the word: "They are those who, having heard the word with a good and honest heart, *hold onto* it. . . ."

edge of salvation and the enlightenment that comes from the persistent retention of the illuminating Word in their hearts. The Gospel lights up the circle of Christ's disciples, shines out from them into the world, and attracts people from its darkness to the light of God's presence. The Church therefore is the place for theophany, the place where divine mysteries are revealed.

PAUL'S TEACHING ON MYSTERY

In his letters Paul speaks about himself as a mystagogue. He picks up the teaching of Jesus and applies it to the life of the Church after the ascension of Jesus. He, too, regards the Christian faith as a mystery, something that is not reached by mental deduction and human understanding, but a hidden reality that is received and held with a clear conscience (1 Timothy 3:9). While that mystery is both concealed and revealed in Jesus the risen Lord, it involves God the Father and the Holy Spirit as well.

The mystery of the faith involves all three persons of the Trinity. Thus Paul speaks about the mystery of God (1 Corinthians 2:1; Colossians 2:2), as well as the mysteries of God (1 Corinthians 4:1). In his wisdom God the Father conceived that mystery before the foundation of the world, a mystery that involves the crucifixion of Jesus, the Lord of glory, a mystery that God reveals through the Spirit (1 Corinthians 2:7–10). It has to do with God's final restoration of all things, the whole universe, under the headship of Christ, the anointed cosmic King (Ephesians 1:7–10).[18] This involves his reunification of heaven and earth,[19] so that people on earth may join together with the angels in one choir that stands in God's presence and praises him for

---

[18] For exploration of this theme in Ephesians, see Chrys C. Caragounis, *The Ephesian Mysterion: Meaning and Content*, Coniectanea Biblica: New Testament Series, vol. 8 (Lund: C. W. K Gleerup, 1977).

[19] See Otfried Hofius, "Gemeinschaft mit den Engeln im Gottesdienst der Kirche," *Zeitschrift für Theologie und Kirche* 89 (1992): 189–90. He argues that in Ephesians 2:19 the phrase "fellow citizens of the holy ones" refers to the angels. Since Christ has removed the dividing wall that separated Jews and Gentiles from each other at the temple and both of them from the heavenly world, the saints on earth, already now in the Divine Service, join with the angels in one song of praise, since they are part of the same assembly, the Church on earth and in heaven.

the riches of his grace.[20] There that choir performs one doxology in praise of God the Father (Ephesians 1:6, 12).[21]

The mystery of cosmic restoration begins with God's creation of a new man in Baptism as an act of renovation (Ephesians 4:24) and his creation of a new humanity by his reconciliation of the Jews and Gentiles with him through the preaching of the Gospel (Ephesians 2:11–12). That new community is the temple of the triune God, the place where both Jews and Gentiles have liturgical access to God the Father through his Son by the Holy Spirit (Ephesians 2:18–22; 3:12). There the mystery of Christ and his role in the restoration of the cosmos is manifest to all people on earth and to all the cosmic powers by the incorporation of the Gentiles as co-heirs with the Israelites in the body of Christ (Ephesians 3:6–10). So the Church plays a central role in God's administration of his mystery on earth, for in it and by it God prefigures and previews the restoration of all creation under Christ.

The mystery of cosmic restoration includes some puzzling features, such as Israel's apparent rejection of Christ (Romans 11:25), the transformation of both the living and the dead at Christ's appearance at the close of the age (1 Corinthians 15:51), and the restricted operation of lawlessness (2 Thessalonians 2:7). God the Father was "silent" about this mystery and kept it "hidden" and "unknown" for ages before the advent of his Son (Romans 16:25; 1 Corinthians 2:7; Ephesians 3:5, 9).

---

[20] By their translation of ἐκληρώθημεν in Ephesians 1:11 as a reference to our election (NIV) or our heavenly inheritance (RSV), most English translations obscure Paul's picture of the Church as a choir that has been given its "allotted place" in God's presence to proclaim his grace (cf. Ephesians 1:6, 12, 14). This sense is confirmed by the following verse, where Paul maintains that God's people are to be praise-singers of God's grace. See Rudolph Schnackenburg, *Der Brief an die Epheser*, Evangelisch-katholischer Kommentar zum Neuen Testament, vol. 10 (Neukirchen-Vluyn: Benziger Verlag; Einseideln and Neukirchener Verlag, 1982), 61. As in Colossians 1:12, Paul here speaks about the allotment of Christians to membership in the heavenly choir, just as the Levitical musicians, like all the priests, were assigned by "lot" into their division for service at the temple in Jerusalem (1 Chronicles 25:8, 9). See John W. Kleinig, *The Lord's Song: The Basis, Function and Significance of Choral Music in Chronicles*, Journal for the Study of the Old Testament, Supplement Series, vol. 156 (Sheffield: Sheffield Academic Press, 1993), 89–95.

[21] See my exploration of this theme in "The Mystery of Doxology" in *Mysteria Dei: Essays in Honor of Kurt Marquart*, pp. 129–47, ed. Paul T. McCain and John R. Stephenson (Fort Wayne: Concordia Theological Seminary Press, 2000).

However, God now gives access to that mystery by the administration of his grace through Paul and the other apostles (Ephesians 3:2). It involves the hidden glorification as those who already now stand with Christ in his glorious presence (1 Corinthians 2:7), their enjoyment of the good things that he has prepared for those who love him (1 Corinthians 2:9), and their reception of the invisible gifts that he has freely given to them (1 Corinthians 2:12).

The mystery of the Christian faith is embodied in the crucified, risen Lord Jesus (1 Corinthians 2:1–2).[22] Paul therefore speaks about "the mystery of Christ" (Ephesians 3:4; Colossians 4:3). The mystery of God is "Christ, in whom are hidden all the treasures of wisdom and knowledge" (Colossians 2:2, 3). All the spiritual riches of God are available in Christ, hidden in his human poverty. Interestingly, in his letters Paul does not concentrate on the revelation of that mystery in the historical events of Christ's life, death and resurrection, but on its present revelation in and through the Church.

In 1 Timothy 3:16 Paul sums up the mystery of Christ, the great mystery of liturgical piety that the Church confesses, in an intricate little hymn with paired couplets that speaks of his paradoxical status as human and yet divine:[23]

> Great, we confess, is the mystery of godliness:
> *he was disclosed*[24] *in the flesh,*
> was vindicated by the Spirit;
> was seen by angels,
> *was proclaimed among the Gentiles;*
> *was believed in throughout the world,*
> was taken up in glory.[25]

---

[22] See Gregory Lockwood, *1 Corinthians*, Concordia Commentary (St. Louis: Concordia, 2000), 81–82, for the reading of μυστήριον (mystery) rather than μαρτύριον (testimony) in 1 Corinthians 2:1.

[23] For a comprehensive analysis of this poem, see Andrew Y. Lau, *Manifest in Flesh: The Epiphany Christology of the Pastoral Principles,* Wissenschaftliche Untersuchungen zum Neuen Testament, series 2, vol. 86 (Tübingen: J. C. B. Mohr, 1996), 91–114.

[24] See, too, the use of φανερόω in Romans 16:26 and Colossians 1:27 for the disclosure of a mystery.

[25] The translation is the author's. This layout of the poem emphasizes its arrangement in three couplets that describe three shifts of location: from earth to heaven, from heaven

Here the mystery of Christ is confessed with six passive verbs that do not tell what he has done but what has been done to him, or, more exactly, what God has done for him.[26] The distinctive feature of this easily memorized poem is the bi-focal location of each of the three couplets. In these couplets we have a shift from earth to heaven, followed by a shift from heaven back to earth, and then from earth back to heaven.

This remarkable little confession of faith shows how the risen Lord Jesus bridges heaven and earth. By his incarnation on *earth* he has been revealed in the flesh, proclaimed among the nations, and believed in throughout the world; by his bodily resurrection and ascension into *heaven* he has also been vindicated by God's Spirit, seen by the angels, and taken up in glory before the Father. The mystery that the Church confesses therefore reaches up bodily from earth to heaven, out to the angels, down to the nations, out to believers all over the world, and back to heaven. Christ has come from the Father to bring people from all over the world back with him into the glory of the Father. Significantly, this poem emphasizes the proclamation of Christ's presence "among the

---

to earth, from earth to heaven. It shows how the risen Lord Jesus joins together the earthly and the heavenly domains. It could also be read as a poem with two parallel stanzas of three lines that deal with his appearance in three domains: the world, the Church, and heaven. It could then be arranged as follows:

> *He was disclosed in the flesh,*
>   was vindicated by the Spirit,
>   was seen by angels;
> *was proclaimed among the Gentiles,*
>   was believed in throughout the world,
>   was taken up in glory.

In this reading the vindication by the Spirit is understood as a reference to what happened at Pentecost.

[26] See Joachim Jeremias, "Der erste Brief an Timotheus," *Die Briefe an Timotheus und Titus,* Das Neue Testament Deutsch (Göttingen: Vandenhoeck & Ruprecht, 1963), 23. He also proposes, rather helpfully, that this poem with its three contrasting couplets is patterned on the ancient Egyptian and wider oriental ritual for the enthronement of a king (23–25). This was enacted in three stages: the king was first exalted as a person with divine status, then presented as king before his subjects, and finally acclaimed as king by his subjects at his enthronement which marked the beginning of his reign. Thus God has exalted his incarnate Son at his resurrection, presented him to the angels in heaven and nations on earth, and has gained the allegiance of believers in him on earth by his enthronement with him in the heavenly realm. Each of these three enactments occurs both on earth and in heaven.

nations" and their faith in him. People on earth have access to that cosmic mystery by the preaching of Christ and faith in him, faith that is produced by God through his Word. Thus the mystery of Christ is cosmic in its extent, for it unites the physical human body with God's Spirit, the angels with people from all nations, and believers on earth with God in heaven.

The mystery of Christ revolves around his hidden presence in the Church. When the disciples of Christ, the saints, gather together for worship, they are involved in a great mystery, something hidden from sight and all the senses, something invisible and yet real. St. Paul speaks of it in this way in Colossians 1:25–28:

> I became the minister (of the Church), according to the task of keeping God's house[27] that was given to me to you, to proclaim the Word of God fully[28], the *mystery* that has been kept hidden away[29] throughout the ages and generations but has now been disclosed[30] to his saints. To them God chose to make known[31] how great among the

---

[27] Paul uses the Greek word οἰκονομία. This term refers to the management of a household and the administration of its business by an οἰκονόμος, a steward or administrator. He envisages the Church both as God's household and his house, his holy temple, the place where he resides with his glory. Both these terms are also used elsewhere in connection with the mystery of Christ (1 Corinthians 4:1; Ephesians 1:10; 3:2, 9).

[28] Rather surprisingly, Paul uses the verb πληρόω here. It normally means to fill or complete or bring to completion. It is used similarly in Romans 15:19 where it refers to a commission to bring the Gospel to its completion by preaching it all over the world. By its use Paul seems to combine two ideas, the full enactment of God's Word and its full proclamation. This corresponds with his use of πληρόω, "fill," in Colossians 1:9; 2:10; 4:17, his use of πλήρωμα, "fullness," in Colossians 1:19 and 2:9, and his use of πληροφορία, which means "full delivery," "full measure," or "full assurance" in Colossians 2:2 (cf. 4:12).

[29] See, too, the use of the passive particle ἀποκεκρυμμένος for God's activity in concealing the mystery of Christ in 1 Corinthians 2:7; Ephesians 3:9; cf. Mark 4:22; Luke 10:21.

[30] The verb φανερόω is also used for the disclosure of a mystery in Romans 16:26; 1 Timothy 3:16.

[31] The verb γνωρίζω is also used for making known of a mystery in Ephesians 1:9; 3:3, 5, 10; 6:19.

Gentiles are the riches[32] of the glory of *this mystery*, which is *Christ among you*[33] (plural), the hope of glory.[34]

Here Paul depicts himself as a mystagogue, a person who initiates others into a mystery. That mystery is the dwelling of the risen Lord Jesus with his people in the Church, the assembly in God's presence that is open to both Jews and Gentiles. Thus, the inclusion of Gentiles in the Church through Christ is part of that mystery (cf. Ephesians 3:4). Since Christ resides among the saints, God's glory is there, too, in all its riches, for the fullness of divinity dwells bodily in Christ (cf. Colossians 1:19; 2:9). Through Christ they therefore have access to God's glory, his manifest presence in the Divine Service. By his preaching Paul discloses that mystery to the saints, those who are united with Christ and so share in his holiness. They alone have access to it. Thus Paul reveals the presence and activity of the risen Lord to the saints by proclaiming God's Word fully to them, the Gospel that proclaims Christ and makes him known to them (cf. Romans 16:26–27; 1 Corinthians 2:1–2; Ephesians 3:6).

Apart from God's Word, his people have no access to the risen Lord Jesus; they have no knowledge or experience of him apart from the Gospel. That word initiates them into the mystery of Christ, something that no eye has seen, no ear has heard, and no human heart has ever conceived (1 Corinthians 2:6–10). The disclosure of Christ's hidden presence in the Divine Service gives the faithful a glimpse of their future glory, a foretaste of heaven here on earth. Thus, since the preaching of the Gospel reveals the hidden presence of Christ, Paul also speaks about "the mystery of the gospel" (Ephesians 6:19).

Both Christ and the Church are part and parcel of the same great mystery. They are, in fact, inseparable from each other, like the head of a body from its body. Thus Paul claims that the union of husband and wife as one flesh in marriage reflects the even greater mystery of the invisible union through Baptism of Christ with the Church, his holy

---

[32] See, too, the reference to the riches of mystery in Ephesians 3:8–13.

[33] Or "in you." If we go with the image of the Church as an assembly, then this phrase is best translated by "among you," but if go with the image of the Church as the temple of God, then it is best translated by "in you."

[34] The translation is the author's.

bride (Ephesians 6:32). Through its union with him the Church does not just make the mystery of God's wisdom known in the earthly realm to both Jews and Gentiles; it also makes it known to angels and demons, the rulers and authorities in the heavenly realms (Ephesians 3:8–12). And the core of that mystery is this: in Christ "we (Jews and Gentiles) have access[35] to God (the Father) in boldness and confidence through faith in him." Thus, just as a wife has access to her father-in-law through her husband, so the Church has hidden access to God the Father through his Son.

The mystery of Christ also involves the work of the Holy Spirit. Paul claims that this mystery was originally revealed by the Spirit to Christ's holy apostles and prophets (Ephesians 3:4–6). The Spirit showed them what they had to say. They, then, were the original custodians of this mystery. But they did not keep it to themselves, nor did they restrict access to some select initiates. They publicized it in the world for the benefit of the whole human race. Their public proclamation of this mystery has been passed on to us through the books that were canonized as the Sacred Scriptures for use in the Divine Service. These books are, if you like, mystery books. Through them the Holy Spirit continues to reveal the mystery of Christ to those who have ears to hear what they have to say.

The Holy Spirit did not just reveal the mystery of Christ to the apostles in the Early Church. Through his Spirit God also revealed the mystery of Christ and his invisible gifts to those who heard their preaching (1 Corinthians 2:7–16). Both the preachers and the hearers are inspired by the Spirit. Through the work of the Holy Spirit the hearers have access to the mystery that Paul proclaimed to them. Like the preachers, they, too, have the Holy Spirit, so that they may know what they receive from God through Christ (1 Corinthians 2:12). The Spirit opens them up to the invisible mystery of God. He attunes their

---

[35] See also Romans 5:2; Ephesians 2:18. Like the verb προσάγω which is used in the LXX for the presentation of an animal as an offering (e.g., Exodus 29:10; Leviticus 1:3; 3:3; 4:14; 7:6; 23:8) or a person as a priest to God (e.g., Exodus 29:4, 8; 40:12; Leviticus 8:9, 10), the noun προσαγωγή is a liturgical term. See K. L. Schmidt, "προσάγω, προσαγωγή," in *Theological Dictionary of the New Testament*, 1:131–33. This verse recalls Ephesians 2:18 with its reference to the access of both Jews and Gentiles to God the Father in his new temple through Jesus by the Holy Spirit for audience with him.

minds to Christ's mind so that they can understand God's thoughts and acts, his hidden dealings with his people. God the Father "enlightens"[36] them by his Spirit, so that in Christ they already now know the riches of their inheritance and experience the resurrecting power by which he energizes them (Ephesians 1:15–23).

The mystery of Christ is revealed in his hidden epiphany, the manifestation of his divinity in human flesh, which is also the theophany of God the Father, his manifestation as God. Unlike the theophanies of pagan gods, that epiphany of Christ does not give us access to God visibly through the human eye in the form of an idol; rather, it gives us access to him *aurally* through his name and Word, the message of the Gospel. The organ for spiritual sight, the organ for the reception of his epiphany, is the faithful heart, the human conscience. It must be cleansed and remain pure if it is to receive and retain the holy mystery of God (1 Timothy 3:9; cf. Matthew 5:8). A clear conscience receives insight into the hidden mystery of Christ that is revealed by God the Father through his Word by the power of the Spirit. The cleansing that is given in baptism and received by faith "enlightens"[37] the eyes of the heart,[38] so that it receives and knows what God the Father gives to the saints both now and in the age to come (Ephesians 1:15–22). Thus the mystery that is hidden from human sight is known by the human heart that receives the life-giving, energizing, revealing light of Christ.

The saints have access to the mysteries of God through the hidden presence of Christ in the Church. The Church is the place where people are led into those mysteries and experience them by virtue of their hidden access to God the Father and his grace in the Divine Service. Those who are ministers of the Gospel are therefore custodians of those mysteries. Thus Paul claims that he and his fellow pastor Sosthenes should be regarded as "stewards of the mysteries of God" (1 Corinthians 4:1). In Greek, the term steward (οἰκονόμος) is quite literally a "housekeeper," the chief slave in charge of his master's household and

---

[36] See 1 Corinthians 4:5; Ephesians 3:9; 2 Timothy 1:10; Hebrews 6:4; 10:32.

[37] See also Ephesians 3:9; 2 Timothy 1:10; Hebrews 6:4; 10:32; cf. 2 Corinthians 4:4, 6.

[38] Paul may be reflecting on the words of congratulation by Jesus to his disciples in Matthew 13:16–17 and Luke 10:23–24. In his Gospel Luke develops the motif of the eyes that see Christ and his salvation (2:30; 10:23–24; 11:34–36; 24:31) in contrast to eyes that are blind and closed to him (4:20; 6:33–42; 19:42; 24:16).

the management of its affairs. Paul's use of this term here for his vocation as a minister of the Gospel recalls his mention of the Church as God's temple in the previous chapter, his place of residence (1 Corinthians 2:16–17). As stewards of God's mysteries they work with what is unseen. The quality and success of their work will therefore only be evident on the day when Christ appears to bring to light the things that are now hidden in darkness (1 Corinthians 4:2–5).

The Lutheran Confessions quite rightly equate the administration of the divine mysteries with the ministry of Word and Sacrament, the ministry of the apostolic Gospel and its enactment (Ap XXIV 80). Like Paul and Sosthenes, all pastors are called to be mystagogues; they all are responsible for the mystery of Christ and for the initiation of people into it. As they lead the Divine Service, they enact and proclaim that mystery. They use the Word of God to reveal what is otherwise concealed until the close of the age. Their task is to proclaim the crucified Christ (1 Corinthians 2:1–2) and gives thanks to God for him as the Lord of all creation (Ephesians 1:15–23).

CONCLUSION

We can, I think, best commend the Christian faith to post-modern people when we ourselves are captivated imaginatively by the wonder of it and live in the mystery of it. This does not mean that we will engage in ritual mystification and intellectual obfuscation, for even though the mystery of Christ is hidden, it is open and accessible to all people. The heart of it is Christ's enlightening presence in the Church. The Church is the place where theophany occurs, the place where the glory of the triune God is revealed here on earth as a preview of the final cosmic epiphany. This happens in the Divine Service. There, through the risen Lord Jesus who brings the Father to us and us to the Father, we have access by the Holy Spirit to heaven here on earth. That heavenly mystery is revealed to us and all the saints by the proclamation of God's Word and its enactment in the Divine Service.

God's Word initiates us and all believers into the mystery of Christ and his wonderful presence with us, which involves us in his work of cosmic restoration. Through God's Word and our faith in it, we get to know the triune God as we are drawn into the fellowship of the Son with the Father and receive all the spiritual blessings that he gives to us in his Son (Ephesians 1:3). We receive those heavenly blessings because we are already now raised with Christ and enthroned with him in the heavenly realms (Ephesians 2:6). We therefore begin to share in the divine life of the Holy Trinity here on earth through our union and communion with Jesus. Through our ongoing reception of the Holy Spirit, "the eyes of our hearts" are enlightened so that we see what is otherwise unseen (Ephesians 1:17–19), the riches and weight of God's glory that is too large for us to take in and enjoy, in all its fullness, here on earth (2 Corinthians 4:17).

By our attention to God's Word and the enlightenment of the Holy Spirit, we begin to see ourselves and the world around us with the eyes of God. And that transforms our imagination. Our vision of God's hidden presence with us, our vision of his glory, colors our perception of reality, so that we begin to see what had previously remained unnoticed and unappreciated by our darkened imagination. We see everything much more coherently as it is in the light of Christ the cosmic King, for he is not only the image of the invisible God but all things also cohere in him (Colossians 1:13, 17). We see how he includes us mere mortals in his work of cosmic restoration.

So as long as we live here on earth, we walk by faith and not by sight (2 Corinthians 5:7). We live as citizens of heaven here on earth. Our vision of God reshapes us and governs our behavior. And that is how we best commend the mystery of Christ to our friends and acquaintances. We know that our life is hidden with Christ in God (Colossians 3:3), even though that is by no means self-evident to others or even to us. We know that wherever we go the triune God goes with us, for Christ is in us as we are in him. We know that when Christ appears, we shall appear with him in glory (1 John 3:2). Then the mystery of Christ will be fulfilled. We shall be like him, for we shall see him face to face (1 Corinthians 13:12). Then the mystery of cosmic restoration will be fully manifest.

THE SUPPOSED PROBLEM
OF A "RIVER OF BLOOD"

Daniel L. Gard

The book of Exodus presents the modern reader with many challenges. Critics of the Bible approach the story of Moses and the liberation of Israel from Egypt with the kind of skepticism that denies *a priori* the historicity of the text, thus relegating Exodus to the realm of myth and legend or to a theological parable told to illustrate something about the God of Israel. Even conservative exegetes often try to explain the narratives, especially the plague narratives, in a way that attempts to reconcile the text with possible naturalistic explanations, perhaps in an effort to make the Exodus narratives more palatable to a skeptical modern world. Such well-meaning efforts ultimately fail to do justice to either scientific theory or the Biblical text. The text must be taken on its own terms, not terms determined from outside the text. Basic hermeneutical principles are still valid and vital in allowing Holy Scripture to tell its story.

My focus in this study is on one verse in particular, Exodus 7:17: "Thus says the LORD, "By this you shall know that I am the LORD: behold, with the staff that is in my hand I will strike the water that is in the Nile, and it shall turn into blood." It has become not only common but standard practice in the last century for conservative exegetes to explain that the word "blood" in this passage means either red algae or red silt and not actual blood. The arguments used for this meaning of the word "blood" are reminiscent of Lewis Carroll's *Through the Looking Glass*. I'll simply call this "Humpty Dumpty Hermeneutics."

With apologies to Mr. Carroll, the discussion goes something like this, with my expansions in parenthesis and italics:

> (*Humpty Dumpty*) "There's glory for you!" (*There's blood for you!*)
>
> "I don't know what you mean by 'glory,' " Alice said. (*"I don't know what you mean by "blood."*)
>
> Humpty Dumpty smiled contemptuously. "Of course you don't—till I tell you. I meant 'there's a nice knock-down argument for you!' " (*"algae for you"*).
>
> "But 'glory' doesn't mean 'a nice knock-down argument,' " Alice objected. (*But "blood" doesn't mean algae.*)
>
> "When *I* use a word," Humpty Dumpty said, in rather a scornful tone, "it means just what I choose it to mean—neither more nor less."
>
> "The question is," said Alice, "whether you *can* make words mean so many different things."
>
> "The question is," said Humpty Dumpty, "which is to be master—that's all."

From the time of the dispersion of the human race at the tower of Babel, communication has been a tricky thing. Words must have meaning if our use of them is to be anything more than senseless chatter. And when it comes to the divine Word, there should be no question as to who is the master—and it is not the exegete.

OVERVIEW OF APPROACHES TO MIRACLES

Before examining Exodus 7:17, it is important to overview the topic of miracles in the Bible. Interpreters approach miracles of the Bible in different ways, largely reflecting their presuppositions regarding the nature of Scripture. John J. Davis identified three schools of thought regarding miracles:

> 1. The miracles are myths that have been recorded to make some sort of point about God. In other words, they are literary creations.
>
> 2. The miracles are natural phenomena that are given theological interpretation. To state it another way, some natural event happened in history that is interpreted by the biblical writer as being an act of God though it was not necessarily caused by God.

3. The miracles actually did happen as the text says they did. This is the position of those that would read the biblical text as an accurate record of history both in what happened and with God as the actor.[1]

To Davis' three schools, I would add a fourth:

4. The miracles happened because God used natural phenomena according to his divine will and to fulfill his divine purpose. Perhaps nowhere is this perspective more common than among conservative scholars who see the plagues of Exodus as caused by God but fully explainable as outgrowths of natural phenomena.

Historically, it is Option 3 that has shaped conservative interpretations of Exodus. However, since the nineteenth century Option 4 has become the standard apologetic among conservative biblical scholars over and against Options 1 and 2.

Strongly influential in the acceptance of Option 4 ("plagues as natural phenomena used by God") is an often cited work by Joseph P. Free.[2] An older source, the 1949 *International Standard Bible Encyclopedia*, based on its 1915 precursor, actually has the same list of unique aspects of the plagues that mark them as miracles:

The miraculous elements in the plagues are no less distinctly manifest than the natural phenomena themselves.

1. Intensification: There was an intensification of the effect of the various plagues so much beyond all precedent as to impress everyone as being a special divine manifestation, and it was so. . . . Merely natural events do not arrange themselves so systematically. In this systematic severity were seen miracles of power.

2. Prediction: The prediction of the plagues and the fulfillment of the prediction at the exact time to a day, sometimes to an hour (as the cessation of the thunder and lightning). . . . Such wonders as the plagues of Egypt can in no wise be explained as merely natural. The prediction was a miracle of knowledge.

---

[1] John J. Davis, *Moses and the Gods of Egypt* (Grand Rapids: Baker Book House, 1971), 79–129.

[2] Joseph P. Free, *Archaeology and Bible History* (Wheaton, IL: Van Kampen Press, 1950).

3. Discrimination: The discrimination shown in the visitation by the plagues presents another miraculous element more significant and important than either the miracles of power or the miracles of knowledge. God put a difference between the Egyptians and the Israelites, beginning with the plague of flies and continuing, apparently, without exception, until the end. Such miracles of moral purpose admit of no possible explanation but the exercise of a holy will. Merely natural events make no such regular, systematic discriminations.

4. Orderliness and Increasing Severity: The orderliness and gradually increasing severity of the plagues with such arrangement as brought "judgment upon the gods of Egypt," vindicating Yahweh as Ruler over all, and educating the people to know Yahweh as Lord of all the earth, present an aspect of events distinctly non-natural. Such method reveals also a divine mind at work.

5. Arrangement to Accomplish Divine Moral Purpose: Last of all and most important of all, the plagues were so arranged as to accomplish in particular a great divine moral purpose in the revelation of God to the Israelites, to the Egyptians and to all the world. This is the distinctive mark of every real miracle. And this leads us directly to the consideration of the most important aspect of the plagues.[3]

The first of these, "Intensification," is central to the more modern attempts to explain the plagues as divine use of natural, scientifically explainable phenomena and presumably to offer an apologetic in light of the skepticism of our age.

An early theory that all of the plagues followed a natural series of phenomena was proposed by W. M. Flinders Petrie in 1911.[4] Particularly influential in the last half of the twentieth century are two articles (1957 and 1958) by a non-theologian, the Danish educator Greta Hort.[5]

---

[3] *International Standard Bible Encyclopedia*, 4 vols. (Grand Rapids: Eerdmans, 1949), 4:2405–2406.

[4] W. M. Flinders Petrie, *Egypt and Israel* (London: SPCK; New York: E. S. Gorsham, 1911), 25–36.

[5] Greta Hort, "The Plagues of Egypt," *Zeitschrift für die Alttestamentliche Wissenschaft* 69 (1957): 84–103, and 70 (1958): 48–59. Hort provided theories for plagues 2 through 9 as well as the first plague. Anthrax infested frogs leave the water and die (plague 2). Either lice breed on the dead frogs or mosquitoes on the infested water to produce plague 3. Plague 4 results from flies breeding in the dead frogs or in plants damaged by the polluted Nile, spreading anthrax which kills the cattle in plague 5 and initiates the

Hort attempted to explain all the plagues from a strictly naturalistic perspective. Her suggestion regarding the first plague is of interest here. Hort theorized that the plague of blood was caused by red algae or clay that killed the fish and provided a culture medium for anthrax (*Bacillus anthracis*) which, in turn, killed the frogs in the second plague.

THE CONTEXT OF EXODUS 7:17

It is important to remember that the text under consideration, Exodus 7:17, is part of a longer narrative involving a series of mighty acts of God in delivering his people. Before beginning that study, it is important to note a few issues pertaining to its interpretation.

The plague narratives of Exodus 7–12 have drawn particular attention to the tension between the Bible and the modern mind. God sent ten plagues upon Egypt, each of which is presented as a miracle designed to force Pharaoh to allow Moses to lead the children of Israel out of Egypt. The plagues begin with the Nile turned to blood (Exodus 7) and end with the death of the first born throughout Egypt, except in those homes marked with the blood of the Passover lamb (Exodus 12). The plagues are framed by an *inclusio*—blood as death and blood as life—marking them as a single, unified literary unit.

The first of the plagues, the turning of the Nile and all the waters of Egypt into blood, was prefigured already in Exodus 4: "If they will not believe even these two signs or listen to your voice, you shall take some water from the Nile and pour it on the dry ground, and the water that you shall take from the Nile will become blood on the dry ground" (Exodus 4:9). When God turns the river into blood in Exodus 7, Moses notes several results: the fish died, the river stank, and the people could not drink the water of the Nile (7:20). In fact, more than the Nile alone, there was blood throughout the land of Egypt including "the waters of Egypt [מֵימֵי מִצְרַיִם] . . . their rivers [נַהֲרֹתָם], their canals [יְאֹרֵיהֶם], and their ponds [אַגְמֵיהֶם], and all their collections of water

---

cultaneous anthrax infections in human beings in plague 6. Plague 7 is a coincidental hailstorm, and plague 8 is a result of the hailstorm as locusts are blown in from other eco-systems. Plague 9 is nothing more than a sandstorm. Plague 10, according to Hort, should probably read the destruction of the first-*fruits* of the harvest rather than the first-*born*.

[כָּל־מִקְוֵה מֵימֵיהֶם] . . . even in *vessels of* wood [וּבָעֵצִים] and in *vessels of* stone [וּבָאֲבָנִים]" (7:19). Clearly, all existing sources of water, natural and stored, were affected, and the Egyptians were forced to dig new wells along the Nile to find water.

Many interpreters have struggled with the fact that the sorcerers [מְכַשְּׁפִים] and magicians of Egypt [חַרְטֻמֵי מִצְרַיִם] were able to duplicate three of the miracles worked through Moses. These courtiers had long been a part of the Egyptian palace; four hundred years earlier at the time of Joseph their predecessors had failed to interpret Pharaoh's dreams (Genesis 41:8). Before the plague of blood, Moses and Aaron encountered these practitioners of secret arts. Aaron had cast down his staff and it became a serpent; when the sorcerers did the same, Aaron's rod swallowed theirs (7:10–12). The sorcerers were able to imitate the first plague of blood (7:22) and the second plague of frogs (8:7). But they were unable to duplicate the third plague of gnats (8:18), ending their involvement in the narrative.

It should not surprise us that satanic powers would be at work to prevent Pharaoh from recognizing the power of YHWH. The sorcerers merely serve ultimately as the instruments of YHWH in working his purposes. The later prophet Macaiah would proclaim that YHWH had sent lying spirits to King Ahab: "Now therefore behold, the LORD has put a lying spirit in the mouth of all these your prophets; the LORD has declared disaster for you" (2 Kings 22:23). God's purposes always will be fulfilled.

There is a sense of ironic humor in the magicians' production of blood and frogs; instead of aiding Pharaoh and relieving the suffering of all Egypt, their actions simply added to the already terrible circumstances. In this way, they become the "Keystone Cops" of the ancient world. When they finally fail in their attempt to replicate the third plague, the sorcerers acknowledge before Pharaoh, "This is the finger of *Elohim*" (8:19). There are two results to this confession. First, Pharaoh refuses to acknowledge what is happening around him. Second, from this point on, the remaining plagues will affect only the Egyptians and not the children of Israel. This then is the narrative context of Exodus 7:17.

Various Interpretations: Non-Lutheran and Critical

How have interpreters understood the first of the plagues? Brevard Childs notes that a shift took place in the nineteenth century, beginning in 1818 with the work of J. G. Eichhorn. Eichhorn "saw the whole affair as arising from natural annual occurrences which Moses exploited with some of his own sleight-of-hand tricks."[6] This father of the higher critical method did indeed mark a new way to read the story of the plagues, one that has continued to influence commentators ever since. The *Jerome Biblical Commentary* concurs with Brevard Childs that a naturalistic reading is relatively recent but also observes that most Roman Catholic exegetes now consider the plagues to be naturally occurring phenomena, though they are usually quick to point out the providential nature of the phenomena.[7]

Not all nineteenth-century commentators conceded the point to Eichhorn. For example, the classic Methodist commentator Adam Clarke wrote: "Verse 20. All the waters—were turned to blood. Not merely in appearance, but in reality; for these changed waters became corrupt and insalubrious, so that even the fish that were in the river died; and the smell became highly offensive, so that the waters could not

---

[6] Brevard S. Childs, *The Book of Exodus, A Critical, Theological Commentary* (Philadelphia: Westminster, 1974), 167. Childs goes on to note, "Perhaps the beginning of the modern period can best be set with the publication of J. G. Eichhorn's classic essay *De Aegypti anno mirabilis* (1818). Naturally many rationalistic arguments to explain the plagues had long been proposed (cf. Bertholdt), but no one had sought to explain the whole cycle so consistently from a rationalistic position in such detail before Eichhorn. He saw the whole affair as arising from natural annual occurrences which Moses exploited with some of his own sleight-of-hand tricks. Moses' initial display with the snake proved to be unsuccessful because he had forgotten that the Egyptian magicians knew the same tricks. Then he sought to impress Pharaoh with the power of the Hebrew God by changing some water contained in a vase into a red color by means of some chemical contrivance which he accompanied with a threat against the Nile as well. Of course, Eichhorn's explanations were so forced and often so outrageous as to call forth dozens of rebuttals from men like Rosenmueller, Hengstenberg, and others."

[7] *The Jerome Biblical Commentary*, ed. Raymond E. Brown, Joseph A. Fitzmyer, and Roland E. Murphy (Englewood Cliffs, NJ: Prentice-Hall, 1968), 51.

be drank."[8] Yet, later in the century, the naturalistic reading of the plague upon the Nile shaped the Keil-Delitzsch commentary: "The changing of the water into blood is to be interpreted in the same sense as in Joel iii.4, where the moon is said to be changed into blood; that is to say, not as a chemical change into real blood, but as a change in colour, which caused it to assume the appearance of blood (2 Kings iii.22)."[9] The commentary then attributes the redness of the Nile to an intensification of the natural phenomena of red earth and micro-organisms into a miracle.

Many conservative scholars have also followed the lead of the naturalistic readings of the critics. Walter C. Kaiser, for example, accepts the theory that the plagues on Egypt coincide with natural phenomena and that the "blood" of the Nile is not actually blood but some reddish contamination.[10] His citation of the work of Greta Hort is indicative of the extent to which her interpretation has influenced biblical scholarship.

In more recent years, critical scholarship has focused great attention on the supposed documentary sources of the plague narratives, seeking to identify the contributions of J, E, and P to the final canonical book. While denying an eye-witness Mosaic authorship, critical scholarship attempts to explain the diverse traditions behind the plague narratives as natural phenomena. For example, *Harper's Bible Commentary* sees the river of blood as a result of red particles of earth intensified by red

---

[8] Adam Clarke, *The Holy Bible Containing the Old and New Testaments with a Commentary and Critical Notes, The Old Testament*, vol. 1 (New York: Abingdon-Cokesbury, 1831), 325.

[9] C. F. Keil and F. Delitzsch, *Exodus. Commentary on the Old Testament in Ten Volumes* (Grand Rapids: Eerdmans, reprinted 1980), 1:478. The comments continue: "The reddening of the water is attributed by many to the red earth, which the river brings down from the Sennaar (cf. *Hengstenberg,* Egypt and the Books of Moses, pp. 104 sqq. Transl; *Laborde, comment.* p. 28); but Ehrenberg came to the conclusion, after microscopical (*sic*) examinations, that it was caused by cryptogamic plants and infusoria. This natural phenomenon was here intensified into a miracle."

[10] Walter C. Kaiser, *Exodus,* Expositor's Bible Commentary, vol. 2, ed. Frank Gabelein (Grand Rapids: Zondervan, 1990), 350.

microorganisms.[11] Likewise, the *Jerome Biblical Commentary* identifies red soil as the cause.[12]

Not all critical commentators agree that the text itself may be read as a naturalistic event. For example, Thomas Dozeman argues:

> Moses is instructed to transform the Nile River into blood. Scholars have sought to interpret this action as a seasonal reddening of the water in the Nile River. But the details of the story argue against such a naturalistic reading. The water is undrinkable and the fish even die. The story takes on significance in the broader context of Egyptian religion. The Nile River is divine, personified in the god Hapi. Its yearly flooding is a source of life in Egypt, associated with the god Osiris, the divine father of the pharaoh. The transformation of the Nile River into blood is an attack against the Egyptian gods. It also renders the land of Egypt ritually impure. The Egyptians themselves use such imagery to signify catastrophe: "The River is blood. . . . The people thirst for water."[13]

A rather interesting perspective is brought by John Durham's masterful critical commentary. After an extended discussion of the documentary sources, Durham observes that the biblical text directly and unequivocally states that the water was, in fact, turned into blood. Furthermore, he explains, the reader must always keep in mind that the biblical narratives of God's mighty deeds are not intended as reports of phenomenological events but are, above all else, theological accounts. While the claims of the Scriptures may prove difficult for modern interpreters to accept, license is not thereby given for the reader to alter the text by means of fanciful explanations.[14] It seems that critical scholars see quite clearly what conservative scholars seek to obscure: the דם of the Nile, according to the text, is nothing other than blood. Perhaps Brevard Childs sums it up the most succinctly:

> In many ways the attempt to defend an historical interpretation of the plagues by means of rationalistic arguments finds its most recent

---

[11] *Harper's Bible Commentary*, gen. ed. James L. May (San Francisco: Harper, 1988), 140.

[12] *The Jerome Biblical Commentary*, 52.

[13] Thomas E. Dozeman, *Exodus*, Eerdmans Critical Commentary (Grand Rapids: Eerdmans, 2009), 216.

[14] John I. Durham, *Exodus*, Word Biblical Commentary, vol 3. (Waco: Word, 1987), 97.

representative in the learned articles of Greta Hort (*ZAW* 68, 1957). However, in the end, this genre of apologetic literature suffers from the strange anomaly of defending biblical "supernaturalism" on the grounds of rationalistic arguments. As a result there is ironic affinity between the arguments of Eichhorn and those of Hort.[15]

INTERPRETATION OF EXODUS 7
IN THE LUTHERAN CHURCH—MISSOURI SYNOD

Over the years, Concordia Publishing house, the publishing arm of The Lutheran Church—Missouri Synod, has provided extraordinarily helpful resources for both scholarly and popular usage. The latest contribution is *The Lutheran Study Bible* (*TLSB*) based upon the English Standard Version and augmented by some of the most thorough study notes available. For Lutheran lay people, *TLSB* is an important resource that combines a high view of Scripture with understandable explanations written by confessional Lutheran theologians. Because *TLSB* has been so successfully marketed and is thus found in many parishes and homes, its influence is and will be profound.

For this reason, the study notes of *TLSB* must be scrutinized. The note for Exodus 7:17 concerning the first of the plagues visited upon Egypt, the changing of the water of the Nile into blood, is more than a little surprising:

> *Turn into blood.* The same sense as Jl 2:31, where the moon will be turned into blood; thus it was not a chemical change into real blood, but a change in appearance, possibly because of red algae. *The Admonition of an Egyptian Sage* (late third millennium BC) refers to the Nile as being turned to blood.[16]

The predecessor to *TLSB*, the 1986 *Concordia Self-Study Bible* (*CSSB*), offers a similar explanation:

> *The water of the Nile ... will be changed into blood.* See Ps 78:44; 105:29. The first nine plagues may have been the miraculous intensification of natural events taking place in less than a year, and

---

[15] Childs, *The Book of Exodus*, 168.

[16] *The Lutheran Study Bible*, gen. ed. Edward A. Engelbrecht (St. Louis: Concordia, 2009), 107.

coming at God's bidding and timing. If so, the first plague resulted
from the flooding of the Nile in late summer and early fall as large
quantities of red sediment were washed down from Ethiopia, causing
the water to become as red as blood (see the similar incident in 2 Ki
3:22).[17]

In 1971 another Concordia Publishing House resource for popular
use, the *Concordia Self-Study Commentary*, said this about Exodus 7:20:

Turned to Blood. The Nile, Egypt's "lifeline," turned into bloody
sewage. At an abnormally high flood stage it carried with it so many
particles of fine red earth and microscopic bacteria as to render it
"foul," undrinkable, and deadly to fish (21, Ps 78:44; 105:29; cf. Jl 2:30;
Rv 16:4).[18]

Taking a step further back in time, Paul E. Kretzmann offers a
radically different perspective in his *Popular Commentary of the Bible*
(1923):

Not merely be given a blood-red color through the presence of
microscopic animals or particles of red clay, but actually be changed
into blood, that the river throughout the length of Egypt would flow
with the liquid that commonly pulses through the veins of men and
beasts.[19]

These four resources, dated 1923, 1971, 1986 and 2009, all have much in
common. All four provide study notes and commentary for use by
Lutheran laypeople. But in regard to the first of the plagues visited upon
Egypt when the Nile was turned to blood, four different answers are
given. Kretzmann in 1923 wrote that it was real blood and emphatically
denied that it was merely red in color due to algae or silt. By 1971, the
naturalistic interpretation makes its appearance, with the CSSB stating
that it was, in fact, both "particles of fine red earth and microscopic
bacteria" that were responsible, rather than actual blood. It seems that
the 1986 CSSB and the 2009 TLSB have split the difference, so to speak.

---

[17] *Concordia Self-Study Bible, New International Version,* gen. ed. Robert G. Hoeber (St. Louis: Concordia, 1986), 95.

[18] *Concordia Self-Study Commentary*, ed. Walter R. Roehrs and Martin H. Franzmann (St. Louis: Concordia, 1971), 66.

[19] Paul E. Kretzmann, *Popular Commentary of the Bible*, 4 vols. (St. Louis: Concordia, 1923), 1:124.

CSSB opts for "large quantities of red sediment," while *TLSB* favors the
theory that, instead of blood, it was "possibly because of red algae." All
three post-1971 resources are united in opposition to the 1923 opinion
of Kretzmann.

This shift of opinion regarding the blood of the Nile is significant,
not only because these textual study notes are taken as authoritative by
those who use these resources but also because they represent a change
in hermeneutics. It is my intention to explore this issue and determine
which, if any, interpretation conforms to historic Lutheran principles of
biblical interpretation.

THE USE OF דָם IN THE PENTATEUCH

To interpret the use of דָם in Moses' narration of the first plague
properly, it is necessary to determine its meaning in actual popular
usage, the *usus loquendi* or *usus generalis*. The word is used 360 times
throughout the Old Testament, including every book of the Pentateuch.
Most commonly, the word applies to the shedding of the blood of
humans in war or homicide and to the shedding of blood in animal
sacrifice. In all these cases, the term always means the literal, physical
blood that flows through the veins of people and animals.

How does Moses use the term דָם elsewhere? Is there an *usus
specialis* found in Moses that is different that the *usus generalis*
throughout the Old Testament? Are there any examples where he uses
דָם to symbolize something else? By far, the most common use of דָם in
the books of Moses is in reference to animal sacrifices, a use that
appears in sixty-three verses.[20] For example, we read in Exodus 24: "And
Moses took half of the blood [הַדָּם] and put it in basins, and half of the
blood [הַדָּם] he threw against the altar" (Exodus 24:6). Or, as we read in
Leviticus 1: "Then he shall kill the bull before the LORD, and Aaron's
sons the priests shall bring the blood [הַדָּם] and throw the blood [הַדָּם]
against the sides of the altar that is at the entrance of the tent of

---

[20] Exodus 22:18; 24:6, 8, 12, 16, 20, 21; 30:10; 34:25; Leviticus 1:1, 5, 11; 3:2, 8; 4:5, 6, 7,
16, 17, 18, 25, 30, 34; 5:9; 6:19, 23; 7:2, 14, 26, 27, 33; 8:15, 19, 23, 24, 30; 9:9, 12, 18; 1:18;
14:6, 14, 17, 25, 28, 51, 52; 16:14, 15, 18, 19, 27; 17:4, 6, 11, 12, 13; Numbers 18:17; 19:4,
5; Deuteronomy 12:27.

meeting" (Leviticus 1:5). In every case of animal sacrifice, the clear and intended meaning of דם is "blood." No other liquid can be meant.

Another use that can only mean actual animal blood is found in Genesis 37:31: "Then they took Joseph's robe and slaughtered a goat and dipped the robe in the blood [בַּדָּם]." In this case, the blood of a goat served to falsify evidence and led Jacob to conclude that Joseph had been killed by a fierce animal. Again, דם can only mean actual blood.

Yet another use of דם in the Pentateuch is in thirteen reference to the shedding of human blood by means of homicide.[21] The first occurrence of murder is in the context of the Cain and Abel, where the word דם is spoken by YHWH: "And now you are cursed from the ground, which has opened its mouth to receive your brother's blood [אֶת־דְּמֵי] from your hand" (Genesis 4:11). The taking of human life by homicide is regularly described by metonomy, a figure of speech here for the shedding of blood: " 'Cursed be anyone who takes a bribe to shed innocent blood [דָּם].' And all the people shall say, 'Amen' " (Deuteronomy 27:25). It is possible to kill using methods that do not produce a flow of blood from the victim. Yet it is, by substitution of the attribute for the specific methodology itself, the shedding of blood, not some other fluid.

A related use of דם is found in criminal proceedings and the punishment that follows (nine verses).[22] The principal is established in Genesis 9:6: "Whoever sheds the blood [דַּם] of man, by man shall his blood [דָּמוֹ] be shed, for God made man in his own image." Other crimes are also punishable by death, described by metonomy as "their blood is upon them," as in Leviticus 20:13: "If a man lies with a male as with a woman, both of them have committed an abomination; they shall surely be put to death; their blood [דְּמֵיהֶם] is upon them." In a closely related usage, Moses writes about the role and limitations of the "redeemer of blood," the relative of a homicide victim, using the term seven times,[23] as in Numbers 35:19: "The avenger of blood [הַדָּם] shall himself put the murderer to death; when he meets him, he shall put him

---

[21] Genesis 4:11; 9:5, 6; 37:22; 42:22; Leviticus 19:16; Deuteronomy 19:10, 13; 21:7, 8, 9; 22:8; 27:25.

[22] Genesis 9:6; Leviticus 20:9, 11, 12, 13, 16, 27; Exodus 22:1, 2 (thief).

[23] Numbers 35:19, 21, 24, 25, 27, 33; Deuteronomy 19:6.

to death." Human blood is also shed in warfare in three verses,[24] such as Deuteronomy 32:42: "I will make my arrows drunk with blood [מִדָּם], and my sword shall devour flesh—with the blood (מִדָּם) of the slain and the captives, from the long-haired heads of the enemy." In no case involving the blood of humans is anything other than actual blood envisioned by the use of דם.

Other usages of the term דם include the laws pertaining to women (six verses).[25] An example is found in Leviticus 12, where Moses writes: "Then she shall continue for thirty-three days in the blood [בִּדְמֵי] of her purifying. She shall not touch anything holy, nor come into the sanctuary, until the days of her purifying are completed" (Leviticus 12:4). Again, it is actual blood, not some other liquid, that is intended by דם. So also with the dietary law, where the eating of blood is prohibited (eight verses).[26] In Genesis 9:4 we read: "But you shall not eat flesh with its life, that is, its blood [דָמוֹ]." Twice in Exodus 4 the term is used to denote the blood of circumcision,[27] which is again real blood: "So he let him alone. It was then that she said, 'A bridegroom of blood [דָּמִים],' because of the circumcision" (Exodus 4:26). There are two metaphorical usages of the word דם in reference to wine, which is referred to as דַּם־עֵנָב ("blood of the grape," Deuteronomy 32:14) or דַּם־עֲנָבִים ("blood of grapes," Genesis 49:11). The connection between what we would call the "juice" that is present in grapes and "blood" in animals is obvious. Such imagery appears also in Revelation 14:20, where "the winepress was trodden outside the city, and blood flowed from the winepress."

Most closely connected with the narrative of the first plague upon the Nile is the tenth plague and the Passover. This is particularly important in determining what is meant by turning the Nile into "blood." We read in Exodus 12:

> Take a bunch of hyssop and dip it in the blood [בַּדָּם] that is in the basin, and touch the lintel and the two doorposts with the blood [מִן־הַדָּם] that is in the basin. None of you shall go out of the door of

---

[24] Numbers 23:24; Deuteronomy 32:42, 43.

[25] Leviticus 12:4, 5, 27; 15:19, 25; 20:18.

[26] Genesis 9:4; Leviticus 3:17; 17:11, 14; 19:26; Deuteronomy 12:16, 23; 15:23.

[27] Exodus 4:25, 26.

his house until the morning. For the LORD will pass through to strike the Egyptians, and when he sees the blood [אֶת־הַדָּם] on the lintel and on the two doorposts, the LORD will pass over the door and will not allow the destroyer to enter your houses to strike you (Exodus 12:22–23).

There is no question that the blood of the Passover is that of a lamb and that it is real blood. As bookends or *inclusio*, the first and tenth plagues surround the plague narratives. Both note at the beginning of the plagues that YHWH hardened the heart of Pharaoh (Exodus 7:13; 11:10). Both involve blood, whether in bringing death (Exodus 7) or preserving life (Exodus 12). In Moses' usage of דם, the word can mean nothing other than actual blood.

The clarity of Moses' use of דם does not permit any other interpretation—it means only blood that flows through the veins of humans and animals. The claim that it actually means algae or silt is to enter the hermeneutical world of Humpty Dumpty: "When I use a word it means just what I choose it to mean—neither more nor less."

SCRIPTURA SCRIPTURAM INTERPRETATUR

If the clear meaning of דם in the Books of Moses is literal blood, are there texts that might allow us to understand the blood of Exodus 7 as something other than actual blood? Three texts are often adduced as solutions to the problem of the Nile turning into literal blood. Those texts are Revelation 6:12, Joel 2:31 (3:4 MT and LXX) and 2 Kings 3:22. But do they actually inform our reading of the first plague? And do they triangulate toward a special meaning (*usus specialis*) that applies to Exodus 7?

This is the explicit claim made by conservatives who attempt to coordinate this plague with natural phenomena. Pointing to Revelation 6:12, where the writer evokes the language of Joel 2:31 in speaking of the moon becoming "as blood," these commentators argue that this approach warrants the reading of Exodus 7 as something other than real blood. As *TLSB* puts it, Exodus 7:17 is to be taken in "the same sense as Jl 2:31, where the moon will be turned into blood; thus it was not a chemical change into real blood, but a change in appearance."[28] A careful reading of the texts in question, however, fails to permit such a decisive conclusion, if for no other reason than the fact that neither Revelation 6 nor Joel 2 is a historical narrative like Exodus 7. Rather, both are apocalyptic texts that require their own hermeneutical approach, one that cannot be transferred to the interpretation of historical narrative like Exodus.

So exactly how does St. John make use of the prophet Joel? The texts themselves are as follows, citing Joel 2:30–31 (3:3–4 MT and LXX) and Revelation 6:12:

Joel 2:30 (3:3 MT and LXX)

וְנָתַתִּי מוֹפְתִים בַּשָּׁמַיִם וּבָאָרֶץ דָּם וָאֵשׁ וְתִימְרוֹת עָשָׁן:

καὶ δώσω τέρατα ἐν τῷ οὐρανῷ καὶ ἐπὶ τῆς γῆς αἷμα καὶ πῦρ καὶ ἀτμίδα καπνοῦ

And I will show wonders in the heavens and on the earth, blood [דָּם, αἷμα] and fire and columns of smoke.

Joel 2:31 (3:4 MT and LXX)

הַשֶּׁמֶשׁ יֵהָפֵךְ לְחֹשֶׁךְ וְהַיָּרֵחַ לְדָם לִפְנֵי בּוֹא יוֹם יְהוָה הַגָּדוֹל וְהַנּוֹרָא:

ὁ ἥλιος μεταστραφήσεται εἰς σκότος καὶ ἡ σελήνη εἰς αἷμα πρὶν ἐλθεῖν ἡμέραν κυρίου τὴν μεγάλην καὶ ἐπιφανῆ

The sun shall be turned to darkness, and the moon to blood [לְדָם, εἰς αἷμα], before the great and awesome day of the LORD comes.

Revelation 6:12

Καὶ εἶδον ὅτε ἤνοιξεν τὴν σφραγῖδα τὴν ἕκτην, καὶ σεισμὸς μέγας ἐγένετο, καὶ ὁ ἥλιος ἐγένετο μέλας ὡς σάκκος τρίχινος, καὶ ἡ σελήνη ὅλη ἐγένετο ὡς αἷμα

When he opened the sixth seal, I looked, and behold, there was a great earthquake, and the sun became black as sackcloth, the full moon became like blood (ἐγένετο ὡς αἷμα).

Several points are worth noting.

---

[28] *TLSB*, 107.

1. Joel 2:30 (3:3 in MT and LXX) speaks of blood in the same way as fire and smoke.

2. The text of Revelation 6:12, while clearly dependent on the images found in Joel 2:31 (3:4 in MT and LXX), does not replicate the earlier text in either its MT or LXX renderings. The LXX reads: ὁ ἥλιος μεταστραφήσεται εἰς σκότος καὶ ἡ σελήνη εἰς αἷμα ("the sun shall be turned [μεταστραφήσεται] into [εἰς] darkness and the moon into [εἰς] blood"), while John writes, ὁ ἥλιος ἐγένετο μέλας ὡς σάκκος τρίχινος, καὶ ἡ σελήνη ὅλη ἐγένετο ὡς αἷμα ("the sun became [ἐγένετο] black as sackcloth, the full moon became like [ἐγένετο ὡς] blood"). The LXX translates the MT quite literally, but John appears to have either a different translation or his own translation or, most likely—and this is the opinion I hold—he simply paraphrases Joel. Unlike Peter in Acts 2:20, who cites Joel by quoting the LXX,[29] John, at most, depends upon Joel for imagery, not as a direct quotation. Still, we can interpret the meaning of Joel 2 as the moon becoming like blood through the words of Revelation 6 by applying the principle that Scripture interprets Scripture.

3. How is Joel 2 connected to Exodus 7 in such a way that allows the interpretation that the Nile, like Joel's moon in John's exegesis, was miraculously changed merely to appear like blood, even if it was really only silt or algae? The preposition לְ is cited as the connection between the two passages. In both Exodus 7:17 and Joel 2:31, the Nile and the moon are respectively changed לְדָם ("to blood"). Defenders of the naturalistic reading of Exodus 7 assume that this preposition לְ here means "like" as an equivalent to John's use of ὡς in Revelation 6:21. Interestingly, the standard Hebrew lexicon of the Old Testament states this regarding the use of לְ: "Into (εἰς), of a transition into a new state or condition, or

---

[29] Compare Peter's speech and his source in Joel:

Acts 2:20 ὁ ἥλιος μεταστραφήσεται εἰς σκότος καὶ ἡ σελήνη εἰς αἷμα, πρὶν ἐλθεῖν ἡμέραν κυρίου τὴν μεγάλην καὶ ἐπιφανῆ

Joel 2:31 (LXX 3:4) ὁ ἥλιος μεταστραφήσεται εἰς σκότος καὶ ἡ σελήνη εἰς αἷμα πρὶν ἐλθεῖν ἡμέραν κυρίου τὴν μεγάλην καὶ ἐπιφανῆ

"The sun shall be turned to darkness and the moon to blood, before the day of the Lord comes, the great and magnificent day."

into a new character or office ... ; ל הפך to change *into* Ex 7:15;
Dt 23:6."[30]

4. The preposition לְ with the noun דם occurs only twelve times in
the Old Testament. Of these, five are in the plague narratives or in
Psalms that recount the plagues (Exodus 4:9; 7:17, 20; Psalm
78:44, 105:29), and in six cases refer to the taking of human life
(Leviticus 16:15; Numbers 35:33; Deuteronomy 17:8; 2 Chronicles
19:10; Proverbs 1:11; Ezekiel 35:6). None can mean something
other than actual blood, including Joel 2:31. The only exception is
the apocalyptic Joel 2:31.

If the logic of connecting Joel and Revelation to Exodus is extended
to other cases, the faulty hermeneutic becomes even more apparent.
Theistic evolutionists have long argued that the term יום ("day") in the
creation narrative of Genesis 1 should be understood in the light of
Psalm 90: "For a thousand years in your sight are but as yesterday [כְּיוֹם]
when it is past, or as a watch in the night" (Psalm 90:4). They cite
2 Peter 3, an apocalyptic text, as support because Peter relies on Psalm
90:4, "with the Lord one day is as a thousand years, and a thousand
years as one day" (2 Peter 3:8). A consistent application of *TLSB*'s hermeneutic in Exodus 7:17 to Genesis 1 would suggest that the theistic
evolutionists have made their case that יום ("day") in Genesis 1 must
mean a long period of time rather than a twenty-four-hour period.

One additional text that several commentators cite[31] as support for
the "blood" of the Nile being something other than actual blood is
2 Kings 3:22: "And when they rose early in the morning and the sun
shone on the water, the Moabites saw the water opposite them as red as
blood [אֲדֻמִּים כַּדָּם]." Since the water of 2 Kings 3 is "as red as blood,"
then, it is argued, the water of the Nile in Exodus 7 may also be
understood to be a trope. This overlooks the use of the preposition כְּ
attached to דם and the presence the word אֲדֻמִּים ("red"). Neither is
used by Moses in the plague narratives. Since the preposition כְּ can be

---

[30] *A Hebrew and English Lexicon of the Old Testament*, ed. Francis Brown, S. R. Driver,
and Charles A. Briggs (Oxford: Clarendon, 1980), 512, 4a; emphasis original. See also
Theological Wordbook of the Old Testament, ed. R. Laird Harris et al (Chicago: Moody,
1980), 463.

[31] Keil and Delitzsch, *Exodus*, 478; *Concordia Self-Study Bible*, 95.

used for the purpose of comparison when attached to a noun, it appropriately describes the color of the water in 2 Kings 3. If Moses had wanted to describe the Nile as being as "red as blood," then he could have used the same preposition.

At this point, it might be of value to consider the Septuagint's translation of Exodus 7 and its implications for how the word דָּם was interpreted by Greek-speaking Judaism. We read in Exodus 7:19 the Hebrew words וְיִהְיוּ־דָם וְהָיָה דָם ("they may become blood, and there shall be blood"). The LXX translates this as καὶ ἔσται αἷμα καὶ ἐγένετο αἷμα ("it shall be blood and it was blood"). Compare this to Matthew 26:26, where Jesus said τοῦτό ἐστιν τὸ σῶμά μου ("this is my body") and τοῦτο γάρ ἐστιν τὸ αἷμά μου ("this is my blood"). If by "ἐστιν" Jesus meant "is" according to the general usage of the Greek verb, then clearly the LXX translators also understood the blood of the Nile to be blood.

It is also worth noting that John 2:9 might help us to understand the LXX translation of Exodus 7:19. There the master of the feast tasted the τὸ ὕδωρ οἶνον γεγενημένον ("the water become wine"), using γεγενημένον, the participle perfect passive accusative neuter singular from γίνομαι. The Greek translators of Exodus 7:19 had likewise written ἐγένετο αἷμα, here the same verb, γίνομαι, as an indicative aorist middle third person singular. The water at Cana became real wine; the water of the Nile became real blood. If γίνομαι could mean something other than "became wine," such as non-alcoholic grape juice, then the pietistic abstinence arguments are strengthened.

CONCLUSION

The plague narratives of Exodus present a defining action of God as the liberating God of history. To the modern, conservative mind, the miraculous actions of God present difficulties that must be defended utilizing theories and explanations that defend the miraculous while accommodating the skepticism of our times. Unfortunately, these well-intentioned attempts fail to take the text on its own terms but resort instead to Humpty Dumpty Hermeneutics: it means just what I choose it to mean—neither more nor less.

Contra Humpty Dumpty Hermeneutics, the text (that is, the words) is the master, not the exegete. Whatever issues a river of blood presents to the modern mind, the clear words of Scripture cannot be explained away by red silt or algae. The fact that modern commentaries, and even popular study bibles, insist that Exodus 7:17 does not mean real blood but possibly red algae is a reminder that only the biblical text in its autograph is inerrant—translations and footnotes are not. Such critiques are helpful in that they provide an opportunity to introduce laypeople to the world of hermeneutics. And that is a good and positive thing.

Traditional Lutheran hermeneutics applied to Moses' narrative of the first plague, the blood of the Nile, results in a reading that is anti-thetical to theories of red silt, red algae, or any other explanation. The word דם means "blood", the fluid that flows through the veins of living creatures. Reading Joel 2:31 through Revelation 6:12 has no bearing at all on the meaning of Exodus 7, nor does 2 Kings 3:22. Simply put, the older commentators were right—the Nile was turned to actual blood. Or, at least, that is what Moses wrote. Of course, he did not have the advantage of reading Lewis Carroll.

CLOUDY SKIES AND CLOUDED EYES

MARK'S SOBER REASSESSMENT OF THE CHURCH

Peter J. Scaer

What can we know of Jesus as he really was? And in what sense can we say that the Christ whom we worship is related to the man who lived in Nazareth? To be honest, these kinds of questions, so popular in modern scholarship, are rarely asked among us. Perhaps, though, we should not feel too bad, or think that we are alone. Until the Enlightenment cast its long shadows, the so-called historical Jesus was known simply by the name of Jesus, whose story was told in the four canonical Gospels. For all of its academic appeal, the historical Jesus debate has a comical side. As Albert Schweitzer noted long ago, scholars have not so much sought the historical Jesus as they have created him in their own image.[1] The result is that we always seem to find the very Jesus that we are looking for. John Dominic Crossan has observed that historical Jesus research has become a joke in scholarly circles, not simply because the Jesus Seminar used colored beads to vote on the authenticity of Jesus' sayings, but because the scholars themselves could never come close to a consensus.[2] As such, it is tempting to treat the historical Jesus debate as kind of sideshow, a spectator sport for believers.

Now, this has not kept the Evangelicals from entering the fray. Craig Keener, for instance, has authored the excellent *The Historical Jesus of the Gospels*, painstakingly sifting through the Gospels' historical

---

[1] Albert Schweitzer, *The Quest of the Historical Jesus* (Minneapolis: Fortress Press, 2001), 478.

[2] John Dominic Crossan, *The Historical Jesus: The Life of a Mediterranean Peasant* (San Francisco: HarperCollins, 1991), xxvii.

details and demonstrating their plausibility.[3] Likewise, Darrell L. Bock
has argued vigorously that the Gospels stand "solidly rooted in what the
historical Jesus actually said and did."[4] The problem, though, for the
Evangelicals is that their scholarship will never be taken too seriously. If
you want a place at the table, you simply must deny some parts of the
story to have credibility or risk being accused of circular reasoning,
uncritical thought, or, worse yet, fundamentalism. What is a Christian
to do? If one becomes convinced of the evangelists' basic claims, much
of what first appeared implausible begins to seem quite likely. And once
a source proves itself trustworthy on the major issues, one tends to give
it the benefit of the doubt on minor matters as well.

On the other hand, if we take the historical Jesus for granted, we
run the risk of taking Jesus for granted. We may become like math students who, having stumbled across the answer key, no longer feel the
need to work out the problems for themselves. The historical enterprise
reminds us that we confess not simply a doctrine or formula, but a man
who was crucified under Pontius Pilate. Our faith is not only Spirit, but
flesh and blood. So, while we who hold to the inspiration of the
scriptures may not feel that we are natural participants in the "historical
Jesus" debate, we surely have a stake in it. Engaging in historical inquiry
includes apologetics, but even more, it is a quest for understanding
Jesus within his historical context. It is taking the incarnation seriously.
As N. T. Wright, among others, has warned, if we do not take history
seriously, we easily fall into theological Docetism.[5] Even more, as
Lutherans, whose doctrine so much depends on the writing of Paul, we
must be doubly alert, lest the Gospels become for us simply background

[3] Craig S. Keener, *The Historical Jesus of the Gospels* (Eerdmans: Grand Rapids, 2009).

[4] Darrell L. Bock, "The Historical Jesus: An Evangelical View," in *The Historical Jesus: Five Views*, ed. James K. Beilby and Paul Rhodes Eddy (Downers Grove: IVP Academic, 2009), 281.

[5] He puts it this way: "It is, after all, the pre-Easter Jesus who goes about doing and speaking the kingdom, and precisely if we say, with the letter to the Hebrews, that Jesus is the same yesterday, today and forever, we cannot use that as an excuse for imagining a docetic Jesus as today's Jesus and then projecting him onto the pre-Easter world, as much as would-be orthodoxy has done." N. T. Wright, "Whence and Whither Historical Jesus Studies in the Life of the Church?" in *Jesus, Paul, and the People of God: A Theological Dialogue with N. T. Wright,* ed. Nicholas Perrin and Richard B. Hayes (Downers Grove: IVP Academic, 2011), 155.

material for the truth we teach. While the Old Testament is more than an appetizer, and Paul more than a dessert, the Gospels are and must remain for us the main course of the Christian diet.

THE HISTORICAL JESUS: GETTING UP TO SPEED

Hermann Reimarus (1694–1768), whose notes were collected by Gotthold Lessing (1729–81), was among the first to argue that the Jesus of history was distinct from the Gospels' picture of him.[6] According to Reimarus, Jesus was a Jewish revolutionary whose goal was to reestablish the kingdom of God on earth. Rather than recording history, the Gospels sprang forth from the imagination and aims of the evangelists, who, disappointed in their failed Messiah, created the Church. The Church, Reimarus contended, was based upon a hoax, and Jesus' body was left lying in Lessing's ditch.

David Friedrich Strauss (1808–74), though also a skeptic, offered a way out of this philosophical predicament. Instead of thinking of the Gospels as "true history," they could be appreciated as "sacred legend."[7] The early Christians interpreted Jesus' life through the lens of the Old Testament, and then, having labeled Jesus "Messiah," they created stories and myths fitting for one so honored. Thus, for Strauss, meaning could be found apart from history, a path popular still today.

As skepticism reigned in the nineteenth century, Jesus became increasingly known as an enlightened teacher and moralist who taught the world about the Fatherhood of God and love for our fellow man. The Gospel of Mark, thought now to have priority, was perfect for a church that cultivated a Jesus apart from the embarrassment of his legendary birth and mythical resurrection. But even that portrait was found to be flawed and wanting. William Wrede (1859–1906), credited by Albert Schweitzer with bringing an end to the first phase of historical

---

[6] In 1778, Lessing published "Von dem Zwecke Jesu und seiner Junger," which may be translated "The Goal of Jesus and His Disciples. These fragments are accessible in Hermann Samuel Reimarus, *The Goal of Jesus and His Disciples*, ed. George Wesley Buchanan (Leiden: E. J. Brill, 1970), 37.

[7] D. F. Strauss, *The Life of Jesus Critically Examined*, ed. Peter C. Hodgson, trans. George Eliot (Philadelphia: Fortress Press, 1972), 56. Strauss notes that the mythical view "leaves the substance of the narrative unassailed; and instead of venturing to explain the details, accepts the whole, not indeed as true history but as sacred legend."

Jesus research, shook up the consensus with his essay "The Messianic Secret." In it, he argued that the Gospel of Mark, far from being a reliable account of Christ's life, was in fact a fiction. Jesus did not tell Peter to be quiet about his identity. Instead, Wrede argued, it is much more likely that Jesus never claimed to be the Christ at all.

It is with William Wrede that Rudolf Bultmann (1884–1976) begins his own *History of the Synoptic Tradition*, a work that perhaps more than any other sowed the seeds of the conservative/liberal division in Lutheranism. For Bultmann the Gospels were the products of an early Christian Church that constructed its gospel stories within the context of its communities and by the light of its post-Easter faith.[8] Thus, with Strauss, Bultmann suggested that the virgin birth could be understood as legend, and the transfiguration as myth. Unlike Strauss, who saw the miracles as expressions of Jewish piety, Bultmann interpreted them as the product of a Christian community reaching out to the Greco-Roman world, whose gods also performed great miracles. For example, the feeding of the 5,000 could be best understood as a "Nature Miracle," which Bultmann compares to examples found in various cultures ranging from Indian myths to Finnish fairy stories.[9] Thus, for Bultmann the Gospels had less to say about Jesus than about the faith of the early Christianity community.

While Bultmann thought he was doing the Church a favor by getting at the core, existential truth of Christ, others demurred. Ernst Kasemann suggested that Bultmann's approach was theologically untenable. As Kasemann wrote, "We cannot do away with the identity between the exalted and the earthly Lord without falling into Docetism."[10] That is not to say that Kasemann and the so-called Second Quest, or New Quest for the historical Jesus, were able to overcome the pessimism of Bultmann. Kasemann's question, nevertheless, was the right one for a church committed to the Jesus of history.

---

[8] Rudolf Bultmann, *History of the Synoptic Tradition,* trans. John Marsh (New York: Harper & Row, 1963), 1.

[9] Bultmann, *History of the Synoptic Tradition,* 236.

[10] Ernst Kasemann, "The Problem of the Historical Jesus," in *Essays on New Testament Themes,* trans. W. J. Montague (London: SCM, 1964), 34.

THE HISTORICAL JESUS: TODAY'S HEADLINES

In more recent times, the quest for the historical Jesus has been undertaken with new vigor, with scholars divided as to whether Jesus' movement was primarily of this world or more eschatological in nature.

Guided by such luminaries as Robert Funk, Burton Mack, and Dominic Crossan, the Jesus Seminar has garnered much sensational press, presenting Jesus variously as a cynic peasant or sage.[11] This Jesus was born in Nazareth, spoke against authority, and inspired the masses with his short, pithy sayings about loving one's enemies, turning the other cheek, and God's special providence for the poor. This Jesus' miracles were largely fabricated, and his healings psychosomatic. He died as one who spoke truth to Roman imperial power. Thus, the Jesus Seminar offers up a type of history and ideology, but with little theology and no eternity.

While the Jesus Seminar offers a minimalist construction, some are still more skeptical. Robert Price, for instance, goes so far as to argue that "it is quite likely that there never was any historical Jesus."[12] Price's work is not without interest. He suggests that "virtually the whole Gospel narrative is the product of a haggadic Midrash on the Old Testament."[13] So, when it comes to the feeding of the 5,000, for instance, Price recognizes it as a rewrite of "Elisha's multiplying the twenty barley loaves for a hundred men in 2 Kings 4:42–44."[14] The fact that the gospel stories hearken back to the Old Testament, is, for Price, evidence that they are not based on the memory of actual events. We might note here that another version of this type of thinking, combined with Jesus' own self-awareness, can be found in the once sensational *The Passover Plot*, in which Hugh Schonfield claimed that the entire Passion Narrative was

---

[11] See, for example, Dominic Crossan, *The Historical Jesus: The Life of a Mediterranean Jewish Peasant* (San Francisco: Harper, 1998).

[12] Robert Price, "Jesus at the Vanishing Point," in *The Historical Jesus: Five Views*, 47. For a full defense of this view, see Robert Price, *The Incredible Shrinking Son of Man* (Amherst, NY: Prometheus, 2003).

[13] Price, "Jesus at the Vanishing Point," in *The Historical Jesus: Five Views*, 67.

[14] Price, "Jesus at the Vanishing Point," in *The Historical Jesus: Five Views*, 71.

a hoax perpetrated by Jesus himself as he ordered his death according to various Old Testament prophecies.[15]

While some scholars draw back, others press forward. Dale Allison takes us to faith's halfway house in such works as *Constructing Jesus*.[16] Allison's knowledge of the scriptures and of the ancient world is breathtaking and his scholarship thorough. Allison reintroduces the eschatological, showing how Jesus preached a kingdom not of this world. Along the way, Allison debunks the myth that Jesus spoke only in short, pithy phrases. Perhaps more significantly, Allison argues, contra the Jesus Seminar, that Jesus actually spoke and taught about himself and thought that he was special. "We should hold a funeral for the view that Jesus entertained no exalted thoughts about himself," writes Allison. Concerning the feeding of the 5,000, Allison deems the event historically possible, with Jesus himself orchestrating the movement: "It is not implausible that he [Jesus] too once retreated into the wilderness in order to stir up memories of the Exodus."[17] Allison's suggestion, while not embracing the supernatural, is helpful, in that he shows, at least, that by feeding the 5,000 Jesus was not only offering up a meal but also teaching about himself. In the end, though, Allison appears to be overcome by the historical enterprise. Thus he finishes his impressive work, *Constructing Jesus*, with this sad coda: "If my deathbed finds me alert and not overly racked with pain, I will then be preoccupied with how I have witnessed and embodied faith, hope, and charity. I will not be fretting over the historicity of this or that part of the Bible."[18] So, in the end Allison engages in a strategic retreat, finding solace not in the unknowable events of Christ life, but in his own life, of which at least he has a more clear and complete picture.

---

[15] Hugh J. Schonfield, *The Passover Plot: New Light on the History of Jesus* (New York: B. Beiss Associates; distributed by Random House, 1965).

[16] Dale C. Allison Jr, *Constructing Jesus: Memory, Imagination, and History* (Grand Rapids: Baker Academic, 2010). See also Allison's *The Historical Jesus and the Theological Jesus* (Grand Rapids: Eerdmans, 2009).

[17] Allison, *Constructing Jesus*, 273.

[18] Allison, *Constructing Jesus*, 462.

James Dunn takes us further down the road in *Jesus Remembered*.[19] Perhaps, Dunn's greatest contribution to the debate has been his challenge to the notion that because the Gospels were written by those who had faith in Jesus, their witness is somehow suspect. Dunn turns this presupposition on its head, explaining, "In direct contrast to this deeply rooted suspicion of faith as a barrier to and perversion of any historical perspective on Jesus, my proposal is that the quest should start with the recognition that Jesus evoked faith from the outset of his mission and that this faith is the surest indication of the historical reality and effect of his mission."[20] Or, to put it another way, the first disciples believed in Jesus precisely because Jesus gave them something to believe in.

Along the way, we should note the work of N. T. Wright, whose *Jesus and the Victory of God* built upon the movement to understand Jesus within the context of Second Temple Judaism.[21] As if that were not enough, Wright went on to write *Resurrection of the Son of God* in which he argues exhaustively for the historicity of the resurrection itself, demonstrating that the New Testament's depiction of the resurrection has no precedent or analogy in other religions. The resurrection simply could not, and would not, have been fabricated by the early Christian community; indeed, if these stories had been fabricated, they would have been told in a much different way. Even more, without the resurrection, the Christian community would have soon disbanded, moving on to the next Messiah, contends Wright.[22]

---

[19] James T. Dunn, *Jesus Remembered*, vol. 1, *Christianity in the Making* (Grand Rapids: Eerdmans, 2003).

[20] James T. Dunn, "Remembering Jesus: How the Quest of the Historical Jesus Lost Its Way," in *The Historical Jesus: Five Views*, ed. James K. Beilby and Paul Rhodes Eddy (Downers Grove: IVP Academic, 2009), 203.

[21] N. T. Wright, *Jesus and the Victory of God* (Minneapolis: Fortress Press, 1996).

[22] N. T. Wright, *The Resurrection of the Son of God* (Minneapolis: Fortress Press, 2003). Wright argues that the pagans had no real notion of bodily resurrection. Old Testament passages such as Daniel 12 would have pointed to a resurrection that emphasized shining glory, as found in the transfiguration, yet the Gospels speak of the disciples finding the resurrected Jesus quite ordinary in appearance.

THE TESTIMONY OF BAUCKHAM

All of this brings us to our man of the hour, Richard Bauckham, whose magnificent *Jesus and the Eyewitnesses* bristles against the assumptions of Bultmann and the despair of ever truly knowing the Jesus of history. Bauckham moves beyond the vagaries of communal memory, arguing that the Gospels are based on the eyewitness testimony of those who actually knew Jesus, including both the apostles, who serve as fundamental guarantors of the gospel tradition, and minor characters who from time to time witnessed events to which not even the apostles were privy. As Bauckham notes, "The Gospels were written within living memory of the events they recount."[23] This means, I suppose, that if you had wanted to know whether Simon of Cyrene actually carried our Lord's cross, you could ask Simon, who might well be sitting, so to speak, in the next pew. Bauckham further argues that Peter provided the eyewitness testimony for much of the Gospel of Mark, and that the Twelve would have functioned as an "official body of eyewitnesses." Thus, Bauckham tears down the wall between the so-called historical Jesus and the Christ of faith. The Gospels, Bauckham contends, "are not some kind of obstacle to knowledge of the real Jesus and his history, but precisely the kind of means and access to the real Jesus and his history that, as historians and as believers, we need."[24] This assertion, taken for granted among us, has made Bauckham avant-garde, a revolutionary in the Society of Biblical Literature. Bauckham's work serves as a bulwark for the historic faith, a reassertion through scholarship that Christ did what he was said to have done and said what he was said to have said. The popular scoffing of Bart Ehrmann need not hold the day.

But, then, beyond the purpose of apologetics, we might wonder what Bauckham's work teaches us theologically, what it might add to our picture of Christ and the Gospels. For starters, his book reminds us that while it is necessary to say that the Gospels are divinely inspired, it is not enough. The question remains: "In what way they are related to the person Jesus?" If the Spirit works simply through an inspired writer, apart from means, then, of course, no eyewitness testimony is needed.

---

[23] Richard Bauckham, *Jesus and the Eyewitnesses: The Gospels as Eyewitness Testimony* (Grand Rapids: Eerdmans, 2008), 7.

[24] Bauckham, *Jesus and the Eyewitnesses,* 473.

We could claim that the Gospels are a revelation of Christ, but not a revelation from the man Jesus. We would be left with a Jesus of history and a Christ of inspiration. Bauckham draws a vivid picture in which the coming of the Spirit is not simply a vertical descent from heaven, but a Spirit who comes from the person and ministry of Jesus himself, who passed on the tradition to apostles whom he taught, who then in turn taught the Church. It has the added advantage, as Bauckham himself writes, that "there is no epistemological chasm between the eyewitness testimony and the theological significance of the events."[25] Theology need not be divorced from history; the two may become one once more.

IF THE GOSPELS ARE TRUE, DOES IT MATTER? HISTORY AND MEANING

We might then say that if we follow Bauckham's lead, we can have our cake and eat it, too. That we can have a Spirit-inspired scripture flowing from Jesus himself. But, perhaps, before we walk away in satisfaction, we may need first to crawl, since we may not be out of the water yet.

Having long been spectators in the historical debate, we may have been shaped by it more than we previously recognized. Even as conservative scholars have through the years bristled against the skeptics, they—the conservative scholars—may have unwittingly bought into their—the skeptics—premises. As we have seen, skeptics have typically dismissed the historicity of Jesus precisely by asserting that the stories have meaning. A good case in point, noted above, is Robert Price. Price argued that nearly all of the Gospel of Mark can be explained away by inventive exegesis and midrashic borrowing. Thus, the story of Jesus' temptation is a creative retelling of Israel's forty years in the desert, and the feeding of the 5,000 can be accounted for as a midrash on Elisha's multiplication of barley loaves in 2 Kings 4, and on the account of Moses and the giving of the manna.[26] By following Bauckham we can argue that the story did indeed happen, and that it was based on the eyewitness testimony of the apostles. But, we should note, it is not

---

[25] Bauckham, *Jesus and the Eyewitnesses*, 473.

[26] Robert Price, "Jesus at the Vanishing Point," 71.

enough simply to say that the event happened, or that the story is based on eyewitness testimony, as if it is the raw recorded data of a tape recorder or video camera. The apostles are not only eyewitnesses, but also preachers, and the evangelists are not only recorders of history, but also theologians. While theology has no foundation without history, neither should we think be satisfied with Gospels that offer history without theology.

Consider for instance the work of R. C. Lenski, rightly held up in our circles as a safe haven from the liberalism of Bultmann and his ilk. His take on the feeding of the 5,000 is instructive. On the positive side, Lenski's Markan commentary offers up a strong defense of the historicity of the feeding. Further, he shows how the evangelists' stories, while differing somewhat in the details, are not ultimately contradictory. On the other hand, when reading Lenski one comes across no Old Testament references at all. Though Mark compares the people to sheep without a shepherd, Lenski makes no mention of Jesus as the fulfillment of David the shepherd; the green grass of Mark does not stir up for Lenski any echoes of Psalm 23; the multiplication of the loaves is not compared with Moses' manna in the desert or to Elisha's multiplication of barley loaves. In ten pages of commentary, Lenski offers not one word on how the feeding fulfilled or pointed back to the Old Testament stories. Lenski summarizes the account in this way: "The story of the miracle is simplicity itself and is so graphically told that comment is hardly necessary."[27] Lenski's silence on the Old Testament should be for us a word of caution. Price's dismissal of the historicity of the Gospels has, rightly, no place among us. But, in the ultimate irony, the unbelieving Price has more to teach us about what the story means, from the perspective of Jesus as Messiah, than does Lenski, who holds to the story's history, but has little to offer us in term of meaning. In fact, it is striking how often Lenksi refers to the "facts" of the Gospel.[28] Lenski heroically asserts again and again that events actually happened. Yet,

---

[27] R. C. Lenski, *The Interpretation of St. Mark's Gospel* (Columbus: Wartburg Press, 1946), 267.

[28] Consider Lenski's description of Jesus' Baptism in Mark, where he begins successive paragraphs in this way: "Mark reports only the fact that Jesus saw the heavens.... Matthew states only the fact.... The plain facts of what occurred," Lenski, *The Interpretation of St. Mark's Gospel*, 47–48.

one is left wondering what it all means. Price suggested that the Church told this story to demonstrate that Christ was the fulfillment of the Old Testament. Allison suggested the Christ himself may have staged the event to make that same point. Lenski does neither. Thus, in a strange way, we are given facts but not faith, and the Jesus of history is once more divorced from the Christ of faith, only this time the union is put asunder by the conservative exegete.

N. T. Wright Offers Up a Challenge

A reading of scripture that emphasizes the facts of the Gospels but downplays their meaning raises some interesting questions. We might ask whether it would matter to our theology if we did not have the Gospels at all. N. T Wright asserts provocatively, "For many traditional Christians it would be quite enough if Jesus of Nazareth had been born of a virgin and died on cross (and perhaps risen again.)"[29] Or, to put it another way, we as a church could do well if we had the Nicene Creed and the Pauline kerygma. Wright plays out the implications in this way:

> But that leaves us with the baffling question, Why then did he [Jesus] go about doing all those things in between? Why did the canonical Evangelists take the trouble to collect and record them? Merely to provide the back story for the cross-based theology of salvation? Merely to show what the incarnate Son of God looked like and got up to? Simply to demonstrate, by his powerful deeds, that he was the second person of the Trinity?[30]

Now, I think that Wright here is playing a little fast and loose, ignoring some prominent evidence. By framing his challenge in terms of "the second person of the Trinity," Wright hopes to avoid the counter-challenge of John's Gospel, which is expressly written "so that you might believe that Jesus is the Son of God" (John 20:31). Yet, we should not so quickly wave off Wright's question. Once Christ's identity is established or faith that he is God's Son is affirmed, what more do the Gospels have to offer? Does each miracle establish yet again Christ's divinity and nothing more? In what sense do the gospel stories enhance

---

[29] Wright, "Whence and Whither Historical Jesus Studies," 131.

[30] Wright, "Whence and Whither Historical Jesus Studies," 131.

our theological understanding and in what way are they profitable for preaching and teaching in the Church?

Wright offers this hypothesis, namely, that the Gospels "are written to convince their readers that he really was inaugurating the kingdom of God."[31] That is to say, when we read the Gospels, we are reading not only about what Jesus accomplished in his life, but we are learning about the kingdom he was establishing for us today. Now, like that of Schweitzer, Wright's kingdom is eschatological, but it is also decidedly this-worldly. The kingdom has to do with Christ's continual work of bringing about the new creation inaugurated by Christ. When speaking of God's kingdom, Wright emphasizes everything from helping the poor and feeding the hungry to tackling such social issues as third-world debt and immigration. As Wright puts it, "Jesus' own mission becomes the template and the energizing force for all that the Church then has to do and be."[32] Or as he puts it in another place, "Jesus is alive again; therefore new creation has begun; therefore we have a job to do."[33] Thus, for Wright the Gospels are the blueprint for our kingdom building, here and now, mainly through the doing of good in society.

THE GOSPELS: A BLUEPRINT FOR THE CHURCH

Wright's proposal has a certain appeal, but ultimately falls short. Ironically, his greatest weakness may very well be historical. He cannot adequately explain how the Church got it so wrong so early.[34] Why is it that the Church, rather than seeing itself primarily in these social terms, came to be defined by her structure, her preaching, and her rituals?

A critic might well note that Wright's vision could surely be held by anyone who wished to promote world peace, recycling, and socialized healthcare. His vision of an earthly kingdom might look to some as the softer side of Calvinism, or perhaps yet another social gospel. Still, Wright has a point. Not only are the Gospels written with a view to the

---

[31] Wright, "Whence and Whither Historical Jesus Studies," 133.

[32] Wright, "Whence and Whither Historical Jesus Studies," 151.

[33] Wright, "Whence and Whither Historical Jesus Studies," 149.

[34] In exasperation he writes, "What then are the Gospels actually all about? I think the Western church has simply not really known what the Gospels were there for." Wright, "Whence and Whither Historical Jesus Studies," 133.

past, but they also point to the future, telling us what the Kingdom of God is like.

Indeed, Wright is not alone in pointing towards the future. Bultmann also thought of the Gospels as forward-looking documents, or at least as a description of the Christian community that followed. Wrede, though a skeptic, saw the Gospels—in a sense rightly—as a blueprint not simply for a conglomeration of social causes and actions, or for a community, but more specifically, for the Church.

Though we find Bultmann's skepticism unwarranted, he was right to note that the words of Jesus were understood rightly and fully only in the light of the resurrection. The Gospels are the product not simply of eyewitnesses, but of evangelists who interpreted and framed the testimony of the eyewitnesses into a theological story. Bauckham, we should note, does not see either Matthew or John as an eyewitness. Bauckham writes, "Not being eyewitnesses themselves, the Gospel writers are less theologically ambitious."[35] Thus, Bauckham attempts to guard against the notion that the evangelists fabricated or tampered with the eyewitnesses. On the other hand, we need to keep in mind that the evangelists were in fact evangelists, not simply recorders of history, but preachers of the faith. They were not simply historians or biographers, but theologians who may even have thought of themselves as writers of scriptures.[36] Though the evangelists did not feel free to alter the stories of the eyewitnesses, they were nevertheless choosing the witnesses whom they would put on the stand and taking those parts of their testimony that they understood to be theologically significant. In Mark's telling of the feeding of the 5,000, the green grass, the picture of Jesus as a shepherd, and the eucharistic actions are not only historically true, they are also theologically significant.[37] The eyewitnesses may have indeed seen many things when Jesus fed the 5,000, but the evangelists offer the details that are theologically significant.

---

[35] Bauckham, *Jesus and the Eyewitnesses*, 472.

[36] Instructive on topic is D. Moody Smith, "When Did the Gospels Become Scripture?" *Journal of Biblical Literature* 119 no. 1 (2000), 3–20, where he argues that Matthew and Luke were self-consciously writing their Gospels as a continuation of the scriptural narrative and meant for their writings to be included in the worship life of the Church.

[37] For this author's take on the story, see Peter J. Scaer, "The Lord's Supper as Symposium," *Concordia Theological Quarterly* 72 no. 2 (April 2008), esp. 123–25.

For an example of how this works, think again about Mark's account of the feeding of the 5,000. In Allison's view, the story may have been Jesus' attempt to offer to the people a sign and to demonstrate that he was a prophet like Moses.[38] Bultmann points the way forward, noting that the story may have served as a kind of evangelism tool to reach out to the pagan community that expected such miracles. But then consider the example of Burton Mack. Mack, a thorough skeptic, contends that the Gospels are creative mythologies. Yet, seeing the documents as charter documents for the Christian movement, his eyes are open to the details. And so, when commenting on the feeding of the 5,000, Mack notes the connections to the Eucharist, the eucharistic actions, and how the broken pieces point to both the Supper to come and to Christ's death.[39] He recognizes the connection between the miracle and what he call the Christian cultus, or what we might call the worship life of the Christians. Just as Price, a skeptic, is able to see the Old Testament connections, so also is Mack able to connect the dots of the feeding of the 5,000 to the life of the Church.

Yet, conservative scholars are often strangely silent as to the story's meaning for the Church today. Perhaps this is due to the worry that by claiming meaning for the story somehow its historicity will be undermined. Consider again the work of Lenksi. Even as he has nothing to say about how the feeding is related to the Old Testament, so also is he silent about what the story might mean for the Church. In recounting the fact that Jesus took bread, blessed it, broke it, and gave it, Lenski makes no reference to the Last Supper, in which these very same words are repeated. In this sense, he does not seem to allow scripture to interpret scripture. But tellingly, Lenski comments that Mark "lets the facts speak for themselves."[40] So, we are left again with the conundrum, and an unnecessary one at that, where one group of scholars finds meaning apart from history, while the other guards history, seemingly by offering or deciphering no meaning. In fact, this type of hesitation can be found in our present day commentaries as well. Gibbs, for in-

---

[38] Allison, *Constructing Jesus*, 273.

[39] Burton Mack, *A Myth of Innocence: Mark and Christian Origins* (Philadelphia: Fortress Press, 1988), 232.

[40] Lenski, *The Interpretation of St. Mark's Gospel*, 268.

stance, in his commentary on the Matthew's account of the feeding of the 5,000 does the reader the service of pointing to the Church when he writes, "In the Blessed Eucharist as well, the Lord of the Church feeds his people, body and soul." But, then he quickly adds, "One should speak cautiously at this point, for Scripture does not provide much explicit elaboration."[41] Such caution though, while having the air of exegetical humility, actually makes the exegete into a better theologian than the evangelist himself, who presumably would not have noticed such an obvious connection. Thus, a similarity is noted, but the Evangelist's voice is muted, and there lays still a ditch between the life of Jesus and its meaning for the Church. Neither is Christ a theologian for performing the miracle, nor is the evangelist given credit for underlining its significance.

In the face of such timid exegesis, Wright's challenge still stands. Do the details of Jesus' ministry really matter? What needs to be explored more fully, I would propose, is the place of the Church, not simply after Jesus, but within the very ministry of Jesus as he carries it out, and as the evangelists record it. That is to say, we must see how Christ establishes the Church within his own ministry and how the evangelists themselves teach about the Church that Jesus is establishing.

THE CHURCH IN THE SYNOPTICS

Matthew alone among the evangelists actually uses the word for church (Matthew 16:18; 18:17). As Matthew presents the matter, everything begins with Christ, who then chooses the twelve apostles. These twelve are foundationally presented, with Peter being primary, the rock upon whom the Church is built. To Peter, and thus to the Church, the keys of the kingdom are given. Peter and the apostles are given the final command to baptize and to teach, with the presumption that the Church will result from their preaching, teaching, and baptizing.

Luke's Gospel proceeds to depict the expansion of the Church. He presents us not only with the Twelve, but with the seventy ministers (Luke 10). In his second book, he shows how the Church developed to

---

[41] Jeffrey A. Gibbs, *Matthew 11:2—20:34*, Concordia Commentary (St. Louis: Concordia, 2010), 752.

include deacons, elders, and even bishops. For Luke, the Church is clearly defined as having started with Christ and his core group of apostles, along with some family members (Acts 1:13–14). This Church then expands with the apostolic blessing of the deacons (Acts 6:1–7) and with the ministry of Paul, who carries forward the apostolic preaching even unto Rome.

What then, if anything, does the Gospel of Mark have to tell us about the Church? For many this question is largely anachronistic. Mark is, after all, the primitive gospel. Consider again, though, Bultmann's assessment of Mark, drawn from Wrede: For Bultmann, the Gospel of Mark offers us not only a historical account but a theological narrative, shaped and formed in light of the faith of the early church.[42] Bultmann, at least in this assessment, was on to something.

There are a number of ways that we can get at the notion that Mark was steeped in the faith and theology of the Early Church. First, we can see the formation of the Church in Jesus' choosing of the apostles, whom he lists in solemn order, beginning with Simon, who is given the name Peter (Mark 3:13–19). As Bauckham is right to observe, the Twelve here serve as a body of eyewitnesses. The numbering of them as twelve, though, also suggests their eschatological significance as the foundation of a new Israel.[43] Furthermore, the naming of Simon as Peter also points to Peter's foundational status.

Second, the churchly nature of Mark can be seen in his sacramental emphasis. Bauckham perceptively notes that Peter appears at the beginning and end of Mark's Gospel, forming a type of inclusio, signaling Peter as an eyewitness to the events of Jesus' life. But there also appears to be a type of sacramental inclusio in Mark's Gospel, in which Baptism and the Supper testify to the meaning of Christ's ministry. John puts it this way in his first epistle: "There are three who testify: namely, the Spirit, the Water, and the Blood" (1 John 5:8). Accordingly, Mark's Gospel is bookended by the witness of the water and the blood. These are the poles by which the life of Jesus is ordered and by which the Church comes into being.

---

[42] Bultmann, *History of the Synoptic Tradition,* 1.

[43] For more on this, see Joel Marcus, *Mark 1–8,* Anchor Bible (New Haven: Yale University Press, 2000), 268.

BAPTISM, BAPTISM, BAPTISM

Mark's Gospel begins baptismally. John steps upon the stage as one who is "baptizing in the desert and preaching a baptism for the remission of sins" (1:4). All the people are said to come out to John precisely in order to be baptized (1:5). Baptism, Baptism, Baptism. After this John the Baptist offers a brief but telling introduction to Jesus' ministry: "I have baptized you with water, but he will baptize you with the Holy Spirit" (1:8). Thus, in Mark's Gospel, Jesus' whole ministry is introduced as an act known and practiced by the Early Church. In doing so, Mark tells us not simply about what Jesus did, but also what he does. In Bultmann's way of thinking, Mark is telling us about the community. Using N. T. Wright's vocabulary, this is an example of Mark telling us about the Kingdom. And in Wrede's view, and ours, Mark is telling us about the Church.[44]

Mark's theology is in no way primitive. In fact, his teaching on Baptism is theologically advanced, linking a churchly act to cross and atonement. Mark notes that as Jesus himself is baptized, the heavens are said to be "torn open," a phrase found again at the end of the Gospel, where at Jesus' death, the temple curtain is "torn open" (Mark 15:38). Thus, the evangelist links Baptism to Jesus' death.

The second part of this sacramental inclusio may, of course, be found in the story of the Last Supper. Mark tells the story of the Supper as a type of Passover, in which Jesus offers himself as the sacrifice of the Passover Lamb (14:12). It is the meal of the atonement, as he offers his blood "poured out for the many" (14:24), even as Jesus had come to "give his life as a ransom for many" (10:45).

What is interesting though is the way Mark links Baptism and the Supper, seeing them as both as a summary of his own work and as a forecast for the work of the apostles. When James and John request seats on honor in the coming glory, Jesus asks them whether they will be able to drink the cup that he drinks and be baptized with the baptism with which he is baptized. The brothers respond affirmatively, to which

---

[44] Compare this view with that of Lenski, who, underplaying the significance of the event, writes, "We should not put too much into Jesus' Baptism." *The Interpretation of St. Mark's Gospel*, 44.

Jesus says "You will drink the cup I drink and be baptized with the baptism I am baptized with" (Mark 10:45–46). In this explicit linking of Baptism and Cup, we may say that Mark is in fact offering a sacramental theology, one that surely would have resonated in the early Christian community. As Joel Marcus puts it, "Mark's Christian readers drink the Lord's cup at communion and thus proclaim his death until he comes (cf. 1 Corinthians 11:26); they also share in that death in a deep sacramental sense (cf. Romans 6:3)."[45] We should also note that Baptism and the Supper are discussed explicitly as an expression of the Kingdom. James and John wish to have special seats in Christ's ruling glory. Also after the Supper, Jesus says that he will not again drink from the fruit of the vine until he does it "anew in the Kingdom of God" (Mark 14:25). Thus, the Kingdom of God preached by Jesus finds its inauguration in Baptism and comes to fruition in the drinking of the Cup, even as the Gospel is framed sacramentally.

SACRAMENTAL BREAD

With mention only of water and blood thus far, one might think that Mark offered up a spiritual Atkins diet. But even as Mark demonstrates the relationship between Baptism and the Cup, so also does he sacramentally combine Baptism and the eating of bread—in an advanced way—whereby he contrasts Christian worship with the practice of the Jews. Thus, we know that Jesus often spoke against the hypocrisy of the Jewish leaders, but he frames that criticism in sacramental terms. Mark writes, "The Pharisees and some of the teachers of the law who had come from Jerusalem gathered around Jesus and saw some of his disciples eating breads with common/defiled, that is unwashed hands." Then Mark adds this aside, "The Pharisees and all the Jews do not eat unless they wash their hands. And when they come from the marketplace, unless they are *baptized*, they do not eat. And they observe many other traditions, including the *baptism* of cups, pitchers, and kettles" (Mark 7:1–4; emphasis added). Thus, Mark critiques the superficiality of a Pharisaic piety that is concerned more with outward purity, specifically in terms that would have made sense

---

[45] Marcus, *Mark 1–8*, 754.

for the Christians' own worship life. The Pharisees baptized their hands and their cups as preparation for the eating of ordinary bread. Christ, Mark shows, offers a true Baptism and a better Bread.

Luke's Gospel has long been recognized for its theme of table fellowship, culminating as it does on the road to Emmaus, where the catalyst for the disciples' spiritual breakthrough is the breaking of the bread. In the breaking of the bread, the disciples eyes were opened, with the result that they saw Jesus as he truly was, the Christ foretold in Scripture (Luke 24:28–35). This positive picture of the eucharistic community is carried on in Acts 2, where the baptized community is gathered together for the breaking of bread, resulting not only in unity but also in generosity.

So also Mark tells the story of how Christ offers a new kind of bread. This story, which culminates in the Last Supper, begins in the feeding of the 5,000, the story of the Canaanite woman, and the feeding of the 4,000. Each story is unique, yet in each case Christ is the source of true bread. Further, in each feeding narrative, the eucharistic actions are present, and the meals are described using language that is both reminiscent of the Old Testament and anticipatory of the New Testament meal.[46]

Nevertheless, Jesus' own disciples do not understand the significance of the bread. While Lukan disciples had their eyes opened, Mark is more sanguine about the persistence of spiritual cataracts. This is seen, almost humorously, in the story of the one loaf (Mark 8:14–21). According to the pericope, the dim-witted disciples forget to bring bread on the boat. They then comically discuss the fact that they have no bread. Now, it should be said, the disciples were not entirely without bread, for they had one bread/loaf. Attempting to turn the discussion in a spiritual direction, Jesus warns his disciples of the leaven of the Pharisees and Sadducees, but to no avail. As Joel Marcus notes, "The disciples completely miss the symbolic force of Jesus' reference to leaven."[47] The disciples carry on with a comically mundane discussion concerning the fact that they have no bread. Jesus then rebukes the

---

[46] See, for example, Jerome Kodell, *The Eucharist in the New Testament* (Collegeville, MN: Liturgical Press, 1988), 44–45.

[47] Marcus, *Mark 1–8*, 511.

disciples, "Why are you discussing the fact that you have no bread? Do you not yet perceive or understand? Are you hearts hardened? Having eyes do you not see, and having ears, do you not hear?" As Joel Marcus notes, this kind of misunderstanding is reminiscent of John's Gospel, where would-be believers misinterpret "living water" (John 4) and "bread from heaven" (John 6). Marcus concludes that the one loaf may well be "interpreted in symbolic, quasi-Johannine manner."[48] We might add that this motif of loaf and leaven is found also in Paul's epistle to the Corinthians, in which yeast is the culprit at the Corinthian Passover and threatens to corrupt their bread of sincerity and truth (1 Corinthians 6:6–8). Paul goes on to speak about this bread/loaf as a "participation in the body of Christ," noting that we all "partake one loaf" (1 Corinthians 10:16–17).

What can we learn from Mark? This story is an amazing, nearly complete reversal of the road to Emmaus, where the words of the Lord resulted in burning hearts, and the breaking of the bread resulted in opened eyes. The disciples, evidently having taken notes, recalled the facts of the feedings of the 5,000 and the 4,000. But like so many commentators, they did not yet understand what the feedings meant. And what did they not understand? That if Jesus was present, they had all they needed. If on the boat, they had one loaf, they indeed had Jesus. For Mark, the Eucharistic bread is the true fulfillment of the Old Testament bread of presence. And, we might add, even as the bread is for Mark the bread of presence, so also does Mark picture the boat as the Church, the place where the bread can be found.

THE CHURCH IN MARK

A BOAT OUT AT SEA

All four of the Gospels speak of the boat in a symbolic way. In Matthew, Jesus calls the first disciples from the boat so that he can make them into "fishers of men." Luke tells the same story, but adds to it the miraculous draft of fish, thus pointing ahead to Pentecost and the growth of the Church. For Luke, the story also offers a picture of church fellowship in which Peter takes the lead, while James and John are

---

[48] Marcus, *Mark 1–8*, 511.

described as being in partnership or fellowship with him (κοινωνοί). So also, in the Gospel of John the boat provides a picture of church unity, when after the resurrection Peter says, "I am going fishing," and the his fellow disciples say, "We will go with you" (John 21:3).

The boat, if anything, plays an even more prominent role in the Gospel of Mark. It has long been recognized that Luke has a theology of pilgrimage. The Christian life is a walk or journey. Disciples are called to take up their crosses daily and to follow Jesus "on the way." The Gospel of Mark, on the other hand, gives the impression that Jesus' chief form of transportation was by boat. Fitting for the beginning of his ministry, Jesus spoke to his disciples on a little boat (3:19). He then taught the seaside multitude while he was sitting in a boat (4:1). He used the boat to get away from the crowds (6:32), though it often did not work, for the crowd often met Jesus as he got out of the boat. All told, Mark mentions Jesus' travel by boat twenty times, in comparison to Luke's paltry six.[49]

A BOAT TOSSED ABOUT

What then does the boat look like in the Gospel of Mark and what does it tell us about the Markan church? To be sure, it is no battleship or cruise liner. Instead, the boat appears to be small, tossed about by the waves. Rather than ark of salvation, it is a place of fear and danger where faith is tested by Jesus' apparent indifference or seeming absence.

Take, for instance the story of Jesus calming the storm (Mark 4:35–41). The story begins with Jesus' exhortation, "Let us go to the other side" (4:35). In this case, the other side refers to the region of the Gerasenes, a territory inhabited largely by Gentiles. Thus, Jesus takes his disciples on a missionary journey, anticipating the Church's movement outwards to the nations. Joel Marcus astutely observes here also "a Jonah typology that permeates our passage."[50] Because of the storm, the

---

[49] Matthew refers to boats fourteen times, and John mentions boats eight times; significantly, four of John's references can be found in the epilogue.

[50] Marcus, *Mark 1–8*, 336. L. C. Cope notes that the parallels include departure by boat, a violent storm at sea, a sleeping main character, badly frightened sailors, a miraculous stilling of the storm, and a marveling response. See *Matthew: A Scribe Trained for the Kingdom of Heaven*, Catholic Biblical Quarterly Monograph Series, vol. 5 (Washington DC: Catholic Biblical Association, 1976), 437.

boat is nearly capsized, and the danger is made more acute by the fact that Jesus is sleeping. Now, this is not just a story about the boat and Jesus, but about the Church as it sailed the stormy seas of evangelism, danger, and persecution. As Marcus puts it, "We may well hear an echo of the community's sense of desperation, therefore, in the anguished appeal of the disciples: 'Teacher, don't you care that we are about to die?' "[51]

Indeed, the theme of persecution permeates the Gospel of Mark. Jesus, for instance, promises his disciples earthly blessings, but notes that such blessings will, of course, come along with "persecutions" (10:30). Later, Jesus will warn his disciples of wars, earthquakes, famines, and persecutions (13:5–13). During this time, Christ's absence will be felt, and his true presence will be longed for as people cry out in vain, "Look, there he is" (13:21). Indeed, this persecution is anticipated even in Mark's telling of Jesus' Baptism, where we are told that having been baptized, Jesus was cast out into the desert, where he was with the wild beasts (1:12–13).[52]

This picture of the Church under persecution can be seen even more clearly in the story of Jesus walking on the water (Mark 6:45–52). In this case, Jesus is not sleeping, he is entirely absent, having instructed his disciples to go off in the boat by themselves. It is as if, through these narratives, Jesus is preparing his disciples for a church in which he will not be visibly present, but present only, as we recall, in the bread of presence. This story emphasizes less the danger and more of the torture and pain. Mark tells us that the boat was in the middle of the lake and that the hour was growing late. They were now at the "fourth watch of the night," Mark writes (6:48). This darkness may well anticipate Christ's own warning of the coming distress and tribulation, as well as his admonition to "keep watch," for one does not know if our Lord will return at midnight or when the rooster crows or at dawn" (14:35–37). The disciples' predicament is captured in Mark's description of them "making tortuous progress" (6:48). In the Apocalypse, the same word

---

[51] Marcus, *Mark 1–8*, 337.

[52] The same word that Mark uses for "wild beasts" can be found throughout the letters of Ignatius, where he speaks about his own upcoming martyrdom in terms of preparing to go to the wild beasts.

describes a time of persecution when the forces of evil are allowed "to torture them [that is, Christians], but not to kill" (Revelation 9:5; cf. 11:10; 12:2). Thus, the disciples, like marines in training, are given a lesson in courage: "Take courage! Ἐγώ εἰμι. Don't be afraid," Jesus says. Why indeed were the disciples afraid? Mark puts it this way: "They were completely amazed, for they had not understood about the loaves, their hearts were hardened" (Mark 6:52). If only they had understood about the loaves they would not have been afraid, for they would have known the Lord was with them.

HISTORY AND THE CHURCH: LESSONS FROM MARK

In this paper, I have attempted in broad strokes to speak about the historical Jesus debate and to explore where we might fit into the discussion. Having begun upon this trail, there is, no doubt, much work to do. What has become clear, at least to me, is that history can become neither the enemy of theology nor a replacement for it. Theology without history is abstract and becomes an ideology. History without meaning has nothing to say or offer. Bauckham puts it this way: "Understanding the Gospels as testimony, we can recognize this theological meaning of the history not as an arbitrary imposition of objective facts, but as the way the witnesses perceived the history, in an inextricable co-inherence of observable event and perceptible meaning."[53] Bauckham's suggestion is more than welcome. History and meaning belong together. We might only improve upon Bauckham's suggestion by thinking of Matthew, and perhaps John, not only as eyewitnesses, but also as evangelists, who both testified to what they had seen and then interpreted it for and within the Church. Matthew after all was a scribe, and all the disciples, as we saw in the story of the one loaf, were taking notes along the way. Good enough notes so that they could recall the number of leftover baskets. With the resurrection, of course, they gained perspective, and their eyewitness testimony, as well as their classroom notes, became for us the story and history of Jesus. If we do not see or understand all of this, Mark would have us know that we are in good company. For even with the bread of Christ's presence, we still

---

[53] Bauckham, *Jesus and the Eyewitnesses*, 5.

sail the seas under cloudy skies, with clouded eyes. We remain like the half-healed blind man; we see men like trees walking. We cry out, along with the man in Mark, "I believe, help my unbelief." And our Lord still points to the loaf and says, "Do you still not understand?"

THE SON AS CREATOR AND SOURCE OF NEW CREATION IN COLOSSIANS[1]

Charles A. Gieschen

Besides the opening lines of the Prologue of the Gospel of John (1:1–3), there is no other biblical text more explicit and profound in its testimony to the Son as creator than the so-called hymn found in Colossians 1:15–20.[2] The first half of the hymn testifies to a clear division between the creator and the creation, whether visible or invisible, with the pre-incarnate Son being the creator of all things (1:15–17). The second half testifies to the incarnate Son as the source of the new creation, proclaiming him to be "the Head of his body, the church" and the "Firstborn from the dead" due to his work of reconciling all things in creation to himself through his atoning death (1:18–20).[3] This study,

---

[1] This study is offered as a tribute to Dean Wenthe with sincere appreciation for his faithful witness to Christ in the entirety of the Scriptures, his untiring service to Christ's Church, and his cheerful friendship over three decades as my teacher, mentor, president, and colleague at Concordia Theological Seminary.

[2] The poetic structure and language of Colossians 1:15–20 has led to the widespread designation of these verses as a hymn. Some scholars have argued that it is a pre-Pauline hymn that was incorporated into the letter, but this is difficult to prove. For purposes of this study, I assume that Paul is the author of both the letter and the hymn, even though some scholars do not include Colossians among Paul's authentic letters. If Colossians 1:15–20 is a pre-Pauline hymn, this Christology is endorsed as Paul's own and is not only earlier than this epistle itself but also a more widespread confession than that of Paul. For a recent treatment of the hymn that includes an extensive bibliography, see Christian Stettler, *Der Kolosserhymnus: Untersuchungen zu Form, traditionsgeschichtlichem Hintergrund und Aussage von Kol 1,15–20,* Wissenschaftliche Untersuchungen zum Neuen Testament, Series 2, vol. 131 (Tübingen: Mohr Siebeck, 2000).

[3] The translation of Colossians provided here and below is my own from the Greek text. Important Greek terms are included in brackets.

therefore, will demonstrate that these themes of creator and source of new creation are central to the Christology of this hymn and also foundational for the Apostle Paul's proclamation of Baptism and sanctification in the rest of this epistle. After discussing the context in Colossae that called for such proclamation from Paul, the primary focus of this study will be the Christology of the hymn. Paul's proclamation of our participation in this new creation through baptism will also be addressed before concluding with some proposals for how the Christology of this epistle continues to speak to our twenty-first-century context.

THE SITUATION AT COLOSSAE

Although this study will include only a brief overview of the historical context for Paul's writing of this epistle, an examination of the context is, nevertheless, critical in discerning possible reasons for Paul choosing to write about the Son as creator and source of new creation.[4] As in other Pauline letters, there is some internal evidence in the letter that provides insight for some of the challenges faced by the Christians at Colossae, even though the extent to which these were internal to the congregation or coming from the outside is not known.[5] The most crucial evidence is found in Colossians 2:16–23.

> [16]Therefore, do not let anyone judge you in regard to food or drink or in the subject of a festival or new moon or Sabbath,[17] which are a shadow of the things to come, but the substance is of Christ. [18]Let no one render a judgment against you, while taking pleasure in asceticism [θέλων ἐν ταπεινοφροσύνῃ] and worship of angels [θρησκείᾳ τῶν ἀγγέλων], what one has seen upon entrance [ἃ ἑόρακεν ἐμβατεύων], causing one to be vainly inflated by his carnal mind [19]while not holding fast to the Head, from whom the entire body, while being nourished and held together through the joints and

---

[4] There are numerous scholarly discussions about the situation at Colossae; see especially Ian K. Smith, *Heavenly Perspective: A Study of the Apostle Paul's Response to a Jewish Mystical Movement at Colossae*, Library of New Testament Studies, vol. 326 (London: T&T Clark, 2006).

[5] For an argument that most of these challenges may have been coming from outside the church at Colossae, see M. Jeff Brannon, *The Heavenlies in Ephesians: A Lexical, Exegetical, and Conceptual Analysis*, Library of New Testament Studies, vol. 447 (London: T&T Clark, 2011), 152–53.

ligaments, grows with a growth from God. [20]If you died with Christ to
the elemental spirits of the world [τῶν στοιχείων τοῦ κόσμου], why do
you submit to regulations while you are living in the world, such as
[21]"Do not handle, do not taste, do not touch"—[22]which reference
things that all perish as they are used—according to the commands
and teachings of men? [23]These regulations have the reputation of
wisdom attained through self-chosen worship [ἐθελοθρησκίᾳ] and
asceticism that is severity to the body [ταπεινοφροσύνη καὶ ἀφειδίᾳ
σώματος], but are of no value against the indulgence of the flesh [i.e.,
sinful condition].

There have been numerous proposals in the past two centuries
about the so-called "Colossians heresy" that Paul is addressing in this
letter.[6] In spite of the variety of scholarly proposals attempting to
identify this heresy, there is one thing that stands out in Paul's own
description of the challenges facing this congregation: several of the
problems seem to be influenced by Jewish practices (e.g., dietary requirements, Sabbath laws, and purity concerns). Much more enigmatic
and the subject of considerable debate are the references to asceticism,
worship of angels, and visionary experience. Also important for our
understanding of the situation in Colossae is the determination of the
referent of "the elemental spirits of the world" (1:20). In light of the
Jewish character of some of the problems that Paul sees, an understanding of these four references should be sought in the context of
first-century Judaism.

The term ταπεινοφροσύνη typically is rendered as "humility" (cf.
usage in Colossians 3:12), but has a more technical meaning of
"asceticism" in the context of Colossians 2:18 and 2:23.[7] The explanation "that is severity to the body" (καὶ ἀφειδίᾳ σώματος) provided after
ταπεινοφροσύνη in 2:23 indicates that the term refers to ascetic

---

[6] John J. Gunther, *St. Paul's Opponents and Their Background: A Study of Apocalyptic and Jewish Sectarian Teachings*, Novum Testamentum Supplement Series, vol. 35 (Leiden: Brill 1973), 3–4. Gunther lists forty-four different proposals from the nineteenth and twentieth centuries, although the differences between some of these proposals is rather minor.

[7] W. Bauer, F. W. Danker, W. F. Arndt, F. W. Gingrich, *A Greek-English Lexicon of the New Testament and Other Early Christian Literature*, 3rd ed. (Chicago: University of Chicago Press, 2001), 989. Most translations and commentators agree that the term carries a more technical meaning in the context of Colossians 2:18 and 2:23.

practices. In light of the mention of the "worship of angels" and visions "that inflate the carnal mind" in 2:18, it is reasonable to conclude that these ascetic practices were preparation for the experience of mystical ascent and visions of the heavenly realms where angels and God dwell. There is considerable literary evidence in Jewish and early Christian literature of fasting and other ascetic practices performed by those seeking to obtain visionary experiences of the heavenly worship.[8]

The interpretation of θρησκείᾳ τῶν ἀγγέλων ("worship of angels") begins by defining how to understand the genitive relationship. Should this relationship be understood as an objective genitive (i.e., worship that is directed towards angels) or a subjective genitive (i.e., worship in which angels are the subjects offering worship to God)? Although the evidence strongly favors the subjective genitive interpretation, the objective genitive should not be dismissed without consideration, simply because it is very doubtful that Jews or Christians would have angels as their sole object of worship in place of God. The evidence is not that neat and clear-cut. Separate studies by Clinton Arnold and Loren Stuckenbruck in 1995 demonstrate that while there is no significant evidence for the worship of angels replacing the worship of God among Jews of this period, there were individuals and groups who venerated angels, sometimes privately, in a manner that usually was not seen as a substitute for the worship of God.[9] Stuckenbruck's examination of the angel worship refusal formula in the book of Revelation (19:10; 22:8–9) and elsewhere uncovered three basic types of venerative activity: "(1) Invocation of angels for assistance, vengeance, or protection; (2) Reverence of angels whose heavenly worship is exemplary; (3) Expressions of thanksgiving in response to various functions or activities attributed to angels."[10] Also instructive is his observation that

---

[8] For example, Daniel 9; *Greek Apocalypse of Ezra* 1:1–5; *4 Ezra* 5:20, 6:35–37, 9:23–25, 12:50–51; *Apocalypse of Abraham* 9; and *Ascension of Isaiah* 2:7–11.

[9] Clinton Arnold, *The Colossian Syncretism: The Interface between Christianity and Folk Belief at Colossae*, Wissenschaftliche Untersuchungen zum Neuen Testament, Series 2, vol. 77 (Tübingen: Mohr Siebeck, 1995), and Loren T. Stuckenbruck, *Angel Veneration and Christology: A Study in Early Judaism and in the Christology of the Apocalypse of John*, Wissenschaftliche Untersuchungen zum Neuen Testament, Series 2, vol. 70 (Tübingen: Mohr Siebeck, 1995).

[10] Stuckenbruck, *Angel Veneration and Christology*, 201–202.

particular "contexts were thought to be capable of breeding an un-
healthy posture which threatened monotheistic belief."[11] These contexts
include the invocation of a prominent angel, the observation or participation in worship that angels are offering, an angelophany during
mystical ascent to see God, and settings with cultic overtones.[12]
Stuckenbruck offers this balanced conclusion.

> These observations do not leave much room for a conclusion that the
> refusal tradition constitutes evidence for a polemic against a veritable
> angel "cult." But it is possible to suggest that it may have functioned as
> *a critique from within* which recognized a danger of angels thought to
> be encountered in heavenly journeys. Since the application of the
> refusal tradition leaves no trace that the notion of an angel's striking
> appearance is being questioned, we may assume that the author and
> the position being opposed shared common angelological ideas. At
> the same time, the intensity of the refusal is hard to explain without
> positing some form of underlying venerative behavior which may
> have been deemed appropriate towards God's messengers, an attitude
> which at least the proponents would probably not have considered
> destructive to a belief in God.[13]

Clinton Arnold has explored literary evidence from this region of
Asia Minor, including pagan worship practices, and builds the argument that some Jews invoked or called upon angels for help, often
without reference to YHWH.[14] Moreover, these Jews who called upon
angels were asking for more than deliverance from evil spirits; they also
sought revelation about the future and specific answers to life (e.g., how
to find a mate or curse an enemy). Arnold characterizes this practice of
"apotropaic magic" as private and argues that it is the result of a
pervasive fear of malevolent powers. Michael was by far the most
frequently invoked angel, but Arnold did not find evidence that Michael
or any of the other angels became the center of cultic veneration jointly
with God. Without dismissing this evidence, the invocation of angels is
probably not the referent of "worship of angels" in Colossians 2:18

---

[11] Stuckenbruck, *Angel Veneration and Christology*, 202.

[12] Stuckenbruck, *Angel Veneration and Christology*, 202.

[13] Stuckenbruck, *Angel Veneration and Christology*, 102–103; emphasis original.

[14] For these conclusions, see Arnold, *Colossian Syncretism,* esp. 59–60.

because the context also mentions ascetic practices and visionary experience.

It is more probable that θρησκείᾳ τῶν ἀγγέλων ("worship of angels") should be understood as a subjective genitive (i.e., worship in which angels are the subjects offering worship to God), with the background for this activity being Jewish mystical ascent and participation in heavenly worship. Ian Smith's recent extensive monograph on this background for the Colossians heresy examines the abundant evidence from Second Temple Jewish apocalyptic literature that demonstrates considerable interest in such activity.[15] Two studies by F. O. Francis have refuted scholarship which argued that ἃ ἑόρακεν ἐμβατεύων ("what one has seen upon entrance") should be interpreted as initiation experiences into mystery religions by demonstrating that ἐμβατεύων ("entrance") in Colossians should be understood as entrance into the heavenly worship in order to experience visually the presence of God.[16] The Book of Revelation's presence in this region after Colossians also testifies to ongoing interest in visionary revelation among some Christians. It is apparent, therefore, that asceticism, worship by angels, and visionary experience in Colossians 2:18 should not be understood as distinct problematic practices but as interrelated. Ascetic practices of fasting and bodily denial were used as preparation for Jewish mystical visionary experiences that began with ascent to heaven and climaxed with seeing the divine chariot throne with the Glory of YHWH seated upon it surrounded by myriads of angels.[17] Paul's rejection of it among Christians may be based on his own past personal experience and Christ's words of warning (2 Corinthians 12:1-10).

There is one other piece of evidence that deserves attention for understanding the situation and the interpretation of the Christology in the hymn. In this same context, Paul poses this question to the Colossians: "If you died with Christ to the elemental spirits of the world

---

[15] Smith, *Heavenly Perspective*.

[16] "Humility and Angel Worship in Colossians 2.18" and "The Background of EMBATEUEIN," in *Conflict at Colossae: A Problem in the Interpretation of Early Christianity Illustrated by Selected Modern Studies*, ed. F. O. Francis and W. A. Meeks (Missoula, MT: SBT and Scholars Press, 1975), 163–95 and 197–207.

[17] For a broad introduction to Jewish mysticism, see Gershom G. Scholem, *Major Trends in Jewish Mysticism*, 3rd ed. (New York: Schocken, 1954).

[τῶν στοιχείων τοῦ κόσμου], why do you submit to regulations while you are living in the world?" (2:20). This rhetorical question builds off of Paul's earlier warning: "See to it that no one takes you captive by philosophy and empty deceit, according to human tradition, according to the elemental spirits of the world [κατὰ τὰ στοιχεῖα τοῦ κόσμου], and not according to Christ" (2:8). The term τὰ στοιχεῖα has been understood in three primary ways.[18] First, it has been interpreted impersonally by many, including Luther, as "elemental principles of the Mosaic law." Second, others have understood the referent to be impersonal "elemental components of the universe such as earth, water, air, and fire." Third, a growing number of scholars see its referent as personal "astral powers or spirits that are identified with fallen angels." This latter interpretation fits well with the immediate context of Colossians 2:15, which mentions "rulers and authorities" (τὰς ἀρχὰς καὶ τὰς ἐξουσίας) conquered by Christ, the interest in invisible spiritual beings among the Colossians, and Paul's cosmology understood in the context of Second Temple Judaism.

To summarize succinctly the situation that Paul faced in Colossae: it appears that members of the church at Colossae were in a context where there was considerable interest in Jewish practices, especially ascetic practices, that led to visionary ascent and worship with "invisible" created angels with the result that Paul was concerned because members influenced by this did not have, or were losing, their focus on the centrality of the incarnate Son in worship and life. It is possible that this worship was motivated, at least in part, by fears of the invisible fallen angelic spirits of this world; ascent to heavenly worship may have been viewed as a means of escaping these spirits. In short, the focus was on creation rather than the creator who has conquered fallen creation. To address the situation, Paul proclaims Christ as the creator of all visible and invisible things who became incarnate and redeemed all things with his blood, making him also the source of new creation. To address some of the experimentation among the invisible cosmos by these Christians, Paul proclaims the Son as the creator and reconciler of the entire cosmos, visible and invisible, heaven and the earth.

---

[18] For a summary of these positions, together with helpful bibliography, see Smith, *Heavenly Perspective*, 80–87.

The Structure of the Colossians Hymn

The subject of the hymn is the Father's "beloved Son," who is introduced at the end of the thanksgiving section of the epistle (τὴν βασιλείαν τοῦ υἱοῦ τῆς ἀγάπης αὐτοῦ in 1:13). The careful structure of this hymn is readily visible in the Greek text.[19] Although there has been some debate among scholars about details of the hymn's structure, it is clear that there are two strophes (1:15–16 and 1:18b–20), each strophe being introduced by the same relative pronoun and verb (ὅς ἐστιν) followed by a variation of the "Firstborn" (πρωτότοκος) title and a series of causal clauses that begin with the same introductory phrase (ὅτι ἐν αὐτῷ). These two strophes are separated by two transition lines that each begin with the same phrase (καὶ αὐτός ἐστιν). The first of these transition statements has content that relates to the first strophe, while the content of the second transition statement is related to the second strophe. The content division, therefore, is between these two transition statements: 1:15–17 has its focus on the pre-incarnate Son as creator and sustainer of all things, and 1:18–20 has its focus on the incarnate Son as source of new creation because he has reconciled all fallen creation and is the Firstborn of the dead. Both strophes make regular use of prepositions (e.g., ἐν and διά) and language inclusive of all creation (e.g., τὰ πάντα).

[15] **ὅς ἐστιν** εἰκὼν τοῦ θεοῦ τοῦ ἀοράτου, **πρωτότοκος** πάσης κτίσεως,

> [16] **ὅτι ἐν αὐτῷ** ἐκτίσθη τὰ πάντα
>
> ἐν τοῖς οὐρανοῖς καὶ ἐπὶ τῆς γῆς,
>
> τὰ ὁρατὰ καὶ τὰ ἀόρατα,
>
> εἴτε θρόνοι εἴτε κυριότητες εἴτε ἀρχαὶ εἴτε ἐξουσίαι·
>
> τὰ πάντα δι’ αὐτοῦ καὶ εἰς αὐτὸν ἔκτισται·

[17] **καὶ αὐτός ἐστιν** πρὸ πάντων καὶ τὰ πάντα ἐν αὐτῷ συνέστηκεν,

[18] **καὶ αὐτός ἐστιν** ἡ κεφαλὴ τοῦ σώματος τῆς ἐκκλησίας·

> **ὅς ἐστιν** ἀρχή, **πρωτότοκος** ἐκ τῶν νεκρῶν, ἵνα γένηται ἐν πᾶσιν   .
> αὐτὸς πρωτεύων,

---

[19] A helpful summary of scholarly proposals is found in Smith, *Heavenly Perspective*, 147–59.

¹⁹ **ὅτι ἐν αὐτῷ** εὐδόκησεν πᾶν τὸ πλήρωμα κατοικῆσαι

²⁰ καὶ δι᾽ αὐτοῦ ἀποκαταλλάξαι τὰ πάντα εἰς αὐτόν,

εἰρηνοποιήσας διὰ τοῦ αἵματος τοῦ σταυροῦ αὐτοῦ,

εἴτε τὰ ἐπὶ τῆς γῆς εἴτε τὰ ἐν τοῖς οὐρανοῖς.

THE PRE-INCARNATE SON AS CREATOR

As stated in the introduction, the pre-incarnate Son as creator of all things is the central theme of the first half of the hymn (Colossians 1:15–17). The first title in the first strophe is very significant for setting the pre-incarnate Son within the mystery of YHWH: "the Image of the invisible God" (1:15). Because of testimony to Wisdom's presence and participation in creation in Proverbs 8:22–31, many scholars have drawn the conclusion that this title is primarily influenced by what is stated about Wisdom elsewhere.[20] For example, Wisdom is described as "an image of God's goodness" in *Wisdom of Solomon* 7:26, but that is considerably different from the Son being "the Image of the invisible God." Although it is very reasonable to argue that testimony about Wisdom's presence before creation and active role in creation influenced early testimony about the Son as creator, wisdom texts are not the source of this exalted title for the pre-incarnate Son.

Adam Christology is sometimes seen in this title because Adam was made "in the image of God, after his likeness" (Genesis 1:26). Colossians, however, is speaking of the pre-incarnate Son here—not the human Jesus as a second Adam—and asserts that the Son *is* the Image of the invisible God, not that he is *in* or *after* the image of God. Furthermore, the assertion that God is "invisible" implies that the Son is not the image of God's visible manifestation, as is the case with Jewish ideas about Adam being created in the image of the Glory. In Colossians, the Son is the only visible image of the invisible God, implying that he is the image after whom Adam was created. Gordon Fee

---

[20] See the critique by Gordon D. Fee, *Pauline Christology: An Exegetical-Theological Study* (Grand Rapids: Baker Academic, 2007), 317–25, and Jarl E. Fossum, "Colossians 1:15–18a in the Light of Jewish Mysticism and Gnosticism," *New Testament Studies*, vol. 35 (1989): 183–201.

misses this point when he jumps to the incarnation to speak of the Son as the image:

> It is through the Son, who alone *by way of his incarnation perfectly bears the Father's image*, that the unseen God is now known (cf. 2 Corinthians 4:4–6). Thus the eternal son, whom the Father sent into the world (Galatians 4:4), has restored the "image" of God that the first Adam bore but that was defaced by the fall.[21]

The most probable background for Paul's usage of "image" is Old Testament testimony about the visible and tangible כְּבוֹד־יְהוָה ("Glory of YHWH") who was seen by Moses and the prophets (e.g., Exodus 16:9–10; 24:15–18; 40:34–38; Ezekiel 1:26–28).[22] It is very noteworthy that Paul identifies Christ as both the Glory of God and the Image of God, most clearly in 2 Corinthians 4.

> [3]And even if our gospel is veiled, it is veiled only to those who are perishing. [4]In their case, the god of this world has blinded the minds of the unbelievers, to keep them from seeing the light of the gospel of the Glory of Christ [τοῦ εὐαγγελίου τῆς δόξης τοῦ Χριστοῦ], who is the Image of God [ὅς ἐστιν εἰκὼν τοῦ θεοῦ]. [5]For what we preach is not ourselves, but Christ Jesus as Lord, with ourselves as your servants for Jesus' sake. [6]For it is the God who said "Let light shine out of darkness" who has shone in our hearts to give the light of the knowledge of the Glory of God [τῆς δόξης τοῦ θεοῦ] in the face of Christ (2 Corinthians 4:3–6).

These lines make it eminently clear that Paul understood Christ to be the Glory. This is especially evident when Paul states in Colossians 4:6 that "the Glory of God" is beheld in "the face of Christ." This is an allusion to Exodus 33:20, where Moses requests to see YHWH's unveiled presence and YHWH responds that no one can see his face

---

[21] Fee, *Pauline Christology*, 301; emphasis mine.

[22] See Charles A. Gieschen, *Angelomorphic Christology: Antecedents and Early Evidence*, Arbeiten zur Geschichte des antiken Judentums und des Urchristentums, vol. 42 (Leiden: Brill, 1998), 78–88, 315–46. The Hebrew term carries the connotation of tangible weightiness. For Paul's use of Glory tradition in Christology, see Carey Newman, *Paul's Glory-Christology: Tradition and Rhetoric*, Novum Testamentum Supplement Series, vol. 69 (Leiden: Brill, 1992). Paul has two brief references to "glory" in Colossians that relate to the restoration of the image of God in Christians on the Last Day (1:27; 3:4).

and live. In this very context where Paul writes of the "gospel of the Glory of Christ," he also identifies Christ as "the Image of God" (4:4). The background for Paul's understanding of the Son as the Image of God is the Glory in the various theophanies recorded in the Old Testament. If Christ is the Glory/Image of God seen now, then the pre-incarnate Son is the Glory/Image of God seen by the prophets of old.

This is the implication of the discussion by Paul that begins in 2 Corinthians 3, where he states that Christians behold the Glory of the Lord in the reading of the Old Testament.

> [17]Now the Lord is the Spirit, and where the Spirit of the Lord is, there is freedom. [18]And all of us, with unveiled faces reflect as in a mirror the Glory of the Lord [τὴν δόξαν κυρίου] and are being transformed into the same Image [τὴν αὐτὴν εἰκόνα] from one degree of glory to another; for this comes from the Lord who is the Spirit (2 Corinthians 3:17–18).

This revelation of the Glory is facilitated through the Spirit in the reading of "the old covenant" or "Moses" (3:14, 15) because the Spirit of Christ has removed the veil from the minds of Christians to see the Son in these Scriptures (3:14–17). It is important to see here, as in 2 Corinthians 2:4, the way that Paul moves between glory and image language: Christians reflect as in a mirror the *Glory* and are being transformed into the *Image*. Glory and Image are different terms for the same reality, namely, the Son. As with the Glory of YHWH in the Old Testament, εἰκών carries an emphasis on material or visual likeness. Why, then, did Paul not use "Glory" terminology in Colossians? He probably used "image" language because it communicated more clearly to his Hellenistic audience. His use of "Image of God" in 2 Corinthians and Colossians is similar to his use of another related term in the Philippians hymn. In Philippians 2:5, he speaks of the pre-incarnate Son as being "in the Form of God" (ἐν μορφῇ θεοῦ). In the background here, once again, is Christ as the Glory.[23] If Paul did not adapt this hymn from another source, he probably chose the language of "form" because it communicated more clearly to that congregation and set up the

---

[23] See Gieschen, *Angelomorphic Christology*, 337–39.

desired parallel in the hymn with the Son later "taking the form of a servant" (μορφὴν δούλου λαβών).

Elsewhere Paul uses the language of "Image of God," while in Colossians an additional adjective is added: "the Image of the invisible [ἀοράτου] God." This is not surprising in light of Exodus 33:20, where YHWH stated emphatically that man cannot see him and live. This testimony became the basis in early Christianity for teaching the invisibility of the Father as reflected especially in the Gospel of John: "No one has seen God at any time, the only-begotten Son, who is at the bosom of the Father, has made him known" (1:18; cf. John 6:46). It is the Son, therefore, who is seen by the patriarchs and prophets in the various theophanies of the Old Testament.[24] Paul regularly uses the title "God" for Father and "Lord" for the Son, for example in the salutations of his letters. To express the meaning of this entire title in a paraphrase: "the pre-incarnate Son is the visible Image (i.e., Glory or Form) of the invisible Father."

Three things seem to guide Paul's use of the next title, "Firstborn of all creation" (πρωτότοκος πάσης κτίσεως). First, it is probable that the parallel structure between the first and second strophe played a major role in Paul's use of the "Firstborn" titles in both strophes. It may be that "Firstborn of the dead" was the more prominent title, as will be argued below, and his use of this term in the second strophe influenced his choice of title in the first strophe. Second, the "firstborn" terminology was used by contemporary Jews and Christians to speak of preexistence, even though Paul does not use it in this manner elsewhere. Third, "Firstborn" was also a messianic title for the eternal Davidic king (MT Psalm 89:27–28; LXX Psalm 88:27–28; English translation Psalm 89:26–27), indicating a unique place of privilege.[25]

The closest example of similar usage of "Firstborn" as a title for the pre-incarnate Son is Hebrews 1: "And again, when he brings the Firstborn (τὸν πρωτότοκον) into the world, he [the Father] says, 'Let all

---

[24] Charles A. Gieschen, "The Real Presence of the Son before Christ: Revisiting an Old Approach to Old Testament Christology," *Concordia Theological Quarterly* 68 (2004): 103–26.

[25] Paul E. Deterding, *Colossians*, Concordia Commentary (St. Louis: Concordia, 2003), 55.

God's angels worship him'" (Hebrews 1:6). Here it is an exalted title that speaks of the Son's preexistence and divine status superior to angels and worthy of worship. An example of similar "firstborn" language in contemporary Jewish usage as an exalted title indicating preexistence prior to creation is found in one of the lists of titles that Philo of Alexandria (first century) ascribes to "the Word" (ὁ λόγος) in his writings.

> And even if there be not as yet any one who is worthy to be called a son of God, nevertheless let him labor earnestly to be adorned according to his first-born [πρωτόγονος] word, the eldest of his angels, as the great archangel of many names; for he is called, the authority, and the name of God, and the Word, and man according to God's image, and he who sees [i.e.,] Israel.[26]

For Philo, all of God's activity in the world, including creation and interaction with the patriarchs and prophets, is accomplished through "the Word." Another Jewish text that dates from the first or second century, the *Prayer of Joseph*, gives the Angel Israel this exalted title: "the firstborn [πρωτόγονος] of every living thing to whom God gives life" (lines 2–3).[27] Evidence from Justin Martyr shows how the firstborn language continued to be used by Christians for the pre-incarnate Son well into the second century: "It is wrong, therefore, to understand the Spirit and the power of God as anything else than the Word, who is also the firstborn [πρωτότοκος] of God."[28] Early usage of this title by Christians and Jews shows that it was a very exalted title, implying pre-existence prior to creation.

Because this title, apart from a context like the Colossians hymn, could be understood to imply a created nature, it is not surprising that the "Firstborn of all creation" of Colossians 1:15 came to be used by the Arians in their attempts to argue that the Son was the first created being who, in turn, was involved in creating the rest of creation.[29] This caused

---

[26] *De Confusione Linguarum*, 28 (146); http://cornerstonepublications.org/Philo/Philo_On_The_Confusion_of_Tongues.html; accessed December 4, 2013.

[27] For further study of this fragmentary text, see Gieschen, *Angelomorphic Christology*, 137–42.

[28] *1 Apology* 33.6; *ANF* 1:174.

[29] See the helpful historical overview in Deterding, *Colossians*, 52–56.

later interpreters to argue that this title actually refers to the *incarnate* Son as the preeminent creature among every creature. Although this exegesis can be understood in the light of history, nevertheless such an exegesis does not stay true to the creation context of Colossians 1:15 nor to how the title would have been understood in the first century. The "Only-Begotten" (μονογενής) of the Gospel of John is an example of a title that may have been used to describe the mystery of the Son's existence before creation specifically because of the possible misunderstanding involved with terminology such as "firstborn" (John 1:18; 3:16).

The majority of the first strophe expresses the Son's central role in creation and is filled with echoes of Genesis 1:1. Three prepositions with the personal pronoun in 1:16 testify to the Son as creator (ἐν αὐτῷ, δι' αὐτοῦ, and εἰς αὐτόν). The inclusiveness of everything being created by the Son is communicated by the language of "all things" (τὰ πάντα) twice, "in the heavens and on earth" (ἐν τοῖς οὐρανοῖς καὶ ἐπὶ τῆς γῆς; cf. Genesis 1:1), and "visible and invisible" (τὰ ὁρατὰ καὶ τὰ ἀόρατα). The latter combination appears to be specifically aimed at the "worship of angels" situation, where part of the invisible creation was receiving undue attention. Even more pointedly directed to the historical situation at Colossae is the further unpacking of invisible creation: "whether thrones, or dominions, or rulers, or authorities" (εἴτε θρόνοι εἴτε κυριότητες εἴτε ἀρχαὶ εἴτε ἐξουσίαι).[30] Nothing is left outside of the Son's creative hands, especially not various angels that drew considerable interest among some members of this congregation.

This theological point is driven home once again in the hymn with the use of the perfect tense verb (in contrast to the use of the aorist ἐκτίσθη earlier): "all things have been created [ἔκτισται] through him and for him" (Colossians 1:16). As any reader of the Old Testament knows, there is a refrain that is repeated throughout the Scriptures: YHWH is creator (e.g., Psalm 104). Even more than the exalted titles of this hymn, Paul's proclamation of the pre-incarnate Son's action as

---

[30] Deterding notes that these are terms used for angelic beings by Paul (cf. Colossians 2:15; Ephesians 1:21) and other Jews in Second Temple literature (e.g., *1 Enoch* 6:7–8; 61:10; *2 Enoch* 20:1; *Testament of Levi* 3:8; *Testament of Simeon* 2:6–7; *Testament of Solomon* 3:5–6; 20:14; *Testament of Abraham* 13:10; *3 Baruch* 12:3; *Apocalypse of Elijah* 1:1–10); see Deterding, *Colossians*, 45.

creator of all things is the most profound way he could have chosen to express that the Son is within the mystery of YHWH, the one God of Israel. Richard Bauckham speaks of this as "creational monotheism."[31] This confession does not imply that the Son only is creator and not the Father; rather, it is a monotheistic and trinitarian confession that the Father creates through the Son. One of the most important Pauline texts that sheds further light on Paul's understanding of the relationship between the Father and the Son as creator is 1 Corinthians 8:5–6. It is especially important to see the careful parallel structure in Paul's statements about the Father and the Son as creator:

> [5]But for us there is one God [εἷς θεὸς], the Father
>   from whom are all things [ἐξ οὗ τὰ πάντα] and we for him,
> [6]and one Lord [εἷς κύριος], Jesus Christ,
>   through whom are all things [δι' οὗ τὰ πάντα] and we
>   through him.

Paul's confession here of "one God, one Lord" is a terse exposition of the Shema confessed daily by pious Jews ("YHWH our God, YHWH is one"; Deuteronomy 6:4). Bauckham explains the Christological and monotheistic significance of Paul's formulation.

> The purpose of what is said about Jesus Christ in 1 Corinthians 8:6 is not primarily to designate him the 'mediator' (a not strictly appropriate term in this context, but frequently used) of God's creative work or of God's salvific work, but rather to include Jesus in the unique identify of the one God. Jesus is included in God's absolutely unique relationship to all things as their Creator. The purpose of the whole verse, in its context, is strictly monotheistic. Its point is to distinguish the God to whom Christians owe exclusive allegiance from the many gods and many lords served by pagans. Just as in all Second Temple Jewish monotheistic assertions of this kind, what is said about God is said as a means of *identifying God as unique*. What is said about Jesus Christ only serves this purpose if it *includes Jesus in the unique identity of God*. Paul apportions the words of the Shema' between Jesus and God in order to include Jesus in the unique identity

[31] Richard Bauckham, *Jesus and the God of Israel: God Crucified and Other Studies on the New Testament's Christology of Divine Identity* (Grand Rapids: Eerdmans, 2008), 194–95.

of the one God YHWH confessed in the Shema‘. Similarly, he
apportions between Jesus and God the threefold description of God's
unique identifying relationship as Creator to all things, in order to
include Jesus in the unique identity of the one Creator.[32]

The first of two transition statements between the first and second
strophes concludes the confession of the pre-incarnate Son as creator:
"And he himself is before all things, and all things hold together in him"
(Colossians 1:17). The language of "before all things" (πρὸ πάντων)
again confesses the mystery of preexistence of the Son from eternity
before creation and puts him firmly on the creator side of the creator-
creation division. The language of "holding together" (συνέστηκεν) all
things is a confession of the Son's ongoing work of sustaining creation.
Against any notion of the Son being active in creation and then turning
the reigns over to the Father and becoming inactive until the incarnation, this phrase confesses the Son's work of preserving creation even to
the Last Day. In a very similar confession, the opening lines of Hebrews
state that God created the universe through the Son, who is "sustaining
all things by his Word of Power" (φέρων τε τὰ πάντα τῷ ῥήματι τῆς
δυνάμεως αὐτοῦ; Hebrews 1:3).[33]

THE INCARNATE SON AS THE SOURCE OF NEW CREATION

The theme of new creation in Colossians is sung out even before the
transition to the second strophe of the hymn begins (Colossians 1:18–
20). At the end of the opening thanksgiving that immediately precedes
the hymn, Paul draws on the creation imagery of darkness and light to
proclaim Christ's saving work as the basis for the restoration of
creation: "Giving thanks to the Father, who has qualified you to share in
the inheritance of the holy ones in *light*. He has delivered us from the
domain of *darkness* and transferred us to the kingdom of his beloved
Son, in whom we have redemption [τὴν ἀπολύτρωσιν], the forgiveness
of sins" (Colossians 1:12–13). This light-darkness new creation

---

[32] Bauckham, *Jesus and the God of Israel*, 216–17; emphasis original.
[33] For a discussion of creation by the Son in Hebrews 1, see Gieschen, *Angelomorphic Christology*, 295–303.

interpretation of Christ's redemptive work at the close of Paul's
thanksgiving serves as a bridge that introduces the body of this epistle,
which begins with the hymn, and theologically prepares the hearer for
the hymn's conclusion, where the basis for the reconciliation of all
creation is "the blood of his cross" (Colossians 1:20).

The transitional phrase that marks the content shift into the second
strophe of the hymn states: "And he himself is the Head of the Body, the
Church" (1:18). Although one might anticipate some mention of Son's
incarnation in a fleshly body in this transition to the strophe about
Jesus' work of reconciliation and resurrection, Paul jumps ahead to the
body that is the result of this work: the Body of Christ, the Church, of
which he is the Head. Paul's understanding of the Church as the Body
of Christ probably resulted, in part, from his experience of Christ on the
road to Damascus. The organic union of Christ with his Church is
apparent in his words to Saul because of Saul's persecution of the
Church: "Saul, Saul, why do you persecute *me*?" (Acts 9:4–5; cf. 22:7–8;
26:14–15). Even though Saul was persecuting individual Christians, he
was also persecuting Christ, the head of the Body, which consists of all
who have been joined to him by Baptism.

The teaching about the Church as the Body of Christ is scattered
throughout the Pauline corpus (1 Corinthians 12:12–13; Romans 12:4–
5; Galatians 3:28), but it is especially in Ephesians that Paul expresses
more fully his understanding of the Body of Christ with Christ as
Head.[34] In speaking about the results of Jesus' resurrection, Paul writes:
"And he [the Father] placed all things under his [Christ's] feet and
appointed him [Christ] the Head over all things for the Church, which
is his [Christ's] body, the fullness [τὸ πλήρωμα] of him [God] who fills
all in all" (Ephesians 1:22–23). This is language very similar to that in
Colossians, including the idea of fullness, but here the fullness of the
Deity dwells not only in the body of Jesus, but also in the Body of
Christ. It is apparent from Ephesians that the temple is an important
metaphor for understanding Body of Christ language: "In him [Christ]
the whole structure is joined together and grows into a holy temple in
the Lord; in whom you also are built together into a dwelling place for
God in the Spirit" (Ephesians 2:21–22). In addition to each believer

---

[34] See further discussion in Gieschen, *Angelomorphic Christology*, 339–43.

individually being a holy of holies in which the Glory/Christ dwells (i.e., Christ is in us; 1 Corinthians 3:16–17; 6:15; 2 Corinthians 6:16), together we are also a huge temple, a huge body with a Head who comprehends us in himself (we are "in Christ"). It is possible that Paul is directing potential mystics away from visionary ascent to see Christ enthroned and toward the Body of Christ on earth in order to see Christ. The Head is the source of new creation or growth for the Body, an idea prominent in Colossians 2:9 that is also expressed in Ephesians 4:

> [15]Let us in every way grow up into him who is the Head, Christ, from whom the whole body, [16]being fitly joined together and united through every joint with which it is supplied, according to the working in measure of each single part, promotes the body's building up of itself in love (Ephesians 4:15–16).

"The Beginning" (ἀρχή) is a title that one would expect to see in the first half of the hymn, used in the context of the Son as the person in whom creation has its origin and source. Besides its usage in Genesis 1:1 (LXX), there is Proverbs 8:22, where the LXX version implies that Wisdom is the first "creation" who then participated in creation, an idea that was very attractive to the Arians: "The Lord created me [Wisdom] as the beginning of his ways." More in line with the use of the term as a title implying the origin or source of creation is its presence in Revelation 3:14, where the risen Christ declares himself to be "the Beginning of the Creation of God" (ἡ ἀρχὴ τῆς κτίσεως τοῦ θεοῦ) in the sense that the Son is the origin and source of all creation. There is evidence that ἀρχη continued to be used as a title for the pre-incarnate Son among some Jewish Christians (e.g., *Acts of Thomas* 10). In the Colossians hymn, however, the title "the Beginning" is found in the second strophe of the hymn as a title that precedes "Firstborn of the dead." In this location, "Firstborn of the dead" can be understood as functioning epexegetically to explain the way in which the incarnate Son is "the Beginning": he is "the Beginning" because his resurrection is the origin and source for the future resurrection harvest. In light of Paul's negative use of τὰς ἀρχάς ("the rulers") in Colossians 2:15, there may also be some contrast implied here between these and Christ as the ἀρχή.

With the title "Firstborn of the dead" (πρωτότοκος ἐκ τῶν νεκρῶν), Paul trumpets out new creation language. The pattern of death, death, death in the fallen creation has been overcome through the Father raising the Son on the third day. Not only does this title stand in parallel with "Firstborn of all Creation" in the first strophe and signal a similar temporal relationship (i.e., the incarnate Son's resurrection is prior to the resurrection of all dead on the Last Day even as the pre-incarnate Son existed prior to all creation), but it also indicates the certainty of the future resurrection (i.e., "firstborn" here indicates that others will be resurrected). As noted above, this title appears to reflect Paul's more widespread interest in using "firstborn" and "firstfruits" language in relation to the *incarnate* Son. When speaking of the people being predestined to be part of God's family in Romans 8:29, Paul writes, "For those whom he foreknew he also predestined to be conformed to the image (τῆς εἰκόνος) of his Son, in order that he be the firstborn (πρωτότοκον) of a large family" (i.e., the eldest son who is the basis for others becoming fellow sons of God). Even more significant for understanding the title "Firstborn of the dead" is Paul's use of "firstfruits" when proclaiming the resurrection of Jesus in 1 Corinthians 15. There he writes of Jesus as "the firstfruits [ἀπαρχή] of those who have fallen asleep" (15:20) and, with regard to proclaiming the order of resurrection, "Christ the firstfruits [ἀπαρχή], then at his coming those who belong to Christ" (15:23). Furthermore, the prominent usage of ὁ πρωτότοκος τῶν νεκρῶν in the trinitarian greeting of Revelation 1:5 indicates that this title was used and recognized among early Christians in Asia Minor, which is the very region in which Colossae is situated.

Not only is the Son preexistent before all things as the Firstborn of all creation, but Colossians 1:18 states that the incarnate Son is the Firstborn from the dead "in order that he himself be preeminent [i.e., of first importance] in all things" (ἵνα γένηται ἐν πᾶσιν αὐτὸς πρωτεύων). It is possible that the incarnation, suffering, and death of Jesus put his divine status in question among some at Colossae. Rather than sidestepping this subject, Paul confronts it head-on in this strophe. Lest invisible angels be viewed by the Colossians as more powerful than the flesh and blood Jesus, Paul proclaims the resurrection of Jesus as the emphatic expression of the incarnate Son's divine identity and unique preeminent status (πρωτεύων). Far from the incarnation diminishing the deity of the Son, Paul emphasizes that "all the fullness (τὸ πλήρωμα) was pleased to dwell in him," that is, in the flesh and blood Jesus. Less there be any confusion about either the "fullness" or the incarnation, Paul restates this truth with even greater clarity later in this letter: "For in him the whole fullness of the Deity dwells bodily" (ὅτι ἐν αὐτῷ κατοικεῖ πᾶν τὸ πλήρωμα τῆς θεότητος σωματικῶς; 2:9).

This clear proclamation about the person of Jesus, his divine and human natures, is vital for proclaiming the work of Jesus in the final lines of this hymn. Having confessed the true identity of Jesus, Paul proclaims the significance of his death by crucifixion as universal reconciliation: "And through him [Jesus] to reconcile [ἀποκαταλλάξαι] all things to him [Jesus], whether the things on earth or the things in the heaven, because he [Jesus] has made peace through the blood of his [Jesus'] cross" (1:20).[35] There can be no doubt that the scope of Jesus' reconciling work includes invisible creation, which also means disarming "the elemental spirits of the world" (2:8, 20) and "the rulers and authorities" (2:15). Paul uses the language of redemption/payment (1:14; 2:14) and reconciliation (1:20–22) interchangeably in this letter to express the significance of Jesus' death:

> In whom we have redemption, the forgiveness of sin (1:14).

> To reconcile all things . . . making peace through the blood of his cross (1:20).

> And you . . . he has now reconciled in his body of flesh by his death (1:21–22).

> Canceling the record of decrees that stood against us . . . nailing it to the cross (2:14).

In a similar manner, Paul uses justification and reconciliation interchangeably in his other letters to express the broad scope of Christ's work, as is very apparent in these texts:

> Because we have now been declared righteous [δικαιωθέντες] by his blood, we will be saved by him from the wrath. . . . Because we have

---

[35] Some translations introduce another subject for some of these pronouns. For a convincing argument that Jesus is the subject of all of them, see Fee, *Pauline Christology*, 309–12.

been reconciled [κατηλλάγημεν], we will be saved by his life (Romans 5:9, 10).

In Christ, God was reconciling [καταλλάσσων] the world to himself, not counting their trespasses against them [universal justification], and entrusting to us the message of reconciliation [καταλλαγῆς]. So we are ambassadors for Christ, God making his appeal through us. We beseech you, on behalf of Christ, be reconciled [καταλλάγητε] to God [individual justification] (2 Corinthians 5:19–20).

The second strophe of the Colossians hymn, which began by trumpeting Jesus' resurrection, climaxes in the proclamation of universal reconciliation accomplished because peace between God and all fallen creation has been made through the atoning blood offered at Jesus' crucifixion (cf. Romans 3:25). Christ's crucifixion and resurrection are the focus of this second strophe because, for Paul, these events are the reason that Jesus is the source of new creation for those baptized into Christ (2 Corinthians 5:17), as will be demonstrated below. Even though the hymn ends, Paul continues his proclamation of reconciliation introduced in the hymn, emphasizing that the Colossians themselves are among the "all things" that Jesus has reconciled: "And you, who once were alienated and hostile in mind, doing evil deeds, he has now reconciled [ἀποκατήλλαξεν] in his body of flesh by his death, in order to present you holy and blameless and above reproach before him" (Colossians 1:21–22).

CHRISTOLOGY IN THE PROCLAMATION OF BAPTISM AND SANCTIFICATION IN COLOSSIANS

To where does Paul point the Colossians for the central spiritual experience of their lives, including those Colossians who may have been tempted to seek escape from evil spirits of this world through heavenly ascent and worship? He points them to Baptism, because that is where their lives were joined to Christ, the source of new creation:

2:11In whom you were also circumcised with a circumcision without hands by the putting off of the fleshly [i.e., sinfully corrupt] body by the circumcision of Christ, 12because you have been buried together [συνταφέντες] with him in baptism, in whom you were also together raised [συνηγέρθητε] through faith by the working of God who raised him from the dead. [13]And you, being dead in trespasses and uncircumcision of your flesh [sinful condition], [the Father] made you alive together with him after he had forgiven us all trespasses. [14]For he has canceled our record of decrees which stood against us and has removed it from our midst, nailing it to the cross. [15]After he disarmed for himself the rulers and authorities, he made a public example [of them], by leading them in triumphal procession (Colossians 2:11–15).

After expressing the broad, cosmic story of creation and new creation in the hymn, Paul helps the Colossians to see where they are joined to this story and experience the new creation that began in this world with the resurrection of Christ: Baptism. In Baptism, one is buried with Christ in a death to sin and raised with him unto life (Romans 6:1–11). For Paul, there is no greater experience of the presence of God than Baptism, because there one is joined to Christ. The mystics may have spoken about mysteries that would be seen through visionary ascent; Paul states that the mystery hidden for ages but revealed now is "Christ in you, the hope of glory" (Colossians 1:27; cf. 3:4). M. Jeff Brannon notes how Paul's teaching of Baptism eliminates the need for mystics to ascend to experience the reign of God.

> It is interesting and significant to note that Paul here combats the realized eschatology of the mystical visionaries with a realized eschatology which is found in Christ when he writes that believers have been raised up with Christ (3.1) and that believers' lives are hidden with Christ in God (3.3). Indeed, Paul's instruction makes it clear that believers already participate in the heavenly reign of God since their lives are incorporated into Christ who is seated at the right hand of God.[36]

This baptismal union with Christ, therefore, becomes the basis for Paul's proclamation of sanctification. The "putting off" language in 3:5–9 is the baptismal life of our sinful condition daily dying with Christ. The "putting on" language in 3:12–17 is the baptismal life of rising with Christ to live out who we truly are in Christ. Especially important here is Paul's teaching about the old and new man: "you have put off the old

---

[36] Brannon, *The Heavenlies in Ephesians*, 151.

man [τὸν παλαιὸν ἄνθρωπον] with his practices and have put on the new man [τὸν νέον] who is being renewed in knowledge according to the image of the one who created him" (3:9–10). For Paul, "the new man" is not "the new self" (ESV), but he is Christ in the Christian and at work through the Christian by virtue of the baptismal union (Galatians 2:20).[37] The "new man" cannot be understood apart from Christ. Paul uses the similar language of "inner man" elsewhere as a reference to Christ in each Christian (Romans 7:22; Ephesians 3:16–17; and 2 Corinthians 4:16).[38]

The link between Christology, baptism, and sanctification is expressed tersely in one of Paul's closing exhortations to the Colossians: "Do everything in the name of the Lord Jesus" (Colossians 3:17). Because they had been baptized in the divine name shared by the Father, the Son, and the Holy Spirit (Matthew 28:19), Paul's command to "do everything in the name of the Lord Jesus" is a call to live one's whole life in the power of the divine name that was invoked upon him when he was baptized and joined to the divine reality of Father, Son, and Holy Spirit present through the invocation of that name.[39] Because the divine name cannot be separated from God himself, it is the very means by which God is present in each Christian (i.e., the baptized is united with Christ and Christ dwells within him via the Spirit). The relationship of the phrase "in the name of the Lord Jesus" to Baptism is explicit in 1 Corinthians: "But you were washed, you were sanctified, you were justified in the name of the Lord Jesus Christ and in the Spirit of our God" (1 Corinthians 6:11). This is not an alternate baptismal formula, but it does reflect that the singular divine name is invoked in Baptism and that this name belongs to Christ, as it also does to the Father and the Holy Spirit. The understanding that the baptized is given and bears the divine name is expressed in 2 Thessalonians where the congregation is encouraged to be worthy of God's call "in order that the

---

[37] I think Deterding's discussion on this point falls short because he see the new man as a reality that is distinct from Christ; see *Colossians*, 151–53.

[38] The presence of Christ defining the identity of the "inner man" in Romans 7:22 is also not clear in Michael P. Middendorf, *Romans 1–8*, Concordia Commentary (St. Louis: Concordia, 2013), 569–70.

[39] For a fuller discussion of the divine name (i.e., YHWH), see Charles A. Gieschen, "The Divine Name in Ante-Nicene Christology," *Vigiliae Christianae* 57 (2003): 115–58.

name of our Lord Jesus be glorified in you and you in him"
(2 Thessalonians 1:12). Through our union with Christ in Baptism, our
everyday life tasks are taken up into his grand work of creation,
redemption, and new creation.

Ian Smith succinctly summarizes the relationship between Christology and the teaching of sanctification (i.e., paranesis) in this epistle:

> This study has seen all four chapters of Colossians as an integrated
> piece of writing. Unlike many previous solutions to the Colossians
> error, we have shown how paranesis relates to doctrine. Paul's
> concern in the letter is that a correct heavenly perspective will lead to
> appropriate Christian behavior. This behavior is seen not in the
> escape from earthly activities but in the midst of them. The lordship of
> Christ over all creation is borne out in everyday relationship of
> church, family and work. A true heavenly perspective results in Chris-
> tian unity despite social, ethnic and class barriers. Such an under-
> standing of heavenly-minded reconciliation is the opposite of the
> practices of the errorists, whose focus on the things of heaven led to
> claims of spiritual elitism that resulted in divisions within the
> Colossian congregation.[40]

THE CHRISTOLOGY OF COLOSSIANS FOR THE CHURCH TODAY

There are several important things that we can learn from Paul's proclamation of Christ in his letter to the Colossians. First, Colossians is
refreshing in its proclamation of the preexistence of the Son before creation and his creative work as a clear confession of his divine identity
which is the firm foundation for the proclamation of his work of universal reconciliation. We live in a culture that views Jesus as a relative
latecomer to the spiritual game. Testimony like the Colossians hymn
helps us ground our proclamation of Jesus in the eternal Son who is one
with the Father and the Holy Spirit as YHWH, the creator of all. If the
Son is not also YHWH, who made the heavens and the earth, then his
blood could not atone, his death could not reconcile, and his body could
not be raised. Paul knows that some took offense to the incarnation,

---

[40] Smith, *Heavenly Perspective*, 207.

suffering, and death of Jesus. He proclaims all of these, but in concert with the proclamation of the Son's preexistence and work of creation. He also understands the Son to be the one present with Israel as history unfolds (1 Corinthians 10:1–11), rather than being the member of the Trinity missing in action after creation until the incarnation. We do well to proclaim the same.

Second, Colossians is a reminder of the importance of always teaching about creation in relationship to redemption and vice versa. There is no more important foundation for the narrative of the Gospels than Genesis 1–3. The work of Christ in redemption cannot be understood properly or fully apart from the proclamation of Genesis 1–3, the creation of all things by God and the fall into sin bringing all creation into bondage. God's goal in redemption is to restore his good creation, which was corrupted and held in bondage by sin, including our bodies. If creation is not taught and proclaimed, then salvation can become more narrowly spiritualized in people's minds as eternal life for humans with God far away from this created world and our bodies. Resurrection and the restoration of creation must not be marginalized in our proclamation of Christ's redemptive work.

Third, although Paul clearly affirms the value of all visible and invisible creation because it was brought about by God through the Son, worship should not stray from its focus on the creator to a fascination with particular aspects or creatures of creation, including invisible creation. Like the Jewish mysticism that Paul addresses at Colossae, there are forms of Christian mysticism that focus more on intermediary figures such as angels or saints than they do on the Christ who created all things. The angel refusal of worship tradition continues to be instructive today: worship is to be centered on the triune God because all others, including the good "angels and archangels" with whom we worship, are creatures whose chief duty, like ours, is to serve and worship the creator. Paul makes the dividing line between creator and creature eminently clear in Colossians, and so should we.

Fourth, Colossians also helps us to see and proclaim the significance of the death and resurrection of Jesus for invisible creation. Fears can arise among Christians over spiritual beings in invisible creation, especially Satan and fallen angels. Sometimes these created beings are viewed as divine and exercising power that rivals that of God. As creator of the creation that is invisible to us, the Son's redemptive work also impacts these creatures. These beings are creatures, no matter what status they may claim, and the creator has defeated their dominion over his fallen creation, as will be fully apparent on the Last Day.

Fifth, Colossians is a vivid reminder to us that the Son must be central in our proclamation of creation and new creation, because he is the source of both. One of the weaknesses of teaching creation strictly from the three articles perspective of the explanations in the Small Catechism is that an unnecessary simplification can result that assigns the work of creation solely to the Father, redemption solely to the Son, and sanctification solely to the Holy Spirit. The proclamation of Paul and the rest of the Scriptures leads us to have a more integrated understanding and proclamation of the one God at work in creation, redemption, and sanctification. As Lutherans, we learn well the distinction between the persons of the Trinity; texts like the Colossians hymn help us in proclaiming the monotheistic oneness of the Trinity.

Finally, Colossians helps us to appreciate Baptism as the greatest spiritual experience that we could ever hope to have before the Last Day: being buried with Christ because we died with him to sin and were raised with him to new life. We do not point people to heaven to be united with Christ; we point them to the font. Through Baptism, Christ now lives in us; he is the new man who daily manifests himself through our lives that show forth the firstfruits of the new creation. Through Baptism, the Son's grand narrative of creation and new creation becomes our story. "For you have died, and your life is hidden with Christ in God. When Christ who is your life appears, then you also will appear with him in glory" (Colossians 3:3–4).

THE EYEWITNESS OF THE OTHER SON OF ZEBEDEE

A PILGRIMAGE WITH JAMES THROUGH SCRIPTURE AND TRADITION

Arthur A. Just Jr.

My pilgrimage with Dean O. Wenthe began in the fall of 1976, my first year at Concordia Theological Seminary, which also happened to be the seminary's first year in Fort Wayne, Indiana. It was Old Testament Bible in Loehe 7, a class packed to the gills, my first seminary class, Dean's last quarter at CTS before leaving for the parish in Atlantic, Iowa. For this New England Lutheran, culture shock was palpable, as this was also my first experience of Fort Wayne, of the Midwest, of this heart of Lutheranism, in a seminary filled with serious, pious people.

What I needed back then was what Dean offered all his students: a sense of humor fueled by a subtle and clever turn of phrase, those unique Wenthe-isms, his "delight" at his own jokes, and the twinkle in his eye as he offered a Christological and sacramental reading of Torah and prophets. At that time, I knew nothing of the controversies over typology and messianic prophecy at our seminary. Dean's teaching about the sacramentality of the temple and the land resonated with this recent college graduate with an English literature major. The richness of his exegesis was evident as he opened up to us Old Testament texts that always pointed to Christ. This entry level class in Old Testament Bible would forever shape the way I would interpret texts, especially the Old Testament.

Little did I realize then that my pilgrimage into the biblical world would start here with this delightful man, with his joy and his jokes, and his incarnational, christological, and sacramental hermeneutic—even though I wouldn't have called it that back then. Later on, when he was president, Dean would begin his little talks with prospective students by calling this pilgrimage into the Biblical world "an adventure." So it was for them, and so it has been for me.

When I returned to the seminary to teach homiletics in the fall of 1984, our studies were close by in Jerome Hall. In 1985, I started doctoral work at Durham University as Dean was finishing up at Notre Dame. He graciously offered to help me get in on the deal at the Notre Dame bookstore for Fat Macs that included Greek and Hebrew fonts, all for only $2,500—what a deal! Back then, we were both pipe smokers, so on Saturdays we'd be in Jerome Hall together, savoring our Balkan Sobraine tobacco, with its distinctive latakia smell, breaking away from our dissertations now and then to discuss the latest Missouri Synod gossip.

Little did we realize during those dissertation days that the next ten years would be the most trying and difficult part of our journey together. I will never forget Dean's kindness when I was taking radiation treatments for cancer in 1994. He would drive me down I-69 to Lutheran Hospital, waiting patiently for me in that room filled with radiation patients—some worse than others—then driving me home, keeping me occupied as the waves of nausea began, providing a unique kind of pastoral care along the way. No matter how difficult the path during parts of the pilgrimage, Dean was first and foremost the pastor, always encouraging us, always hopeful, always the optimist.

With any pilgrimage, there are surprises along the way. By far the biggest surprise was Dean's election as president of the seminary. Over his fifteen years in that office, Dean would become a visionary for theological education—evidenced by our new curriculum   a very effective fundraiser, and a master at promoting the seminary in both Church and world. He tirelessly served his faculty, giving our seminary room to be what it most wanted to be: a place of lively, theological debate, a center for biblical and confessional Lutheranism, and, most important of all, a place where Christ is present in Kramer Chapel with all his gifts—in Lutheran liturgy and Christ-centered hymns that are central to our seminary life. Dean gave us the freedom to be authentically Lutheran and authentically catholic, which, in the words of *Lutheran Service Book,* means "the whole Church as it confesses the wholeness of Christian doctrine."[1]

As for my contribution to his festschrift, I could think of no better way to honor him than with an essay that embraces both our Lutheran and catholic roots. Dean would certainly resonate with this statement, one that I believe he has embodied in his own pilgrimage as pastor, professor, and president. We are all looking for home, prodigals wandering in the wilderness of sin, looking for our Father's house. Emmaus disciples all, we journey towards home only to return back to Jerusalem. We are always on pilgrimage, to Eden restored, to paradise regained, from the Jordan to Jerusalem, from font to table. This longing is so deep, so human, that Christians throughout the ages have felt compelled to pilgrimage, walking from their homes to Jerusalem, to Rome, to Santiago, to Canterbury.

Home is where Christ is with his saints, and so where Christ is present at font, pulpit, and table, his saints come home to God in him. But even so, that did not stop the baptized from wandering across the world in search of home, especially to sacred spaces built over the tombs of the saints. If the tomb is empty, as in the Church of the Holy Sepulcher in Jerusalem, so much the better. Rome, of course, is Peter's city, her first bishop and pope, a natural destination for pilgrimage to his tomb under the altar of St. Peter's in Vatican City. Andrew, Peter's brother, is patron saint of Patras, Greece, Russia, and Scotland, with relics of his body found in all those places. Origen suggests that Andrew preached around the Black Sea; both Romania and Kiev claim him as their founding apostle. With so many far-flung places from which to choose, pilgrimages to Andrew's resting places were rare, requiring either deep pockets or sturdy legs. St. Mark lies under the altar in Venice, transferred there from Alexandria, as tradition has it. Venice is a nice place for tourists to visit, so a pilgrimage of sorts is made to his tomb. Matthew lies buried in Salerno, Italy. Enough said.

---

[1] *Lutheran Service Book* (St. Louis: Concordia, 2006), 158.

The patron saint of Lutherans is Paul, and Wittenberg is our pilgrimage destination, not because Paul is buried there, but because the tomb of his greatest disciple is found in the Castle Church. Since justification by grace through faith is the doctrine upon which the Church stands and falls, we honor Luther, the re-discoverer of this central doctrine of the Church. Paul's tomb was an object of pilgrimage as he is also buried in Rome, first interred with Peter in the catacombs, and then transferred to St. Paul Outside the Walls. He is, actually, the patron saint of London, where St. Paul's Cathedral holds the tombs of Lord Nelson and the Duke of Wellington, who are not Lutherans.

And then there is John, son of Zebedee and the alleged beloved disciple and evangelist, companion to Peter in Acts, youngest and last of the apostles to die. He is patron saint of Asia Minor, for he is buried near Ephesus. It was there that he spent the last years of his life, taking care of Mary, Jesus' mother (and perhaps his aunt), and seeing visions at Patmos and writing them down so that endless bible studies could contemplate their meaning. Like Venice, Ephesus is worthy of a pilgrimage, although not many of the ancients thought so.

Finally, there is James, the other son of Zebedee, the first of the twelve to be martyred when Herod Agrippa I was tetrarch of Judea, Galilee, and Samaria. James was martyred in Jerusalem during Passover, as recorded in Acts 12:1–3: "About that time Herod the king laid violent hands on some who belonged to the church. He killed James the brother of John with the sword, and when he saw that it pleased the Jews, he proceeded to arrest Peter also. This was during the days of Unleavened Bread." This little episode, often overlooked, changed the entire life of the Church. James is buried in Santiago de Compostela, a long way from Jerusalem; his burial is the story of legend. But more on that later.

As for the rest of the apostles, and even for the seventy from Luke 10, Pseudo-Hippolytus gives a list of their burial places, which are scattered throughout the known world of that time: Philip in Hierapolis, Bartholomew in Armenia, Thomas in India, James, son of Alphaeus, next to the temple in Jerusalem, Thaddeus in Mesopotamia, Simon the Zealot and Matthias also in Jerusalem.

But this paper is about James, the other son of Zebedee, exploring why he is a significant eyewitness of the life and ministry of Jesus of

Nazareth and why his burial in Santiago de Compostela continues to bear witness today.

So, what do we know about James, this brother of John, this son of Zebedee?

KNOWING THE END OF THE STORY

If you know the end of the story, then you can read back knowing how it all comes out. That is how many of us read the New Testament and the Old, from knowing the end of the story, from knowing that each week at the Eucharist the Church heard the story of the cross, resurrection, and ascension from the beginning. What we know about James is that he was the first of the apostles to be martyred. James died during the third significant persecution of Christians, a persecution from a source other than the religious establishment of Israel, namely, from Herod Agrippa I, the grandson of Herod the Great. Herod's persecution lasted from AD 41 to 44. During this same persecution, Peter was imprisoned, miraculously escaping to the house of Mary, the mother of John Mark, the very John Mark who would later accompany Barnabas on his missionary journeys and then author the second Gospel (Acts 12:6–19). At the end of this episode the simplicity of Luke's record of Peter's statement belies its significance: "But motioning to them with his hand to be silent, he described to them how the Lord had brought him out of the prison. And he said, 'Tell these things to James and to the brothers.' Then he departed and went to another place" (Acts 12:17).

The one to be told these things, of course, was not James the son of Zebedee, but James the brother of our Lord. Richard Bauckham, in his chapter "James in the Jerusalem Church" in *The Book of Acts in Its Palestinian Setting*, notes that "12:17 is a key verse in the development of the narrative of Acts."[2] He observes that this is the first time James the brother of Jesus was referred to in Acts, and that in this same verse Peter is described as moving to an unknown location. Peter is mentioned again in Acts only at the Apostolic Council. The persecution of Herod Agrippa seems to indicate that a shift was taking place in the

---

[2] Richard Bauckham, *The Book of Acts in Its Palestinian Setting* (Grand Rapids, MI: Eerdmans, 1995), 434.

leadership of the Jerusalem Church from Peter and the apostles to James, the brother of our Lord, and the elders. This shift in leadership forever changed the shape of the Church, a change that occurred because James, the son of Zebedee, was martyred by Herod Agrippa I.[3] The seedbed of the Church is indeed the blood of martyrs.

Now here's the rub. James' (the son of Zebedee) martyrdom at the hands of Herod Agrippa I is the only time Luke mentions James in the book of Acts. During the first fourteen years of the Church's life, Peter and the apostles were the clear leaders in the Jerusalem Church, staying behind in the city during the persecution of the Diasporan Jews that was led by Saul when everyone else was scattered. The reconstitution of the Twelve in Acts 1 with the selection of Matthias to replace Judas indicates the symbolic significance of the Twelve as the representation of reconstituted Israel in the post-resurrection, post-Pentecost era. The pillars of the Church were Peter, John, and James (the sons of Zebedee), the only members of the Twelve mentioned in Acts, though only Peter and John are mentioned in Acts 1–11 when they are persecuted and imprisoned for their preaching. James suddenly appears for the first time in Acts 12 as the first apostle killed for the faith.

Following Proverbs 9:1 ("Wisdom has built her house; she has hewn her seven pillars."), Bauckham suggests that along with the three apostolic pillars—Peter, James, and John—the other four pillars were the four brothers of Jesus—James (the eldest), Joses, Jude, and Simon. The "pillars" of the Church are significant in light of Paul's language in Galatians 2:9, where he refers to "James and Cephas and John, who seemed to be pillars," although this James is the brother of our Lord. Throughout the New Testament, the metaphorical language of the church as a building with Christ as the cornerstone and the apostles as the foundation was common (1 Corinthians 3:11; Ephesians 2:20; 1 Peter 2:4, 6–7). For Bauckham, this image of Christ and the apostles expresses the belief that "the early Christian church . . . saw itself as the place of God's eschatological presence, destined to supersede the temple in Jerusalem."[4]

---

[3] Bauckham, *The Book of Acts*, 434–41.
[4] Bauckham, *The Book of Acts*, 442–43.

The question remains: why is James arrested with Peter and then martyred? One might expect John to be arrested with Peter, since he is Peter's silent companion in their work in Jerusalem and Samaria with the healing of the crippled man by the beautiful gate (Acts 3:1–10), their witness before the Jewish council (4:1–22), and their mission to Samaria (8:14–25). There is no mention of James in any of these significant moments in the Church's earliest ministry, yet he is the unfortunate one to be with Peter when Herod Agrippa I decides to arrest and kill them.

James is significant because he is the first apostle martyred and because he is one of the inner three—Peter, James, John. His martyrdom shifts the Church's focus from Jerusalem and the Jewish mission to Paul and his mission to the Gentiles.

THE INNER THREE

Peter, James, and John are the inner circle of Jesus' disciples who, during his ministry, witnessed the raising of Jairus' daughter, Jesus' transfiguration, and his agony in the Garden of Gethsemane, and, after his ascension, provided leadership for the Jerusalem Church as described in the first twelve chapters of Acts.[5] Looking at the lists of the apostles in Matthew, Mark, Luke, and Acts, it is either the inner three— or the inner four, if you include Peter's brother Andrew—who are always listed as first in the catalogue of the apostles.

MATTHEW 5:2	MARK 3:16–17	LUKE 6:14	ACTS 1:13
Simon, the one called Peter	**Simon** Peter	**Simon**, the one named Peter	**Peter**
Andrew, his brother	**James**, the son of Zebedee	**Andrew**, his brother,	**John**
James, the son of Zebedee	**John**, the brother of James (and placed on them the name of Boanerges, which is, Sons of Thunder)	**James**	**James**
John, his brother		**John**	**Andrew**
	Andrew		

---

[5] Ironically, the pillars mentioned in Galatians 2—James, Cephas and John—are not the three pillars noted in the Gospels. Peter and John are the same, but this is a different James. By this time, leadership had shifted from James the son of Zebedee to James the brother of the Lord.

So what does this all mean? Matthew preserves the family relationships, listing the brothers in order—Peter and Andrew, James and John. As we shall see, Mark has the most interest in reporting the actions of the inner three, and so he places them together in his list, separating Peter and his brother Andrew. Most significantly, we only know the nicknames of James and John, the sons of Zebedee, as Boanerges, sons of thunder, by Mark's qualification of them in his list of the apostles. As for Luke, he follows Matthew in keeping the brothers together, but curiously makes no mention of them as sons of Zebedee, since they have already been named as such in their calling to be apostles in the great catch of fish (5:10). Luke's apostolic list in Acts 1 appears to reflect their significance in the Church's life. Here he reverses the order of the brothers, and places John ahead of James, presumably because Peter and John are the only apostles to be named in Acts 1–11.[6] Luke anticipates Peter and John going it alone without James in Acts 1–11 in his account of the preparations for the Passover, for only Luke tells us which disciples—Peter and John—Jesus sent to prepare it (Luke 22:8).

What happens to the inner three when they appear together in the Gospels? They are privy to epiphanic moments: a resurrection with Jairus' daughter, the glory of Jesus in the transfiguration, apocalyptic prophecies about the temple on the Mount of Olives, and suffering in the garden of Gethsemane. The inner three are portrayed as Jesus' closest companions, allowed a glimpse of him in intimate moments where something is revealed about him that is concealed from the other nine. They are marked as leaders; thus, it is no surprise that they are the only apostles among the Twelve mentioned in Acts.

THE SONS OF THUNDER AND MARK 10:35–45

In discussing "The Petrine Perspective in the Gospel of Mark" in his book *Jesus and the Eyewitnesses*, Richard Bauckham notes that "Peter is not only typical of the disciples to some degree, but also the most fully

---

[6] As for Andrew, he does make an appearance with the big three in Mark, in the healing of Peter's mother-in-law (1:29) and in Jesus' apocalyptic discourse on the Mount of Olives (13:3), but what distinguishes Andrew from Peter and James and John is that he does not get a special name.

characterized individual in the Gospel, apart from Jesus."[7] Although
James and John, the sons of Zebedee, are not as fully characterized as
Peter and Jesus, we get a sense of their personalities from the nickname
given to them by Mark. Simon, of course, receives his nickname from
Jesus, becoming Peter, the rock upon which the Church is built.

In his book *John, the Son of Zebedee, the Life of a Legend*,
R. A. Culpepper notes that when James and John appear apart from
Peter, "they do not depict intimate experiences with Jesus or secret
manifestations"; rather, they come across "as intolerant and hot-
tempered." As to why they are called "Boanerges, or Sons of thunder,"
Culpepper says that "explanations have ranged from the suggestion that
James and John spoke with loud voices to the conjecture that as followers of John the Baptist they had witnessed the voice from heaven,
spoken with thunder."[8] More likely, Culpepper argues, "sons of
thunder" is a more positive assessment of the significance of their
nickname:

> Jesus may have called the brothers "sons of thunder" not as a dis-
> paraging nickname but as a promise of what they could become. Peter
> is the only other example of a disciple to whom Jesus gave a new
> name. In his case, the name is ironic. Peter was anything but rock-like
> in his faithfulness to Jesus, but he would become the leader of the
> disciples and a leading figure in the early church in Jerusalem. The
> suggestion that the name, as in the case of Peter, is a promise or a
> forecast of the greatness of the sons of Zebedee has a great deal of
> merit. By the giving of the name Boanerges, Jesus announced that
> James and John would become "sons of thunder," mighty witnesses,
> voices as from heaven.[9]

Two examples of the personalities of the two disciples as "sons of
thunder" occur in the Gospels. When the days were fulfilled for his
being taken up, Jesus set his face to journey to Jerusalem—the famous
turning point in Luke's Gospel (9:51). Within Luke's journey motif,

---

[7] R. Bauckham, *Jesus and the Eyewitnesses: The Gospels as Eyewitness Testimony* (Eerdmans: Grand Rapids, 2006), 175.

[8] R. A. Culpepper, *John, the Son of Zebedee, the Life of a Legend* (Minneapolis: Fortress Press, 2000), 39–40. Culpepper also notes that some suggest the two sons of Zebedee were "sons of thunder" because of "the impetuosity of their natural character."

[9] Culpepper, *John, the Son of Zebedee*, 40.

with Jerusalem as Jesus' inexorable destiny, Jesus' death is in full view as he enters Samaria. This seems to be the intent of the Samaritans not offering hospitality, "because his face was journeying to Jerusalem" (9:53), although the liturgical rivalry between Mount Gerizim and Mount Zion is the source of the unwelcoming attitude of the Samaritans. James and John are incensed at the rejection of Jesus by the Samaritans; their impetuous call to rain fire down on Samaria shows them to be Mark's "sons of thunder" as they seek to fulfill the role of Elijah in 2 Kings where he wants to rain fire on the enemies of God.

James and John, like John the Baptist when he sent his emissaries to ask Jesus if he was the coming one (Luke 7:18–23), do not understand that the vengeance of God is not on Jesus' enemies but on Jesus. Isaiah's day of vengeance is when the fire of eschatological wrath kills Jesus, not his enemies, as Jesus takes upon himself the wrath of God for our sin. The fire cast down upon Jesus on the cross baptizes him in his own blood, as he himself predicted later on in his journey to his death: "Fire I came to throw on the earth, and how I wish that already it were kindled. But a baptism I have to be baptized with, and how I am in distress until it is accomplished" (Luke 12:49–50). Jesus rebukes James and John for not understanding that he is not like Elijah, the fiery reformer; rather, his death on a cross is the locale of God's fiery restoration of creation that is both holocaust and bloody bath. Like Peter, James and John are typical of all the disciples in their misunderstanding of Jesus' destiny in Jerusalem.

Mark's Gospel provides the most incisive look into the characters of James and John, what Bauckham calls "the most substantial instance of a focus in the Gospel on named male disciples other than Peter."[10] It comes as a request to Jesus by James and John:[11] "Teacher, we want you to do for us whatever we ask of you .... Grant us to sit, one at your right hand and one at your left, in your glory" (Mark 10:35–37). Jesus' response is not what they expected. In his mild rebuke of them, he speaks of his death as a cup he must drink and a baptism with which he must be baptized.[12] The disciples are willing to drink this cup and be

---

[10] Bauckham, *Jesus and the Eyewitnesses*, 171.

[11] Note that James is listed first here in this programmatic passage of their personalities.

[12] This is a parallel to Luke 12.

baptized with this baptism, for they are, after all, "sons of thunder," although they do not yet fully understand that to share Jesus' glory they must first share in his sufferings. Here Jesus prophesies James's martyrdom and how he, James, will learn what it means to suffer and then enter into glory. What Jesus cannot grant them is what they requested—to sit on his right and on his left—although they are being prepared for that by Jesus in this very scene. As one might expect, the other disciples were indignant of James and John, suggesting that their status as a family of wealth and influence in Bethsaida,[13] as well as their being chosen along with Peter as the inner circle of Jesus' disciples, gave them the right to ask such a thing of Jesus.

This exchange between Jesus and the sons of Zebedee is an occasion not only for a catechesis for James and John on the meaning of discipleship, but also for the most profound statement of the atonement in the Gospels. If they want to be great and to be first—that is to sit at his right and sit at his left—they must become servants like Jesus: "For even the Son of Man came not to be served but to serve, and to give his life as a ransom for many" (Mark 10:45). Though the request made by the "sons of thunder" totally misses what Jesus is all about, he uses it to teach them the most profound meaning of his life and his death: only through suffering and death will they receive honor, only through the cross will there be glory.

James and John come to learn that honor and glory are received as gift at the eucharistic table where, as St. Paul says, we proclaim the Lord's death until he comes again (1 Corinthians 11:26). In Luke's institution narrative, the language of substitutionary atonement is placed at the breaking of the bread: "This is my body, which is being given on behalf of you" (τὸ ὑπὲρ ὑμῶν διδόμενον), and in the offering of the cup, "This cup is the new testament in my blood, which is being poured out on behalf of you" (τὸ ὑπὲρ ὑμῶν ἐκχυννόμενον). The language of service comes in the dialogues after the Supper, in Jesus' final pastoral

---

[13] The parallel in Matthew's Gospel (Matthew 20:20–28) has the mother of the sons of Zebedee asking Jesus about her sons. James and John are never named in Matthew. Our sense of James and John as coming from a family of means is surmised from Mark 1:16–20, where their father Zebedee is described as having hired servants. The mother of James and John could have been Salome, one of the women at the foot of the cross, a sister of Mary, meaning James and John were cousins of Jesus and nephews of Mary.

theology. After this sublime moment in which Jesus gives his body and pours out his blood on their behalf, the disciples argue among themselves as to who is the greatest. Jesus' response is similar to what he said to James and John in Mark 10: "For who is greater, the one who reclines [at table] or the one who serves? Is it not the one who reclines? But I am in the midst of you as the one who serves" (ἐγώ εἰμί ἐν μέσῳ ὑμῶν—Luke 22:27–28). Christ now serves sinners at a table where, in the words of Ernest Best in *Following Jesus: Discipleship in the Gospel of Mark*, "all believers participate sacramentally in the passion of Jesus; there cannot then be special seats in glory for special believers."[14] By offering sinners his body and blood at the eucharistic table, Jesus serves us as he gives his life as a ransom for many.

THE SANTIAGO CREED

The eyewitness testimony of James, the son of Zebedee, continues today, but in a way even James would not have expected. As we indicated earlier, tradition tell us that St. James the Elder, the son of Zebedee and the first martyred apostle, is buried in the cathedral in Santiago de Compostela on the western coast of Spain. This is a legend worthy of our consideration, for legends have consequences. The pilgrimage to Santiago de Compostela is one of the three greatest pilgrimages in Christendom, alongside Jerusalem and Rome, dating back to AD 812. In the Jubilee year of 2010, an estimated 270,000 *peregrinos*, which is Spanish for pilgrim, walked to Santiago de Compostela. Some began as far away as France or Germany, although the traditional place to begin the journey is San Jean Pie de Pord, 800 kilometers from Santiago, a distance of approximately 500 miles. Medieval pilgrimages to Santiago were said to swell to hundreds of thousands.[15]

The pilgrimage to Santiago de Compostela clearly captured the imagination of the Medieval Church for all the right reasons and for all

---

[14] Ernest Best, *Following Jesus: Discipleship in the Gospel of Mark*, Journal for the Study of the New Testament, Supplement Series, vol. 4 (Sheffield: JSOP Press, 1981), 124.

[15] For a history of the pilgrimage to Santiago de Compostela during the Middle Ages, see Jonathan Sumption, *The Age of Pilgrimage: The Medieval Journey to God* (New Jersey: Hidden Spring, 2003), especially pp. 162–63, 237–38, 248, 252–53.

the wrong reasons. Sorting out the difference means unraveling the mysteries of what is known as "The Santiago Creed," that is, what the saints in Spain believe and confess about their patron saint. The two parts of the creed that interest us are these, as formulated by T. D. Kendrick in his erudite study, *Saint James in Spain*:

> firstly, that he preached Christianity in the country . . . thirdly, that after his execution in Jerusalem the apostle's body was taken to Galicia in northwest Spain and buried at the place where now stands the cathedral of Santiago de Compostela.[16]

The details of "The Santiago Creed" concerning James' preaching the Gospel in Spain and his burial there are really quite simple. Working with the date of his martyrdom in Jerusalem during the reign of Herod Agrippa I, between AD 41 and 44, James had a window of eleven to fourteen years after the ascension of Jesus to travel to Spain and back. There is certainly no reason to believe that such a trip would have been impossible because of time. The question, however, is when such a trip might have occurred.

---

[16] T. D. Kendrick, *Saint James in Spain* (London: Methuen and Company, 1960), 13. Remarkably, of all the books on the *camino* to Santiago de Compostela, most give a narrative of the legend of St. James' mission to Spain, but none of the sources. Only Kendrick has provided them, thus our dependence on him. The other parts of the Santiago Creed stretch the capacities of most Lutherans, but need to be included here because they are intimately tied to the two parts cited above. Most Spaniards wholeheartedly affirm every part of this creed:

> . . . secondly, that during his mission there the Virgin Mary, while still a living woman, was miraculously transported, accompanied by angels bearing a marble pillar, to the banks of the River Ebro; that she talked with St James and told him to build a church dedicated to herself on the site where the pillar had been placed, a church that is now the basilica of Nuestra Senora del Pilar in Zaragoza. . . . Fourthly, that in the ninth century St James appeared on earth and helped a Spanish army to win a decisive victory over the Moors.

Raphael J. Collins, in *The Roman Martyrology* (Westminster, MD: The Newman Bookshop, 1946), 162–63, affirms "The Santiago Creed":

> St. James the Apostle, brother of the blessed evangelist John, was beheaded by Herod Agrippa at about the feast of Easter. He was the first of the apostles to receive the crown of martyrdom. His sacred bones were on this day carried from Jerusalem to Spain, and placed in the remote province of Galicia, where they are devoutly honored by the far-famed piety of the inhabitants, and the frequent concourse of Christians, who visit them through piety and in fulfillment of vows. . . .

It is unlikely that James traveled to Spain before the martyrdom of Stephen, since it appears that the apostles remained in Jerusalem immediately after the ascension of Jesus. Although James is not mentioned in the first part of Acts, his brother John is, and one could easily assume that James was still part of the inner three with Peter and John, even though he is not mentioned alongside them. Would not James be one of the apostles referred to in Luke's summary statements, as in Acts 4:32–37, where they provide testimony to the resurrection and assist in distributing goods to the poor, as well as Acts 5:12–16, where they perform signs and wonders among the people? Would not James be one of the apostles arrested by the high priest (5:12), beaten, and charged not to speak in the name of Jesus (5:40)? Would not James be among the Twelve when seven were appointed to serve tables and hands were laid upon them by the apostles (8:6)? Then there is Acts 8:3, after Stephen's martyrdom in AD 36, when Luke emphatically states that many were scattered throughout Judea and Samaria, except the apostles (πλὴν τῶν ἀποστόλων). This conforms with Luke's intentions to preserve Jerusalem as the apostolic Church, the birth mother of all missions. Would James be the lone exception among the apostles, fleeing to Spain after this persecution? Had he started a mission in those early post-Pentecost years, would not Luke have recorded such a mission endeavor as he did with Philip in Samaria? A case could be made that James is as much a part of the apostolic activity in Acts 1–8 as Peter and John.

Yet why does Luke not name him alongside Peter and John? After all, there are three moments in Luke's Gospel where they appear together: at the great catch of fish (5:8–10), the raising of Jairus' daughter (8:51), and the transfiguration (9:28), although we noted that Luke changes the order in his list of the apostles present at the transfiguration, placing John before James, which is different from Matthew and Mark. We also noted that Luke lists James after John in the list of apostles in Acts (1:13), the only list of apostles in which this occurs. Could Luke be acknowledging James' absence in the apostolic work of Acts 1–11, raising the possibility that the reason James is not included alongside Peter and John is because he is off to Spain to evangelize Spaniards? Arguments from silence are always less than persuasive, but James is always listed before his brother John, except in the two Lukan exceptions, and the one that seems most telling is the list of apostles in the first chapter of Acts.

Assuming that James was in Jerusalem from Pentecost through the martyrdom of Stephen, it is more likely that he may have embarked on a Spanish mission during the peace that reigned among the churches throughout Judea, Galilee, and Samaria as the Church was built up and multiplied, which Luke indicates in another summary statement in Acts 9:31: "So the church throughout all Judea and Galilee and Samaria had peace and was being built up. And walking in the fear of the Lord and in the comfort of the Holy Spirit, it multiplied." Just before this announcement of peace, Saul had escaped from Damascus (9:23–25) and appeared before the apostles in Jerusalem, where he testified concerning his conversion on the road to Damascus (9:27). This Jerusalem visit is the one Paul refers to in Galatians 1:18, about three years after his conversion, or in AD 38–39. This time of peace would have allowed James to leave Jerusalem and travel to Spain and back, giving him anywhere from two to six years for such a missionary journey. Kendrick offers a reasonable description of what the Medieval Church thought James's mission to Spain might have looked like during these years:

> After the first Pentecost Spain was allotted to St James the Greater as his mission-field and he sailed for Andalusia at a date generally said to be one of the three years AD 38–40. From southern Spain he journeyed by way of Merida and Braga to Iria Flavia, now Padron, on the River Sar near its confluence with the Ulla and about ten miles from the Galician coast. . . .[17]

So it was possible for James, the son of Zebedee, to travel to Spain and back either before Stephen's martyrdom or after it. Kendrick offers this assessment: "At least it is humanly possible that St James visited Spain. The country was a Roman province already possessing some good roads and it could be reached from Palestine by an established sea-traffic. The mission could have been undertaken and carried out."[18]

But if this is true, why does Luke not mention any of it in the book of Acts? Perhaps it did not fit his neat agenda of showing a Jewish,

---

[17] Kendrick, *Saint James in Spain*, 16.
[18] Kendrick, *Saint James in Spain*, 26.

Petrine mission in Acts 1–12, with excursions to Samaria (Acts 8) and among the Gentiles in Acts 10–11, and then a Gentile, Pauline mission in Acts 13–28.

Spain was an interest of Paul's, as he indicates in his epistle to the Church in Rome, and it is entirely possible that after his house arrest (Acts 28) he made his way to Spain and then back to Rome. Paul's desire to carry the Gospel to Spain, after delivering the collection from Macedonia and Achaia to Jerusalem and then visiting Rome, is what he reports to the Romans: "I hope to see you in passing as I go to Spain, and to be helped on my journey there by you, once I have enjoyed your company for a while. . . . When therefore I have completed this and have delivered to them what has been collected, I will leave for Spain by way of you" (Romans 15:24, 28).

Did Paul ever visit Spain as part of his missionary journeys? Paul could have left Rome in AD 63 after the imprisonment described in Acts 28:16–31, returning to Rome during the persecutions of Nero when he was martyred along with Peter in AD 64–65. There was sufficient time between those two visits to Rome for him to make his way to Spain. It was certainly his heartfelt desire, as he wrote the Romans in AD 58, and there is no indication that he ever changed his mind. There is evidence early on of a very well-organized church in Spain in the fourth century that hosted a pre-Constantinian church council in Elvira, outside Granada, with nineteen bishops and twenty-four presbyters in attendance. Such a church could have come from the evangelization of Spain by Paul and maybe even by James. In the late first century, Clement of Rome wrote of Paul's visit to Spain, calling it the "extreme limit of the west": "Paul also obtained the reward of patient endurance, after being seven times thrown into captivity, compelled to flee, and stoned. After preaching both in the east and west, he gained the illustrious reputation due to his faith, having taught righteousness to the whole world, and come to the extreme limit of the west, and suffered martyrdom under the prefects."[19]

Spain was clearly an apostolic destination; unfortunately no such evidence exists to corroborate a mission to Spain by James, the son of

---

[19] Clement of Rome, *First Epistle to the Corinthians*, chap. 5; *ANF* 1:6.

Zebedee. Again, Kendrick suggests why, pointing out that since the seventeenth century many, even within the Roman Church, have doubted that James evangelized Spain:

> The reason for this doubt is that it is historically improbable, in the highest degree improbable, that St James visited Spain; for there is nothing in the history of the early apostolic church to suggest that by the time of St James's execution in Jerusalem, that is to say before AD 44, Christianity had been preached or had obtained converts in Greece and Rome and on the far side of the Mediterranean. But in the Santiago creed we are asked to believe that a missionary journey to the northwest of Spain, over 6,000 miles there and back from Jerusalem, was made by an apostle within years of the Crucifixion, and, that this prodigious missionary endeavor having been made, it was nevertheless not considered worth recording in the Acts of the Apostles. . . .
>
> And who, we may ask, had heard of St James's journey? St Jerome and two other writers of the fourth and fifth centuries believed an apostle, whom they did not name, had been in Spain; but no one said St James had been there until the seventh century, nearly six hundred years after his mission is supposed to have taken place.[20]

THE PILGRIMAGE TO SANTIAGO DE COMPOSTELA

As for James' burial in western Spain, legend holds that, after his bones were buried in Jerusalem where he was martyred, saints from the church in Western Spain came to Palestine to transfer his relics to the place where he evangelized Spain. There in Galicia they were carefully preserved, then lost, then found again in the ninth century by means of a star and an angelic announcement.

---

[20] Kendrick, *Saint James in Spain*, 26–28. Kendrick goes on to present the other evidence in history of James's mission to Spain, but all no earlier than AD 600. His most damaging evidence to "The Santiago Creed" is from Julian of Toledo (AD 642–690) whose book describes apostolic missions but never mentions James, the son of Zebedee, as a missionary to Spain, saying only that "he preached to the Jews and wrote them an epistle." He concludes by saying that "what all this seems to imply is that at the end of the seventh century there was an archbishop of Toledo, the first Primate of Spain, and a churchman of outstanding administration and scholarly ability, who had never been told that St James the Greater had preached in Spain . . ." (30).

Truth be told, there is no internal evidence and very little external evidence to support the proposition that James traveled to Spain or that his body is buried there in the cathedral at Santiago de Compostela. But there is no evidence that it is not true either. So to believe this is no different than accepting many things that tradition hands down to us through the church that are impossible to verify through Scripture and history.

This much I know is true. That the Gospel reading for the feast of St. James on July 25 in the cathedral of Santiago de Compostela is Matthew 20:20–28, in which pilgrims hear the most profound statement on the atonement by Jesus in the Gospels, "For even the Son of Man came not to be served but to serve, and to give his life as a ransom for many."

This much I know is true: that sermons may be heard in the cathedral on Matthew 20 that suggest that at his martyrdom James may have recalled, even recited, those profound words of Jesus.

This much I know is true: that countless pilgrims who have walked over 500 miles to visit this sacred space have "participated sacramentally in the passion of Jesus" by eating his body, given on their behalf and drinking his blood, poured out for them.

In this way, perhaps, the eyewitness testimony of James, the other son of Zebedee, lives on and on and on . . .

REVELATION OF GOD IN CHRIST

Walter Obare Omwanza

In 1958, the Nigerian writer Chinua Achebe published *Things Fall Apart*, widely regarded today as the finest novel to come out of Africa. Indeed, it is a classic text in world literature. Its setting is pre-colonial Nigeria, seen through the eyes of the character Okonkwo. In Okonkwo's experience of rapid change, the tribal ways and the values of the clan lose their former pattern of meaning, and Okonkwo himself, rather than grow and adapt, comes to a shameful end.

This story has much to say to our generation. It captures a theme that is universal in human experience. Its title comes from the famous poem by the Irish poet William Butler Yeats (1865–1939), "The Second Coming":

> Things fall apart; the centre cannot hold;
> Mere anarchy is loosed upon the world,
> The blood-dimmed tide is loosed, and everywhere
> The ceremony of innocence is drowned;
> The best lack all conviction, while the worst
> Are full of passionate intensity.[1]

I say this to introduce us to a larger subject. We live in a world that is falling apart. Whether we feel this at the level of culture or society, tribe or clan, family or self, disintegration is a symptom of a deeper, more virulent disease, namely, this world's defection from its Creator. Every time a preacher of God's Word speaks a word of Law, he is making a diagnosis. Accordingly, the Gospel in its broadest significance is God's promise of the only remedy for the rupture between creation

---

[1] "The Second Coming," in *The Poems of W. B. Yeats*, ed. William York Tindall (Westport, CT: The Easton Press, 1976), 108.

and Creator. The apostle Peter refers to the common taunt given by the unbelieving world to the Christian in these words: *"Where is the promise of his coming? For ever since the fathers fell asleep, all things are continuing as they were from the beginning of creation"* (2 Peter 3:4). The notion that the world has an unbroken continuity is called uniformitarianism.[2] It is false. In fact, this world, which is God's creation, has been radically broken, and God has done and is doing still and will do ultimately in the future something truly radical to heal it. All of this he does in Christ.

My subject is the broadest possible theme of the Bible: IN CHRIST ALL IS MADE NEW. To address this subject properly, I would like to propose seven theses or propositions. My purpose in doing this is so that in our work together in the Lord's vineyard we may better keep our eye at all times on his abiding purpose in Christ our Savior.

1

The universe as a whole is not the product of blind chance but is the ordered design of a provident Creator (Genesis 1–2; Psalm 19:1–4; Psalm 139; Acts 14:17; 17:24–27; Romans 1:18—2:16; Hebrews 3:4).

If we do not start here, where the Scriptures start, where the creeds also begin, nothing that follows will make any sense. Indeed, if we do not always begin at this starting point in our thinking and speaking, our communication of the Gospel will seem irrelevant and pointless to modern people. Most secular people today operate on the basis of an unfounded assumption—that the universe as a whole and in all its parts is self-existing and self-explanatory. The name for this prejudice is materialistic naturalism.[3]

Darwinism is only a part of this prejudice. It has dominated the Western imagination for nearly a century and a half. Charles Darwin

---

[2] Uniformitarianism assumes that the same natural laws and process that operate in the universe today have always operated in the same way and intensity in the past and apply equally everywhere in the universe.

[3] Materialistic Naturalism rejects the existence of the super-natural. It holds that nothing exists beyond the natural world and that everything that does exist is matter or energy.

(1809–82) taught that (1) life came from non-life, (2) complex life evolved from simple life, (3) plants, animals, and humans all have a common origin, and (4) change occurs through the survival of those life forms that adapt to changing conditions. In his day, a single cell was regarded as being as simple as a ping-pong ball filled with a jelly called *protoplasm*. No one uses the word "protoplasm" anymore, because we all now know that the complexity of the cell nucleus, as well as the interior of the cell, is beyond description. There is no such thing as a "simple" life form! Indeed, the evidence is mounting daily that, as a theory of explanation, Darwinism is tottering toward collapse. Thus, as intellectually bankrupt as it is, even more so must be the notion of theistic evolution, that a God infinitely wise and good would have used chance and death to order a good creation, for death and randomness is precisely what the idea of natural selection entails.

We simply cannot explain the mystery of life on the basis of natural selection. Darwinism simply has no capacity to account for the organic complexity of God's creation.[4] Today, we have looked at the intricacies of the human genome; we observe the information-bearing properties of DNA and its writing of a genetic code that gives precise instructions for the assembly of the amino acids into proteins required by a given organism. How can the mutation of protein form new organisms if the specific code required for assembling these proteins must be present for this in the first place? The irreducible complexity of life itself tells of an intelligent design to the universe.

Darwin wrote that the fossils of transitional forms in the so-called tree of life must be found in the geological record or his theory would be proven to be false.[5] But, after more than a century of exploration, paleontologists have not found such forms. Instead, even in the so-

---

[4] See Michael Denton, *Evolution: A Theory in Crisis* (Bethesda, MD: Adler and Adler, 1985), 328, where he describes in vivid imagery the complexity of a single cell.

[5] Darwin could admit that the most serious challenge to his evolutionary theories was the fact that the geological evidence did not provide evidence of a "finely-graduated organic chain." See Charles Darwin, *On the Origin of Species*, vol. 49 in *Great Books of the Western World* (Chicago: Encyclopedia Britannica, 1952), 152.

called Cambrian strata, we discover dense populations of fully differentiated phyla without precursors in the geological record.[6]

Since 1960 and the first modern attempts at Cornell University, the Search for Extra-Terrestrial Intelligence (SETI) has made use of radio telescopes to search for intelligent life on other planets. But when we think of the many and exceedingly rare coincidence of conditions necessary for life of any kind to exist on any planet, we must feel astounded at what the Lord God has provided for us on this good earth. The new science of astrobiology is just beginning to discover and categorize these conditions. A partial list of conditions for sustainable life, based upon the unique properties of the carbon tetrahedron, includes the following: a terrestrial planet, of correct mass, in a nearly circular orbit, with proper proportion of rocky crust to molten interior, enabling circulation of an iron-nickel core productive of a protective magnetic field to shield harmful radiation, with life-renewing plate tectonics, orbiting a spectral G2 dwarf main sequence star, protected from comets by outer gas giant planets, within the circumstellar habitable zone, a planet abundant in liquid water for assimilation and transport of nutrients, with a proper ratio of seas and continents to provide a complex biosphere, and seas of sufficient depth that a planetary moon produces in them tides and currents providing a kind of circulatory system to the biosphere, with an oxygen-rich atmosphere, yet one predominantly of nitrogen, with moderate rate of rotation, and moderate tilt for seasons, orbited by a relatively large moon to stabilize this tilt, belonging to a solar system that lies within a stable, flattened ("pinwheel") disk galaxy, a star system located midway between the bulging core and the outer rim where heavy elements are not to be found, nowhere close to the highly energetic galactic center and potential black hole, but within the habitable galactic zone, yet between and not within the spiral arms themselves with their active star-forming regions, nebulae and super-novae, inimical to life, and within a galaxy

---

[6] The argument in this section is drawn from the article by Thomas V. Aadland, "*Baptizatus sum*: Radical Lutheranism and the Divinely Engendered Life," to be included in a forthcoming publication in honor of Lutheran theologian James Arne Nestingen.

not gravitationally compromised by colliding neighbors. The list is growing as the science of astrobiology matures.[7]

Today, visually stunning documentation shows that human conception and birth also bear witness to the majesty of God in his creation. Alexander Tsiaras, who wrote the algorithms for virtual surgery so that astronauts could be cut in robotics pods in deep space flights, has now produced, using new scanning technology, striking images of structures in the human body on a wide scale.[8] As he concentrated his study on collagen—that rope-like material in the human body that typically swirls and twirls but forms into a grid and is thus transparent only in the cornea of the eye—he saw it as "so perfectly organized, it was hard not to attribute divinity to it." Tsiaras used these non-invasive techniques *in utero* for his video presentation, *From Conception to Birth*. The results have left him in awe. You can tell that he struggles to find the right words to describe God's handiwork. "The magic of the mechanisms inside each genetic structure saying exactly where that nerve cell should go—the complexity of these mathematical models is beyond human comprehension. Even though I am a mathematician, I look at this with marvel: How do these instruction sets not make these mistakes as they build what is us? It's a mystery. It's magic. It's divinity." Millennia earlier, the psalmist had already confessed this truth: "You have knit me together in my mother's womb" (Psalm 139:13).[9]

Whether we look at it microscopically or telescopically, the universe bears witness to an infinite intelligence that has designed it. That intelligence is God. Space does not permit us to examine the many ways in which the creation also gives evidence of its purpose. When the apostle Paul spoke to the Athenians on Mars' Hill at the foot of the Acropolis, he argued on the basis of these things, that God had so

---

[7] Cf. Guillermo Gonzalez and Jay W. Richards, *The Privileged Planet: How Our Place in the Cosmos is Designed for Discovery* (Washington DC: Regnery Publishing, 2004).

[8] Aadland, *Baptizatus sunt*. The annual TED award was presented to Tsiaras in December 2010 at the INK conference. His presentation at that conference is available at http://www.youtube.com/watch_popup?v=fKyljukBE70 (accessed March 16, 2012). For this work, Tsiaras has been hailed as a "digital-age Leonardo da Vinci." Succeeding quotations also come from this presentation.

[9] The study of the microscopic structures of bodily tissues is called *histology*, which comes from the Greek word (ἰστός), a cognate that means "weaving" or "knitting."

created this vast universe that we might know that he exists and thus long for a relationship with him. Atheism may endure over time, but it will always be intellectually illegitimate—irresponsible and untenable on the basis of the evidence that is writ large over the things that God has made. All of it speaks of an incredible Providence elegantly defined in the words of the prophet Isaiah: The LORD "formed the earth and made it (he established it; he did not create it a chaos, he formed it to be inhabited!)" (Isaiah 45:18 RSV).

2

This creation, however, is not now as God first intended it. Sin and death are the twin manifestations of a disorder that is not the original will of the Creator. This corruption is principally due to the rebellion of one who stood at the crown of God's creative work, Adam. To the sinful children of Adam speaks the voice of doom, the Law of sin and death (Genesis 3; Romans 3:23; 5:12–21; 6:23; 8:19–22).

When God created the heavens and the earth, he did not leave anything to chance. By his almighty word, he spoke into existence the things that are out of nothing. In six days, God ordered the creation, setting out all things necessary for life on this planet, each kind of living thing reproducing after its kind and not another. God looked upon that which he made—light, earth and seas, plants and the lights in the heavens, the birds in the sky, the animals upon dry land, the swarming creatures of the deep—and he saw that it was *good* (Genesis 1:4, 10, 12, 18, 21, 25). Finally, to put the crown on all that he had made, God said, "Let us make man in our image, after our likeness" (1:26). Then, when God had looked upon all that he had made, including humankind—Adam and Eve, created in his own image and likeness—he called it *very good* (1:31)!

There was nothing out of place, nothing chaotic or morally evil in God's finished work of creation. Yet in the world as we know it, there is much that is not good. A corrupt police force is not good. A dishonest businessman is not good. A man who beats his wife does something not good to his marriage. Civil disorder is not good. The damage these things do to the fabric of the created order is obvious. There are other things, however, not easily apparent that are equally damaging to the life of God's creation—envy and wrath, lust and covetousness, pride and self-righteous religiosity. All of these things come out of the heart of man, as our Lord tells us. "For from within, out of the heart of man, come evil thoughts, sexual immorality, theft, murder, adultery, coveting, wickedness, deceit, sensuality, envy, slander, pride, foolishness. All these evil things come from within, and they defile a person" (Mark 7:21–23).

The heart of man is the heart of what has gone wrong in God's creation. This heart has a natural prejudice against God. Our first parents listened to the voice of the tempter and believed his vague and empty promises rather than the clear and certain Word of God. With that, a radical breach was opened between the creation and its Creator. This breach is what the Bible terms "sin." It is a bondage out of which man is not free to be in communion with his Creator. Martin Luther put it this way: "Man by nature is unable to want God to be God. Indeed, he himself wants to be God, and does not want God to be God."[10] If Adam, fresh from his creation, was nevertheless able to be tempted and able to sin (*posse peccare*), after that radical breach with his Creator, in his wretched state of misery, man is not able not to sin (*non posse non peccare*). Sin is anti-creative. It is invariably destructive, damaging of all that is good. By its very nature, sin is ungodly and unloving.

Two additional remarks are pertinent here. First, a doom has fallen upon humanity because of Adam's fall. The wrath of God rests on all forms of unrighteousness (Romans 1:18). "The wages of sin is death" (Romans 6:23). The unity of the human race consists in this, that we are born of Adam, born in that lost and sinful condition, for which we are also personally responsible. "The soul who sins shall die" (Ezekiel 18:20). Insofar as someone stands apart from the living God, he must feel the anxiety of approaching death and the eternity that awaits. For just as, according to Solomon, God has placed eternity in our hearts, so he has put in us a conscience that becomes uneasy and, literally, "bites back" at us in remorse (Ecclesiastes 3:11).

---

[10] Martin Luther, "Disputation against Scholastic Theology," Thesis 17; AE 31:10; WA 1:225.

The second remark is similar to the first. A doom has fallen likewise on the whole of creation. We also relate to this creation in which there is disintegration and decay, so that we feel its doom. We feel it in the sweat of the brow by which we must win our bread from the earth. We feel it in the anguish of childbirth and the anxiety that attends the raising of our children, knowing that we do not need to teach them how to be selfish, but must labor long to train them not to be overcome by self-centeredness. We feel it whenever we attempt anything creative, expending as much energy on fighting disintegration as we do on production. The farmer tends his wheat, but he must also give attention to the weeds. Paul writes: "For the creation waits with eager longing for the revealing of the sons of God. For the creation was subjected to futility, not willingly, but because of him who subjected it, in hope that the creation itself will be set free from its bondage to decay and obtain the freedom of the glory of the children of God. For we know that the whole creation has been groaning together in the pains of childbirth until now" (Romans 8:19–22).

These two consequences of the fall are together expressed in what the Bible names "the law of sin and death" (Romans 8:2). This present eon, this fallen creation, is addressed by that voice of the Law, the voice of doom. That voice is continuously demanding, threatening, accusing, terrifying, damning, and killing us.

3

As recorded in the Sacred Scriptures, God has promised the restoration of his creation. Just as the first creation was spoiled through the willful rebellion of the first Adam, so the new creation is brought about through the perfect obedience of the second Adam, Christ. The news of that restoration is the Gospel (Genesis 3:15; John 3:16; Acts 3:19–21; 4:12; Romans 10:4; 1 Corinthians 15:22).

In Adam, we are despoilers of God's good creation. In Adam, we all die (1 Corinthians 15:22). But God did not abandon his fallen creation, nor did he forsake that one who had been made to bear his image as the righteous and intelligent creature, representing God before the creation, and who is assigned dominion over it. Immediately, in Paradise God gave the first promise of the Gospel as recorded in Genesis 3:15, the promise of One strangely described as the Seed of the woman, who would crush the head of the serpent, and by him, be bruised in his heel.

All God's promises find their fulfillment in Jesus. God entered his spoiled creation at the level of our own humanity in the person of Jesus. As incarnate, he, the Son of God, did two things simultaneously, giving the answer to two questions. Do you want to know who a true Man is? Look to Jesus. Do you want to know who God truly is? Look to Jesus. He enters into the waters of the Jordan to be baptized by John. As their lowly Servant, he identifies with sinners and so becomes marked as one of them. He did not seek to give his words authority by deferring to that of the rabbis, but spoke as did no other man. In his acts of healing for those who were blind, deaf, mute, and afflicted with paralysis or leprosy, he did God's work of restoration. He was absolute master over wind and wave and all creation, multiplying loaves and fishes to feed the hungry—even raising the dead. All of this demonstrated God's kindly intention to restore the life he first gave. What did Jesus do? He forgave people their sins, as only God can do. Finally, he took the sum total of that sin belonging to the whole of humanity and, just as foretold at his baptism by John, took away the sin of the world in his own sacrificial death as the Lamb of God (John 1:29). He was perfectly obedient even unto death (Philippians 2:8). And, therefore, God the Father put his seal of approval on his own beloved Son, raising him up from death and the grave and bestowing on Jesus the highest honor in heaven and earth. This Jesus is our true Lord, the One who restores creation.

That all may know and believe this, Jesus sends out the Gospel, the good news of his work. Those he sends out, his apostles, all speak of his saving death, his resurrection, his ascension to the right hand of the Father, and his coming in unspeakable power and great glory to judge the living and the dead.[11] He himself is the basis of that judgment, acknowledging those who are his own as distinct from those who are not. The distinction between them is a matter of faith. Is one trusting that he or she is justified before God by his grace alone through faith

---

[11] Cf. C. H. Dodd, *The Apostolic Preaching and Its Developments* (New York: Harper and Row), 1964.

alone and for the sake of this same Lord Jesus, the Christ of God, alone? Or is one seeking to justify himself?

We see this apostolic preaching begin immediately, such as in the sermons of Peter in the temple precincts immediately after the Day of Pentecost. Peter and John continue to bring the name of Jesus to people, so that a man who has been crippled leaps for joy. His speech, the preaching of the Gospel, enables his hearers to respond in the way that acknowledges what God has done. "Repent therefore and be converted, that your sins may be blotted out, so that times of refreshing may come from the presence of the Lord, and that he may send Jesus Christ, who was preached to you before, whom heaven must receive until the times of restoration of all things [ἀποκαταστάσεως πάντων], which God has spoken by the mouth of all his holy prophets since the world began" (Acts 3:19–21).

Restoration of all that had been spoiled by human rebellion is promised here. Yet that restoration comes only in Christ. As Peter stated to the temple authorities who had arrested them: "There is salvation in no one else, for there is no other name under heaven given among men by which we must be saved" (Acts 4:12).

These two passages give the framework for God's restoration of the creation. It will be done, but it will be done for us only in Christ. This Gospel is truly good news for all humanity, totally distinct from the voice of the Law. The Gospel bestows, promises, forgives, consoles, saves, and gives life. When one has been granted faith in Christ, the demanding, threatening, accusing, terrifying, damning, and killing voice of the Law is ended, for Christ is the end of the Law (Romans 10:4).

4

By his death and resurrection Christ is establishing a new creation. But he begins this work first among humankind, those created in God's image (Mark 10:45; Luke 19:10).

Christ has completed his atoning work. We do not yet see the full effect of this work. But it has already begun to have its effect, even though, for now, that effect is hidden from the eyes of sinful men. It is the work of God the Holy Spirit, as we shall speak of more below.

This work takes place in the human heart, effecting a change of orientation. Sinful existence is blasphemous existence. It speaks falsely about God, denying his ultimacy and Godhood by thought, word, and deed. When God first seeks Adam the sinner in the garden, he asks, "*Adam, where are you?*" (Genesis 3:9). No longer was Adam conversing with God in the cool of the day. He had fallen silent and was hiding. But the conversion of the human heart restores the communion with God that God has always been seeking. This communion we call prayer.

We must learn anew to see how significant this is. We may not think of genuine prayer as being indicative of a coming new heavens and earth, but it is. Prayer is characteristic of faith's humility and openness, its purely passive and receptive character. Christ's work is to reunite heaven and earth, and his Gospel brings the renewal of communion between heaven and earth.

5

The Holy Spirit now bestows the deliverance Christ purchased and won for us from sin and death through the proclamation of the Gospel and the administration of the Sacraments. Because these means of grace bring the forgiveness of sins, they are also a foretaste of the future life and salvation (Matthew 28:18–20; John 3:5–7; Titus 3:5–7; 1 Corinthians 11:23–25; 1 Peter 1:3).

We have spoken in a provisional way of the effects of Christ's death and resurrection in the conversion of human hearts. But how does this conversion happen? How does God communicate his saving grace? He does this through means, through the proclamation of the Gospel and the administration of the sacraments. As the Confessions of our church say, through these means God the Holy Spirit grants faith when and where it pleases him in those who believe the Gospel (AC V).

In Holy Baptism, God puts his name on us, claims us as his own children, "in the name of the Father and of the ✝ Son and of the Holy Spirit." This is nothing less than a whole new life, a new engendering (John 1:12), one not constituted in Adam but in God. In the Holy Supper, the risen Christ bestows his body and blood, that which was given and shed for the forgiveness of our sins. And, as the Small

Catechism teaches us, "where there is forgiveness of sins, there is also life and salvation."

Sometimes Christians think of salvation individualistically. They are thinking of heaven, of course, but only of the benefits of salvation for themselves personally and not the restoration of the whole creation. We might think of it the other way round. Through his means of grace, God is saying, "I forgive you." He is stripping away all guilt and bestowing a new and open relationship that lives on into eternity. The sacraments are bringing into the present the future life when God will be all in all. Thus, the sacraments are eschatological. They bring the blessings of the eschaton, the end of the old age and the beginning of the new.

Living in light of this future brings a new energy and hope to us even now, what the apostle Peter calls a "living hope" (1 Peter 1:3). How do we live now in the light of eternity? What do God's children do? They forgive. "Be kind to one another, tenderhearted, forgiving one another, as God in Christ forgave you" (Ephesians 4:32). "Put on then, as God's chosen ones, holy and beloved, compassion, kindness, humility, meekness, and patience, bearing with one another and, if one has a complaint against another, forgiving each other; as the Lord has forgiven you, so you also must forgive" (Colossians 3:12–13). Such forgiveness brings Jesus' work and the new, restored creation into our present relationships.

A visitor to a certain region was traveling with his host by car up through a winding valley. As they drove, he noticed the houses along the way and their dilapidated condition, their windows broken, paint peeling—these and other signs of disrepair and neglect. As they climbed higher out of that valley, the man noticed that the homes in the higher elevation were neat and well cared for. He asked his host about this. The difference was that all the homes in the lower elevation stood upon ground that had been condemned in order to make way for a new reservoir. A dam had been built lower down on the river and its waters would soon rise and flood them over. We could say these houses had no future, no hope.

When we know by faith that our destiny is for good and not for evil, we care not less but more deeply about this life and its bodily welfare. Christians, just because they are by faith children of God and have received such mercy, will also show mercy to others. This is why we build hospitals, establish clean facilities, and care for widows and orphans, those who are especially in need. In some substantial way, we will want to continue the healing ministry of Jesus, bringing in his name the mercy we ourselves have also received. Because the scope of God's concern reaches out to the whole of his creation, we also care for the earth—not because we worship it as do the neo-pagans, but because it belongs to God. We use it as that over which we are to have dominion, but not exploiting it in a devastating way. Rather, we work to eliminate pollution of air and water and the filthy littering of our streets and villages. Christians ought to demonstrate a concern for beauty, tilling and keeping the garden God has given us. Never standing idle, they will be good stewards of their time and talents.

Faith issues forth in a life of love and service to the neighbor. Such service is rendered freely, not by a compulsion or anxiety that implies that one must, by his service, justify himself. In this way, the child of God actually pleases the Father, not through a life that is perfect, for even our best acts are always tainted with sin. But God accepts such good work for the sake of the faith it demonstrates in him who is Mercy incarnate, our Lord Jesus Christ. All such endeavors are but signs of God's new creation that will burst forth upon this world in its full-bodied glory only with the visible return of Christ and a new creation brought by his omnipotence. Living by this grace, a believer in Christ actually pleases God. He is graciously enabled, able in measure not to sin but in faith to please God (*posse non peccare*).

6

When Christ returns, he will fully restore the fallen creation to a state surpassing even the first (1 Corinthians 2:9; 15:28; Revelation 7:14–17; 21:1–7).

There will come a day soon when the time of faith will have ended and God's glory will be seen in the face of Christ. Then he will separate the sheep from the goats, the believers from the unbelievers, and the fate of each individual will be sealed for all eternity. There is much to be said about that Day, but we wish only to say here that it will be the end of the old and the beginning of the new in a visible and perfect way. God will remove all the damage done to his creation by the rebellion of Adam, the destruction done by the murderer and liar, the destroyer of men's souls and the chief despoiler of God's good creation. God will then fill his new creation with his presence. Two passages from the last book of the Bible especially speak of this:

> These are the ones coming out of the great tribulation. They have washed their robes and made them white in the blood of the Lamb. Therefore they are before the throne of God, and serve him day and night in his temple; and he who sits on the throne will shelter them with his presence. They shall hunger no more, neither thirst anymore; the sun shall not strike them, nor any scorching heat. For the Lamb in the midst of the throne will be their shepherd, and he will guide them to springs of living water, and God will wipe away every tear from their eyes (Revelation 7:14–17).

> Then I saw a new heaven and a new earth, for the first heaven and the first earth had passed away, and the sea was no more. And I saw the holy city, new Jerusalem, coming down out of heaven from God, prepared as a bride adorned for her husband. And I heard a loud voice from the throne saying, "Behold, the dwelling place of God is with man. He will dwell with them, and they will be his people, and God himself will be with them as their God. He will wipe away every tear from their eyes, and death shall be no more, neither shall there be mourning nor crying nor pain anymore, for the former things have passed away." And he who was seated on the throne said, "Behold, I am making all things new." Also he said, "Write this down, for these words are trustworthy and true." And he said to me, "It is done! I am the Alpha and the Omega, the beginning and the end. To the thirsty I will give from the spring of the water of life without payment. The one who conquers will have this heritage, and I will be his God and he will be my son (Revelation 21:1–7).

We who are inured to the effects of sin and death cannot even begin to imagine such a life that is promised us. "But, as it is written, 'What no eye has seen, nor ear heard, nor the heart of man imagined, what God has prepared for those who love him' " (1 Corinthians 2:9). All that is presently out of joint will be put right. Our bodies, which have suffered the growing weakness and infirmities of the human race, will be perfectly whole forever. Our minds and hearts, often divided against themselves, especially in the child of God who battles against the flesh, will be healed. Our time, so divided up at present and suffering recurrent conflicting demands, will be totally devoted to one ceaseless act of praise and creativity and enjoyment of God, at whose right hand, says the psalmist, are pleasures forevermore (Psalm 16:11). We will not be able to sin (*non posse peccare*). We will not be able to die.

The sustaining blessing of the inexhaustible life of God will interpenetrate all things, and life will begin in all possible and growing fullness. "When all things are subjected to [God], then the Son himself will also be subjected to him who put all things in subjection under him, that God may be all in all" (1 Corinthians 15:28).

7

In so defeating the mystery of evil, the mystery of God's triune being and life will be revealed.

Creation or life as God intends is endowed and enriched by relationship. The very being of our personhood is in reality communion with others. Sin damages this. So when restoration happens in its eternal fullness, we shall participate in the divine life in a way only anticipated now by faith. Jesus promises: "If anyone loves me, he will keep my word, and my Father will love him, and we will come to him and make our home with him" (John 14:23).

We who have heard God's word by faith have a revelation of the Holy Trinity. At Jesus' baptism by John in the Jordan, the Father speaks and says, "You are my beloved Son; with You I am well pleased" (Mark 1:10–11), as the Spirit descends on him in the form of a dove. We have received the peace the Holy Spirit gives us by faith in God's Son, who is the Father's gift.

We have often heard that the Gospel bestows on us priceless and sacred gifts: the forgiveness of our sins, adoption in God's family, an inheritance in heaven. It is true. But the Gospel is more than giving. It is God's *self*-giving! The Father gives himself to us in his Son; the Son gives himself to us in his incarnation, on the cross on behalf of our sins, and in his Supper; the Spirit gives himself to us as he takes what belongs to Christ and gives it to us, so bringing us back to the Father. We see real and genuine glimpses of the life of the Holy Trinity in the sacred scriptures, but a full enjoyment of their life together still awaits us. The Father lives for the Son, the Son lives for and from the Father, the Spirit lives for and from and with the Father and the Son. Even so shall we.

The apostle Peter writes: "His divine power has granted to us all things that pertain to life and godliness, through the knowledge of him who called us to his own glory and excellence, by which he has granted to us his precious and very great promises, so that through them you may become partakers of the divine nature (θείας κοινωνοὶ φύσεως), having escaped from the corruption that is in the world because of sinful desire" (2 Peter 1:3–4). I could not believe this were it not written in the Word of God, which cannot lie. We will become partakers of the divine nature. What we have now by faith will be granted us forever—God's own life and strength, holiness and immortality.

What will life in the triune God be like? Hints are given us in the Bible. It is enough for now. We will till and keep the garden. But it will not bring forth thorns and thistles. Rather, it will blossom and flower in growing splendor and God's creation will have been perfectly restored in Christ. "To him be glory in the church and in Christ Jesus throughout all generations, forever and ever. Amen" (Ephesians 3:21).

THE VISITATION OFFICE
IN THE CHURCH'S REORGANIZATION

Werner Elert

Translated by

Matthew C. Harrison
with Roland F. Ziegler

What follows is an extraordinary essay that I've long wanted to translate.[1] It has become especially significant for me since assuming the task of ecclesiastical supervision in The Lutheran Church—Missouri Synod. The Synod's constitution essentially defines the task of the president (and the district presidents as an extension of the office of president) as one of "visitation" for the assurance of confessional fidelity. While Elert's prescriptions are historically defined by the postwar period of the German situation, the essay is nevertheless filled with historical and theological insights concerning the fundamental task of oversight in the Lutheran Church. His broader concerns are completely consonant with the constitution of the LCMS.

It is a pleasure to present this essay in honor of Dean Wenthe. It was in 1983 or so that I first visited the seminary in Fort Wayne, eagerly contemplating study to be a pastor. On a blizzardy day in January or February, a student named Rick Suggitt from my home congregation in

---

[1] First published as "Das Visitationsamt in der kirchlichen Neuordnung," in *Jahrbuch des Martin Luther-Bundes* (Münich, 1948), 66ff. Reprinted in *Ein Lehrer der Kirche: Kirchlich-theologische Aufsätze und Vorträge von Werner Elert*, ed. Max Keller-Hüschemenger (Berlin and Hamburg: Lutherisches Verlagshaus, 1967): 139–50. The footnotes throughout are the work of the translator.

Sioux City took me to the first seminary class I'd ever attended. Dean Wenthe was the lecturer. I was captivated. Little could I have known what a powerful imprint this deceptively good natured-man of iron Lutheran disposition, wrapped in velvet countenance, would have on my life. It is with the very joy over texts that animates Dean's Hebraist being that I joyously make this offering to my dear teacher in Christ, friend and colleague in the Lutheran confession.

                                                        Matthew C. Harrison

1

The reorganization of the church[2] in Germany is not taking place in the free realm of utopian constitutional experimentation. It is a churchly event, first and foremost under the absolutely binding mandate of the Lord of the church, that his Gospel be proclaimed, that Baptism take place, the Holy Supper be celebrated, and the Office of the Keys administered. Where this rightly takes place, there is the communion of the saints [*communio sanctorum*].[3] Only where this rightly takes place can there be Christian faith, love, forgiveness, suffering, confession, and the sure expectation of the coming of the kingdom. But we are not the first who have borne this mandate. The church of Christ is not an oft-repeated momentous experience. As the communion of saints it is rather an enduring fellowship. So the apostles and their congregations [*Gemeinden*] already experienced and understood the church. This is because only as a continuum could and can it also be a community of brotherly love and discipline. And only thus could it grow and also be maintained as an external institution.

But we cannot, in the second place, arbitrarily abandon the place assigned to us within all the ages of the continuing, enduring, and binding communion of saints. This assignment of place always happens in a defined geographical space, in a designated century, in a legally constituted church [*Kirchentum*]. But it is binding only if and when we are

---

[2] Because Elert uses the word "church" is so many different ways, it is lowercased throughout this essay except in cases where conventional practice calls for uppercasing.

[3] In every case, Elert's use of *communio sanctorum* is translated here as "communion of saints."

claimed for the church through the ecclesiastical action in Word and Sacrament by which the mandate of Christ is fulfilled. If we hear the Gospel delivered in accordance with its mandate and receive the Sacrament according to its institution in the legally constituted church to which we belong, then we cannot separate ourselves from her without at the same time forsaking our place in the communion of saints.

But if this is so, it is determined by the "confessional standard" of this church [as an institution]. Here we mean the church's doctrine, which is publicly in force as it is expressed in its confessions and to which all bearers of the ecclesiastical office [*Amt*] are pledged. This certainly does not mean that this doctrine is always actually preached and administered accordingly. But it depends on whether or not in this church clergy who contradict [the church's public doctrine] can be called to account according to the confession. Where the confession obliges [pastors] to proclaim the Gospel and use the Sacraments in accordance with their institution, and where what happens in the church accords with this confession, there we may believe the marks of the communion of saints are to be recognized. Not geography, not canon law, but the confession determines the place that is assigned to us in the continuity of the church.

The confession serves the historical continuity of the church. It joins us in the great *Te Deum* with the choir of the orthodox confessing church of all times. This is why the Lutheran confessors at the time of the Reformation made the orthodox confessions of the ancient church their own without questioning whether or not they were actually timely or relevant. For the same reason, neither can we deny the confessions of the time of the Reformation, lest we sever the bond between us and the communion of saints. It is, incidentally, an untrue assertion when one hears today that the confessions should hold merely an historical significance for those who hold the pastoral office and especially for congregations. On the contrary, the confessions have demonstrated their enduring existential significance over the past century in the defense against theological liberalism and most recently in the church struggle [*Kirchenkampf*] [in Germany]. Even more, they have been in uninterrupted use through the catechism, agendas, and hymns. They guide every preacher to the correct understanding of the Scriptures as he prepares his sermon, even if he is not always conscious of this. A Lutheran congregation should be just as surprised if one day the dogma of Trent were preached in its pulpit than were it asked to confess a new theological declaration in place of the Apostles' Creed.

The confessions articulate the obligation and the readiness to fulfill the mandate of Christ. These confessions bound their subscribers at the time of their origin not because they were current or up to date, but because they were in accord with the Scriptures. If they were in agreement with the Scriptures at that time, then they still are today. We can and indeed must change the external polity [Ordnung] of the church if it contradicts the confession, but the confession also establishes the goal and boundaries when the ordering of the church is changed for other reasons.

2

Suppose for example that all previous institutions reaching beyond the local congregation—and that means all ecclesiastical structures, including the government of the church—were no longer extant. The church of Christ, the communion of saints, would remain, nevertheless, provided the mandate [Auftrag] of Christ, corresponding to the correct confession, continued to be fulfilled. The churchly action would only happen in the local congregation, with all of the congregations interconnected by the common confession in the true unity of the church according to the satis est of our Augsburg Confession.[4] What could force us to establish an order beyond the individual congregations?

It was this question that Luther believed he faced when in 1528 he wrote the preface to the "Instruction to the Visitors," authored by Melanchthon.[5] It is certainly correct that in the early years of the Reformation he regarded as possible an independent, individualistic existence [independentistisches Fuersichsein] of the local congregation. But already in the document he wrote to the Bohemian Utraquists, "De

---

[4] "For the true unity of the church it is enough to agree concerning the teaching of the Gospel and the administration of the sacraments." AC VII 2.

[5] Martin Luther, "Instructions for the Visitors of Parish Pastors in Electoral Saxony" (1528), AE 40:269–320; WA 26:195–240. Translations of Luther are from Elert's text, not the American Edition.

instituendis ministris," he pointed out a way that could extend beyond [the local congregation] (1523; WA 12.169ff.). The occasion to answer the practical question for his own situation was, to be sure, a result of the externally disordered condition of the congregations [*Gemeinden*] that had been seized by the Gospel in Electoral Saxony after the elimination of their former episcopal jurisdiction.

From 1526 visitations were undertaken to move beyond the disorder for which Melanchthon had penned the "Instruction." Luther's preface developed the starting point, which would necessarily lead to a church polity [*Ordnung*] beyond the local assemblies [*Versammlungen*]. He gets the counsel of the apostolic witness—how could it be otherwise—and demonstrates how the biblical unity of the first Christian congregations had also led to an overarching order for the entire church. "What a divine salutary work it is," the preface begins,

> to visit the pastors [*pfarhen*] and Christian congregations by intelligent, skillful people, is shown to us sufficiently in both the New and Old Testaments. For thus we read that Saint Peter traveled about in the Jewish land (Acts 9[:32, 38]). And Saint Paul with Barnabas in Acts 15[:36][6] also visited anew all the places where they had preached. In all his epistles he testifies how he is concerned for all congregations [*gemeinen*] and pastors. He writes letters, sends his disciples, and acts just like the apostles. When they hear in Acts 8 how Samaria had accepted the Word, they sent Peter and John to them" [Acts 8:14].[7]

Then follow examples out of the Old Testament, where Samuel, Elijah and Elisha had acted similarly. Thus, Luther continues:

> These examples have been diligently used also by the old fathers, the holy bishops of former times, and many of them are still found in papal law. For out of this work originally came bishops and archbishops, who accordingly were required to visit many or few. For originally a bishop was an overseer or visitor [*visitator*], and an archbishop was the one over these very overseers and visitors, just as each

---

[6] "And after some days Paul said to Barnabas, 'Let us return and visit the brothers in every city where we proclaimed the word of the Lord, and see how they are' " (Acts 15:36).

[7] WA 26:195; cf. AE 40:269. "Now when the apostles at Jerusalem heard that Samaria had received the word of God, they sent to them Peter and John" (Acts 8:14).

pastor [*Pfarher*] visits his parishioners [*pfarkinder*] and inspects and oversees how his people teach and live. And the archbishop should visit, inspect and oversee such bishops as to how they teach.[8]

Luther proceeds to show how the office of overseer of the bishops and archbishops gradually decayed as they instead had come to serve their own selfish interests. Indeed, he blames the entire decay of the Christian church, which made the Reformation necessary, on the failure of the office of the visitor. Here it is to be taken into account that for Luther every parish pastor [*Pfarrer*] is a bearer of the bishop's office of the Early Church. Through Melanchthon's *Treatise on the Power and Primacy of the Pope* this identification [of the office of every pastor with that of bishop] also came into our confessions.[9] What Luther says here may not be understood as an attempt to re-establish the old hierarchy as canon law. What he intends is that just as the individual Christian or the individual congregation, so also the individual parish pastor [*Pfarrer*] should not simply be left to himself. Parish pastors require oversight of doctrine and life and to this end should be visited.

Luther's preface has often been noted because in it he also develops the first theological foundation for government of the church by territorial princes [state church] that followed. "Because no one among us is called or has a certain mandate," namely to exercise the most necessary visitation, therefore the territorial princes have been asked, "out of Christian love (for according to secular authority they are not bound to do it) and for the sake of God's will . . . certain capable persons are chosen and placed for such an office or action [*Amt*]."[10] It is correct, that church government by territorial prince actually developed as an enduring institution on the basis of an emergency situation. But it is

---

[8] WA 26:196; cf. AE 40:269–70.

[9] Tr 61–62 notes: "By the confession of all, even our adversaries, it is evident that this power belongs by divine right to all who preside over the churches, whether they are called pastors, presbyters, or bishops. Accordingly Jerome teaches clearly that in the apostolic letters all who preside over the churches are both bishops and presbyters. He quotes from Titus, 'This is why I left you in Crete, that you might appoint presbyters in every town,' and points out that these words are followed by, 'A bishop must be married only once'" (Titus 1:5–7); *The Book of Concord: The Confessions of the Evangelical Lutheran Church*, ed. Theodore G. Tappert (Philadelphia: Fortress Press, 1957), 330.

[10] WA 26:197; cf. AE 40:271.

more essential that the re-establishment of the office of the visitor [*Amtes der Visitatoren*] demanded by Luther also formed the origin of the constitution involving superintendenture [*Superintendentur-verfassung*] of the Lutheran churches in Germany. For all church orders gave to the superintendents (superintendent, dean, arch-priest, inspector, provost) the visitation duties demanded by Luther.

In the secondary literature the superintendents appear as the legitimate organ of oversight of the territorial prince. Considered from a legal standpoint, they became just that. Luther's preface, however, demonstrates on the other hand quite clearly that for him the functions of the territorial prince stand in the service of the office of the visitors. He does not demand superintendents (visitors) because the territorial prince requires them; rather, he turns to the territorial prince only because the church needs visitors (superintendents). He translates "bishop" with "overseer" or "visitor." "Superintendent," furthermore, is the translation of "*episkopos*," "bishop." But it is not the territorial princes in their office later described as "summepiscopacy" who are the bearers of this office of overseer newly required by Luther.[11] It was the superintendents. As the office of oversight of doctrine, it had its norm in Scripture and Confessions—authorities that did not have their force or authority based upon the will of the territorial prince. Nor did the rule "*cuius regio eius religio*" [whose rule, his religion][12] alter any of this, for it presupposed that the territorial princes for their part submitted to the authority of Scripture and confession.

While "secular" councilors also occupied positions in the consistories, the superintendents were always clergy [*Geistliche*] (only in Riga was there once for a brief period an exception to this), because in the office of overseer over other bearers of the office the same requirements are necessary as in the case of the bearers of the office themselves (according to 1 Timothy 3:2ff.). On the other hand, the superintendent,

---

[11] That is, supreme ecclesiastical authority exercised by political rulers. See Hermann Sasse, "Church Government and Secular Authority," in *The Lonely Way: Selected Essays and Letters*, 2 vols. (St. Louis: Concordia, 2001), 1:173–241.

[12] See Hermann Sasse, "*Cuis Regio Eius Religio?* On the Four Hundredth Anniversary of the Religious Peace of Ausgburg," Letters to Lutheran Pastors 38 (Pentecost 1955), trans. Andrew Smith, to be published by Concordia Publishing House in a forthcoming collection of Sasse's letters.

because he was likewise a bearer of the office in relation to the other bearers of the office, was only first among equals [*primus inter pares*]. He himself in the assemblies of the clergy in his district, in the conventions or synods[13] that were required by the church orders (in the old Lutheran church orders there are assemblies of pastors), was also counseled and instructed by the other bearers of the office.[14] The introduction of the title of "bishop" for the first pastors of the Lutheran territorial churches after the end of the system of church governance by the territorial prince [in 1918][15] cannot and could not be justified by asserting they are the successors of the territorial princes. On the contrary, the *Summepiskopat* or church governance by territorial prince arose from the basic Lutheran thought of the constitution of the superintendents.

3

If Luther was right in his demand for an office of ecclesiastical visitation—or for him what is the same, the office of overseer [*Aufsichtsamtes*]—then the office brings about an order that encompasses, beyond the individual congregation, the entire church. But did he have it right?

If one takes his derivation "of the bishops and archbishops of this word, that is, from the apostolic custom of the visitation"[16] strictly historically, then it is very easy to raise an objection from the history of law. But he does not think of describing the bishops and archbishops from the institutional perspective of canon law as hierarchical steps or levels of offices. All that matters is the practice of visitation, which is the same for any form of the spiritual office. Each pastor [*Pfarrer*] is a visitor because he "is to visit, care for and oversee his parishioners

---

[13] Throughout this document, Elert uses the word "synod" in the sense of an assembly or convention of representatives from congregations, i.e., a meeting. I have often rendered it simply "convention."

[14] The superintendent presided but also took instruction from the other pastors.

[15] The democratization of Germany after World War I with the Weimar Republic ended the rule of territorial princes and with it their leadership of their respective churches.

[16] WA 26:196; cf. AE 40:270.

[*pfarkinder*] as he teaches and lives there."[17] Yet, because the pastor [*Pfarrer*] himself must not be unsupervised, he also must be visited. But by whom?

The hyper-independent [*independentistische*] doctrine makes the congregation the overseer of the bearer of the office [*Amtsträger*]. Rightly so! Paul makes every congregation responsible for everything that transpires in its midst. But why "does he testify that he is deeply concerned for *all* congregations [*gemeinen*] and pastors [*pfarhen*]? Why does he write letters, send his disciples, even visit himself?"[18] With these few pen strokes Luther sketches out the true apostolic ordering of the *entire* church. The ancient church knows of no hyper-independent, solitary existence of the local congregation for its own sake, no matter how often it is asserted. All its congregations understand their membership in the body of Christ, which means membership in the entire church. The only question is if and how this understanding also found its external expression. Rudolf Sohm[19] once placed great emphasis on the fact that the apostolic church in each congregation—in every assembly [*Versammlung*] of the body of Christ, that is, Christianity—is not present partially but *in toto*. This is incontrovertible. But it was never deduced from this that one could not intervene in the internal dealings of a local congregation from outside.

The examples that Luther uses from the Book of Acts are completely valid. The apostles did not leave any congregation to itself. It could be argued that the Early Church was a mission church; the congregations were not yet mature, so the apostles had to be concerned continually for their children, even when separated by distance (1 Corinthians 4:14ff; 2 Corinthians 6:13; 1 Thessalonians 2:11). But this objection is not valid. Paul wrote to the congregation at Rome before he had even seen it, and, although he could not say, it was not yet mature. On the contrary, he gives it an excellent evaluation (Romans 1:8).[20] First

---

[17] WA 26:196; cf. AE 40:270.

[18] WA 26:196; cf. AE 40:269.

[19] Sohm (1841–1917) was a Lutheran who taught Roman and ecclesiastical law at the University of Leipzig.

[20] "First, I thank my God through Jesus Christ for all of you, because your faith is proclaimed in all the world" (Romans 1:8).

Peter in its preface addresses such a wide circle of hearers that its author can in no way be regarded as the founding missionary of all the congregations of this circle.[21] It also already presumes strongly ordered structures within the congregations (1 Peter 5:1ff.). The same is true of the letters in Revelation written to the seven congregations of Asia Minor. Here an authority is always claimed that does not stop at the parochial boundaries or jurisdiction of a congregation.

This authority is of course apostolic, insofar as it was present only in the beginning of the church, and as such is not repeatable. But it lives on in the written Word of the apostles and it requires that this Word continues to be preached unabated. This is the task of the spiritual office [Amt], and this task is identical with the mandated teaching task which Christ himself gave to his disciples. But from this it is impossible to conclude that the act of teaching and hearing ever concerns only the appropriately locally defined circle, the pastor and his local congregation. Though there are no longer any apostles present among us either, still the state of the congregation, including that of its office bearers, has remained the same. This renders necessary the apostolic function of oversight, which expresses itself in critique, admonition, and encouragement.

In this respect the Early Church thought and lived not as hyperindependent [independentistic] [congregations] but as a total church. The church lives from the Gospel. The church is healthy where the Gospel is rightly taught. It is ill where the Gospel is adulterated. If poison forces itself into a congregation, it proceeds to infect the body of the whole church. In the heresy of one pastor, the unity of the entire church is broken. This obvious insight is already presupposed by the polemical letters of Paul, especially the pastoral letters, and 1 John, 2 Peter, and the Book of Revelation. Conversely, the sick member can only become healthy if powers of healing flow to it from the whole. Luther became not only the Reformer of the Wittenberg congregation but of the entire church. The presupposition is always the com-

---

[21] "Peter, an apostle of Jesus Christ, To those who are elect exiles of the Dispersion in Pontus, Galatia, Cappadocia, Asia, and Bithynia, according to the foreknowledge of God the Father, in the sanctification of the Spirit, for obedience to Jesus Christ and for sprinkling with his blood: May grace and peace be multiplied to you" (1 Peter 1:1–2).

munication [i.e., church fellowship] of all congregations with each other, just as was doubtless the case in the Early Church. There is no congregationalistic, independent existence, concerned only for itself in the individual congregation.

Just how a congregation orders itself in external matters can be a matter of indifference to the other congregations. But whether things are right with Word and Sacrament, this is a matter of concern for all other congregations, for Word and Sacrament constitute the unity of the church in its entirety [*Gesamtkirche*]. If there exists here a genuine responsibility of the one [congregation] for the others and all for the one, then allowance for this must be made in an ordered way. In the church *everything* must happen in an orderly fashion. The First Letter of Clement, written at the end of the apostolic era from the congregation at Rome to the congregation at Corinth, is the classic example of the supervision of one congregation over another. The motivation was good, but the method could not be carried through in practice. There has to be an oversight of the entire church, and therefore the church must be visited in totality. The apostles in no way reserved this task for themselves. They had already appointed their helpers for the task. Paul is informed by them concerning the state of congregations. On the other hand he reminds the congregations through these helpers of the apostolic doctrine and order [*Ordnung*] (1 Corinthians 4:17; 16:10; 2 Corinthians 7:7, 13; Philippians 2:19; Colossians 1:8; 1 Thessalonians 3:2ff.). And if Titus, to whom was entrusted the filling of the offices [of the ministry] in a number of city congregations, was to pay careful attention to see that a bishop must be able to admonish in sound doctrine and deal effectively with those who contradict it, then to this supra-congregational overseer or visitor not only is authority attributed, but he is also to be capable and to have thoroughgoing understanding with respect to sound doctrine. We conclude from this that in spite of the general priesthood not every Christian is invited to exercise the function of overseer. Supervision of doctrine requires thorough theological understanding.

Here, accordingly, there can be no further doubt that Luther was correct in his demand of a visitation office for the entire church. In any case, in doing so he demanded nothing other than what the apostles themselves had done. This office [Amt], as stated, is in its function nothing other than the spiritual office [geistliche Amt] in general by which authority every pastor visits his own congregation. It possesses no higher rank. It is distinguished from the pastoral office [Pfarramt] of the local congregation only by its wider realm of visitation.

4

All present plans toward a new ordering of matters of the church do not seek to reorder the local congregation. They seek legal forms for larger ecclesiastical entities. For this, neither the apostles nor Christ himself impart concrete directions that might be compared somehow with the constitutional prescriptions for the Old Testament theocracy. Nor can the practice of visitation by the apostles be correlated directly to any canonical configurations. Neither for Luther do they have legislative authority, but only significance as an example. But even though there are no constitutional prescriptions given to us for larger ecclesiastical entities, still, all ecclesiastical acts and all planned legal forms have to prove their legitimacy for the task that the Lord of the church has imparted. Therefore, even now our first question cannot be how one can, without enormous turmoil, create a constitution against which no party can raise legitimate legal concerns. Rather, it has to be developed from the final necessities that determine the life of the church according to the mandate [of Christ].

One necessity is, as we have presupposed, the commitment to the confessional standard, because the confession expresses the obligation and the willingness to fulfill the mandate of Christ in Word and Sacrament. This confessional commitment forms the solid bond between every local congregation and the office bearers who belong to it. The commitment is, however, at the same time the bond of the true unity of the entire church, which is liable for the totality of its members. From this follows as the second necessity the supervision of the whole [church] and over individual churchly acts in the local congregation. In contradistinction to all sorts of external usages and institutions, the individual churchly acts, properly speaking, are the performance of Word and Sacrament in accordance with the confession. Only through this will the mandate of Christ be fulfilled.

For this reason no atomistic, side-by-side—though isolated—existence of individual local congregations would be justifiable, even if, according to our hypothesis, the existing church governments and other super-congregational institutions were suddenly no longer to exist. The overseers, Greek "*episcopi*," Latin "superintendents," or in the language of Luther, "visitors," would have to be placed in office for the purpose of oversight of the actual ecclesiastical acts in congregations. For the oversight (here in a fixed sense, which supposes that such oversight is similar to the oversight of each pastor over his congregation, only exercised over a greater area) cannot be exercised by an anonymous and bureaucratic board, but only by bearers of the spiritual office [*Amt*] and in a personal way. The visitor must first of all have the same qualifications for the office [of the ministry] as the office bearer whom he visits. He must, therefore, among other things be "apt to teach" (1 Timothy 3:2; Titus 1:9).[22] Second, he must be sworn to the same Confessions as the clergy. And third, he must know the ministry of the pastor [*Pfarrers*] in the congregation from personal experience.

The office [*Amt*] of the visitor can only be effective if his area of oversight is not too large. Theodor Kaftan,[23] who as the former general superintendent for Schleswig had not only the corresponding experience but also expertise in matters theological, once rendered the judgment that such a district of supervision should not exceed 300 pastors or congregations. But one could just as well halve this number. Historical reasons, travel limitations, and the like could demand still smaller districts. It is self-evident that each district [*Bezerk*] can be made up only of congregations of the same confession, for a Reformed visitor, for instance, cannot oversee pastors who are sworn to the Lutheran confession regarding the doctrine of the use of the sacraments, or vice versa.

The visitation office can only be understood as a function of the general spiritual office [*geistlichen Amtes*]. For this reason, as members of the clergy of their district, the visitors would be only first among equals [*primi inter pares*]. On the other hand, however, they administer

---

[22] Note, for instance, the texts used for the installation of district presidents in *Lutheran Service Book: Agenda* (St. Louis: Concordia, 2006), 330–36.

[23] Kaftan (1847–1932) was superintendent of Schleswig-Holstein from 1886 to 1917.

their office as an office of the entire church, because it indeed encompasses the individual congregations. In this respect they also are joined
more tightly together to each other. They would prevent any new particularism through common counsel and mutual encouragement, and
come together into a *Council of Visitors*. They would be in the front line
of responsibility to see that all the church's proclamation and the corresponding use of the sacraments are oriented toward the confession of
their church. Everything would belong to their circle of duties that the
church order is to regulate with respect to the doctrine and the sacraments: the care for the theological education of those with the necessary
gifts; continuing education of those already in the office; theological
examinations; ordination; the examination of the agendas and hymnals
according to the confession; and of course, also the visitations, from
which they get their name "visitor." The Council of Visitors would
express the genuine unity of the church. Unity in Word and Sacrament
would be expressed to those outside [the church]. And their common
word would have special weight for those inside the church as those
who have the first line of responsibility for the unity of confession.

In this way, an order for the entire church of our confession would
be developed out of the visitation office already exercised by the apostles
and their assistants [*Gehilfen*]. This would let the church recognize its
unity precisely in the essential marks of the church, the *notae ecclesiae*.
Is it utopian for us to envision in such a way the new order that we seek?

5

It could be argued that none of this is new. The right of oversight understood as the right of visitation is provided for in the constitutions of
our present territorial churches, and it is actually exercised in proven
subdivisions [of the office] (general superintendent, provincial deans,
deans, etc.). This is of course correct, provided one can also ask whether
law and practice in general are born from a theologically justifiable
understanding of the church. There is certainly a difference whether the
right of visitation as law (entitlement) is claimed by an administrative
body in the style of a territorial princely government of the church, or
whether it is viewed as analogous to the duty of visitation incumbent
upon every pastor over against his congregational members. Over-

coming the particularism of the territorial churches is a matter of obtaining greater ecclesiastical unity.[24] The question is about what contribution the visitation office can bring to this problem.

The present territorial churches cannot be ignored in these proceedings for unification. This is not because they are the only entities capable of action in this matter of church law, but also because, as was stated at the beginning of this paper, they are in general the confessionally defined locus of our ecclesiastical legislative actions. Their confessionally defined character is expressed not least in that their ecclesiastical institutions have the right of oversight of doctrine and the use of the Sacraments. This justifies—and this alone it seems to us—the fact that up to this point they have been so jealous to guard their independence. For whatever else is still laid claim to under the words "church government," is, to put it carefully, of little significance. This is the reason why in 1934 they had to resist "integration" into the National [*Reichs*] Church. They could not hand over the supervision of doctrine and sacraments to the confession-less National [*Reichs*] Church government. Corresponding to this, the Synod of Barmen in its legal declaration formulated this fact, that "in the constitution, participation of territorial churches in the DEK [German Evangelical Church] is confessionally determined" (Ziff. 3).[25] Thus viewed, the right of oversight, *because* it until now is truly the basis for the individual existence

---

[24] This "particularism" of the territorial churches involved the fact that these churches had developed variously with respect to their varying confessional commitments. There were a dozen or so churches legally constituted as Lutheran churches. They formed the VELKD (United Evangelical Lutheran Church) within the EKD (Evangelical Church in Germany—the broader union of all state churches in Germany). Others were historically either Reformed or "Union" churches, where both the Lutheran and Reformed confessions had legal status. In the "consensus union" churches, a new hybrid confession was formed. Since World War II, the Lutheran character of the VELKD has continued to diminish within the EKD soup, such that some have recently been asking why such an entity should exist any longer. Sasse predicted it all.

[25] The reference here is not to the well-known Barmen Declaration of 1534 ("Die Barmer Theologische Erklärung") but the "Erklärung zur Rechtslage der Bekenntnissynode der Deutschen Evangelischen Kirche" ("Declaration on the legal status of the confessing convention of the German Evangelical Church") of the same year. This document can be found in *Die erste Bekenntnissynode der Deutschen Evangelischen Kirche zu Barmen*, vol. 2: *Text, Dokumente, Berichte*, ed. Gerhard Niemöller, Arbeiten zur Kirchengeschichte; 6 (Göttingen: Vandenhoeck & Ruprecht, 1959), 203.

of the territorial churches in a truly churchly fashion, is a bulwark of particularism. Or, as it is similarly stated here, it is an *obstacle* on the path to a more encompassing ecclesiastical unification.

This obstacle should not be overcome, such that the centralizing methods of the National Church of 1933 [i.e. the D.E.K.] be repeated. Whoever advocates this makes the entire effort of opposition, not least of which was that of the Barmen Synod, finally duplicitous. A centralized leadership of a National [*Reichs*] Church governance must claim supervision of doctrine and administration of the sacraments. For without this there is no church governance. It must then declare the present divergence of the confessions as trivial, and in so doing deny, at least in part, the binding nature of the valid confession. Or it must give up the right of supervision. But in so doing, the confession would be rendered completely impotent as the *norma normata* [the norm that is normed] that also determines the constitution.

But the right of supervision, which hitherto has formed the bulwark of the particularism of the territorial churches because it justified it as genuinely churchly, does not need to render this particularism permanent. If supervision is not or no longer can be understood as a function of an administrative body, but rather as a necessary function of the entire church, then the entire church ought thus to speak as the one that commissions it. Individual church entities, legally independent but united in a common confession with the broader church [*Kirchentümer*], could then, without violating the commitment to the confession, exchange their visitors at any time, just as pastors can change congregations. And if indeed each visitor was assigned a defined circle of visitation, then this would all be done for the practical reasons of effective implementation, but no longer out of a fundamental legal particularism. The office [*Amt*] of overseer would be changed from a pillar of particularism into an instrument of unification.

In applying this to our situation, we must now limit ourselves to the scope of the Lutheran confession, because objections would have to be expected for the Reformed doctrine of [church] constitution. Then we would have, for example, the following picture. The present territorial churches delegate in their area the incumbents of the office of oversight who are entrusted with the corresponding authority (the right of examination, ordination, and visitation in the narrower sense, etc.) to the council of visitors. This corresponds in a sense to the bishops' conference of the United Evangelical Lutheran Church [of Germany; *Vereinigte Evangelische-Lutherische Kirche*; VELKD] as it is planned; only the larger territorial churches have to be represented by more visitors, corresponding to the numbers Kaftan suggests. Also, in the areas of the united churches[26] in which the Lutheran confessional standard is maintained, areas of visitation will be formed where henceforth the oversight of doctrine and the administration of the sacraments will be exercised exclusively according to the Evangelical Lutheran confession. Equipped with the appropriate authority for visitation, visitors will also join the council of visitors. Prerequisite, of course, is that with respect to the doctrine and administration of the sacraments, they not continue to be bound to other administrative authorities or mandates. For with the task of unification of the total church that is posed to the council, it would be irreconcilable if they were subject to mandates in doctrine and administration of the Sacraments—or also would carry out visitation in congregations—with another confessional standard. The solutions necessary for this require a certain period of transition. Visitors, whose function in this respect is not yet clearly regulated, would take part in the council only as guests.

Granting the concerns indicated by Kaftan's numbers, for Germany we come to perhaps 60 (median of 40 to 80) visitors of the Evangelical Lutheran confession. The accession of the Lutheran free churches would also be very welcome. Their extraordinary significance for the orientation of all ecclesiastical events, also all proceedings toward unification in confession, goes far beyond the weight of their mere numbers. They also need not fear that they are being swept away in a general stream of the union. What is proposed here is precisely the implementation of the basic principal proclaimed by the Barmen Synod that "a church's constitutional form [*äussere kirchliche Ordnung*] always has to be justified by its (the church's) confession."

---

[26] The "united" or union churches do not displace either the Lutheran or Reformed confessions, but allow both to exist in the church. A "consensus union" put forth a new, combined confession.

The present territorial churches (and free churches) retain their independent realms of administration, which is indeed necessary for guarding legal continuity. Also, the formation of the council of visitors in no way excludes the goal of a confederation of all protestant churches [*Kirchentümer*] in Germany, pursuing again unified federated leadership. But this proposed way of proceeding would achieve a suggested path where the entire realm of doctrine and the administration of the sacraments would be represented by one entity, bound exclusively to the same confession. The associations [*Moderamen*][27] of the Reformed Federation can serve as a model here, though it rests on other internal presuppositions. And the united areas [*konsensusunierten Gebiete*][28] could, if they regarded it as necessary, create a similar type of representation. At first the result might perhaps not achieve what is desired, which today for many is the formation of a united National Church [*Reichs Kirche*] along the lines of the German Evangelical Church [DEK] of 1933. In reality, however, more would be accomplished precisely for a genuine churchly unity. The particularism of the territorial churches would no longer preclude it, because subscription to the confession, which up to now has justified such particularism, would be overtaken by the greater unity. And conversely, the greater unity would be real ecclesiastical unity according to the apostolic example, because it would be born of the responsibility of the whole for a confessionally faithful execution of the mandate of Christ by all her members.

6

This proposed polity [*Ordnung*] has an episcopal nature by virtue of the task of unification that it entrusts to the visitors. We will need to be prepared for the charge of episcopalism, which for its critics is virtually the same as clericalism and hierarchism. On similar grounds, the associations [*Moderamen*] of the Reformed Federation have raised the

---

[27] *Moderamen* formed a sort of para-church organization, including Reformed congregations, both within and independent of the union. They were not a synod or convention as such.

[28] "Consensus Union" meant a new confession of former Lutheran and Reformed Churches (e.g., Baden), unlike the Prussian Union where both confessions obtained.

accusation that the controversial draft constitution for the United Evangelical Lutheran Church of Germany [VELKD] is "against the word of God" (Declaration of March 14, 1947; The Reformed [*Moderamen*] are, via this censure, [ironically] exercising the right of oversight over the Lutheran churches). Their declaration states concerning the proposed powers granted to the leading bishop by the draft constitution that "the congregation is largely disenfranchised." We do not need to defend the constitution of the United Evangelical Lutheran [VELKD] here. But this complaint shows the kind of opposition that often arises against the suspicion of episcopalism. By "bishop" they understand a cleric who desires to dominate the congregations. He assumes powers, which belong to "the congregation." Jealousy and suspicion against a bishop are the expected fruits of the Spirit.

Now it is certainly correct that there is to be in the church of Christ no "domineering rule" [*Herrschaft*] of one over the other. The New Testament provides very intense warning against this. But its warning is directed to the presbyters [i.e., the local pastors] (1 Peter 5:3). We conclude from this that a purely presbyterial constitutional polity can no more provide a guarantee against the lust for power [*Herrschaftsgelüste*] of ecclesiastical office bearers. Whoever has carefully studied certain areas of more recent church history will easily find examples of this. In order to "dominate" [*beherrschen*] the congregation, one need be no theologian. And a theologian can, without being a bishop, also tyrannize the whole church. According to biblical understanding, the presbyters are also "overseers," for Paul addresses the Ephesian presbyters as "bishops" (Acts 20:17, 28).

It would also be extremely important to ask if the visitors, not only as a result of a personal lust for power [*Herrschaftsgelueste*] but also through their episcopal function for the sake of the office [*Amt*], assume for themselves tasks that belong to "the congregation." Here two things must be stated. First, their office [*Amt*], like everything in the church, fulfills the mission of Christ, *diakonia, ministerium*, service [*Dienst*]. They serve the Lord *by* serving "the congregation." They demonstrate their ministry [*Dienst*] like any other pastor [*Pfarrer*], only with the particular additional concern [*Auflage*] to see that false doctrine and misuse of the Sacraments do not creep in. Thus their ministry [*Dienst*] is a protective task for the congregation. They exercise it, however, with no other means than the pastor [*Pfarrer*], for they use only the means of the Word. Disciplinary measures like those granted by the Calvin's constitution to the presbyters over against the "congregation" are not granted to the Lutheran visitors or bishops.

In the second place, they [the bishops] represent no hierarchy, for a hierarchy enlarges itself by co-opting [power], as it were. At least the Lutheran bishops of the German territorial churches, according to the current applicable constitutions, are chosen by their conventions [*Synod*]. They therefore not only serve "the congregation" but also exercise this service [*Dienst*] on their behalf. All the critics of an episcopal system of governance are in agreement that a convention represents "the congregation." Nothing would prevent all bearers of the office of oversight from being elected by their area conventions [*Synod*].

Thereby, however, also the practical counter thesis will be touched upon, to which the polemic against episcopalism has tended. Not bishops, so it goes, but rather synods represent "the congregation." But to what extent here are the conventions preferred? Because so-called "laity" belong to them? That they take part in conventions is certainly necessary for more than one reason. But are they fundamentally better suited to represent "the congregation" than "clergy" [*Geistliche*], who are, to be sure, also members of the congregation? Nobody can seriously maintain that. In the New Testament one finds neither mandate nor model for the present polity for conventions [*Synod*]. The reference to the so-called apostolic council would be out of place here. That assembly [*Versammlung*] did not consist of elected representatives of a plurality of congregations, but rather bearers of the apostolic office and the entirety of the Jerusalem congregation, whose elders [*Älteste*] were particularly prominent. The Jerusalem congregation was distinguished here in a manner that contradicts the form of our polity with respect to constitutions of conventions that assume equal rights for all local congregations. The particular dignity [of the Apostolic Council] is that its members had the Lord himself in their midst and that they had experienced the first coming of the Holy Spirit. The congregation at Antioch did not send its representatives to take part in a vote. They were there to participate in bringing about an authoritative decision [*votum*] "of the apostles and elders [*Ältesten*] (Acts 15:2). The participation of the entire Jerusalem congregation was thereby not expected. Their participation, therefore, cannot be regarded as a condition for the validity of the decision. The New Testament knows plenary assemblies [*Vollversamm-lungen*] of the entire local congregation [*Ortsgemeinde*]. It makes them responsible for all internal happenings in a congregation. But it knows no conventions in the present sense, as a representative total organ of a larger number of congregations. The preferred position that is commonly given today to the conventions [*Synod*] in the entire order of the church has no better biblical justification for itself than the proposed council of visitors.

With this we are not saying that conventions should cease to exist. There are plenty of churchly tasks to justify them also in their present form. The participation of non-clergy is just as indispensable as in the polity of the local congregation. But their natural realm is the territorial churches that have existed up to this point. If today, however, a polity for the general convention is advocated that has the imprint of a national [*Reichs*] church and claims an authority with respect to doctrine without consideration for its composition normed by confession, it must be decisively opposed. Because the evangelical Lutheran confession accords with Scripture, it is intolerable for an entity not bound to this confession to have jurisdiction in the realm of doctrinal matters. We cannot sacrifice the true unity of the church for an imaginary union unity [*Unionseinheit*] or in favor of the horizontal connections of a theological school.[29] In order to meet the accusation of offering only a negative critique, we have sought a constructive counterproposal through a concern for the necessary office of doctrinal oversight.

---

[29] The confessionally Lutheran critique of the Union, which Elert shares, opposed what Sasse called the "Calvinization of Lutheranism," that is, the reduction of the Lutheran Church to a school of Lutheran concern within a broad union of various theological viewpoints within one church. Elert's proposal was, of course, completely ignored.

CHRISTIAN INVOLVEMENT IN THE PUBLIC SQUARE

David P. Scaer

June 2011 brought a conclusion to the tenure of Dean O. Wenthe as president of Concordia Theological Seminary in Fort Wayne, Indiana, a remarkable period in which the institution thrived administratively, collegially, educationally, and financially. Dean has been a leader not only in the Church but in the community. In his honor this essay discusses choices that Christians, especially Lutherans, faced leading up to the 2012 national elections as expressed in two leading political voices, the Tea Party movement and the *New York Times*.

Since colonial days, American churches have been forces in the political life of the nation. For years it was proverbial that the Lutheran Church was the Republican Party at prayer. This may only be true now of The Lutheran Church—Missouri Synod. Conversely, the Evangelical Lutheran Church in America may find its societal agenda in the pages of the *New York Times*. On its website the Tea Party favors items that appeal to a politically conservative mind-set: limited federal government, individual freedoms, personal responsibility, free markets, and returning political power to the states and to the people. Individual freedoms are already guaranteed in the Bill of Rights. Success results from a sense of personal responsibility, and failures often are of our making, but not always. Trimming pork from the federal budget has an appeal, but limits on some programs like national security could have serious consequences. While absolutely free markets probably never really existed except among pirates, excessive regulations are annoying impediments. Unspecified by the Tea Party are those political powers to be returned to the people.

One-hundred fifty years ago a war was fought on our soil to deprive the states and people of the right to enslave others. Government rights at any level are not absolutes. Paying fewer taxes is not a part of Christian ethics, but keeping as much of what we have acquired belongs to that human condition called original sin. Government exists to restrain evil, the law's first use according to a Lutheran definition. Evil can be restrained but not eradicated. Nearly all governments tolerate evil of some sort and some promote it. Whatever good they accomplish is temporary; civil righteousness is never as good or permanent as the divine kind. Libertarianism, associated wrongly or rightly with the Tea Party, tends towards unbridled freedom, but this is not an option for Christians. We do not have the right to drive drunk, neglect our infant children, or kill our unborn. Bearing arms is a constitutional right, but in some cases it can be morally wrong (e.g., allowing gun ownership to volatile persons). What is moral, legal, and constitutional may overlap, but these are not synonyms.

Implied in the creed of the *New York Times*, "All the News That's Fit to Print," is that other media are not bound by the self-restraints and high standards of objectivity it sets for itself. To state the obvious, the *Times* is not the *New York Post*, and in any case its creed is an overstatement and self-serving. There must be news that is fit to print that does not make the pages of the *New York Times*. Even the gospels acknowledge some things Jesus said and did that were omitted if for no other reason than for lack of space or, as John puts it, all the books in the world could not contain them—another overstatement. Whatever was included in the gospels was done at the expense of what was excluded. Such exclusions gave license to the writers of the apocryphal gospels to fill in the gaps with fascinating fiction. All writing is selective. A thin line is drawn between intentional and unintentional omissions. Underlying the *New York Times* creed is the eighteenth-century rationalist philosophy of common sense realism that events possess their own meaning. Upon reflection, people of average intelligence will come to the same conclusions; those who disagree have less than normal intelligence. Opinions, however, have to do more with convictions, not IQ.

The *New York Times* defines its goal as a quest and publication of the truth; the Tea Party sets for its goal a better society. Thus the *Times* is no different from other news media and the Tea Party is no different from other political movements. One presents itself as a gospel for a better world and the other proposes principles for an ideal society. Their goals are similar, but their plans to achieve them are different. If all agreed on what an ideal society would look like, there would be no need for a political movement like the Tea Party or newspapers like the *Times* or even for the church. Secular endeavours have this churchly character in that they recognize that the current situation is less than desirable and offer programs to perfect society. What this world will look like and how it will come about are the points of disagreement.

The *New York Times* is not alone in its claims to objectivity. The self-evident truth that all men are created equal with inalienable rights, a rationalist principle that found its way into the Declaration of Independence, was not that self-evident to the slave holders who signed the document. Differences over this self-evident truth led to our nation's bloodiest war. A claim to objectivity hardly guarantees it. Optimistic estimations of human potential do not fit the Christian perspective of humanity estranged from God by sin. Passive voice sentences like "All the News That's Fit to Print" omit the subject of the action, but the implied subjects are the editors of the *New York Times* who determine what is fit and what is not fit. Almost synonymous with "All the News that's Fit to Print" is "Fair and Balanced," the banner that flies over Fox News.

Putting one's hands on what is fair is as difficult as agreeing to what is fit to print. Translated into theological terms, if one item is chosen for inclusion on the printed page, another is not. So our first response to self-proclaimed objectivity is that no oral or written account, what the Germans call *Geschichte*, corresponds precisely or in all details to what happened, *Historie*. No oral or written report exhausts an event's meaning. This would apply to such faith-determining events as the crucifixion and the resurrection. Objectivity does not belong more to one part of a newspaper than another. Editorials are typically found on the third page from the back of a newspaper's first section, but editorial opinion begins with the decision on what to print on page one. Omission of an event qualifies as an editorial, in that the reader is not given the opportunity to evaluate it. Similarly, no scientifically proven

fact is ever so perfect that it cannot be adjusted or eventually discarded
(e.g., PSA tests for males, not eating before swimming). Subjectivity
belongs to the scholarly and scientific quests for knowledge as well as its
preservation.

This principle is applicable to which words and deeds of Jesus are
included in the Gospels. The evangelists were not collectors of dis-
connected data from the life of Jesus; rather, they interpreted them so
their readers (hearers) would see that in Jesus God was reconciling the
world to himself. As an event in history, the cross does not project one
self-evident truth. To Jesus' adversaries, crucifixion was a well-earned
penalty for a man who made himself equal to God. For Pontius Pilate
this was the easiest way to eliminate a political nuisance that threatened
the Pax Romana in Judea. To Paul it was the power of God to salvation.
A writer's perspective and intent are factors in reporting an event. So
while the *Times*, especially in its Sunday edition, is a delightful source of
information about topics beyond the reach of most, its editors intend to
win readers to their points of view. They want to be the evangelists of
our times.

Rather that pitting the platform of the Tea Party against the
editorial policies of the *New York Times*, a more obvious contrast might
be Joe Solmonese's Human Rights Campaign with its advocacy of same-
sex marriage and the Manhattan Declaration prepared and signed by
leaders of various Christian traditions defending marriage as a union
between one man and one woman as well as advocating pro-life positions. These groups do not grab the attention given the Tea Party and
the *New York Times*, but each group works at converting the public to
its points of view. Friedrich Daniel Ernst Schleiermacher, recognized as
the founder of liberal Protestantism, defined church as community, but
this definition can be reversed so that every community is a church
converting the unconverted and proselyting members of other communities. Political parties are communities of like-minded people working for a common goal, a definition close to Schleiermacher's definition
of church. These secular associations are pseudo-churches promising a
taste of the good life now as an Ersatz for eternal life. Unmentioned is
the fact that any good results are temporary and, more often than not,
undelivered. In this scheme, newspapers function as Scriptures with an

implied infallibility. Correction notices are rare and placed so inconspicuously that newspapers protect their assumed inerrancy.

Which comes first, newspapers or political parties, is a chicken and egg question. While newspapers took up the abolitionist cause before a political party was formed to advance it, the consciences of New England Congregational churches were the seed bed from which the abolitionist newspapers sprang. Philosophical movements, often with religious overtones, give birth to newspapers, which in turn give birth to political parties. So it was with the origin of Christianity and its propagation. Jesus did or said something. Someone heard it and passed it around and then someone else wrote it down. Ideas spring from the minds of people who publish newspapers like the *New York Times* or form political movements like the Tea Party. Listening to all sides in political debates is the best way to determine a course of action, even though we may never know with certainty that the path chosen is the best possible one. In our context it means reading a variety of newspapers, listening to a variety of television and radio commentators, and in the mix attempting to locate a course of action. Undigested raw material is rarely a call to arms. Uninformed opinion is like overworked vocal chords detached from the center of thought, what St. Paul calls a clanging bell.

A church stepping into the political arena is in danger of a misstep; but since the fourth century, church and state have not avoided this symbiotic relationship. On the surface the Emperor Constantine saved the Church from persecution. A clerical entitlement from Caesar was more dependable for the clergy than living off the free will donations of the faithful. The bishop of Rome could hardly resist the imperial gift of the Lateran palace. Christian martyrdom was redirected to giving one's life for the empire. Financial support for the Church came with the price of government involvement. No church has been able to avoid this completely, but the Roman Church has done this better than those in the Lutheran tradition. By soliciting the aid of the princes, Luther followed in the steps of Orthodox communions in the East, where princes determined church agendas. Reformation scholar Mark Noll notes, "Because of the large role given to secular rulers, Lutherans have had difficulty resisting political authority that compromised or contradicted the Christian gospel."[1] The electors of Brandenburg forced Lutherans into ever closer alliances with the Reformed. An egregious example of government control was Hitler's use of a state church alliance to redefine Protestant Christianity with the pagan elements of the old Norse religion. Since his version of Christianity did away with the Old Testament, it was no Christianity at all, as Dietrich Bonhoeffer recognized.[2] Since the 1930s, Scandinavian governments have appointed bishops and deans who were in tune with their socialist agendas that led to ordaining women and now homosexuals and the blessing of same-sex marriages. These churches lost their Lutheran identity and, some would say, their Christian identity. Government assistance to the church comes with a price. Monasteries had their advantages. In the West, secularization comes from infusions of an increasingly secular culture, a point Dean Wenthe has often made in his sermons.

Rather than the government or culture setting the agenda of the church, there are cases where the reverse happens and the church has worked to change the direction of government. Examples include Dietrich Bonhoeffer, who tried unsuccessfully in Hitler's Germany, and American abolitionists, who succeeded in their fight against slavery. So convinced that their cause to end slavery was divine, the Union armies could sing "The Battle Hymn of the Republic," belting out with Christian conviction that "God's truth is marching on." As a political force in America's large cities, Catholicism replaced Protestantism in the twentieth century, but its diminished influence was evident in New York's legalizing same-sex marriages in July 2011. Add to this the up-to-now ineffective opposition of the U.S. Conference of Catholic Bishops to the proposed government requirement that its churches fund insurance plans covering birth control and abortion. Currents between church and state can flow in both directions. Consider how some church's services begin to resemble patriotic celebrations. In some congregations the pledge of allegiance is recited in place of the creed, the national flag has a greater prominence than the cross, and "The Star

---

[1] Mark A. Noll, "The Place of Scripture in the Modern Christian University," *The Cresset* 74, no. 5 (Trinity, June 2011), 11.

[2] Eric Metaxas, Bonhoeffer: Pastor, Martyr, Prophet, Spy: A Righteous Gentile vs. Third Reich (Nashville: Thomas Nelson, 2010).

Spangled Banner, "God Bless America," and "The Battle Hymn of the Republic" function as hymns. "Amazing Grace" is so often used in secular settings that its Christian content may already be compromised. Patriotism as an Ersatz for faith destroys it, as it did in Germany in the 1930s.

In an attempt to reassert religion into the political world, multi-denominational alliances have been established. Among these were Jerry Falwell's Moral Majority and the presidential aspirations of Pat Robertson. Promise Keepers had a moral agenda. In 1988 Os Guinness organized a moral phalanx of Christians, Jews and Muhammadans.[3] Mormons desired an alliance with conservative Christians in opposing the Equal Rights Amendment. The Manhattan Declaration gathers Christians from various traditions to oppose abortion and support the traditional view of marriage. Apart from ideological convictions, strength is found in numbers, so it is reasoned. With the election of Jimmy Carter, 1976 was to be the year of the Evangelicals; it turned out not to be the case. Evangelicals still look back with nostalgia to what might have been. European Lutherans contravened their two kingdoms doctrine in exchange for government support. Calvinism is constructed to welcome such support to further its adherents idea of God's kingdom on earth (e.g., sixteenth-century Geneva and then Puritan New England). In such alliances, it is thought things might go better for the church with help from the state. Richard John Neuhaus was a valiant warrior in these matters. *First Things* was intended to bring those of different and even opposing religious and philosophical views together in reaching common moral goals. He succeeded in bringing Catholics and Evangelicals onboard, but Jewish participation was never as full throated as he liked, and followers of the prophet never joined.

Bonhoeffer's active opposition to National Socialism continues to fascinate. Early Christians refused to worship the emperor and the im-perially approved gods. Bonhoeffer went further and worked to assas-sinate the Führer, something that was not on the minds of the early Christians, but this situation was different. Hitler had used the church to foster National Socialism by appointing one bishop of the Third

---

[3] David P. Scaer, "Response to Os Guinness," in *Evangelical Affirmations*, ed. Carl F. H. Henry and Kenneth Kantzer (Grand Rapids: Academie Books, 1990).

Reich and by folding church youth organizations into his German Youth Movement. Neuhaus was on a reverse mission, not in curbing state control of the church, but in bringing the church into the public conversation from which after his death it seems increasingly excluded. His mission may have been compromised by the secularization of theology in such American mainline denominations as the Episcopal Church and the Evangelical Lutheran Church in America. The timbre of pitches of the voices of the mainline churches was indistinguishable from what was already heard in the public square. In bringing classical Christian views into that square, Neuhaus fought a rear guard action against churches whose agendas were being promoted by those who made no claim to being Christians.

The secularization of Europe began with eighteenth-century rationalism, which defined the world by material causes and effects and obviated the need for supernatural explanations like God. Communism restricted the spread of religion in anticipation that those with well-fed bodies could discover for themselves that non-existent souls would no longer be obsessed with religious questions. A prosperous Western Europe needed no prodding to reach the same goal. Benedict XVI noted that the constitution of the European Union made no mention of its Christian past in which popes and bishops crowned emperors and kings and where Lutherans, Catholics, and Calvinists fought each other for the proper understanding of the Christian truth. Europe's Christian past no longer defines how its inhabitants see themselves.

The First Amendment of the American Constitution was intended to keep the state from controlling the church, but more commonly it is used to canonize a secularism that keeps God out of the public conversation. Constitutional objections to crosses and copies of the Ten Commandments in public places are periodic. Though not as radical as government involvement in 1930s German church affairs, governments today set standards for acceptable prayers in the civil sphere. Such prayers dare go no further than speaking of the divine as "Father" or "God" (maybe "Mother God"), but use of the "J" word is unacceptable. With restrictions on using the name of Jesus, Wenthe declined an invitation to offer an invocation from a neighboring state institution of higher learning. Left unaddressed, political correctness threatens to emasculate the message of the Church, and secularism allows God less playing time on the public field.

In choosing among the various political ideologies, we might consider Solomon: "I have seen everything that is done under the sun; and behold, all is vanity and a striving after wind" (Ecclesiastes 1:14). The world is in flux, but Christian faith is a constant. Winds of human thought are unpredictable. Running after the wind and latching on to one particular political gust is never permanently satisfying. Like Don Quixote, it is a case of jousting with windmills. Life in the political sphere has a note of non-reality. We try to control, preserve, or advance a certain way of life, but we cannot. What appears to be permanent soon passes away. This is as true of the opinions of newspapers as it is of the goals of political movements. From the case of Australian newspaper mogul Rupert Murdoch, we learn that positions taken by the press are determined by prior biases. He who pays the piper calls the tune. In choosing among political options there should be an awareness that what is judged to be legal and constitutional may not be moral or advance the common good. What some states call marriage exceeds the biblical definition to the point of contradicting it. Moral and legal discrepancies belong to human existence, and so hitching our moral wagon to this or that political star is not without its problems. Newspapers like the *New York Times* cannot be read as gospel, and the kingdom promised in Tea Party-like platforms may attract millennialistic minded Evangelicals but less so Lutherans, who hold that God's kingdom is found in the cross and continued in the Church's worship life in anticipation of its full revelation at the end of time.

The creed's claim that Jesus was crucified under Pontius Pilate places the Church's origins in a Roman province whose governor knew what was the right thing to do but then did the wrong thing. The Church's dilemma is that of never being able to identify fully with her surroundings. She is not given, however, the option of freeing herself from them. The Lutheran distinctive is that Christians participate in the civil sphere knowing that it is not the theater where the final act of the drama of salvation will be played out. Judaism, Reformed and Evangelical Protestantism, Orthodoxy, Islam, and Mormonism share a common view that God's kingdom is made visible in society or government. Lutherans do not. Whatever role Catholicism plays in world politics, it does not presage imperial ambitions. Currently, self-survival in a secular culture absorbs its energies.

Lutherans coming to America had to decide for the first time how they would govern, support, and organize themselves without government. The American democratic climate was a factor in their adopting the congregational form of church organization for which biblical mandates were conveniently discovered. Luther's doctrine of the two kingdoms provided a reason for minimal involvement in political issues, but political hesitancy later proved to be morally embarrassing as in the slavery issue. Congregationalists, Methodists, and Catholics were stepping up to the plate on political issues long before Lutherans knew where the ballpark was. Heading right to the plate to take their turns at bat were Bonhoeffer in Germany and Neuhaus in America. Intriguingly, both were brought up as Lutherans, and in the case of Neuhaus it is arguable that his later ordination as a Roman Catholic priest did not eradicate the indelible character imprinted on him during his formative years when he grew up in a Lutheran parsonage.[4]

One cause of Lutheran hesitancy in political involvement may be an underdeveloped doctrine of the Law's third use. For some time there have been those who claim that the third use as defined in the Formula of Concord is not in keeping with Luther. Others give such little attention to the third use that it has no significant function, and so they quickly slip back into the second use in God's accusing the believer of sin. A full understanding of the Law's third use requires a Christological component in that Christians engage in indiscriminately doing good, especially to the helpless. Before aiding the stricken traveler, the good Samaritan did not ask the man about his religious convictions. Today, governments provide for the public welfare, but not in the ancient world. In developed countries, the church and the state may have

---

[4] Timothy George, Neuhaus's Baptist friend, said that in joining Rome Neuhaus "remained 'the Lutheran [he] used to be.' " "The Radical Conservative," *Christianity Today*, 53 no. 3 (March 2009): 50–51. This was in response to Neuhaus's "How I Became the Catholic I Was," *First Things* 22 (2002): 14–20, an essay first delivered at Concordia Theological Seminary, Fort Wayne, IN, during the presidency of our honoree.

common goals and so one may assist the other, but in undeveloped countries churches are often the major providers.

Here comes the rub. We may be agreed that the church, the government, newspapers, and political movements are committed to the common good, but they may disagree among themselves what that good is. Here the church must resist giving prior approval to the agenda of any non-church group. Christians may differ among themselves over what that common good is. A parting of the ways has come about with certain state governments no longer using Lutheran and Roman Catholic adoption services because they refuse to place children with same-sex couples. The church can never enter an alliance that does not allow her to speak a prophetic word condemning an immoral public policy. What the church and world view as good and evil may not be co-terminus, but Christians can no more let the world determine what is good and right than she can let the world determine her theology. The church can no more let the world instruct her on what she believes than she can let the world instruct her about morality or ethics.

Using his "While We're At It" column, Neuhaus often took the *New York Times* to task. In its embryonic stage the Tea Party probably escaped his notice, but he formed alliances with Carl F. H. Henry and Charles Colson, leaders for Evangelicalism who have come to be associated with the Tea Party. By joining the Roman Catholic Church, Neuhaus found a platform to create alliances with other religious groups that would have been difficult to form from within the ELCA. Rather than walking the tight rope of moral neutrality, he tied his bungee cord to what he believed was right and plunged headlong into the public square. With every bounce he came closer to the classical Lutheran faith of the Canadian parsonage in which he was brought up.

In her first three centuries, the Church's energies were absorbed with confessing Christ in the expectation that her members would be persecuted and even martyred, all in the public square. Worship of the one God, accessible only in Jesus, was countercultural in a world filled with gods, not the least of whom was the divine Caesar who had little use for Christian exclusivity. By legalizing Christianity, Constantine made the church respectable and increasingly indistinguishable from its environment. Living now in what many regard as a post-Christian era, a church separated from her governmental benefactor faces diminishing privileges. In a secular world that by definition does not allow for God—or ironically allows for a multitude of gods—the Church's continued existence depends on her insistence on the exclusivity of her message.

To retain or regain her place in the public eye, Christians may be tempted to identify with culture, though with that act she signs her own death warrant. Identifying with culture is always a fool's journey for the Church, since culture is never monolithic but a constantly moving kaleidoscope of recombining of a people's past and present experiences. When biblical Israel did just that, God's people became no people. A church not distinct from its culture is destined to be submerged into it. By rejecting one aspect of the culture and choosing another, the Church lets society determine who she is. The scepter of failure must not become a reason for the Church not to speak the prophetic word where it needs to be spoken, but with the awareness that whatever good is accomplished and whatever evil is hindered is only temporary. We should disabuse ourselves of the self-satisfying belief that the world desires to listen to the Church's message unless it endorses what the world proposes. For the world, the Church should tend to its own affairs and not impose her views on those not in her fellowship. With decisions on abortion and same-sex relations, it has become evident that the Church has standards that the world cannot understand. Faced with the displeasure of the world, some Christians may succumb to this siren call with a chorus that goes something like this: "As a Christian I am opposed to such actions, but not as a citizen." Moral bifurcation for Christians is impossible.

In August 2011, the *New York Times* may have been comprised in printing all the news that fit to print. In his review of *Absolute Monarchs: A History of the Papacy* by John Julius Norwich, executive editor Bill Keller vented the frustrations of his Catholic youth. Editors of newspapers have the right of freedom of expression. After all, this is what newspapers are all about, but the right should be exercised with caution. The author may not be the "renowned historian" Keller takes him to be. More likely, he is not credentialed at all. In his review, Keller describes how when he was growing up he believed that a priest could

turn a bread wafer into the actual flesh of Christ. Catholic belief concerning the Eucharist for him was analogous to believing in aliens. As a
widely recognized intellectual, *Times* editor Keller should have thought
through the consequences of this. Discovery of extraterrestrial intelligent life, though not probable, is at least not impossible for those who
assume that finding water on a planet would be enough to ignite the
engine of evolution. At least this is a topic of learned conversation. For
theological reasons finding such life is unlikely, but should it happen,
Keller would have to eat a large portion of crow in telling his Catholic
priest that he had returned to the faith of his youth and again believed
that the Eucharist bread is indeed changed into the body of Christ.

Historians, like the ideologues who write newspaper columns and
organize political movements, are not above critique. *First Things* editor
R. R. Reno notes that the *Times* has used clerical abuse to assert "in one
way or another that the Catholic Church is too morally compromised
and internally corrupt to function as a legitimate voice in American
public life." He adds, "We see something of the same in treatments of
the 'religious right' and the enthusiastic evangelical piety of various
Republican politicians. An ardent faith, it is suggested, makes one unfit
to govern." Then he concludes,

We live, as many have said, after Christendom. Our age is secular.
The old establishments have been replaced by others, ones that have no
need for alliance with religious leaders . . . . The church did not seek the
divorce, but it is nonetheless now a largely accomplished fact. With the
loss of the status and influence once by integration into political power,
however, comes an opportunity to engage the city of man in a new way.[5]

We can expect church credentials in civil matters to be ignored and
besmirched, but where society condones, promotes, and requires evil,
the Church must continue to make that society uncomfortable.

---

[5] R. R. Reno, "The Public Square," *First Things* 27 (November 2011): 5.

THE PSALTER IN CHRISTIAN WORSHIP

A REVIEW AND A REAPPRAISAL

Paul J. Grime

A little more than a quarter-century ago, I was honored that Dean Wenthe consented to preach at my ordination. For his sermon text he pointed us to Ezekiel: "I will set up over them one shepherd, my servant David, and he shall feed them: he shall feed them and be their shepherd. And I, the LORD, will be their God, and my servant David shall be prince among them. I am the LORD; I have spoken" (34:23–24). In the course of the sermon, he spoke of how he believed that David was a "remarkable model for every ministry,"[1] and how at every moment in his life David was visited by God's presence. Yet, Wenthe went on, "for all his skills as a warrior, David also loved God's house." As evidence, he cited not only the provisions David made for moving the ark of the covenant to Jerusalem but also his stated desire to build a permanent home for the ark, namely, the temple. Dr. Wenthe also mentioned in his sermon an additional piece of evidence concerning David's love for the Lord's house and that was his authorship of nearly half of the 150 psalms. As Wenthe so eloquently put it, "In loving the hymnody of Israel, even as you have loved it, he loved the presence of Yahweh."

For my contribution to this festschrift in honor of my mentor, colleague, and friend, I can think of no better topic than the psalms. The sheer size of the Psalter—only a few Old Testament books come close to it in length—and the frequency with which writers of the New Testament quote it (comprising nearly 40 percent of all Old Testament

---

[1] The quotations from the sermon are from a videorecording (November 8, 1987) that is in the author's possession.

quotations) testify to its significance. Over the course of history, as I will describe below, the Psalter has been the subject of constant inquiry, with massive commentaries written by a number of theologians. Even more significant, however, is the pervasive use of the Psalter in the worship of the Church through the centuries. There is much, I believe, that we can learn from that usage.

HISTORICAL OVERVIEW[2]

The writings of the early church fathers give ample testimony to their high estimation of the psalms.[3] Documents as early as the *Didache* (c. AD 100) and the writings of Justin Martyr (c. AD 150) make considerable use of the psalms. Several centuries later, Augustine devoted thirty years to the completion of his massive *Exposition on the Psalms*.[4] In the intervening years, theologians from Irenaeus to Athanasius demonstrated a remarkable familiarity with the Psalter. And in the centuries that followed these early fathers, nearly every theologian of significance either wrote specifically on the psalms or integrated them into his writings in substantial ways.[5]

---

[2] There are a number of resources that provide significant discussion on this topic, including Massey H. Shepherd Jr., *The Psalms in Christian Worship: A Practical Guide* (Minneapolis: Augsburg, 1976); Arthur A. Just Jr., *Heaven on Earth: The Gifts of Christ in the Divine Service* (St. Louis: Concordia, 2008), 98–115; Quentin Faulkner, "Psalm/Psalmody," in *Key Words in Church Music*, rev. and enlarged, ed. Carl F. Schalk (St. Louis: Concordia, 2004), 499–501; John Harper, "Psalmody," in *The New Westminster Dictionary or Liturgy and Worship*, ed. Paul Bradshaw (Louisville: Westminster John Knox Press, 2002), 391–93; Philip H. Pfatteicher, *Commentary on the Lutheran Book of Worship: Lutheran Liturgy in Its Ecumenical Context* (Minneapolis: Augsburg Fortress, 1990), 381–85; Philip H. Pfatteicher and Carlos R. Messerli, *Manual on the Liturgy—Lutheran Book of Worship* (Minneapolis: Augsburg, 1979), 19–21; and Pius Parsch, *The Breviary Explained*, trans. William Nayden and Carl Hoegerl (St. Louis: B. Herder Book Co., 1952), 48–84.

[3] See the helpful summary in William L. Holladay, *The Psalms through Three Thousand Years: Prayerbook of a Cloud of Witnesses* (Minneapolis: Fortress Press, 1993), 162–74.

[4] William C. Weinrich, "Speech of the Heart; Speech of God: Augustine's Use of Psalm 4 in *Confessions* 9.4" in *Day by Day We Magnify Thee: Psalms in the Life of the Church*, ed. Daniel Zager (Fort Wayne: Concordia Theological Seminary Press, 2003), 49.

[5] For a fascinating examination of the use of the psalms through the centuries, see Bruce K. Waltke and James M. Houston, *The Psalms as Christian Worship: A Historical Commentary* (Grand Rapids: Eerdmanns, 2010).

In contrast to the extensive written testimony that exists concerning the use of the psalms in the theological endeavor during those early centuries of the Church, evidence of the actual use of the psalms in worship during this same time period is quite scant. There are simply few extant references to worship in the Early Church that provide sufficient detail. That the early Christians used the psalms in worship is fairly certain; what is not as certain is how they used them. For example, in the late second century Tertullian hints at the use of the psalms in conjunction with the reading of Holy Scripture in the main Sunday service.[6] Which psalms were used or how they were presented, however, is not clear. By the fourth century, details begin to emerge. Augustine's sermons, for example, reveal which psalms were regularly read on certain festivals of the year.[7] Available evidence also reveals that the location of the psalm in the service continued to be near the reading of the Scriptures, though the precise location varied depending on location. In Rome, for example, the psalm occurred after the first reading, whereas in Augustine's church in Hippo the psalm came after the second reading.[8]

More instructive for our investigation is the manner in which the early Christians sang the psalms. It is also in the fourth century that we find evidence of a form of presentation that has come to be known as responsorial psalm singing. Most likely drawn from Jewish models, responsorial singing consists of a back and forth movement between leader and congregation in which the leader sings the verses of the psalm with interruptions by the congregation, which sings a single line from the psalm as a refrain. Psalm 136 is the prime example of how this method of presentation might look, with the congregation repeating the phrase "for his steadfast love endures forever" after each verse. Many other psalms have built-in refrains, though with far less repetition, such as Psalm 67 (with the refrain "Let the peoples praise You, O God" in vv. 3 and 5) and Psalm 46 ("The Lord of hosts is with us" in vv. 7 and 11). The responsorial form of singing was eminently congregational, not to

[6] Peter C. Cobb, "The Liturgy of the Word in the Early Church," in *The Study of Liturgy*, 179–88, ed. Cheslyn Jones, Geoffrey Wainright, and Edward Yarnold (New York: Oxford University Press, 1978), 186.

[7] Holladay, *The Psalms through Three Thousand Years*, 167–68.

[8] Cobb, "The Liturgy of the Word in the Early Church," 186.

mention practical, in an age when printed books were not available for large groups of people and when many people were illiterate.[9] After learning a simple refrain, even the least educated in a congregation could easily participate in singing any psalm.

The flowering of the responsorial form of psalm singing occurred with the rise of daily prayer for the masses in the fourth century. This setting for worship is often referred to as the "cathedral office," the people's service. It was during this time, however, that an alternate—and eventually, competing—venue for worship developed, namely, the monastic office. Already in a nascent form in the late third century, monasticism grew considerably in the coming centuries. Though at first it was not in competition with the people's public gathering, eventually worship in these communities became a private affair, due in part to the tendency to establish monastic communities away from the centers of population.[10]

Central to the monastic experience was inculcating in each monk a disciplined life of continuous prayer." In order to accomplish that goal, members of the community gathered eight times a day for prayer that centered around the recitation of the psalms. Though there were different practices from one monastic community to another, most eventually settled on the common practice of praying through the entire Psalter every week. Since the purpose for the continual repetition of the psalms was to form a life of prayer in the individual, it was necessary for the individual to participate thoroughly in the daily exercise. Thus, the monks sang not just refrains to the psalms but the entire psalm texts. The method for praying the psalms was, therefore, not responsorial, but antiphonal, singing. Divided physically into two halves, the community would alternate the singing of the two halves of each psalm verse. Because of the constant repetition, the monks could eventually commit the entire Psalter to memory.

---

[9] Paul Westermeyer, *Te Deum: The Church and Music* (Minneapolis: Fortress Press, 1998), 18–19.

[10] For an overview of this development, see W. Jardine Grisbrooke, "The Formative Period: Cathedral and Monastic Offices," in *The Study of Liturgy*, 358–69, ed. Cheslyn Jones, Geoffrey Wainright, and Edward Yarnold (New York: Oxford University Press, 1978).

Before moving on in this admittedly brief overview of the use of the psalms in worship, it will be helpful to draw one important contrast in the use of the psalms in the Early Church. In the monastic tradition, the psalms were assigned to the various services of the day and week with little regard for their content. Except in a few cases where certain psalms suggested themselves for a particular time of day (such as Psalm 4 for Compline at the end of the day), the psalms were simply distributed in canonical order over the course of the days of the week.

In contrast, the use of the psalms in the main service on Sunday came to be associated with the readings assigned to a particular Sunday in the developing Church Year. This tendency toward a thematic use of the psalms continued with the eventual adoption of specific texts for each Sunday of the year. By the fifth century, the Introit was on its way to being well established, with a different portion of a psalm assigned as the entrance music for each week. The use of the psalm between the readings eventually evolved into what became known as the Gradual. Psalm verses were regularly sung at the gathering of the offering, and in many places psalms were appointed for use during the distribution of the Sacrament.[11] In the course of the Middle Ages, it was the choir that assumed the task of singing these texts. As composers expanded the complexity of the musical settings of these Propers, they gradually shortened the length of the psalms texts that they used, reducing most of them to no more than a verse or two. Thus, by the end of the Middle Ages, the service incorporated the psalms in numerous places, though only brief excerpts of these psalms were sung.

Like theologians before him, Martin Luther valued the psalms quite highly.[12] As a member of the Augustinian order, he had an intimate familiarity with them through his participation in the Daily Office. His first university lectures were on the psalms, a topic to which he returned several times later in his career. Far beyond any scholarly interests in the psalms, however, was Luther's practical appreciation of their content. In his preface to the Psalter, he suggested that the Holy Spirit had compiled the Psalter as a short summary of the entire Scriptures—the

---

[11] Holladay, *The Psalms through Three Thousand Years*, 175.

[12] For a general overview, see Holladay, *The Psalms through Three Thousand Years*, 192–95.

perfect resource for a person who did not have the time to read the whole Bible![13]

In his liturgical reforms of 1523 and 1526, Luther referred only briefly in several places to the use of the psalms. He spoke approvingly of the Introits that had been handed down through the centuries, though he offered the caveat that his preference was for the singing of full psalms rather than the very abbreviated versions preserved in the historic Introits. Likewise, he acknowledged the importance of retaining the use of the psalms in the daily services, though he cautioned against the monastic practice of requiring the singing of too many psalms, lest the people be overburdened.[14] Beyond these general comments, however, Luther provided no additional directions. The Lutheran practice that ensued was one of conservative reform, with the retention of many of the ancient chants of the Introits and Graduals and the provision of only general principles regarding the use of the psalms in the Daily Office.

The reformation movements of the sixteenth century produced two other lines of development that reinvigorated the use of the psalms. The first occurred in the English Reformation through the work of Thomas Cranmer. One of his most significant liturgical reforms was the reinvigoration of the Daily Office for the common people. Whereas Luther gave only general directions about the restoration of daily services for the common folk, Cranmer provided specific details on how a cathedral office for the sixteenth century might look. Recognizing the impossibility of adhering to a weekly recitation of the Psalter in such a context, Cranmer proposed a plan for praying through the whole Psalter each month. The prominence that Cranmer gave to the psalms resulted in the development later in the century of what is commonly referred to today as Anglican chant, a simple but effective method of singing the psalms. In addition, English composers took up the task of writing countless choral settings of the psalms.

---

[13] Martin Luther, "Preface to the Psalter," AE 35:254.
[14] AE 53:22, 38, 69.

A second line of development that had tremendous impact on the use of the psalms came through the reforming efforts of John Calvin.[15] As with many theologians before him, Calvin treasured the psalms quite highly; his massive commentary on the psalms provides ample testimony. Coupled to this appreciation was his understanding of the value of congregational song, an insight he shared with Luther. Unlike Luther, however, whose own hymn texts demonstrated his desire to draw hymnody from a variety of sources,[16] Calvin believed not only that the psalms were the best source for the congregation's song but that they should be the only source. Thus, in the Reformed tradition metrical paraphrases of the psalms were to be the only hymns of the people.

The results of Calvin's initiative are impressive. By 1562, the entire Psalter appeared in metrical translation (French) in the *Genevan Psalter*. The richness of the collection was beyond doubt, with 125 different melodies and 110 distinct meters for the 150 psalms. Just as significant was the fact that this Psalter was eventually translated into nearly two dozen languages. Yet even before others were able to translate it, the concept of metrical paraphrases had caught on, especially in England, where the complete Psalter appeared in hymn form in a collection by Thomas Sternhold and John Hopkins also by the year 1562. With this flowering of creative activity, the Psalter was well on its way to a new level of use in the worship life of the church.[17]

Though there were further developments in the use of the psalms in worship during the ensuing centuries, I must move on to conclude this survey with a brief review of recent developments, specifically the use of the psalms among Lutherans in America. In comparison to the *Book of Common Prayer*, which has included the text of the complete Psalter since the 1662 edition, few Lutheran hymnals included any psalm texts until approximately a century ago. Within The Lutheran Church—Missouri Synod tradition, the first hymnal to include psalm texts was

---

[15] See Holladay, *The Psalms through Three Thousand Years*, 194–200; Westermeyer, *Te Deum*, 153–58.

[16] And that included about a half-dozen paraphrases of psalms, such as "From Depths of Woe" (*LSB* 607) for Psalm 130 and "May God Bestow on Us His Grace" (*LSB* 823/824) for Psalm 67.

[17] For more background, see Robin A. Leaver, "Metrical Psalmody," in *Key Words in Church Music*, 423–430.

the music edition of the *Evangelical Lutheran Hymn-book*, published in 1930. Like its successor, *The Lutheran Hymnal*, the psalms appeared with little formatting that might assist those who used them. A colon, often hidden in the middle of a line, separated the verses into their two halves, and the hymnals provided no directions or musical vehicle that would enable users to sing the psalms.

The publication of *Lutheran Book of Worship* (1978) and *Lutheran Worship* (1982) signaled a new expectation regarding the use of the psalms. The editors of these volumes designed a layout of the Psalter that emphasized the poetic nature of the text. More importantly, they provided a system for "pointing" the psalms that made it possible for worshipers to join in singing them with relative ease. This layout, which proved to be quite successful, was most recently carried forward in the successor worship books, namely, *Evangelical Lutheran Worship* (2006) and *Lutheran Service Book* (2006), respectively.

Given the fact that the Lutheran Church has for its nearly five-century history focused primarily on hymn singing, what might account for this renewed interest in the use of the psalms?[18]

RENEWAL OF PSALMODY IN THE SUNDAY LECTIONARY

To answer this question, we must first take a brief excursion into the world of lectionary revision at the end of the twentieth century. One of the many outcomes of the Second Vatican Council (1962–65) was the renewal of worship in the Roman Catholic Church. The first decree promulgated by the Council, the Constitution on the Sacred Liturgy (*Sacrosanctum Concilium*), launched numerous reforms that continue to impact the Church to this day. Pertinent to our topic was the call for a richer fare of readings from the Scriptures in the weekly Mass, a call that led to the development of a new lectionary commonly referred to today as the three-year lectionary.[19] Published in 1969, the *Ordo*

---

[18] This assertion does not deny the fact that the Lutheran Church has historically used psalmody in the Divine Service in such places as the Introit and Gradual. For the most part, those propers were handled by a choir that sang on behalf of the congregation. The recent interest in the psalms, by contrast, has focused much more intently on congregational participation in one form or another.

[19] Literature on this lectionary is extensive. For helpful background on its development, see Normand Bonneau, *The Sunday Lectionary: Ritual Word, Paschal Shape*

lectionum Missae quickly had an impact well beyond the boundaries of the Roman Church. Just four years later, the Inter-Lutheran Commission on Worship (ILCW) released its own version of this lectionary for the purpose of field testing it for a new, pan-Lutheran hymnal for Lutherans in North America.[20] Four decades later, its impact is still felt, with the vast majority of Lutherans in the United States and Canada using one form or another of the three-year lectionary.[21]

The most basic premise behind the organization of the three-year lectionary was the "in course" reading of the Synoptic Gospels over the span of three years—each Synoptic (Matthew, Mark, Luke) assigned to three series (A, B, C), respectively, with readings from the Gospel of John interspersed over all three years, especially during the seasons of Lent and Easter. The next most important feature, and in some ways its most significant contribution, was the reestablishment of readings from the Old Testament, readings that had not been heard with any regularity in the Sunday service since the sixth century. The drafters of the lectionary chose Old Testament texts that "complemented" the Gospel reading in some fashion in order to demonstrate the unity of the Scriptures.

It is here that we now return to our topic of psalmody, for in addition to the three readings assigned to each Sunday and festival, a psalm was also appointed. When the ILCW issued its test materials in 1973, it provided a brief explanation of the purpose of this psalm:

(Collegeville, MN: Liturgical Press, 1998). For a more in-depth examination of the hermeneutics behind the three-year lectionary, see Fritz West, *Scripture and Memory: The Ecumenical Hermeneutic of the Three-Year Lectionaries* (Collegeville, MN: Liturgical Press, 1997).

[20] Inter-Lutheran Commission on Worship, *The Church Year: Calendar and Lectionary*, Contemporary Worship 6 (Minneapolis: Augsburg; Philadelphia: Board of Publication, Lutheran Church in America; St. Louis: Concordia, 1973).

[21] Like the members of the Inter-Lutheran Commission on Worship, those who prepared *Lutheran Service Book* wrestled with the competing interests of the historic, one-year lectionary and the three-year lectionary. As the ILCW acknowledged in its 1973 proposal, "There are good precedents *both* for the annual repetition of a single set of well-chosen lessons *and* for the use of a greater variety of biblical passages over a longer span." *The Church Year: Calendar and Lectionary*, 14; emphasis added. In the end, those who prepared *LSB* opted to provide revised versions of both lectionaries.

1. Psalms sung in conjunction with readings from Scripture is a practice stemming from the synagogue. These Psalms are a major part of the service, not merely convenient transition pieces. . . .

2. Liturgically, the Psalms are to be corporate utterance, sung or spoken. In no case should they be used as additional lessons.[22]

Similarly, when the lectionary was revised in 1992 and published as the Revised Common Lectionary, the editors again gave explicit, albeit brief, instructions regarding the nature and purpose of the appointed psalm, namely, that the psalm functioned as a meditative response by the congregation on the first reading.[23] And, most recently, the guide for the use of *Evangelical Lutheran Worship* describes the psalm in this way: "The appointed psalm is meant to be not a fourth Bible reading but rather the communal response to the first reading. Having heard the Old Testament Reading, the assembly enters into the word with the words of a psalm. We might think of the psalm following the first reading as something like the hymn of the day that follows the gospel and sermon."[24] Though the various introductory resources for the three-year lectionary did not go into extensive detail explaining the nature of the appointed psalm, each did make it clear that the general purpose was to provide the congregation a response to the Old Testament Reading by means of a psalm.

How has the appointed psalm faired in congregations of The Lutheran Church—Missouri Synod? In visiting congregations, I get the sense that the psalm is seldom used as it was originally conceived as a response to the Old Testament Reading. There are various reasons that may be contributing to this state of affairs. First, if a congregation already uses the Introit, the use of an additional psalm may seem redundant (even though the appointed psalm is nearly always different from

[22] *The Church Year: Calendar and Lectionary*, 28–29.

[23] *The Revised Common Lectionary* (Washington DC: The Consultation on Common Texts, 1992), 11. The "Principles for Psalm Selection" as recorded in the CCT minutes from November 10, 1990, stated: "1. The psalm shall be chosen as a liturgical response to the first lection. 2. The psalms shall fit harmoniously within the general tenor of the celebration." Consultation on Common Texts, *The Revised Common Lectionary: 20th Anniversary Annotated Edition* (Minneapolis: Fortress Press, 2012), 217.

[24] Gail Ramshaw and Mons Teig, *Keeping Time: The Church's Year*, vol. 3 in the series *Using Evangelical Lutheran Worship* (Minneapolis: Augsburg Fortress, 2009), 54.

the Introit for the day). Second, when the three-year lectionary first appeared, and along with it the reintroduction of readings from the Old Testament, many pastors may have felt that including a psalm in addition to the Old Testament Reading was just a bit too much. Third, including the appointed psalm does lengthen the service, especially if it is sung. I have some sympathy for this concern, recognizing that pastors and church musicians do have to take the length of service into consideration.

REINTRODUCING THE PSALM IN THE SUNDAY LECTIONARY

Though the three-year lectionary has been in use among us now for nearly four decades, there is no time like the present to reacquaint ourselves with the appointed psalm and the role it can play in drawing us back into the lectionary itself, especially the Old Testament Reading. This exercise is not limited, however, only to those using the three-year lectionary. The working group that made revisions to the one-year lectionary for *LSB* also followed the same principle of choosing a psalm that provides commentary on or echoes the thoughts of the Old Testament Reading for the day.

I will begin by addressing a few practical matters related to the use of psalmody in worship.[25] One of the benefits of using the appointed psalm is that it provides an opportunity for congregational participation. The psalms as printed in the hymnal, along with the musical tones that are provided, offer a simple way for the entire assembly to participate. The best practice, however, is not simply to revert to this form of using the psalms every week. There are a host of options available, including all kinds of psalm settings that church publishers make available. These include, in particular, choral settings of psalms that involve the congregation by means of the repetition of a simple antiphon. There are also many strictly choral settings of psalms that, while not providing an opportunity for congregational participation, can be employed from time to time. Pastors would do well to consult

---

[25] Note that all of these suggestions also apply to the use of the psalms in the Daily Office, specifically in the section marked "Psalmody" under the heading "Additional Psalms."

with their church musicians, perhaps even perusing with them the latest catalog offerings from the music publishers in order to identify potential psalm settings.

Another source of psalm settings for the congregation consists of hymn paraphrases of the psalms. In the topical index of *LSB*, there is an entry for psalm paraphrases (p. 996). Some of these hymns cover only a portion of a psalm, so one must look carefully at the hymn text to ascertain its appropriateness for a given Sunday.

Regarding the concern over the length of the service, there are several practical suggestions to consider. First, if the Introit is regularly used, a congregation might consider omitting it and using the ap-pointed psalm (after the Old Testament Reading) instead. One would not have to follow the practice uniformly, but might institute it for one or more seasons of the church year, thus accentuating the change in seasons in the process. Second, if the church's choir typically sings an anthem during the service, on those occasions when the choir director schedules a psalm setting for a particular Sunday, one could move the "anthem" to the place immediately after the Old Testament Reading, thus allowing the psalm setting to perform double duty. If the psalm is sung by the congregation using one of the musical tones in *LSB* (p. xxvi), the use of one of the double tones (Tones I, J, and K) might be helpful. Singing a psalm in two-verse segments allows it to move along more quickly and is especially helpful when the psalm text is longer.[26]

For the remainder of this essay, I will examine specific examples from the lectionary in order to demonstrate some ways in which the appointed psalm flows out of the Old Testament Reading, specifically considering how it provides the congregation (and the preacher) the opportunity to reflect on the reading. Admittedly, the correlation of

---

[26] The only caution regarding the use of double tones is that there must be an even number of verses in the psalm in order for the tone to work correctly. Careful preparation requires more than simply checking the number of verses to see whether it is divisible by two. The versification of the psalms in *LSB* does not always follow the division for chanting. For example, Psalm 48 has 14 verses. Verses 12–14, however, are divided into only two couplets, thus resulting in an odd number of chanting couplets that will not work with a double tone. Conversely, while Psalms 42 and 100 have an odd number of verses, the division of the verses results in an even number of couplets, thus making it possible to sing them to a double tone.

psalm and Old Testament Reading for each Sunday is not always a perfect match; some Sundays the match seems made in heaven, while on other Sundays the relationship may not be all that obvious. For purposes of supporting my call for a greater use of the appointed psalm, the examples I will provide here, drawn fairly evenly from both the three- and one-year lectionaries, fall into the "made in heaven" category.

To begin, I will consider a few examples that are found in both lectionaries. On both Trinity 5 (in the one-year lectionary) and Proper 8 in Series C, the Old Testament Reading is the story of Elijah as he is running for his life from Queen Jezebel (1 Kings 19:9b–21; the reading for Trinity 5 begins with v. 11). Fearing that he was the only one left who feared the Lord, Elijah was near the point of despair. The appointed psalm in both lectionaries is Psalm 16. The first verse nicely sets the tone: "Preserve me, O God, for in you I take refuge." The entire psalm functions almost as a prayer of Elijah after receiving assurance from the Lord that he was certainly not the last, that there were still 7,000 who remained faithful. Thus might Elijah—and we—pray: "As for the saints in the land, they are the excellent ones, in whom is all my delight" (v. 3). As we pray this psalm, we come to understand better both the fears that Elijah faced as well as the comfort and hope that was his. Thus, v. 11 concludes the psalm—and also serves as the antiphon—with this note of joy: "You make known to me the path of life."

On Trinity 6 and Lent 3 in Series B, the Old Testament Reading is the giving of the commandments at Mount Sinai (Exodus 20:1–17). The appointed psalm for both lectionaries is Psalm 19, with v. 8 serving as the antiphon: "The precepts of the Lord are right, rejoicing the heart; the commandment of the Lord is pure, enlightening the eyes." Throughout, the psalmist rejoices in the goodness of God's Word. In vv. 12–13 the psalm ventures into what we would speak of as the second use of the Law: "Who can discern his errors? Declare me innocent from hidden faults. Keep back your servant also from presumptuous sins; let them not have dominion over me!" The psalm then concludes with a fitting prayer for us as we consider our lives in light of God's commandments: "Let the words of my mouth and the meditation of my

heart be acceptable in your sight, O Lord, my rock and my redeemer"
(v. 14).

A stunning pairing of reading and psalm occurs on Trinity 16 and
Proper 5 in Series C. Here the raising of the widow's son at Zarephath
(1 Kings 17:17–24) is followed by Psalm 30. The psalm gives full expression to the wide-ranging emotions that the widow must have experienced. The antiphon (v. 5b) encapsulates both extremes quite well:
"Weeping may tarry for the night, but joy comes with the morning." In
one verse after another, one can almost hear the widow's voice. Not surprisingly, the appointed Gospel for the day is the account of Jesus'
raising of the widow's son at Nain (Luke 7:11–17). For the pastor who
preaches on either the 1 Kings or Luke passage, this psalm offers ample
opportunity to draw his hearers into the story in order to understand
the utter joy that came upon these women who had found themselves in
the depths of despair: "You restored me to life from among those who
go down to the pit. . . . You have turned for me my mourning into
dancing" (vv. 3b, 11a). It is then but a short distance for the preacher to
make application to our own lives, demonstrating in the process how
the psalms wonderfully speak to us in our varied needs and experiences
in this life.

For Proper 6 in Series C, the Old Testament Reading is the story of
the prophet Nathan confronting David with his sins of adultery and
murder (2 Samuel 11:26—12:10, 13–14). One would expect Psalm 51 to
be the obvious choice since the inscription to that psalm specifically indicates that these were the words of David "when Nathan the prophet
went to him, after he had gone in to Bathsheba." Yet, the appointed
psalm for this day is not Psalm 51 but Psalm 32:1–7, another that flowed
from the pen of David. While Psalm 51 would certainly complement the
reading nicely, it is difficult to argue against Psalm 32. Consider these
words of v. 3: "For when I kept silent, my bones wasted away through
my groaning all day long." Given the fact that David was able to keep
his sin hidden from others for so long, one can only wonder what the
internal struggle must have been like for him. Could his thoughts,
however, have been those that we hear in the following verse: "For day
and night your hand was heavy upon me; my strength was dried up as
by the heat of summer" (32:4)? The antiphon chosen for this psalm

clearly embodies the main thrust of the reading, namely, David's confession: "I acknowledged my sin to you, and I did not cover my iniquity; I said, "I will confess my transgressions to the Lord," and you forgave the iniquity of my sin" (32:5). Given that the second half of this verse is familiar to anyone who has spoken the Confession and Absolution in Divine Service, Setting Three (the familiar Page 15 service from *TLH*), the preacher has an immediate point of contact in drawing his hearers into David's confession.[27]

Many psalms perform double duty in that they are paired with more than one Old Testament Reading; Psalm 103 services as a good example. In the one-year lectionary, it is paired with the Micah 7:18–20 reading for Trinity 3, which is nicely summarized in the opening sentence: "Who is a God like you, pardoning iniquity and passing over transgression for the remnant of his inheritance?" The antiphon assigned to this psalm is v. 8, that marvelous declaration of God's mercy that appears no less than eight times in the Old Testament:[28] "The Lord is merciful and gracious, slow to anger and abounding in steadfast love" (103:8). Yet, in the three-year lectionary this psalm is paired with no less than three different readings. Of particular interest is its use with two pericopes from the Joseph narrative, first when Joseph reveals his identity to his brothers for the first time (Genesis 45:3–15 for Epiphany 7 in Series C) and then also after the death of their father Jacob when Joseph's brother beg for his forgiveness for all that they had done to him (Genesis 50:15–21 for Proper 19 in Series A). For this second example, the antiphon assigned to the psalm shifts from v. 8 to v. 13: "As a father shows compassion to his children, so the Lord shows compassion to

---

[27] The decision to pair Psalm 32 to this reading rather than Psalm 51 was not an innovation of the Lectionary Committee for *LSB*; rather, that choice dates back to the original release of the three-year lectionary in 1969 and appears to have been the consistent choice ever since. This move demonstrates the rather obvious fact that there are other psalms that could be chosen; indeed, in some cases there are probably better choices waiting to be identified. In the case of the pericope recounting David's confession, for example, another psalm that would work admirably is Psalm 38. Another of the penitential psalms, this psalm would provide the preacher with a lengthy lament that encapsulates the thoughts that may have gone through David's mind as he came to the realization that his sin had finally been exposed.

[28] Exodus 34:6; Numbers 14:18; Nehemiah 9:17; Psalm 86:15; 103:8; 145:8; Joel 2:13; Jonah 4:2.

those who fear him." In a rather interesting twist, this verse calls to mind the dreams that Joseph had told his brothers years before, the very dreams that had stoked the enmity that they harbored toward him (Genesis 37:5–11). The twist in the story, however, is that despite the fact that the brothers had indeed bowed down to their brother, Joseph used his position not to lord it over them but to show compassion, even as God had shown compassion on him! It should not be lost on the preacher that the Gospel reading for this day contains Jesus' instructions to love one's enemies (Luke 6:27–38).[29]

While I could give many other examples of felicitous pairings of Old Testament texts and psalms, these few should suffice to demonstrate the riches that the appointed psalm in both the one- and three-year lectionaries offers. While there would be great benefit in giving the congregation the opportunity to sing the psalm occasionally, if not regularly, preachers should also take note of the psalm and the unique insights that it can bring to their understanding of the readings for the day.

The Psalter is indeed a rich treasury of prayer and praise, one that the lectionary is waiting to open to us.

---

[29] In the one-year lectionary this reading from Genesis 50 is paired with Psalm 138 on Trinity 4. I find this choice far less convincing than the choice of Psalm 103.

BONHOEFFER ON PSALM 119

John T. Pless

My first classroom experience with Dean Wenthe was in a summer course he taught at Concordia Theological Seminary in 1982 on "Preaching the Old Testament." In that course he drew upon Dietrich Bonhoeffer's devotional classic, *Prayerbook of the Bible: An Introduction to the Psalms,* to lead students into the depths of the psalms in the light of Christ Jesus who prayed them and enables us to pray them now. Throughout his career, Dr. Wenthe has prayed, taught, and studied the psalms, often making reference to Bonhoeffer's little book.[1] It seems good and right that this essay reflect something of my teacher, president, and now colleague's interest in the psalms. Like Bonhoeffer, Dean Wenthe understands the Christology of the psalms and the way that these sacred texts shape the life and character of those who belong to Christ. This essay will examine Bonhoeffer's treatment of one psalm in particular, Psalm 119.

HISTORICAL CONTEXT

In his American diary entry of July 9, 1939, Bonhoeffer identified Psalm 119 as his favorite psalm.[2] His "meditation" on Psalm 119 is fragmentary; he only completed the first twenty-one verses and offered two bare-bone outlines of his intentions for the whole psalm. Bonhoeffer

---

[1] See Dean O. Wenthe, "The Psalms as Homiletical Resources," *Concordia Pulpit Resources* 22 (November 27, 2011–February 19, 2012): 3–4.

[2] *Dietrich Bonhoeffer Works, Volume 15: Theological Education Underground: 1937–1940,* ed. Victoria J. Barnett, trans. Victoria Barnett, Claudia Bergmann, Peter Frick, and Scott Moore (Minneapolis: Fortress Press, 2012), 496 (hereafter DBW 15).

worked on his manuscript in the winter of 1939–1940; he never brought
it to completion in the form of a publishable document, though it would
influence his *Prayerbook of the Bible*, which appeared later in 1940. It
was during this tumultuous period that Bonhoeffer was drawn to the
psalms for strength and direction; Psalm 119 was especially compelling
for Bonhoeffer. Eberhard Bethge, Bonhoeffer's close friend and later his
biographer, notes that while Bonhoeffer was pastor to the German
congregations in London, he visited the Community of the Resurrection
in Mirfield in March 1935, where Psalm 119 was recited liturgically
every day. According to Bethge, this psalm became the biblical passage
most frequently quoted by Bonhoeffer."[3]

In *Prayerbook of the Bible*, Bonhoeffer describes Psalm 119 as a
repetitive doxology of divine love that invites ongoing meditation:

> Psalm 119 becomes especially difficult for us perhaps because of its
> length and uniformity. Here a rather slow, quiet, patient movement
> from word to word, from sentence to sentence is helpful. We recog-
> nize, then, that the apparent repetitions are in fact always new varia-
> tions on one theme, the love of God's word. As this love can have no
> end, so also through all of life, and in their simplicity they become the
> prayer of the child, the adult, and the elderly.[4]

---

[3] Eberhard Bethge, *Dietrich Bonhoeffer: A Biography*, rev. ed., trans. Eric Mosbacher et
al. (Minneapolis: Fortress Press, 2000), 412. Bethge also notes that in the late winter of
1938, Bonhoeffer "was finally able to make some progress with his meditation on Psalm
119. At the university he had learned that this was the most boring of the psalms; now
he regarded its interpretation as the climax of his theological life. For years he had tried
to penetrate the mystery of its verses" (667).

[4] *Dietrich Bonhoeffer Works, Volume 5: Life Together and Prayerbook of the Bible*, ed.
Geffrey B. Kelly, trans. James H. Burtness (Minneapolis: Fortress Press, 1996), 165
(hereafter DBW 5). Bonhoeffer's appreciation for Psalm 119 is in contrast to Artur
Weiser's claim that "this psalm, the most comprehensive of all the psalms, is a
particularly artificial product of religious poetry," representing an early stage in the
development of a legalistic spirituality of which "one cannot fail to realize that a piety
such as that expressed in the psalm, according to which God's word and law take the
place of God himself and his wondrous works (v. 13), are even worshiped (v. 48) and
become the source of comfort which as a rule is bestowed upon man by divine saving
grace (vv. 50, 92), carries with it the germs of a development which was bound to end in
the self-righteousness of the Pharisees and scribes." Artur Weiser, *The Psalms: A
Commentary*, trans. Herbert Hartwell (Philadelphia: Westminster Press, 1962), 740–41.
Far from seeing Psalm 119 as an artificial and ultimately legalistic religious construct,

Because the psalm deals with the "way" of the Lord and his righteous ones, it encompasses the whole of Christian existence. It frames the life of faithfulness from birth to death.

Bonhoeffer first lectured on the psalms at the Preachers' Seminary in Finkenwalde in 1935. Bethge observes that "this had become necessary for the entire seminar because its daily and detailed reading of the psalms—unusual within the German Evangelical tradition—had raised a number of questions."[5] It was the Old Testament scholars, in particular, who objected to Bonhoeffer's unscientific reading of the psalms. Patrick D. Miller notes, "His biblical interpretation has not been taken very seriously by biblical scholars, whose attachment to historical-critical methods has kept them from seeing how Bonhoeffer read the text not literally but seriously and saw in it a constant witness to Jesus Christ."[6]

The advocacy of the psalms as appropriate for liturgical and devotional use appeared in the eyes of many of Bonhoeffer's contemporaries to be archaic at best and religiously offensive at worse.[7] After all, it was Bonhoeffer's great teacher, Adolph von Harnack, who had not only marginalized the Old Testament but suggested that it was theologically deadweight to be abandoned by an enlightened church. It was Harnack

---

Bonhoeffer understood the psalm as an inexhaustible benefaction of God's favor that anchors the believer in life with God.

[5] Bethge, *Dietrich Bonhoeffer: A Biography*, 434.

[6] Patrick Miller, "Dietrich Bonhoeffer and the Psalms," *Princeton Theological Seminary Bulletin* 15 (1994): 274. See also Martin Kuske, *The Old Testament as the Book of Christ: An Appraisal of Bonhoeffer's Interpretation*, trans. S. T. Kimbrough Jr. (Philadelphia: Westminster Press, 1976). Kuske offers a positive assessment of Bonhoeffer's reading of the Old Testament in contrast to the Old Testament scholars and theologians of Bonhoeffer's day who saw the Old Testament as pre-Christian writings that, at best, stood in dark contrast to the brightness of the New Testament Gospel. For a critical assessment, see Walter Harrelson, "The Source of Answers to the Question Concerning Jesus Christ: Bonhoeffer and the Bible," in *The Place of Bonhoeffer: Problems and Possibilities in His Thought*, ed. Martin E. Marty (New York: Association Press, 1962), 113–39.

[7] For a brief but helpful overview of the fate of the Psalter after the Reformation, see "History of Interpretation since the Reformation: 'Accredited Exegesis,' " in Bruce K. Waltke and James M. Houston, *The Psalms in Christian Worship: A Historical Commentary* (Grand Rapids: Eerdmans, 2010), 80–112. See also Brevard S. Childs, "The Impact of the Critical Approach on the Psalter," in *Introduction to the Old Testament as Scripture* (Philadelphia: Fortress Press, 1979), 508–11.

who declared, "To reject the Old Testament in the second century was a mistake which the church rightly repudiated; to retain it in the sixteenth century was a fate which the Reformation could not yet avoid; but to continue to keep it in Protestantism as a canonical document after the nineteenth century is the consequence of religious and ecclesiastical paralysis."[8] Bonhoeffer's insistence that the psalms be maintained in the Church and understood as Scripture that bears Christ, is fulfilled by him, and is prayed by him so as to incorporate the Church into these petitions of supplication and doxology cut against reigning exegetical and dogmatic opinion, thus earning him the label of a "biblicist."[9]

In contrast to this dismissive tagging of Bonhoeffer, John Webster offers a salutary corrective:

> In interpreting Bonhoeffer's work, it is fatally easy to take insufficient account of the fact that "most of Bonhoeffer's work is biblical exposition" (E. G. Wendel, *Studien zur Homiletik Dietrich Bonhoeffers*) apart from his two dissertations, *Sanctorum Communio* and *Act and Being*. Most scholars of Bonhoeffer have gravitated towards other issues: sociality and ethical, most of all. One result of this is the over-theorized picture of Bonhoeffer: the practical directness of Bonhoeffer's biblical writings and the sense that biblical exposition is the task of the theologian in which theory may be a hindrance has been lost from view.[10]

---

[8] Cited by Kuske, *The Old Testament as the Book of Christ*, 9.

[9] Such is the judgment of Wolf Krötke, "Bonhoeffer and Luther," in *Bonhoeffer's Intellectual Formation*, ed. Peter Frick (Tübingen: Mohr Siebeck, 2008), 59. "Krötke writes: "Bonhoeffer seems to accept unquestioningly the word of Scripture—which he now identifies with Jesus Christ himself—and thus assigns it priority in the act of understanding before the Spirit of Christ. Hence he falls prey to Biblicism."

[10] John Webster, *Holy Scripture: A Dogmatic Sketch* (Cambridge: Cambridge University Press, 2003), 78–79. Also note Bonhoeffer's striking comments in a letter written on April 8, 1936, to his brother-in-law Rudiger Schleicher, whose theological position was more reflective of the older liberalism of Adolph von Harnack. After explaining to his brother-in-law that God's Word reveals the cross, thus spelling death and judgment of all our ways before God, Bonhoeffer says,

> Does this perspective somehow make it understandable to you that I do not want to give up the Bible as this strange Word of God at any point, that I intend with all my powers to ask what God wants to say to us here? Any other place outside the Bible has become too uncertain for me. I fear that I will only encounter some divine double of myself there. Does this somehow help you understand why I am

In his work on Psalm 119, we see Bonhoeffer the biblical expositor working pastorally with the scriptural text for the sake of the life of the Church created by the Word of God and for Christians called to the life of discipleship that is sustained by God's Word.

WHY PSALM 119?

Bonhoeffer considered mediation on Psalm 119 "the climax of his theological life."[11] It is this psalm that served as a hermeneutic for Bonhoeffer's understanding not only of the whole Psalter but of Christian existence itself. Here Bonhoeffer's thought parallel's Luther.[12] Oswald Bayer has noted the significance of Psalm 119 for Luther: "In Luther's eyes, the individuality of our own life's journey reflects the

---

> prepared for a *sacrificium intellectus*—just in these matters, and only in these matters, with respect to the one, true God! And who does not bring to some passages his sacrifice of the intellect, in the confession that he does not yet understand this or that passage in Scripture, but is certain that even they will be revealed one day as God's own Word? I would rather make that confession than try to say according to my own opinion: this is divine, that is human." Dietrich Bonhoeffer, *Meditating on the Word*, trans. David McI. Grace (Cambridge: Cowley Publications, 2000), 37.

Bonhoeffer continues, describing how this approach has opened the Scriptures to him:

> And now let me tell you quite personally that since I learned to read the Bible in this way—and that was not so long ago—it has become daily more wonderful to me. I read it mornings and evenings, often also during the day. And each day I take up a text, which I have before me the entire week, and I attempt to immerse myself in it completely, in order to really listen to it. I know that without this I could no longer rightly live, let alone believe" (37–38).

This newfound approach to reading and meditating on the Scriptures is evident in Bonhoeffer's work with Psalm 119 less than two years after writing this letter.

[11] Bethge, *Dietrich Bonhoeffer: A Biography*, 667.

[12] Brian Brock writes: "There is ample evidence that Bonhoeffer's approach to the Psalter was influenced by Luther, who thought of the Psalter as a divinely given form for addressing God. Bonhoeffer follows Luther in understanding the book as a 'children's primer' for learning to talk to God, in assuming that only one book in the Bible is devoted to training our speech and affections towards God and in his Christological approach to the Psalms. There are striking parallels between Bonhoeffer's exegesis of Psalm 119 and Luther's treatment of it in his first lecture series, especially regarding the central place of the undivided heart, the primacy of the petition for grace, and the centrality of relying on God's Word rather than our own interpretations of Scripture." Brian Brock, " 'Success and Failure': Public Disasters, Works of Love, and the Inwardness of Faithfulness," in *Who Am I? Bonhoeffer's Theology through His Poetry*, ed. Bernd Wannenwetsch (London: T&T Clark, 2009), 63.

universality of the course of God's word. He finds this connection between the individual and the universal prefigured in Holy Scripture,
especially Psalm 119. Those who pray this psalm fully surrender their
own destiny to the destiny of God's word. They see their relationship to
God as nothing else than a relationship to his word."[13]

THE PATH OF THE TORAH

Bonhoeffer sees this theme of the believer's destiny comprehended in
God's Word in the opening section of his meditation on Psalm 119:

> The path between the beginning and this end is the turn [Wandel]
> within God's law. It is the life under the word of God in its utter mul-
> titude of forms, in its richness, in its exhaustible fullness of knowledge
> and experiences. In truth there is only one danger on this path,
> namely, to want to step back behind this beginning or to lose sight of
> the goal, which is the same thing. In a moment the path ceases to be a
> path of grace and faith. It ceases to be God's own path.[14]

Only God creates the beginning and determines the ending.

For Bonhoeffer, both beginning and ending are given. Here
Bonhoeffer's reading of the psalm is completely anti-synergistic.
Christians are delivered from "never-ending beginnings."[15] So Bon-
hoeffer writes,

> To wait for a new beginning, day after day, thinking that one has
> found it countless times only to declare it lost in the evening: this is
> the complete destruction of faith in God who has set the beginning
> once through his forgiving and renewing word in Jesus Christ, that is,
> in my baptism, in my rebirth, and conversion. God has converted me
> to himself once and for all: I was not the one who converted myself to
> God once and for all. God has set this beginning; this is the joyful

---

[13] Oswald Bayer, *Theology the Lutheran Way*, ed. and trans. Jeffrey G. Silcock and Mark
C. Mattes (Grand Rapids: Eerdmans, 2007), 39. Note Bonhoeffer: "Truly, these are the
ones who have ventured to accept God's deeds as having happened for them, who
proceed from the beginning God has accomplished. They are like the victors after a
battle won. They are like the living who have come through the valley of death. They are
like the wanderers for whom the sun rises after a dark night and who have found their
way. Now they reach forth toward a new future; now they walk from victory to victory;
now they are on the path in the light" DBW 15, 500.

[14] DBW 15, 497.

[15] DBW 15, 497.

certainty of faith. Therefore, I am not to attempt setting countless beginnings of my own next to the one beginning of God.[16]

Using the Old Testament imagery of "the way," Bonhoeffer confesses that the believer is one whose feet God has set on a path or way of which Christ is himself the Alpha and the Omega. The Christian determines neither his beginning nor his ending; rather, he is taken up into Christ, living and moving in him as one who is created for life with God. From Psalm 119, Bonhoeffer develops an understanding of the Christian life as shaped by the Law of the Lord, that is, the Torah.

Bonhoeffer is not completely consistent in how he understands the nature of the Torah.[17] At points in the manuscript, he seems to equate it with *nomos*, while at other junctures he appears to see the Torah as inclusive of both God's judgment of sin and his promise of forgiveness. Bonhoeffer can speak of the difference between life under the Law and life in the Law: "Whoever is caught in the search for a new beginning is under the law and is worn down and killed by it. Whoever comes from the found beginning [*sic*] is within the law of God, is upheld and preserved by it for life."[18] The language of being "under the Law" echoes the Pauline usage (e.g., Romans 3:19; 6:14; Galatians 3:23–25; 4:4). To be under this Law is condemnation and death, but those who are in Christ—the One who has fulfilled the Law and by his atonement is "the end of the law" (Romans 10:4)—are now "within the law of God" according to Bonhoeffer. For Bonhoeffer, God's Law is inseparable from its fulfillment in Jesus Christ: "Whoever asks about the law will be

---

[16] DBW 15, 497.

[17] Here note Hans-Joachim Kraus' discussion of the difficulty in determining a precise definition of Torah. See Hans-Joachim Kraus, *Psalms 60–150: A Continental Commentary*, trans. Hilton C. Oswald (Minneapolis: Fortress Press, 1993), 413–14. See also the chapter "The Torah as Mediator" in Walter Brueggemann, *Theology of the Old Testament* (Minneapolis: Fortress Press, 1997), 578–99.

[18] DBW 15, 498. For a further clarification of Bonhoeffer's statement, see his *Prayerbook of the Bible*: "The three psalms (1, 19, 119) that in a special way make the law of God the object of thanksgiving, praise, and petition, wish above all to make clear to us the blessing of the law. Under 'law,' then, is to be chiefly understood as the entire redemptive act of God and directions for a new life in obedience. Joy in the law, in the commandments of God, fills us when God has given to our life the great transformation that comes through Jesus Christ" DBW 5, 164. Also see Bernd Janowski, "Freude an der Tora. Psalm 1 als Tor zum Psalter," *Evangelisches Theologie* 67 (2007): 18–31.

reminded of Jesus Christ and the redemption from servitude to sin and death that in him has been accomplished for all human beings and will be reminded of the new beginning set by God in Jesus Christ for all human beings."[19]

Bonhoeffer goes on to explain that the Law is not reduced to a teaching of morality, an ethical norm, or an ideal existence to be achieved. Instead,

> God's law is inseparable from his redemptive deed. The God of the Ten Commandments is the God who has led you out of the land of Egypt (Exod. 20:2). God gives his law to those whom he loves, whom God has chosen and accepted (Deut. 7:7–11). To know God's law is grace and joy (Deut. 4:6–10). It is the way of life for those who accept the grace of God (Lev. 18:5)."[20]

Bonhoeffer seeks to avoid any legalistic rendering of the Torah:

> Only when we realize that the decision has already been made, that the beginning has already occurred, that the deed has already been done by none other than God, only when we have been affected and drawn into the decision, the beginning, and the deed of God, can we hear God's commandment as the law of life [Lebensgesetz] of those for whom God has already done everything and who are now "within the law."[21]

Being "within the law" is not a moral or spiritual achievement; it is the gift of the God who justifies the ungodly by grace through faith alone. These are the blessed or happy ones.[22]

Bonhoeffer's discussion of the Torah gives evidence of the influence of Karl Barth.[23] Bonhoeffer reflects Barth's synthesis of Law and Gospel when he writes, "The great wonder in God's law is the revelation of the

---

[19] DBW 15, 499.

[20] DBW 15, 499.

[21] DBW 15, 499.

[22] "Happy are those, for they are freed from the agony of their own beginnings; happy are those because they have overcome all the internal divisions that arise from discrepancy between their own beginnings and the beginning by God; they are 'complete,' 'whole,' undivided, unassailable" DBW 15, 500.

[23] Note, for example, Barth's formulation: "The Law is nothing else than the necessary form of the Gospel." Karl Barth, "Gospel and Law," in Community, Church, and State: Three Essays, ed. Will Herberg (New York: Doubleday Anchor, 1960), 80.

Lord Jesus Christ. Through him, the word receives life, contradictions receive unity, revealed things receive unfathomable depth."[24] Statements like this would indicate that theologically Bonhoeffer might be situated somewhere between Luther and Barth.[25]

ATTENTIVENESS TO GOD'S WORD

A key aspect of Bonhoeffer's work on Psalm 119 is his focus on the believer as one who is attentive to the Word of God. While Bonhoeffer does not make an explicit use of Luther's triad, *oratio, meditatio, tentatio*,[26] all three are found in his exposition of the psalm.

Oratio is seen under the aspects of prayer, praise, and thanksgiving. Christians are recipients of God's gifts in body and soul; they are enabled to acclaim him as the giver of every good and perfect gift. Bonhoeffer cautions against a Christianity that would attempt "to be more spiritual than God himself,"[27] using piety as an excuse for not acknowledging material blessings. Of these people Bonhoeffer says, "They want to be the schoolmasters of the Holy Scripture and thus deny themselves the full joy of their Christianity and deny God the thanks-

---

[24] DBW 15, 521.

[25] Here it is important to recall Bonhoeffer's partnership with Barth in the production of the "Barmen Declaration," which confessed "Jesus Christ, as he is attested to Holy Scripture, is the one Word of God which we have to hear in life and which we have to trust and obey in life and in death," cited in Eberhard Busch, *The Barmen Theses Then and Now* (Grand Rapids: Eerdmans, 2010), 19. This leads Oswald Bayer to observe that the theologies of both Barth and Bonhoeffer bear "a distinctively Hegelian stamp." Bayer, *Theology the Lutheran Way*, 82; see also 193–96. Gerhard Ebeling, who studied with Bonhoeffer at Finkenwalde, also provides a discussion of Bonhoeffer's theological relationship to Barth. See Gerhard Ebeling, "The 'Non-religious Interpretation of Biblical Concepts,' " in *Word and Faith* (Philadelphia: Fortress Press, 1963), 98–161. Also see Andreas Pangritz, "Dietrich Bonhoeffer: 'Within, Not Outside the Barthian Movement,' " in *Bonhoeffer's Intellectual Formation*, ed. Peter Frick (Tübingen: Mohr Siebeck, 2008), 245–82, and Michael DeJonge, *Bonhoeffer's Theological Formation: Berlin, Barth, and Protestant Theology* (Oxford: Oxford University Press, 2012).

[26] See Luther's "Preface to the Wittenberg Edition of Luther's German Writings," AE 34:279–88. Luther speaks of *oratio, meditatio, tentatio* "as three rules amply presented" throughout Psalm 119 (285). For an extensive and insightful treatment of this triad, see Oswald Bayer, "Theology as *Askesis*: On Struggling Faith," in *Festkrift für Peter Widman: Gudstankens aktualitet*, ed. M. W. Petersen, B. K. Holm, and A. Jacobsen (Copenhagen: Forlaget ANIS, 2010), 35–54; Oswald Bayer, *Theology the Lutheran Way*, 33–65.

[27] DBW 15, 500.

giving that is owed to his great kindness."[28] Knowing the truth—
Bonhoeffer cites 1 Timothy 4:3—Christians are enabled to give thanks
as those "who walk in the law of the Lord."[29]

This thanksgiving is not self-directed; this would be carnal
thanksgiving or worldly thanksgiving. "The thanksgiving of the world
always refers ultimately to itself; through gratitude one seeks merely the
higher confirmation and consecration of one's own happiness."[30] Such a
thanksgiving, Bonhoeffer argues, would be in the way of the Pharisee in
Luke 18, "because in his thanksgiving he saw only himself and did not
receive the gift in humility but abused it against his neighbor."[31]

Echoes of Luther's *meditatio* are to be heard in Bonhoeffer as well.
Meditation involves the ear hearing and the heart dwelling on the words
of the Lord:

> Because his commandments are supposed to remind us daily and
> witness to us that God is the Lord, a purely external fulfillment of the
> commandments is not enough. Not only lips and hands but an entire
> undivided heart must be involved. It must search continuously for the
> one of whom the testimonies speak. In commandments, worship
> services, and prayers, the heart is seeking the one who gives every-
> thing."[32]

There is permanence to this meditation that engages the Christian. "We
are to hold on to the commandments when they come from God to us,
diligently, earnestly, with all our strength, so that they cannot be lost to
us or torn away from us. God's commandment is there not only for the
moment but permanently. It wants to enter us deeply and wants to be
held fast in every condition of life."[33]

---

[28] DBW 15, 501. Also note Brock: "During this period Bonhoeffer was deeply immersed in the psalms, especially Psalm 119, where the blessedness of the righteous has a particularly high profile. As he comments on Ps. 119:1 ('How blessed are those whose way is blameless, who walk in the Law of the LORD!') Bonhoeffer becomes more certain that, correctly understood, the blessedness of God's children is a very concrete, earthly flourishing." Brock, "Success and Failure," 54.

[29] DBW 15, 502.

[30] DBW 15, 508–509.

[31] DBW 15, 509.

[32] DBW 15, 503.

[33] DBW 15, 505.

This is meditation governed by the First Commandment. "When God's Word has struck us, we may say: I seek you with my whole heart. For we would seek an idol halfheartedly, but never God himself. God needs the whole heart."[34]

Drawing on the psalmist's language in verse 11 that God's Word is treasured in the heart, Bonhoeffer alludes to the parable of the sower and the seed in Matthew 13 to make the point that "when God's word comes to us, it wants to be secured in fertile ground."[35] Essentially, meditation moves beyond the mind to the heart for Bonhoeffer:

> If I have God's word only in my mind, my mind will often be pre-occupied with other things, and toward God, I will be missing. There-fore, it is never enough to have read God's word. It must enter us deeply, dwell in us like the Holy of Holies in the sanctuary, so that we do not stray in thoughts, words, and deeds. Often it is better to read little and slowly in the Scriptures, and to wait until it has penetrated into us, than to know too much about God's word but not to 'treasure' it.[36]

Meditation is necessary for genuine proclamation. The words of the Lord lodged in the heart are to be expressed with the mouth: "The whole heart must belong to the word of the God before we learn to place our lips also entirely into the service of Jesus Christ."[37] This means that for Bonhoeffer proper exegesis is impossible apart from meditation:

> Meditation, that is, prayerful consideration of the Scriptures, and exegesis are indispensable for the one who honestly seeks God's pre-cepts, and not his own thoughts. A theologian who does not practice both denies his office. But every Christian will be granted the time that he needs if he truly seeks it. Meditation means to take God's word prayerfully in my heart; exegesis means to recognize and understand God's word in Scripture as God's word. The one does not exist

---

[34] DBW 15, 513.

[35] DBW 15, 513.

[36] DBW 15, 514. Compare Bonhoeffer with Luther's description of meditation in his commentary on Deuteronomy 14:1 of 1525: "To chew the cud, however, is to take up the Word with delight and meditate with supreme diligence, so that (according to the proverb) one does not permit it to go in one ear and out the other, but holds it firmly in heart, swallows it, and absorbs it into the intestines" AE 9:136.

[37] DBW 15, 515.

without the other. Both are reflections, which need to be practiced daily."[38]

This daily practice is rooted in a "delight" (Psalm 119:16) in the Lord's words. "I do not forget the things in which I delight."[39] Hence Bonhoeffer sees mediation as an exercise in both remembrance and repetition. Where these are lacking there can only be unbelief.

The remedy for unbelief is God's faithfulness to and in his words; thus, Bonhoeffer speaks of the Christian's meditation as a prayerful receptivity of God's mercy in Christ so that "each new day it is a new prayer, when we open our eyes in the morning and close them at night, that God may give us illumined eyes of the heart, eyes wide open when the day wants to deceive our natural eyes and when night dupes us with bad dreams, eyes opened and enlightened, filled at all times with the wonder of God's law."[40] So Bonhoeffer describes the Christian as living with the petition of blind Bartimaeus (Mark 10:46–52), praying for sight. "It is a gift of grace," writes Bonhoeffer, "to recognize one's own blindness to God's word and be able to pray for opened eyes."[41] This prayer is answered when "within the human words I hear God's eternal word; in past history I recognize the present God and his work for my salvation."[42]

Less clear in Bonhoeffer's reading of Psalm 119 is the place of *tentatio*, but it is not absent. Bonhoeffer warns against a preoccupation with the agonizing aspects of life: "There are Christians who want to be more spiritual than God himself. They like to talk about struggle,

---

[38] DBW 15, 517. Here see the chapter "Bonhoeffer: Exegesis as Meditation on the Torah of the Lord," in Brian Brock, *Singing the Ethos of God: On the Place of Christian Ethics in Scripture* (Grand Rapids: Eerdmans, 2007), 77–95. Here Bonhoeffer is reclaiming ground lost to Johann Salomo Semler (1725–91), who denounced Luther's triad as unscientific. See Bayer, "Theology as *Askesis*," 38.

[39] DBW 15, 518.

[40] DBW 15, 520. See also the discussion of Bonhoeffer's understanding of God's faithfulness in Psalm 119 in Brock, *Singing the Ethos of God*, 59. For the centrality of this theme in the Psalter, see Rolf Jacobson, "The Faithfulness of the Lord Endures Forever: The Theological Witness of the Psalter," in *Soundings in the Theology of the Psalms: Perspectives and Methods in Contemporary Scholarship*, ed. Rolf Jacobson (Minneapolis: Fortress Press, 2011), 111–37.

[41] DBW 15, 521.

[42] DBW 15, 521.

asceticism, suffering, and cross, yet it is almost embarrassing to them that the Holy Scripture does not talk exclusively about that, but that it cannot speak often enough about the happiness of the pious, about the well-being of the righteous."[43] Yet he recognizes the author of Psalm 119 as one who has experienced misery and affliction that leads him to be thankful for God's gracious dealings with trust and contentment.

The primary image that parallels Luther's *tentatio* in Bonhoeffer's treatment of Psalm 119 is that of the Christian as a "stranger." Citing the biblical examples of Abraham, Jacob, and David, Bonhoeffer writes, "When God's word first encountered me, it made me a stranger on this earth."[44] Being a stranger entails displacement and suffering, making us totally dependent of the One who calls us to a guest-like existence: "But because I am nothing on earth but a guest, without rights, without support, without security, because God himself has made me so weak and lowly, he has given me one pledge for my goal: his word."[45]

God has given the promise that his Word will not be withdrawn. But this promise is contested by our own imagination:

> For the one who has become a stranger on earth according to God's will and call, there is in truth only one thought that can fill him with deep fear, namely, to no longer recognize God's will, to no longer know what God demands of him. Certainly, God is often hidden to us in our personal lives or in his actions in history; this is not what is alarming. But when God's revealed commandment is obscured, so that we no longer recognize from God's word what we are to do, it is a severe trial.[46]

For Bonhoeffer, it is precisely at this point that we are tempted to "act according to my own principles" rather than God's Word.[47] Therefore the psalmist teaches sojourning believers to pray, "do not hide your commandments from me" (Psalm 119:19).

---

[43] DBW 15, 501.

[44] DBW 15, 521.

[45] DBW 15, 522.

[46] DBW 15, 523.

[47] DBW 15, 523. Here also see Bonhoeffer's 1938 "Bible Study on Temptation," in DBW 15, 386–415, and his commentary on the temptation of Eve in "Creation and Fall" in DBW 3, 103–20.

CONCLUSION

Bonhoeffer's treatment of Psalm 119 came at a particularly crucial juncture in his life. The seminary communities he sought to nurture at Zingst and Finkenwald had been disbanded a few years earlier. No doubt, some of his reflections on the time spent with the training of pastors for the Confessing Church, embodied in his 1938 book, *Life Together*,[48] informed his exposition of Psalm 119. Just months before (July 1939), Bonhoeffer made the fateful decision to leave Union Seminary in New York and return to Germany. He worked on his *Ethics* in proximity to the time he produced the fragment on Psalm 119.[49] There is little doubt that these and other factors shaped and sharpened his engagement with this biblical text so dear to him. Bonhoeffer's book on the psalms, *Prayerbook of the Bible*, published in 1940 as the last of his works published during his lifetime, condensed and carried forward numerous themes from his fragmentary work on Psalm 119. Bonhoeffer has left Christians in general, and pastors in particular, with a profound and evocative reading of Psalm 119 that promises to enrich our praying, speaking, and living in Christ.

---

[48] Bonhoeffer provided concrete instructions for how the psalms were to be prayed corporately in *Life Together*; see DBW 5, 53–58. His earlier work on Psalm 119 is reflected in this book: Here Bonhoeffer heightens the repetitive nature of the Psalm indicating that prayer is not simply an expression of human need or a gushing from one's heart but a continual process of hearing, appropriating, and impressing of God's will in Christ Jesus on the mind.

[49] Here see the insightful essay by Brian Brock, "Bonhoeffer and the Bible in Christian Ethics: Psalm 119, the Mandates, and Ethics as a 'Way,' " *Studies in Christian Ethics* 18, no. 3 (2005): 7–29.

THE LITURGICAL HYMNODY
OF ST. AMBROSE OF MILAN

Timothy C. J. Quill

INTRODUCTION: A SERMON AGAINST AUXENTIUS[1]

[The Arians] declare that the people have also been led astray by the strains of my hymns. I certainly do not deny it. That is a lofty strain, and there is nothing more powerful than it. For what has more power than the confession of the Trinity which is daily extolled by the mouth of the whole people? All eagerly vie one with the other in confessing the faith, and know how to praise in verse the Father, Son, and Holy Spirit. So they all have become teachers, who scarcely could be disciples.[2]

Ambrose preached these words to calm the fears of people in the wake of the imperial decree demanding the basilica be turned over to the anti-trinitarian Arians. This brief quote on the nature and purpose of Christian congregational hymnody has few rivals. The more one probes the theological, historical, musical, poetic, and pastoral context in which Bishop Ambrose preached these words, the more one can appreciate their brilliance and relevance. They summarize the approach

---

[1] Auxentius should not be confused with Bishop Auxentius who died in AD 373 and was succeeded by Ambrose. This Auxentius was "recognized by the Arians of Milan as their bishop, but for convenience, and to avoid unpopularity with the Catholics, had ceased to call himself Auxentius, since that name brought with it the recollection of the Arian predecessor of Ambrose, and adopted the name Mercurinus." Robinson Thornton, *St. Ambrose: His Life, Times, and Teaching* (London: Wyman and Sons Printers, 1897), 54.

[2] Ambrose, "Sermon Against Auxentius on the Giving Up of the Basilica," *NPNF*[2], 10:436.

to congregational singing used by the man who is often called the father of western liturgical hymnody.[3] In this essay I will examine the homiletical text of St. Ambrose within its historical and theological context, asking whether and how the authentic hymns of Ambrose reflect the views expressed by the bishop in his sermon against Auxentius.

CONTEXT: QUOD PERSECUTIONIS TEMPORE (QUANDO CONFESSION FIDEI EDENDA EST)

Ambrose (AD 340–397) was born fifteen years after the Council of Nicea, four years after the death of Arius, and one year after the death of Constantine the Great. Throughout Ambrose's life, the Church was engaged in a fierce struggle with the Arian heresy. When he was just over thirty years old, Ambrose was appointed "Consular" of *Aemilia Liguria*. Milan, its capital city, was an important political and ecclesiastical center. After Constantine moved the capital of the empire from Rome to Constantinople in AD 330, Milan became the new seat of the imperial government in the West. Subsequent bishops of Milan would be, in effect, the emperor's "pastor." When Ambrose moved to Milan, the sitting bishop was an Arian named Auxentius. Under Auxentius, none of the Orthodox or Nicene congregations were allowed to hold services in the city's church buildings. Three years later, Auxentius died and Ambrose was chosen the new bishop. The churches would now be returned to orthodox Christians. The western emperor at the time, Valentinian I, was a strong ruler and solid Nicene Christian. Valens, his brother and co-emperor in the East, was a staunch Arian. Valentinian's wife Justina was an Arian who kept her beliefs concealed while her husband was alive (or possibly had them restrained by him). After the death of Valentinian and the assassination of his son Gratian, Justina (mother of the new twelve-year-old emperor Valentinian II) demanded that the Portian Basilica located outside the walls of Milan be

---

[3] Erik Routley, *A Panorama of Christian Hymnody* (Collegeville, MN: Liturgical Press, 1979), 56. Ruth Messenger demonstrates that Ambrose's hymnody provided the inspiration for early medieval hymnody as well, with his hymns enjoying widespread use and considerable imitation. Ruth E. Messenger, "The Mozarabic Hymnal," *The Hymn* 16, no. 2 (April 1965): 50. See also Maurice P. Cunningham, "The Place of Hymns of St. Ambrose in the Latin Poetic Tradition," *Studies in Philology* 52, no. 4 (October, 1955): 509.

surrendered for use by the Arians. Ambrose refused. Justina made a second attempt, this time demanding the new and larger basilica located within the walls. The year was AD 385, just four years after the second Council of Constantinople. During Holy Week, Justina ordered soldiers to surround the church. Inside were Ambrose and the Nicene Christians. The possibility of martyrdom loomed. The people kept the church filled night and day. To pass the time they sang psalms and hymns. Augustine reported in his *Confessions*:

> That was the time when the decision was taken to introduce hymns and psalms sung after the custom of the eastern Churches, to prevent the people from succumbing to depression and exhaustion. From that time to this day the practice has been retained and many, indeed almost all your flocks, in other parts of the world have imitated it (*Confessions* IX vii. 15).[4]

Whether or not this was the first time hymns were sung by alternating stanza or whether or not Ambrose found time to craft hymns during the siege will be left to others to debate. What is pertinent is that it was an age of intense struggle over the doctrine of the Holy Trinity that affected the lives of everyone from the men on the throne to the people in the "pews." It was during this time that Ambrose had a great impact on the formation of hymnody and chant. His hymns were intentionally and explicitly trinitarian and Christological in nature. However, there were other historical and theological issues that gave shape to Ambrose's hymns. The end of the fourth and beginning of the fifth century was a time when the post-Constantinian Church was experiencing immense growth. It was the golden age of the great Easter Vigil. Cyril of Jerusalem, Chrysostom, Ambrose, and others each delivered their impressive mystagogical catechesis during this period. Pagans were pouring into the churches who required not only doctrinal instruction but instruction and formation in Christian life and discipline. In the opening words of his mystagogical address to the newly baptized, Ambrose wrote:

We have spoken daily upon subjects connected with morals, when deeds of the Patriarchs or the precepts of the Proverbs were being read,

---

in order that being taught and instructed by these you might grow accustomed to enter the ways of the ancients and to walk in the paths, and obey the divine commands; in order that being renewed by baptism you might hold to the manner of life which beseems those who are washed.[5]

Arianism was not the only danger that threatened the Church. The attempt of the heathen members of the Roman Senate to have the Altar of Victory restored in the Senate House (before which all oaths would be made)[6] and the brief but alarming reign of Julian the Apostate (AD 361–363) are reminders that the old pagan religions were still an active part of the religious and political milieu.

It is ironic that almost fifty years after the death of Arius it would be his followers who complained "that the people have been led astray by the strains" of Ambrose's hymns. It was, after all, through his own songs that Arius was so successful among the laity. The field of ritual studies recognizes the power of song in re-constructing the way people think and believe. It is true of social and political as well as religious trans-formation. In a 1990 workshop on worship and hymnody,[7] hymn-writer Brian Wren lectured a group of church workers on the theological reasons why it was necessary, in his opinion, to broaden the traditional trinitarian language in liturgy and song to include titles like "God the Mother" and other inclusive metaphors when referring to God. He con-cluded his presentation with the thought-provoking observation that some things can only be really known by praying them. Copies of a new, inclusive liturgy were distributed at this workshop, including the hymn "Bring Many Names." Stanza two reads:

> Strong mother God, working night and day,
> planning all the wonders of creation,
>> setting each equation,
>> genius at play:

---

[5] Ambrose, "On the Mysteries," *NPNF*[2], 10:317.

[6] See "Memorial of Symmachus, the Prefect of the City" and Letters XVII and XVIII of Ambrose to Valentinian II; *NPNF*[2] 10:411–422.

[7] The seminar took place at Eden Theological Seminary, Webster Groves, Missouri.

Hail and Hosanna

strong mother God![8]

There is a big difference between merely hearing and repeating theological information and praying theology. When music is added to the text, the emotional and communal effects are intensified. *Lex orandi lex credendi.*

So also with Ambrose. His hymns complemented catechesis, sermon, and liturgy. Ambrose appears fully aware of the reciprocity between confession and prayer. Words function in worship on different levels—some deeper than others. Ritual studies speak of liminality. Ambrose would be more at home in *coram deo* categories. He pushed the connection beyond the realm of anthropology to that of faith and theology, for example, when he states: "For what has more power than the confession of the Trinity which is daily celebrated by the mouth of the whole people."[9] While it is important and beneficial for the "whole people" to confess the faith together in verse, nevertheless, the most essential thing is the confession of the Holy Trinity. The congregation is created by the Word. The Word is not the creation of the congregation. Such is the way of idolatry. We do not bring names; God reveals his name, which is put on us in Holy Baptism and confessed (ὁμολογέω). We merely say back what he has revealed to his people. The congregation is dispensable. The proclamation of Christ and the Holy Trinity is indispensable and will go on even if God has to make stones cry out. Ambrose told the congregation on another occasions that if the praise of Christ goes silent, "the stones will cry out." It was true when Jesus received the praise of the children as he entered Jerusalem and it is true today. Ambrose drew on the Gospel reading for the day:

> You have heard it read that when Christ sat upon the foal of the ass, the children cried aloud, and the Jews were vexed. At length they spoke to the Lord Jesus, bidding Him to silence them. He Answered: "If these should hold their peace, the stones will cry out." Then on entering the temple, He cast out the money-changers . . . That passage

---

[8] Brian Wren, *Piece Together Praise: A Theological Journey—Poems and Hymns Thematically Arranged* (London: Stainer and Bell Ltd.; copublished with Hope Publishing Co., Carol Stream, IL, 1996), 162.

[9] *NPNF²*, 10:436.

was read by no arrangement of mine, but by chance; but it is well fitted to the present time. The praises of Christ are ever the scourges of the unfaithful. And now when Christ is praised, the heretics say that sedition is stirred up. The heretics say that death is being prepared for them, and truly they have their death in the praises of Christ. For how can they hear His praises, whose weakness they maintain? And so today, when Christ is praised, the madness of the Arians is scourged.[10]

Ambrose continued, saying that the demonic "Gerasenes could not bear the presence of Christ." Auxentius and the Arians are even worse than the Gerasenes. The praise of Christ by both young and old cannot be stopped in Milan. If they hold their peace, "the stones will cry out." Ambrose then added, " 'The stone which the builders rejected is become the head of the corner.' Invited, then, by these praises, Christ enters his temple, and takes his scourge and drives the money-changers out of the temple."[11]

Ambrose's sermons are profoundly Christological and liturgical. His sentences are shaped by the conviction that the Lord is present where his Word and name is proclaimed. His Word of promise— present in his name—is efficacious. It forgives. It drives out. This is all the more reason for the baptized to sing orthodox praises to the Trinity. "For what has more power than the confession of the Trinity. . . . All eagerly view one with another in confessing the faith, and know how to praise in verse the Father, Son, and Holy Spirit." The passage ends with the delightful conclusion, "So they all have become teachers, who scarcely could be disciples."[12] It was an age of disciple making. As noted above, it was a time when great numbers of converts were going through the extensive process of catechesis.[13] Ambrose knew how dif-

---

[10] NPNF[2], 10:433.

[11] NPNF[2], 10:433.

[12] NPNF[2], 10:436.

[13] In a letter to his sister, Ambrose explains some of the early events in the unfolding basilica crisis. "The day after, which was Sunday, when the Catechumens were dismissed, I was teaching the creed to certain candidates in the baptistery of the basilica. There it was reported to me that they had sent decani from the palace, and were putting up hangings, and that part of the people were going there. I however, remained at my ministrations, and began to celebrate mass." Letter 22, NPNF[2], 10:423.

ficult a task it was to make disciples. Instruction and admonition to live as disciples did not end at Baptism.

Another significant ingredient that contributed to the formation of Ambrose's hymns and Ambrosian hymnody is reflected in the opening quote: *quae* **quotidie** *totius populi ore celebratur* ("which is **daily** extolled by the mouth of the whole people").[14] While this could certainly be applied to the congregational singing during the siege of the basilica, it is also descriptive of the wider and on-going liturgical life of the Church in the fourth and fifth centuries. The daily (*quotidie*) extolling of the Trinity by the whole people also describes the Daily Office before it became dominated by the monastics. It was still a "peoples' office." The "peoples' service" (also referred to as the parochial, cathedral, or ecclesiastical office) took place in urban churches and was attended by clergy, laity, and monks. The structure was different from that developed by the Egyptian cenobites. It was designed for working people, with prayer in the morning to give thanks for the new day and prayer at night to confess one's sins for that day and to ask for protection during the night.[15]

Ambrosian hymnody was born before daily worship was taken over by the "professionals." Monastic daily worship was shaped by the canonical hours and the *lectio continua* of Scriptures and the Psalms. The peoples' office was shaped by the rhythm of morning and evening, as well as the liturgical seasons. The themes of light and darkness, morning and evening, were effectively used to admonish and comfort people. In the peoples' office, the people sang. Ambrose could thus boast that the whole people "all eagerly vie one with the other in confessing the faith, and know how to praise in verse (*versibus praedicare*) the Father, Son and Holy Spirit."[16] Marilyn Stulken comments: "Like the hymns of Luther many centuries later, Ambrose's hymns were written for congregational use, for the strengthening of faith in a period of ad-

---

[14] *PL* 16, III, p. 1060.

[15] *The Liturgy of Hours in East and West* (Collegeville, MN: Liturgical Press, 1986), 56.

[16] *NPNF*[2], 10:436.

versity. Immediately popular, Ambrose's hymns were soon imitated by others, creating a collection of over ninety 'Ambrosian hymns.' "[17]

What was it about Ambrose's hymns that made them so popular and so widely imitated? What was it that inspired the people to "eagerly vie one with another in confessing the faith?" The first element was the introduction of the practice of alternating the singing of the hymn stanzas that, in a sense, allowed the people to teach each other. Second, the hymns were accessible to the people. William Reynolds describes how the language Ambrose used in his hymns drew on the common expressions of his audience in a style that was unassuming, yet dignified.[18] Arthur Walpole offers this thoughtful description of the literary character of four hymns ascribed to Ambrose,

> They are, as we should expect from a man of Ambrose's character and education under the best masters of Rome, sharp cut, clear, concise, nervous and strong. As the themes are high, so the thought is profound. As Archbishop Trench happily put it: "The great objects of faith in their simplest expression are felt by him so sufficient to stir all the deepest feelings of the heart, that any attempt to dress them up, to array them in moving language, were merely superfluous. The passion is there, but it is latent and repressed, a fire burning inwardly, the glow of an austere enthusiasm, which reveals itself indeed, but not to every careless beholder ... how truly these poems belonged to their time ... [when] the faith which was in actual conflict with, and was just triumphing over, the powers of this world found it utterance in hymns such as these, wherein is not softness, perhaps little tenderness; but in place of these a rock like firmness, the old Roman stoicism transmuted and glorified into the nobler Christian courage, which encountered and at length overcame the world.[19]

The rhythmic style was also a major reason for the popularity of Ambrose's hymns.

---

[17] Marilyn Kay Stulken, *Hymnal Companion to the Lutheran Book of Worship* (Philadelphia: Fortress Press, 1981), 127.

[18] William Jensen Reynolds, *A Joyful Sound: Christian Hymnody,* 3rd ed. (New York: Holt, Rinehart and Winston, 1978), 7.

[19] Arthur S. Walpole, *Early Latin Hymns: With Introduction and Notes* (Cambridge, MA: Cambridge University Press, 1922), 24–25. The Trench quote is from Richard C. Trench, *Sacred Latin Poetry* (London: Macmillian and Co., 1864), 88.

In contrast with the irregular, asymmetrical prose form of the psalms, these hymns appeared in a new symmetrical form. Each hymn was made up of a number of stanzas, usually eight, and each stanza contained four lines of iambic dimeter, a popular folk like rhythm rather than a classical metrical form.... The melodies were constructed with one note to each syllable.[20]

What accounted for the popularity of eight stanzas? Walpole offers two explanations as plausible. It was a length not "so long as to weary the singers ... [nor] so short as to preclude the teaching."[21] Second, antiphonal hymn singing required an even number of stanzas. A third reason for the popularity of Ambrose hymns was that the use of metrical hymnody was well suited for memorization in an age when most of the worshipers were illiterate.[22] Naturally, as discussed in this paper, an additional reason for the enduring popularity of Ambrose's hymns was his poetic skill.[23]

---

[20] Walpole, *Early Latin Hymns*. Concerning the melodies used for Ambrosian hymnody, see *The New Oxford History of Music*, 10 vols., vol. 2: *The Early Middle Ages to 1300*, ed. Richard Crocker and David Hiley (Oxford: Oxford University Press, 1990), 2:236. "Concerning the melodies used for hymns we are even more in the dark than with antiphons and responsories. We have a large repertory of melodies preserved in sources after 1000, and virtually no way to decide which of these is older or younger. The essential fact of Ambrosian hymnody, and of the tradition dependent upon it, is that every strophe is sung to the same melody; this has the corollary that any text can be sung to any tune (of the same structure), and with that, the connection that might be presumed between a tune and a text (the basic tool in research on antiphons and responsories) is rendered of no effect. Sorting out the hymn tune tradition can only be done on purely intrinsic evidence. This has not yet been done, perhaps never can be done."

[21] Walpole, *Early Latin Hymns*, 23.

[22] See Allen Cabaniss, "The Background of Metrical Psalmody," *Calvin Theological Journal* 20, no 2 (1985): 196.

[23] For more on Ambrose's competence in using iambic dimeter with poetic imagination, see Jan den Boeft, "Delight and Imagination: Ambrose's Hymns," *Vigiliae Christianae* 62 (2008): 425–40. See also Jan den Boeft, "*Cantatur Ad Delectationem*: Ambrose's Lyric Poetry," in *Poetry and Exegesis in Premodern Latin Christianity: The Encounter Between Classical and Christian Strategies of Interpretation*, ed. Willemien Otten and Karla Pollmann (Leiden and Boston: Brill, 2007): 81–97 where he summarizes Ambrose's poetic and musical influences: "Producing truly poetical Christian hymns required technical literary skill and a lyrical perception of the created world. Ambrose's classical education had taught him the first of these and his talent for the second was further inspired and deepened by his view of creation as a source of delight and imagination, which could also be explored for literary objectives. Rhetoric and poetry had to provide delight in order to be efficient. The biblical psalms had clearly demonstrated this and

Having discussed historical, theological, liturgical, literary, and musicological elements that contributed to the hymnody of Milan at the end of the fourth and beginning of the fifth centuries, the next step will involve a textual study of Ambrose's hymns. The number of authentic hymns is still a matter of debate. Five hymns "have been identified with scholarly confidence as his": *Aeterne rerum conditor* (Eternal Maker of all Things), *Splendor paternae gloriae* (O Splendor of God's Glory Bright), *Deus creator omnium* (O God, Creator of All Things), *Iam surgit hors tertia* (Now Appears the Third Hour), *Veni redemptor gentium* (Come Redeemer of the Nations).[24] This study will examine the first two hymns.

AETERNE RERUM CONDITOR

1   Aeterne rerum conditor,
    noctem diemque qui regis,
    et temporum das tempora,
    ut alleves fastidium;

Eternal creator of the world,[25]
you govern night and day and give
changes of time and season to
relieve man's boredom.

2   Praecox diei iam sonat,
    noctis profundae pervigil,
    nocturna *lux* viantibus
    a **nocte noctem** segregans.

Now the bird that has been like a
light to travelers during the
night and marked off for them the
Nightwatches, is heralding the day
and calling on the sun to shine.

3   **Hoc** exitatus *lucifer*
    soluit polum caligine,
    hoc omnis errorum chorus
    viam nocendi deserit.

When the cock crows, the sun
wakes up and frees the skies from
darkness; when he crows, all night
Prowlers leave the path of sin.

4   **hoc** nauta vires colligit

    pontique mitescunt freta;

At cock-crow the sailor again finds
    courage,
the angry seas become calm.

---

the hymnode profits from this experience by following the tracks of the psalmist. Therefore Christian lyrical poetry proved to be an eminently viable experiment" (97; used by permission: Koninklijke BRILL NV).

[24] Walpole, *Early Latin Hymns*, 23.

[25] The translation of stanzas 1–4 and 6 are from Joseph Connelly's *Hymns of the Roman Liturgy* (Westminster, MD: The Newman Press, 1957), 16–18; stanzas 5, 7, and 8 are the author's. The translations are an attempt to reflect the literal meaning of the original and do not imitate the iambic dimeter.

hoc ipse petra ecclesiae	It was at cock crow that the very Rock of the Church
canente culpam diluit.	washed away his sin.

5	surgamus ergo strenue:	Let us arise therefore with vigor;
	gallus iac*entes* excitat	the cock awakens the sleepers,
	et somnol*entos* increpat:	and upbraids the drowsy;
	gallus neg*antes* arguit.	the cock rebukes the deniers.

6	**Gallo** canente spes redit,	When he crows, hope comes back,
	aegris salus refun**ditur**	a feeling of health returns to the sick,
	muncro latronis con**ditur**	the robber sheathes his sword
	lapsis fides rever**titur**.	and trust makes its way back to sinful souls.

7	Iesu, labantes **respice,**	Jesus, when we fall, look upon us
	et nos videndo corrige;	and with your gaze restore us;
	si **respicis** lapsus cadunt,	if you look our sins fall away,
	fletuque culpa soluitur.	our guilt is washed away in tears.

8	**Tu** *lux* refulge sensibus,	O Light, illumine our senses,
	mentisque somnum discute;	drive sleep from our souls;
	te nostra vox primum sonet,	may our tongue's first act be to herald you
	et vota solvamus **tibi**.	and may we discharge our vow to you.

The hymn "Eternal Maker of the World" illustrates the literary style of early Latin hymnody. The absence of the definite and indefinite articles in the Latin language adds to the economy and terseness of expression. Ambrose's use of rhetorical repetition makes for good poetry and good hymnody that lends itself to memorization. Each stanza stands by itself as a complete thought, yet flows naturally into the next in context and syntax, making it ideal for responsive singing by the congregation. For example, *noctem* (night) in stanza one, is repeated four times in the second stanza. The five-fold *noctis* is then echoed in stanzas three and four with the four-fold use of *hoc* (referring to the cock crow). The repetition is continued with the three-fold use of *gallus* (cock) in stanzas five and six, the three-fold *-itur* verb ending in stanza six, and the use of *tu, te,* and *tibi* in stanza eight.

Stanza five reflects the depth of both poetic style and theology that contributed to the popularity, imitation, and staying power of Ambrose's hymns. The nouns and verbs in lines two, three and four build to a climax in the final line: *iacentes* (sleepers), *somnolentos* (drowsy), *negantes* (deniers); *excitat* (awaken), *increpat* (upbraid), *arguit* (rebuke, accuse, expose, convict). In the Middle Ages, the cock became "the standing emblem of a preacher. . . . As the lion was said to be unable to withstand the crowing of the cock, so Satan, the roaring lion, fled preaching."[26] In his *Book of Pastoral Rule*, Gregory the Great writes:

> For that cock, too, whom the LORD in his manner of speech takes to represent a good preacher, when he is now preparing to crow, first shakes his wings, and by smiting himself makes himself more awake; since it is surely necessary that those who give utterance to words of holy preaching should first be well awake in earnestness of good living.[27]

The repetition of imagery is also seen in the allusion to Peter's denial of Jesus. The first comes in stanza five, line four, "The cock rebukes the deniers (*negantes*)." Both *gallus* and *negantes* are found in Luke 22:61b, "*Priusquam gallus cantet hodie, ter me negabis.*" The biblical image is picked up again in stanza seven. This time it is applied to the worshippers with the plural *labantes*. The effect is powerful! "Jesus, look upon us when we fall" (*Iesu, labantes respice*). Here is evidence that Ambrose was dealing directly with the Latin biblical text: *Et conversus Dominus respexit Petrum* (Luke 22:61a). Ambrose replaces *Domini* with *Iesu*, but appropriates the soul-chilling *respicio*. Ambrose then surprises us with a Gospel reversal. *Respice* becomes the *respicis* (look) that makes our sins go away. It is literally a play on words: falling (*lapsus*, meaning sins) falls away. A similar reversal is performed on Luke 22:62, "And he [Peter] went out and wept bitterly (*flevit amare*).

---

[26] F. A. March, *Latin Hymns with English Notes* (New York: Harper and Brothers Publisher, 1888), 224.

[27] Gregory the Great, *Book of Pastoral Rule*, 3.40, NPNF[2] 12:71 (second numbering). Ambrose also writes in *Hexameron* 6.4.26, "The lion fears the cock, especially the white one." *PL* 14:252. My thanks to John Nordling for this translation.

The verb *fleo* becomes *fletuque* in the final line of stanza seven. Tears wash away our fault.

The final stanza returns to where the hymn begins—to the boredom and weariness of time and to the normal human experience of waking from sleep and drowsiness. The first mutterings of the day are transformed into praise. The light of Jesus' forgiving look shines into the waking mind and drives sleep from the soul. The tongues' first true act is praise. Here one sees similarities with the daily monastic use of Psalm 51 to mark the end of the Great Silence observed by the monks since Compline the previous evening. Unless the Lord open our lips, we have nothing to say. Psalm 51 was a "hymn" of repentance and forgiveness, and so also was *Aeterne rerum conditor*. It comes as no surprise that Ambrose's hymn would eventually be appropriated by the Roman Catholic Breviary.[28]

Aeterne rerum conditor ("Eternal Maker of All Things") is addressed to Jesus. Stanza seven makes this clear. While this is not a hymn written explicitly to teach the Holy Trinity, it is noteworthy that the first word of the hymn is "Eternal." The Arians acknowledged Jesus as creator but not as God eternal. Not only is it good literary style to place the word "eternal" first in the sentence, it also stresses the deity of Jesus Christ. Even as the hymn effectively speaks to "everyman," it simultaneously incriminates the Arians as *negantes* par excellence.

SPLENDOR PATERNAE GLORIAE

1 Splendor **paternae gloriae,**   O Splendor of God's glory bright[29]
de **luce lucem** proferens,   O Thou that bringest light from light
lux lucis et fons **luminis,**   O Light of light, light's living spring
dies dierum **inluminans,**   O Day, all days illumining;

2 Verusque sol inlabere   O Thou true Sun, on us thy glance
micans nitore perpeti   let fall in royal radiance,
jubarque sancti Spiritus   the Spirit's sanctifying beam
infunde nostris sensibus   upon our earthly senses stream.

---

[28] Matthew Britt, ed., *The Hymns of the Breviary and Missal* (New York: Benziger Brothers, 1922).
[29] Translation by Robert Bridges as found in Ruth Ellis Messenger's, *The Medieval Latin Hymn* (Washington DC: Capital Press, 1953), 84–85. It captures the iambic dimeter of Ambrose's hymns, but sacrifices literal accuracy.

3 Votis uocemus et **Patrem**—   The Father, too, our prayers implore,
   Patrem perennis **gloriae,**   Father of glory evermore,
   Patrem potentis gratiae   the Father of all grace and might,
   Culpan releget lubricam.   to banish sin from our delight.

4 Informet actus strenuos,   To guide whate'er we nobly do,
   dentem retundat invidi   with love all envy to subdue,
   casus secundet asperos,   to make all-fortune turn to fair,
   donet gerendi gratiam.   And give us grace our wrongs to bear.

5 Mentem gubernet et reget,   Our mind be in his keeping placed,
   casto fideli corpore;   our body true to him and chaste,
   fides calore ferveat,   where only faith her fire shall feed
   fraudis venes nesciat,   to burn the tares of satan's seed.

6 Christusque nobis sit cibus,   And Christ to us for food shall be,
   potusque noster sit fides;   from him our drink that welleth free,
   laeti bibamus sobriam   the Spirit's wine, that maketh whole,
   ebrietatem spiritus.   and mocking not, exalts the soul.

7 Laetus dies hic transeat,   Rejoicing may this day go hence,
   pudor sit ut diluculum,   like virgin dawn our innocence.
   fides velut meridies,   like fiery noon our faith appear,
   crepusculum mens nesciat,   nor know the gloom of twilight drear.

8 **aurora** cursus provehit,   Morn on her rosy car is borne;
   aurora totus prodeat,   let Him come forth our perfect Morn,
   in Patre totus Filius,   the Word in God the Father one,
   et totus in Verbo Pater.   the Father perfect in the Son.

According to Julian's *Dictionary of Hymnology, Splendor paternae gloriae* is "a beautiful morning hymn, to the Holy Trinity, but especially to Christ as the Light of the World, and a prayer for help and guidance throughout the day."[30] Julian also notes that it is a "companion and sequel to *Aeterne rerum conditor.*" The opening line, while mentioning the Father (*paternae*), is addressed to the Son. The Father is explicitly

---

[30] John Julian, *Dictionary of Hymnology: Origin and History of Hymns and Hymnwriters,* 2nd ed. (Grand Rapids: Kregel Publications, reprinted in two volumes, 1985), 2:1080.

and individually addressed in stanza three: *Votis cocemus et Patrem* ("In our prayers let us also ask the Father").

Splendor paternae gloriae is very likely drawn from Hebrews 1:3: *"qui, cum sit splendor gloriae et figura substantiae **eius** et portet omnia verbo virtutis suae."* But who is the splendor of his glory and the exact figure of his substance who upholds all things by the power of his word? The antecedent of *eius* is *Deus* (θεός, Heb. 1:1). Ambrose correctly interprets *Deus* as a reference to the Father: "The sun represents the Father, and the rays issue from it is the procession of the Son. But there is no inequality of nature, for the Son also is *verus sol*."[31] The *verusque sol* seems to indicate that lines three and four (light of light, the source of light; the day that gives the days) are a predicate along with true sun."[32] Thus, stanzas one and two form a single prayer asking the Son to come as the light, the day, and the true sun. "The eternal relation of the Son to the Father is often illustrated in early Christian writers by the relation of the rays of light to the central source whence they stream. Ambrose frequently uses *splendor* thus."[33]

The hymn strives to reflect the unity of the Godhead (εἷς θεός) while yet maintaining the three distinct persons in the one divine essence. It must be understood in the light of the ecumenical councils of Nicea and Constantinople. It was Emperor Theodosius I who called the second council at Constantinople in AD 381. Bishop Ambrose had a great influence on Theodosius, who spent considerable time at the royal palace in Milan. At one point, Ambrose refused Theodosius communion until he repented for his rash order that precipitated the massacre in Thessalonica. Theodosius repented.[34] No bishops from the West attended the Council.[35] The Council of Constantinople did, however, send a letter addressed to the Western bishops who assembled in Rome for a synod. Ambrose's name appears second on the list of addressees behind that of Pope Damasus of Rome. The congenial synodical letter

---

[31] Connelly, *Hymns of the Roman Liturgy*, 21.

[32] See Wolpole, *Early Latin Hymns*, 36, note 3. "The *–que* of v. 5 seems to indicate that *lux*, like *sol* is intended to be a predicate, 'Come as the Light.' " See also Connelly, *Hymns of the Roman Liturgy*, 21, note 5.

[33] Wolpole, *Early Latin Hymns*, 35. See also Ambrose, *de Fide* 1.79; *Hexaemeron* 6.42.

[34] See Letters LXI and LXII to Theodosius, *NPNF*², 10:455–456.

[35] *NPNF*², 14:162.

was carried to the synod by three Eastern bishops and carefully reported on the doctrinal issues. "Through them [the three bishops] we wish to make it plain that our disposition is all for peace with unity for its sole object, and we are full of zeal for the right faith." After reaffirming the Nicene Creed, the letter continues:

> It is the faith that teaches us to believe in the name of the Father, of the Son, and of the Holy Ghost. According to this faith there is one Godhead, Power and Substance of the Father and of the Son and of the Holy Ghost; the dignity being equal, and the majesty being equal in three perfect hypostases, i.e. three perfect persons. Thus there is no room for the heresy of Sebellius . . . the Eunomians, of the Arians . . . and the Pneumatomachi.[36]

In view of Nicea and Constantinople, *verus sol* leaps from the text and from the lips as a rejection of Arianism and Monarchianism. To sing *luce lucem* followed immediately by *lux lucis* is to sing twice the Nicene Creed's *lumen de lumine* and the Constantinopolitan's φῶς ἐκ φωτός.[37] Thus could Ambrose preach, "For how can they bear his praises, whose weakness they maintain? And so to-day, when Christ is praised, the madness of the Arians is scourged."[38]

The characteristic repetition is observed with the word "light." *Luce lucem, lux lucis, luminis,* and *inluminans* is obvious. Less obvious is that *lux* flows out of *splendor*. It is more apparent with the Greek ἀπαύγασμα (brightness, radiance). More subtle is the repetition of the theme of light throughout the entire hymn—inconspicuous yet unifying. *Splendor . . . luce . . . dies . . . sol . . . meridies . . . aurora.* The hymn ends where it began—with light and the Holy Trinity. The coming light of dawn (*aurora*) harkens back to the light of stanza one. Connelly writes:

> The natural dawn is coming; may the Dawn come—and in His entirety. *Totus* is explained by the next two lines and by *ego in Patre et Pater in me est,* John 14:10. The hymn ends where it began—with the divinity of Christ.[39]

---

[36] From "The Synodical Letter of the Council of Constantinople," *NPNF²*, 14:189.

[37] For the text, see J. N. D. Kelly, *Early Christian Creeds,* 3rd ed. (New York: David McKay Company Inc, 1972), 297–98.

[38] *NPNF²*, 10:433.

[39] Connelly, *Hymn of the Roman Liturgy,* 23.

In between the opening and closing stanzas, the hymn prayerfully addresses the sorrows and joys of life. There is sin, temptation, Satan, envy, and wrongs to bear. There is also joy, purity, faith, Christ for food and drink (John 6:50), and the Spirit's wine (Ephesians 5:18). Weal and woe will vary in the life of the congregation and among the individual lives of the worshipers; what does not change is the Holy Trinity, whose light and grace begins and ends all things.

CONCLUSION

Ambrose's hymns are trinitarian, biblical, didactic, poetic, and congregational. They possess theological, liturgical, and pastoral integrity. They are not private or independent pieces of devotional activity; rather, they are intimately connected to those things that make up the life of the Church: doctrine and creed, liturgy, sermon, life and discipline, and ecclesiastical warfare against heresy. They faithfully reflect the orthodox confession and, in turn, reinforce it upon the people. In his examination of *Deus creator omnium*, Eric Routley identifies both of these themes. Not only does this hymn set forth a clear trinitarian doxology but also applies it directly to the people.[40] Ambrose's hymns are didactic poetry, rich in biblical imagery. They are not theological treatises arguing the finer points of the trinitarian debates. For that, Ambrose chose other forms of communication. He preached sermons, taught catechesis, wrote letters, and attended synods. He wrote dogmatic works, such as *De Fide, De Spiritu Sancto, De Incarnationis Dominicae Sacramento, De Mysteriis,* and *Libri duo de paenitentia.* It was, however, concern for and knowledge of the finer points of theology that gave shape and content to his hymns.

The hymns are didactic poetry, but didactic on a different level then what goes on in the classroom or lecture hall. "Some things can only be really known by praying them." The God to whom one prays is and will be the God of one's confession. *Lex orandi lex credendi.* "All eagerly vie one with the other in confessing the faith, and know how to praise in verse the Father, Son, and Holy Spirit."[41]

---

[40] Routley, *A Panorama of Christian Hymnody,* 56.
[41] *NPNF*[2], 10:436.

Eleven centuries later, the theological movement known as the Reformation would again restore song to its rightful place among the laity. It, too, was "a time of persecution, when the confession of faith is to be made" (FC SD X 2).[42] It is quite astonishing to read a description of hymnody from another era and language that comes so close to being a description of Ambrose's hymnody.

> Luther's hymns were meant not to create a mood, but to convey a message. They were a confession of faith, not of personal feelings. This is why, in the manner of folk songs, they present their subject vividly and dramatically, but without the benefit of ornate language or other poetic refinements. They were written not to be read but to be sung by the whole congregation.
>
> The language and vocabulary are therefore simple and direct. Like the ancient Hebrew poets he knew so well, Luther used few adjectives and formed brief pungent lines consisting almost exclusively of verbs and nouns. Most of the words are monosyllables. The thought is condensed and concentrated. Frequently every line forms a sentence of its own. Enjambment, i.e., carrying over of one or more words from one line to the next so as to bridge the break between verses, is quite uncommon. There is never a break in the middle of a verse. This again agrees with the nature of mass singing. A crowd sings a verse at a time, and so each verse must make sense as a unit.[43]

Both Ambrose and Luther exhibited a high degree of musical and literary sophistication. Where they differ is due mainly to the difference in language (German and Latin) and the differing styles of music.[44] The poetry of German hymnody relied on rhyme and was not as strictly tied to iambic meter.

Both Ambrose and Luther crafted their hymns as theological expressions of Scripture and Creed. Good theology cannot remain silent. It must have good song. Pure theology must have pure hymnody by

---

[42] *Concordia Triglotta: Die symbolischen Bücher der evangelisch-lutherischen Kirche* (St. Louis: Concordia, 1921), 1053. The Latin reads, quod persecutionis tempore (quando confessio fidei edenda est)." See *Die Bekenntnisschriften der evangelische-lutherischen Kirche* (Göttingen: Vandenhoeck & Ruprecht, 1982), 1054.

[43] AE 53:197–98.

[44] Unfortunately, due to the lack of musical notation from the fourth century, the original tunes accompanying Ambrose hymns remain unknown.

which those in whom faith has been created are able to confess, give witness, thanks, and praise in song. Ambrose understood the singing of psalms and hymnody as a communal activity that brought unity and concord to the church.[45] Ambrose was driven to write hymns for his congregation during a time of suffering and persecution for the sake of Christ and the Holy Trinity. Luther discovered his gift for writing congregational song when he wrote the ballad for Heinrich Voes & Johann Esch, the first Lutheran martyrs who were burned at the stake for their confession of the pure Gospel. From this was unleashed a phenomenal composition of hymns in which Luther put song into the mouths of God's people who came to receive the Lord's gifts at the purified evangelical mass.

As with Ambrose and Luther, the twenty-first-century global Church, representing many cultures and languages, continues the ongoing enterprise of "inculturation." It also faces continuous threats to the true confession of the Holy Trinity from sects and heresies both within and outside of the Church. A visit to Milan would well serve all those entrusted with the Church's liturgy and song:

All praise to God the Father be,
All praise, Eternal Son, to Thee,
Whom with the Spirit we adore,
For ever and for evermore. Amen.[46]

Good theology must have a good song. During the presidency of Dean Wenthe, the liturgical life at Concordia Theological Seminary flourished. To experience the liturgical hymnody at the Annual Theological Symposia, the Good Shepherd Institute Hymn Festival, Call Day and Graduation services, not to mention the Daily Office, is to experience heaven on earth. The irony is that while Dean Wenthe is not

---

[45] John Moorhead, "Ambrose and Augustine on Hymns," *The Downside Review* 128, no. 451 (April 2010): 79–92.

[46] *Splendor paternae gloriae*, by Ambrose, translation from *Hymns Ancient and Modern: Historical Edition with Notes on the Origin of both Hymns and Texts* (London: William Clowes and Sons, Limited, 1909), 3. The Latin text reads:

Deo Patri sit Gloria
eiusque soli Filio
sancto simul cum Spiritu
nunc et per omne saeculum

known for his vocal aptitude, nevertheless, under his leadership liturgical song was not only restored after a period of decline, but carried to new heights.

We live by faith, not sight. By faith we sing with the angels, archangels, and all the company of heaven. All who have had the privilege of singing the hymns of the church in Kramer Chapel know what it means to live, if not by sight, at least by sound—faith in the Word yes, but the Word put to the sound of heavenly music. Pure theology longs for pure doxology. Thank you, Dean.

WOMAN IN THE IMAGE OF GOD

EXPLORING GREGORY NAZIANZEN'S REFERENCE TO EVE IN HIS CONFESSION OF THE HOLY SPIRIT

James G. Bushur

It has been my pleasure to know Dr. Dean Wenthe since I was a student at Concordia Theological Seminary in the late 1980s. For me, Dean's greatest contribution to the Church consists in his conviction that theology is more than mere loyalty to a uniform, authoritative system; rather, theology is a conversation that is personal, reciprocal, and collegial. This conversation begins with God's creation of humanity in his own image and after his own likeness. "Let us make man ..." (Genesis 1:26). For Dean, this means that God creates man to be a participant in a divine conversation—even the personal, reciprocal conversation between the Father, Son, and Holy Spirit. It is this divine conversation that reaches its fullness in the incarnation, where God engages us face-to-face in the reciprocal exchange of his love. In this conversation, God opens himself up to human sin, anger, rebellion, grief, shame, and death; at the same time, humanity is opened up in Christ to God's love, mercy, righteousness, holiness, and eternal glory. For Dean, the blessed and delightful exchange between God and man in Christ is the setting in which the Church's theological task is constituted. In the Church's baptismal and eucharistic life, humanity is invited to take part in a blessed conversation with our Father in prayer and praise and with one another through the "mutual conversation and consolation of the brethren" (SA III IV).

On more than one occasion, I remember Dean emphasizing that the Church carries on its theological conversation even with those who have died in Christ. For Dean, this perspective informs his task as an exegete. To interpret Jeremiah or one of the prophets is not to treat the text as an impersonal artifact from which to extract certain facts or information. Rather, for Dean, to read the text is to enter into living conversation with the person of the prophet and the Spirit by whose inspiration he spoke. Yet, the exegetical task is not merely an interaction between the individual exegete and the text, but also a conversation that includes the whole fellowship of the Church—angels, archangels, and all the company of heaven. In this essay, I, too, seek to enter into theological conversation with the dead in Christ. I wish to explore Gregory Nazianzen's contemplation of the Holy Trinity, especially in terms of his bold confession of the Spirit's consubstantial divinity. For Gregory, the Spirit's divinity is the very foundation without which the Church's whole theological architecture must crumble. The Spirit ensures that our conversation with the prophets and apostles is not merely human, but divine. While our knowledge comes from the Father and through the Son, it can only be received in the Spirit. The Spirit is the place or fellowship where the Church, joined to Christ, can call God "Abba, Father." Thus, this essay is offered in praise of the Spirit who spoke by the prophets and becomes, therefore, the foundation for the Church's confessional and doxological life. In addition, this essay is offered in thanksgiving for the ongoing theological conversation of the Church. Into this conversation I was introduced by faithful professors like Dr. Dean Wenthe, and it continues to be my great privilege to participate in this divine conversation as Dean's student, friend, and colleague.

THEOLOGICAL CONVERSATION
VS. SOCIOLOGICAL CONSENSUS

"For I received from the Lord what I also delivered to you, that the Lord Jesus on the night when he was traditioned received the bread and, giving thanks, broke it and said, 'This is my body . . .' " (1 Corinthians 11:23–24).[1] For St. Paul, the life of the Church consists in the act of divine traditioning; the Father hands over his Son to be received in the

---

[1] Bible translations are the author's.

Spirit. This act of traditioning is grounded in Jesus' cross. The Gospels testify that the language of tradition (παραδίδωμι) originates in Jesus' own descriptions of his impending passion. "The Son of man is being handed over (παραδίδοται) into the hands of men . . ." (Mark 9:31). Yet, for Paul, the reality of Christ crucified persists in the institution of the Lord's Supper. The Father's traditioning of his Son in the Spirit does not end with the crucifixion, but remains the divine activity in which the Church subsists, "proclaiming the Lord's death until he comes" (1 Corinthians 11:26).

For ancient Christians, the life of the Church was defined from within the act of divine traditioning. In the latter half of the second century, Irenaeus, against his "Gnostic" opponents, identifies "true gnosis" with

> the doctrine of the apostles [ἡ τῶν ἀποστόλων διδαχή] and the ancient constitution of the Church [τὸ ἀρχαῖον τῆν ἐκκλησίας σύστημα] throughout the world, and the reproduction of the body of Christ [ὁ χαρακτὴρ τοῦ σώματος τοῦ Χριστοῦ] according to the succession of the bishops by which they tradition [tradiderunt] the church in every location and which has come even to us . . . .[2]

Irenaeus' words echo Acts 2:42 and define the Church dynamically as that which is traditioned with the "reproduction of the body of Christ" by a succession of bishops. For Irenaeus, to be a Christian is to subsist within that humanity of Jesus that continues to be handed over from one generation to the next.

However, with the arrival of the Enlightenment, tradition was no longer considered a reliable path for truth. Enlightenment scholars sought to replace tradition with the scientific method. The scientific method promised a knowledge that was immediate and objective and, therefore, independent of human prejudice and protected from the biased process of human traditioning. Applying the scientific method to the humanities gave rise to the social sciences. Anthropology would no longer be defined theologically with reference to the incarnation, nor would humanity be perceived to be in accord with the Scriptures as the expression of God's own character. Instead, humanity was defined

---

[2] Irenaeus, *Adversus Haereses*, iv, 33, 8; *ANF* 1:508.

sociologically as the expression of a specific community's cultural values. Rather than a theological discipline that wrestled with humanity's creation in the image of the triune God, anthropology became a secular, scientific discipline subject to changing social consensus. In this way, social concerns trumped theological ideals. Karl Rahner writes, "The behavior of Jesus and his apostles can be adequately explained by the cultural and social environment of their day, in which they not only acted but could not have acted otherwise than they did."[3] Rahner's words betray a sociological fatalism. Man no longer lives and moves personally within the freedom of God's image, but is fatalistically conformed to the impersonal whole and becomes an expression of collective values. From the fate of such social predestination not even Jesus himself could escape.

The triumph of the secular sociological viewpoint over traditional theology has manifested itself most clearly in feminist studies. Feminist theologians often assert that an inherent connection exists between society's patriarchal oppression of women and the traditional theological emphasis on God as Father and Son. Rather than eliminating traditional theology altogether, feminist theologians have sought to explain it by means of a sociological hermeneutic.[4] From this perspective, traditional trinitarian language—Father and Son—is not rooted in God's own self-revelation, nor is it a true description of divine ontology; rather, the trinitarian names are merely human metaphors that originate in the social values of an unenlightened humanity. In this way, sociological assumptions have become the presupposed condition for all theological reflection. As Haye van der Meer, Rahner's student, puts it:

---

[3] Karl Rahner, "Priestertum der Frau?" *Stimmen der Zeit* 195 (1977): 299, as translated in Manfred Hauke, *Women in the Priesthood? A Systematic Analysis in the Light of the Order of Creation and Redemption* (San Francisco: Ignatius Press, 1988), 22.

[4] See Manfred Hauke, *Women in the Priesthood?*, 21ff. After introducing several scholars who argue for a sociological reading of the Church's theological history, Hauke writes, "There is no need here to criticize these authors' attempts to account for the exclusion of women from the priesthood in terms of restrictive social factors. Such factors certainly deserve extended attention, and the relevance of their influence will have to be critically examined. What appears questionable is only the reduction of the terms of the inquiry to the social situation. Through such reduction, theology basically renounces the use of its own proper cognitive methodology and runs the risk of turning into (amateurishly practiced) sociology."

"Perhaps theology should be content to place its trust in the results of secular psychosocial developments."[5] Such a statement waves the white flag surrendering theology into the hands of secular social sciences.

Thus, for feminist theologians gender distinction is no longer a subject for theological contemplation, but is reduced to its utilitarian, sociological significance. Scientifically, gender simply functions as that which allows for the procreation of the human animal, but is not constitutive of one's true inner identity. "Differences in behavior between the sexes are determined not by nature," writes Helga Horz, "but by social conditions."[6] Catharina Halkes, in more provocative terms, asserts, "Both sexes have the potential ability . . . to integrate (the polarities of male and female) within themselves, and thus to become autonomous individuals, developing toward wholeness and androgyny."[7] Here the male-female distinction is not rooted in the creative will of God, nor is it the expression of God's own character and life. Instead, the significance of gender distinction is ever-changing, being defined and redefined by utilitarian interests, collective values, and social consensus. Thus, the feminist argument for male/female equality basically consists in an argument for their social interchangeability.

In light of the present circumstances, this essay wishes to explore the intimate connection between theology and anthropology in the trinitarian arguments of the fourth century. It is hoped that the anthropological theology of the pre-enlightenment church may help in the recovery of a theological anthropology by post-enlightenment Christianity. Gregory of Nazianzus's *Theological Orations* played a central role in the development of the word *hypostasis* (person) as essential to the theological grammar of the Church's trinitarian confession. This essay seeks to explore Nazianzen's argument in terms of the following

---

[5] Haye van der Meer, *Priestertum der Frau? Eine theologiegeschichtliche Untersuchung*, Quaestiones Disputatae, vol. 42 (Freiburg, Basel, and Vienna: Herder, 1969), 176, as translated in Manfred Hauke, *Women in the Priesthood?*, 22.

[6] Helga Horz, *Die Frau als Personlichkeit. Philosophische Probleme einer Geschlechterpsychologie* (Berlin: VEB Deutscher Verl. der Wissenschaften, 1968), 119, as translated in Manfred Hauke, *Women in the Priesthood?*, 31.

[7] Catharina J. M. Halkes, *Gott hat nicht nur starke Sohne. Grundzuge einer feministischen Theologie* (Gütershloh: Gütersloher Verlagshaus, 1980), 26, as translated in Manfred Hauke, *Women in the Priesthood?*, 65–66.

question: what is the relationship between personhood as it is within the communal life of the Holy Trinity and personhood as it resides within humanity? In other words, how do theological personhood and anthropological personhood interrelate? In the aftermath of Nicea, this interrelation became evident in the debates that surrounded the Son's generation from the Father. However, less explored is how this interrelation between theology and anthropology functioned in the arguments over the divinity of the Holy Spirit. Thus, this essay will consider Nazianzen's bold argument for the Spirit's "consubstantial" relation to the Father and the Son; his argument reaches its crescendo in his fifth and final theological oration (*Oration* 31) delivered in Constantinople in preparation for the ecumenical council of AD 381. This oration stands as the standard for the Church's confession of the Spirit's consubstantial divinity and certainly contributed to the recognition of Gregory as *The Theologian*, a posthumous honor bestowed at the Council of Chalcedon (AD 451).

THE CAPPADOCIAN CONTEXT: ARIUS AND EUNOMIUS

In the first two of his *Theological Orations* (*Oration* 27 and 28), Gregory Nazianzen demonstrates the impossibility of rationally comprehending God's essence. This point is emphasized against the Eunomians, who represent the latter fourth century's most difficult and dangerous intellectual challenge to the faith of Nicaea. At the beginning of the fourth century, Arius began his argument with the transcendence and, therefore, ineffability of God's essence.[8] He reasoned from this premise that God's essence is incommunicable, so that every relation is fundamentally external to his essence. For Arius, God relates to nothing essentially. Every relation by which God interacts with another must

---

[8] See the reconstruction of Arius's *Thalia* in Rowan Williams, *Arius: Heresy & Tradition* (Grand Rapids: Eerdmans, 1987, rev. 2001), 100–103. According to the reconstruction of Williams, Arius's first proposition is as follows: "So God himself is inexpressible to all beings. He alone has none equal to him or like him, none of like glory. We call him unbegotten on account of the one who by nature is begotten" (101). The inexpressibility of God's being is fundamental for Arius and controls his understanding of the term "unbegotten." Unbegotten does not express God's essence in any positive way, but arises from the revelation given in the begotten.

collapse into an external activity of the divine will or power.[9] In other words, every relation is reduced to the *ad extra* interaction of the Creator with his creatures. The *creatio ex nihilo* not only describes God's relation to creation, but also defines his relationship to the Son. Jesus' relationship to God is just as external to God's essence as that of the created cosmos;[10] such a relation is grounded in God's external will and consists in the *ad extra* communication of God's legal commands. Arius's denial of the Son's essential divinity is a necessary consequence of his fundamental premise that God's essence is a transcendent mystery beyond human comprehension.

In the latter half of the fourth century, however, Eunomius, the bishop of Cyzicus, argued in a fundamentally different manner.[11] While Arius maintained that God's essence was absolutely unknowable, Eunomius claimed that God's essence could be described philosophically. For Eunomius, God did not merely transcend creation; he was essentially opposed to created being.[12] Eunomius located this absolute opposition in the attribute of God's unbegotten or unoriginate being. For Arius, the term unbegotten was a negative or *apophatic* attribute; it did not describe what God is in his essence, but only what he is not. Unbegottenness as a divine attribute simply expressed the fact

---

[9] Arius, *Thalia*: "By God's will the Son is such as he is, by God's will he is as great as he is." Williams, *Arius: Heresy and Tradition*, 103.

[10] Arius, *Thalia*: "To put it briefly: God is inexpressible to the Son. . . ." Williams, *Arius: Heresy and Tradition*, 103. Arius uses the same word—"inexpressible (ἄρρητος)"—to describe God's relation to the Son as he does to describe God's relation to "all beings."

[11] Concerning Eunomius, see Lewis Ayres, *Nicaea and Its Legacy* (Oxford: Oxford University Press, 2004), 144ff.

[12] See Khaled Anatolios, *Retrieving Nicaea* (Grand Rapids: Baker Book House, 2011), 41ff. Anatolios points out that while Arius resisted the language of "image" in relating the Son to the Father, Eunomius embraced it as long as it was defined with precision. In his discussion of Arius, Anatolios suggests that Arius views the Son as "the supreme negative theology in person." I think this perspective better fits Eunomius. Arius resisted the Son as "image" of God because for him the utter transcendent and ineffable character of the divine essence does not work well with the idea of an accessible image. The divine nature is not exactly the opposite of created nature; it transcends created nature. Thus, for Arius nothing in creation can be a genuine image of the divine essence. The suggestion of Anatolios that the Son is like a negative photograph perhaps better fits Eunomius. For him, Jesus is a truly negative image that, because of its *heteroousian* character, actually reveals the divine nature itself. The Son, precisely in his begottenness, manifests the Father as the only unbegotten essence.

that God in his essence transcended any notion of generation with which humanity is familiar. Yet, what was a negative attribute for Arius becomes a positive attribute for Eunomius. For the bishop of Cyzicus, God's essence is unbegottenness itself.[13] Arian mysticism has morphed into Eunomian rationalism. Unbegottenness, in the Eunomian way of thinking, establishes an absolute boundary for God's essence, a boundary he cannot transgress without ceasing to be God. Thus, God's unoriginate character not only denies that God's essence has a beginning or a source or a cause, it also removes the possibility that God's essence can generate or produce another like unto itself.[14] Unbegottenness excludes the activity of generation at both ends. On the level of essence, God is neither generated nor is he generative.

Thus, Eunomius's rejection of Nicaea was more definitive and more radical than that of Arius. Arius's objection to Nicaea's confession that the Son is *homoousias* with the Father was focused chiefly on the language of *ousia*. Most in the Arian camp preferred an *apophatic* stance when speaking of the essence of the Father or that of the Son.[15] To attempt a description of the divine essence was to replace theological confession with philosophical speculation. Essences are unknowable; true theological confession begins only when God engages in external

---

[13] See Eunomius, *Liber Apologeticus* 8, in *Eunomius: The Extant Works*, trans. Richard P. Vaggione, Oxford Early Christian Texts (Oxford: The Clarendon Press, 1987), 41. Eunomius writes, "So then, if, as shown by the preceding argument, the 'Unbegotten' is based neither on invention [ἐπίνοιαν], nor on privation [στέρησιν], and is not applied to a part of him only [ἐν μέρει] [for he is without parts], and does not exist within him as something separate [ἕτερον] [for he is simple and uncompounded], and is not something different alongside him [for he is one and only he is unbegotten], then 'the Unbegotten' must be unbegotten substance [οὐσία ἀγέννητος]."

[14] "But if God is unbegotten in the sense shown by the foregoing demonstration, he could never undergo a generation [γένεσιν] which involved the sharing [μεταδοῦναι] of his own distinctive nature [τῆς ἰδίας φύσεως] with the offspring of that generation [τῷ γεννωμένῳ], and could never admit of any comparison or association [σύγκρισιν καὶ κοινωνίαν] with the thing begotten." Eunomius, *Apology* 9, in *Eunomius: The Extant Works*, 43.

[15] Concerning the post-nicene *homoian* theology as supported by Emperor Constantius, see Ayres, *Nicaea and Its Legacy*, 133ff. Ayres includes the statement from the Council of Sirmium (AD 357): "But as for the fact that some, or many, are concerned about substance [*substantia*] which is called *ousia* in Greek, that is, to speak more explicitly, *homoousion* or *homoiousion*, as it is called, there should be no mention of it whatever, nor should anyone preach it" (138).

activity.[16] Thus, the fundamental ground of all theological knowledge is God's creative will by which he produces all creatures *ex nihilo* and redeems them through the activities of Christ.[17] For Arians, even the knowledge of God revealed in Jesus Christ is a knowledge grounded in the Creator's will as it works *ad extra*.[18] From this perspective, Arians wanted to replace *ousia* language with that of *thelema, dunamis,* or *energeia.* Consequently, many Arians were content with the simple elimination of the *ousia*-language from the Nicene Creed. Salvation did not depend upon the Son's essential relation to the Father; it depended on the Son's agreement with the Father's creative and redemptive will. Jesus Christ, precisely in his perfect obedience to the Father, is a true and complete manifestation of God's creative will.

In contrast to Arius, Eunomius and his followers could not accept a simplistic silence concerning the divine *ousia.* The Eunomians did not merely want to replace the language of essence with that of will or energy; they wanted to replace the *homoousias* with the language of *heteroousias.* The Father and the Son were essentially divided from one another. The Father's essence does not merely transcend the Son's being; it is the absolute antithesis of the Son's being.[19] While, for Arius,

---

[16] For the theological perspective of Arius, see Williams, *Arius: Heresy and Tradition,* 95ff. Williams emphasizes the centrality of the divine will in Arius' thought. He writes, "For Arius, the notion of the sovereign divine will resolves the problem of the monad's relation to all else. . . ." (197–98).

[17] See Anatolios, *Retrieving Nicaea,* 47ff. Antolios suggests that Arius' theological difficulty may have its origins in his soteriology. Arius was too soteriological in that he defined the Son's very origin and essence as being "for us." Anatolios writes, "For Arius, the Son and Word comes to be as the first and preeminent created manifestation and mediator of the glory of the Unbegotten; precisely inasmuch as his being is bound up with this work of mediation, he is 'for us' through and through" (51). From this soteriological perspective, the Son's essence comes into being in God's will to create and redeem the world.

[18] See Anatolios, *Retrieving Nicaea,* 41ff. Anatolios demonstrates that the "unity of will" characterized Arian theologians.

[19] "And yet not even an attribute such as shape, say, or mass and size can exist in this essence because God is altogether free from composition [συνθήκης ἐλεύθερον]. But if it neither is nor ever could be lawful to conceive of these or anything like them as being joined to the essence of God [συμπεπλεγμένον τῇ οὐσίᾳ], what further argument is there which will permit the likening [ὁμοιοῦν] of the begotten to the unbegotten essence?" Eunomius, Apology 11, *Eunomius: The Extant Works,* 47. Eunomius' words not only conflicted with the *homoousian* position of Nicaea but also challenged the *homoiousian* and *homoian* positions toward which a majority of bishops had gravitated

Father and Son terminology described the external production of the
Son from the Father *ex nihilo,* for Eunomius such terminology
described the essential differences between the Father and the Son. The
Father's essence consists precisely in his unbegottenness and the Son's
in his begottenness. For Arius, the confession of the Father and the Son
expresses a relationship rooted in the external will; for Eunomius, however, the Father's begetting of the Son establishes an eternal and essential division between them.[20] The respective essences of the Father and
the Son are mutually exclusive. "But after all, there is no one so ignorant
or so zealous for impiety," writes the Bishop of Cyzicus,

> as to say that the Son is equal [ἴσον] to the Father! The Lord himself
> has expressly stated that "the Father who sent me is greater than I."
> Nor is there anyone so rash as to try to yoke [συζεῦξαι] one name to
> the other! Each name pulls in its own direction [ἀνθέλκοντος] and the
> other has no common meaning with it at all: if the one name is
> "Unbegotten" it cannot be "Son," and if "Son" it cannot be
> "Unbegotten."[21]

While Arius understands "Father" to refer figuratively to the external
generative activity of God's creative will, Eunomius understands it to be
a definition of the divine essence itself in terms of his unoriginate
character. Father and Son are names designating radically different
essences.

   Within such a theological context, the Cappadocian Fathers are
compelled to engage the theological description of divine fatherhood
and sonship in a more acute way than any before them. In order to
counter Arian arguments in the middle of the fourth century,

---

in the middle of the fourth century. For Eunomius, there can be no likeness between the
Father and the Son on the level of their respective essences.

[20] "Accordingly, if this argument has demonstrated that God's will is an action [τὴν
βούλησιν ἐνέργειαν] and that this action is not essence [οὐκ οὐσίαν] but that the Only-
begotten exists by virtue of the will of the Father [ὑπέστη βουλήσει τοῦ πατρὸς ὁ
μονογενής], then of necessity it is not with respect to the essence but with respect to the
action [πρὸς τὴν ἐνέργειαν] [which is what the will is] that the Son preserves his
similarity [τὴν ὁμοιότητα] to the Father." Eunomius, Apology 24, *Eunomius: The
Extant Works*, 65. Like Arius, Eunomius grounds the Son's being in the will or activity
of the Father. However, Eunomius gives special emphasis to the notion that the Father's
willing of the Son makes him external to the Father's essence.
[21] Eunomius, Apology 11; in *Eunomius: The Extant Works*, 47.

Athanasius was challenged to distinguish the Father-Son relation from the external activity of God's creative work.[22] Perhaps more important to Athanasius than the language of *homoousias* was the Nicene distinction between begetting and making. Christ is "begotten, not made [γεννηθέντα, οὐ ποιηθέντα]." For Athanasius, this distinction was made clear through the use of *ousia*.[23] The creed formulated at Nicaea originally stressed this distinction by confessing that Christ is "begotten from the essence [*ousia*] of the Father."[24] In this way, the Fathers at Nicaea emphasized the ontological difference between creating and begetting. God's creative work functions outside the divine essence and ensures the absolute and eternal distinction between God and his creation on the level of essence. Essentially, creation comes into being from nothing and, therefore, has its ground in the external will of the Creator. Creation does not exist as a result of natural necessity (as the Greeks maintained), but of God's voluntary and radical freedom.

In contrast, for Athanasius, begetting functions within the divine essence itself. The Son is not generated out of nothing (*ex nihilo*), but

---

[22] The distinction between "begetting" and "making" is fundamental to Athanasius's argument. For instance, he writes, "Thus does divine Scripture recognise the difference between the Offspring and things made, and shew that the Offspring is a Son, not begun from any beginning, but eternal; but that the thing made, as an external work of the Maker, began to come into being." Athanasius, *Discourses* 2.58; *NPNF*[2] 4:380. Cf. also *Discourses* 1.33–34; *Discourses* 2.69–70.

[23] See John Zizioulas, *Communion & Otherness* (New York: T&T Clark, 2006), 181ff. Zizioulas makes the point that *ousia* is employed by Athanasius and the Nicene Fathers as an exclusionary term. The Son's *homoousias* relation to the Father simply says that the Son is not a creature deriving his existence *ex nihilo*. Zizioulas is certainly correct to recognize that the Nicaean use of *ousia* language is fundamentally negative, excluding the Son's classification as a creature. However, Athanasius's spirited defense of this language suggests that his devotion to the language expresses more positive notions. For Athanasius, the communicability of the divine *ousia* is not merely fundamental for a true confession of Christ, but also fundamental for his understanding of Baptism. In Baptism, an external slave becomes a son because he is incorporated into the Son's own generative relation to the Father. Thus, *ousia* language for Athanasius ensures the reality of the Church's baptismal and eucharistic communion with God.

[24] See John Zizioulas, *Communion & Otherness*, 129, note 52. Zizioulas suggests that the elimination of *ousia* from this part of the Nicene Creed at Constantinople may bear some theological significance. At Nicaea, the use of *ousia* helped exclude the Arian confession that Christ was a creature deriving his existence *ex nihilo*. However, it is eliminated at Constantinople in order to prevent the Eunomian confession that identified fatherhood with the divine *ousia*.

generated out of the Father's own being. "Creatures are from without and are works of the Maker; but the Offspring is not from without nor a work, but from the Father and proper to His Essence."[25] For Athanasius, fatherhood is not merely an activity God chooses to do, but an internal movement in and through which God subsists. Thus, God is Father at the depth of his being and subsists within an eternal generation by which he relates to his Son. The Son's relation to the Father is not reduced to the Father's external will, but is fundamental and essential. For Athanasius, the Son does not merely possess a similar essence to the Father, but subsists in one and the same essence with the Father. While God's creating consists in the communication of his will and commands to creation, the Father's begetting consists in the communication of his own being to the Son. Within the relation of begetting, the Father and Son both possess the same essence though in different ways. The Father possesses divinity in the way of one who begets and generates, and the Son possesses the same divinity in the way of one who is begotten and generated.

However, at the end of the fourth century, the Cappadocian Fathers must engage this theological discussion concerning divine fatherhood and sonship in a fundamentally new light. While Arius identified fatherhood and sonship with the external activity of God's will, Eunomius identified them with diverse essences that were absolutely distinct. Eunomius seeks to use Athanasius's own argument against the Nicene confession. For the bishop of Cyzicus, fatherhood describes the divine essence in such a way that it is identified with unbegottenness itself. This identification of fatherhood and the divine essence ensures that the Son must subsist outside the divine being. Following an Aristotelian principle, Eunomius assumes that the effect must be external to its cause.[26] "Order is secondary [τάξις δευτέρα] to the one who

---

[25] Athanasius, *Discourses* 2.57; *NPNF²* 4:379.

[26] See Basil, *Against Eunomius*, in *St. Basil of Caesarea: Against Eunomuis,* The Fathers of the Church, vol. 122, trans. Mark DelCogliano and Andrew Radde-Gallwitz (Washington DC: Catholic University of America Press, 2011), 119ff. Because Eunomius assumes that effects are external to their causes, he rejects the notion that there is any order within God. "For order is secondary to the orderer," Eunomius writes as quoted by Basil, "but nothing which belongs to God has been ordered by another." *St. Basil of Caesarea: Against Eunomuis,* 121. Basil responds by pointing out that there are two different kinds of order. One kind is an order imposed upon something from the

orders, but nothing which pertains to God has ever been ordered by
another [ὑφ᾽ ἑτέρου τέτακται]."²⁷ The Son in his begottenness must
subsist outside of God's essential unbegottenness. While the Nicene
Fathers distinguished begetting from creating, the Cappadocians must
distinguish divine fatherhood and sonship from the divine essence
itself. Father and Son cannot be metaphorical names for the creative
will; yet, neither can they be names designating diverse essences. In
other words, Eunomius' argument demands the development of
hypostasis or person as a distinct ontological category.

THE BAPTISMAL PNEUMATOLOGY
OF BASIL OF CAESAREA

In the latter decades of the fourth century, the arguments concerning
the divinity of the Son were moving toward a theological and scriptural
clarity. The concepts of fatherhood, sonship, and begetting expressed a
relationship with which humanity could resonate. Even if the bishops of
the Church could not always give a detailed and definitive proof, it
seemed clear enough that begetting entailed something different from
creating. A father's relation to his son cannot be reduced to the external
will. Man does not make a son in the same way that he constructs a
plow. The plow is an external work; its existence or non-existence has

---

outside by another. However, another kind of order is that which is natural and inherent, such as the relation between fire and its light. Light is not an effect that is
separated or imposed upon the fire, but rather inherent in the fire itself. Therefore, Basil
maintains that "the Father is ranked prior to the Son in terms of the relation that causes
have with what comes from them, not in terms of a difference of nature or a pre-
eminence based on time." *St. Basil of Caesarea: Against Eunomuis*, 121. Basil rejects the
notion that effects must be external to their causes; the Son is an eternal effect that
eternally resides within the Father who is his cause, source, or *arche*. This same discussion is taken up by Gregory Nazianzen in *Oration 29*, where he writes, "Because they
are *from* him, though not *after* him. 'Being unoriginate' necessarily implies 'being
eternal,' but 'being eternal' does not entail 'being unoriginate,' so long as the Father is
referred to as origin [ἀρχὴν]. So because they have a cause they are not unoriginate
[ἄναρχα]. But clearly a cause is not necessarily prior to its effects—the Sun is not prior
to its light." *Oration* 29.3; author's translation. Cf. *NPNF*² 7:302. Gregory's discussion of
cause and effect within God is part of his argument that there is and must be "order"
within God. Against Eunomius, Gregory argues that if God is "anarchical" in his
essence, then all that comes from him will necessarily end in anarchy.
²⁷ Eunomius, *Apology* 10; *Eunomius: The Extant Works*, 45.

no consequence for the farmer's inward being; therefore, it is a tool wholly subject to the farmer's will. The begetting of a son takes place in a fundamentally different way. The son's existence has consequences for the father's identity; without the begetting of a son, a man cannot be called father in the true sense. While the construction of a plow is an external act that leaves it subject to the farmer's choice, the begetting of a son is an internal relationship that consists in the communication of the father's very being and life to his son. The numerous biblical texts expressing Jesus' sonship and the common experience of fathers generating sons gave the defenders of Nicaea an advantage in their arguments for the Son's essential divinity.

However, this advantage enjoyed by the Nicene Fathers in the defense of the Son's divinity was utterly lacking when the argument moved to the Holy Spirit. Scriptural citations concerning the Spirit's divinity were comparatively sparse, and the manner of the Spirit's derivation from the Father seemed hopelessly hidden under a theological cloud and within a philosophical darkness. Arian and Eunomian supporters sought to take advantage of this theological ambiguity. Losing the battle for the Son, such heretics turned to the Spirit. Many of the arguments against the Spirit's divinity follow the same path as earlier arguments against the Son. However, it seems that opposition to the Spirit's divinity assumed two new attacks that were certainly effective and in need of orthodox answers. The first attack was the apparent silence of Scripture concerning the Spirit's essential divinity; the second, more serious objection concerned the meaning of the Spirit's "procession" from the Father as a distinct mode of existence from the Father's begetting of the Son.

The first new attack revolved around the apparent silence of Scripture in regard to the Spirit's essential divinity. The Son's essential relation to the Father was grounded in the act of begetting. Scriptural texts testifying to Jesus' filial generation from God could be multiplied from the beginning of the biblical narrative to its end. However, the Spirit's essential divinity appeared to be at best an implication of prophetic and apostolic texts. Early arguments often focused on the titles, "Holy" and "Spirit." For orthodox Fathers, such titles implied the Spirit's divine identity; however, for heretical challengers such deductions were interpreted to be nothing but foreign and self-serving inferences imposed by biased readers. Such theological challenges caused the orthodox defenders to follow a more cautious course in their defense of the Spirit.

Basil of Caesarea acknowledged the apparent silence of the Scriptures concerning the essential divinity of the Spirit. In his classic work, *On the Holy Spirit*,[28] he never explicitly calls the Spirit "God," nor does he demand the confession of the Spirit as *homoousias* with the Son and the Father. Many interpreters claim that this characteristic of Basil's work is a matter of political diplomacy.[29] His refusal to refer to the Spirit's divinity with a bold and explicit label is thought to be a concession to those of a more moderate perspective. However, it is possible that Basil's silence is a rhetorical attempt to use his opponent's strategy against them. Basil's opponents seem to be using the scriptural silence concerning the Spirit's essential divinity in order to paint trinitarian defenders as overzealous innovators.[30] Proponents of the Spirit's divinity were being characterized as extremists who were aggressively demanding a confession of the Spirit that lacked explicit testimony from the Scriptures. However, for Basil, the apparent silence of the Scriptures could be interpreted in different ways. The Scriptures may not explicitly affirm the Spirit's divinity in *ousia* terminology, but neither do they

---

[28] For the original Greek, see Basile De Cesaree, *Sur Le Saint-Esprit*, Sources Chrétiennes, vol. 17 (Paris: Les Editions Du Cerf, 1968). For English translation, see St. Basil the Great, *On the Holy Spirit*, trans. David Anderson, Popular Patristics Series, no. 42 (Crestwood, NY: St. Vladimir's Seminary Press, 1980). Hereafter, this translation will be referenced by the translator's name.

[29] One exception is John Zizioulas, *Communion & Otherness*, 183ff. Zizioulas suggests that Basil's silence concerning the *homoousias* language is evidence of his preference for *hypostatic* relations. Instead of locating the unity of the Trinity in the *ousia*, Basil locates it in the *hypostasis* of the Father and, therefore, deemphasizes the *ousia* language. This suggestion is interesting and worthy of investigation. It is certainly true that for Basil and the Cappadocians the divine *ousia* is unknowable. Only the Father, Son, and Spirit know each other on the level of the *ousia*. Christians know God in and through the *hypostases* of the Father, Son, and Spirit. Thus, a silence concerning the divine *ousia* may be a natural tendency when arguing against Eunomius and others claiming to know God on the level of the essence.

[30] See Basil, *On the Holy Spirit*, 6.13. Basil characterizes his opponents' attacks this way, "They call us innovators, revolutionaries, phrase-coiners, and who knows how many other insults." Anderson, 28. Basil's characterization of his opponents may not be far from the truth as both sides sought to claim the support of the Church's tradition.

explicitly deny it. Basil's silence may be a rhetorical attempt to paint his
opponents as the aggressive innovators (the true *pneumatomachi* as he
calls them)[31] who explicitly reject what the Scriptures do not reject. Basil
strategically demands that his opponents acknowledge what Scripture
itself demands, namely, that the Spirit is to be "worshipped and
glorified together with the Father and the Son."

For Basil, the divine ranking of the Spirit is grounded in the liturgy
of Baptism. Matthew 28 is not merely a single scriptural text for Basil,
but the foundation for the Church's entire life. For the bishop of
Caesarea, the Church's life is doxological. In the baptismal formula,
Basil sees the warrant for a new kind of doxology. The Church's
worship rightly praises the Father *through* the Son and *in* the Spirit; but
she must also praise the Father *together with* the Son and the Spirit. The
first doxology expressed the economy of God's salvific relationship to
humanity. Every gift comes to the faithful from the Father through the
Son in the Spirit; likewise, the Church's prayers and offerings proceed in
the Spirit through the Son to the Father. The second doxology, however,
expresses the inward life of the Holy Trinity, the so-called immanent
Trinity. The inward life of God consists in the correlation of the Father
with the Son and Spirit in a true equality of honor. It is this doxology
that is grounded in the baptismal waters and, therefore, demanded of
the Church. For Basil, the grammatical correlation between the three
persons of the Trinity in Matthew 28 and the Church's baptismal
formula must be reflected in her doxological life.

For Basil, the baptismal liturgy is the *arche*[32] or first principle from
which his argument for the divine dignity of the Spirit proceeds. The
correlative relationship between the three persons within the divine
essence is the proper context for interpreting the soteriological economy of the Gospel. The ordering of the three persons in the economy of
the Gospel must not be interpreted to mean the essential subordination
of the Spirit. The Spirit is just as essential to the divine illumination of

---

[31] See Basil, *On the Holy Spirit*, 11.27, Anderson 47–48.

[32] Basil describes the purpose of his treatise as presenting "a suitable beginning [ἀρχήν]"
for the discussion on the Spirit. *On the Holy Spirit*, 1.3; Anderson, 18. Thus, Basil is
explicitly not writing an exhaustive treatment of the question; he seeks to provide the
foundation from which the question of the Spirit can be answered. For Basil, this theological foundation is the liturgy of Baptism.

humanity as the Father and the Son. The light of the Son comes forth from the Father, but can only be received and perceived by humanity in the Spirit. The Spirit is the light in which the Church can perceive Jesus as the icon of the Father. Thus, the Spirit is the place or atmosphere in which humanity can be brought into communion with the Son and offered to the Father.

For Basil, the divinity of the Spirit is necessary for the true illumination of humanity. If the Spirit is merely a creature, then the theological knowledge he communicates is merely an external revelation inherently subject to time and corruption. Apart from the gift of the Spirit, who is acquainted with "the depths of God," humanity's theological knowledge remains grounded in the external will of the Creator. Such a "natural knowledge" must remain a partial or vague glimpse through a dark mirror. Pagan idols testify to this kind of knowledge as humanity creates its own external metaphors or images for God. Yet, all such images fall short of the truth because they are foreign to God's being, originate within the creaturely world, and are imposed from the outside. For Basil, the Christian knowledge of God is qualitatively superior to that of pagan idols.[33] While the pagan knowledge of God is grounded in the creative will and approaches God from the outside, the Christian knowledge of God is grounded in the Son and the Spirit. Jesus' flesh is the one true icon that derives from the Father's own hands and, therefore, provides an internal revelation of God's own being. "He who has seen Me has seen the Father" (John 14:9). However, the full perception of Jesus as the true icon of the Father cannot take place ex-

---

[33] "He is the Spirit of wisdom, revealing Christ, the power of God and the wisdom of God, in His own greatness. As the Paraclete, He reflects the goodness of the Paraclete (the Father) who sent Him, and His own dignity reveals the majesty of Him from whom He proceeded. So on the one hand, there is a natural [φυσική] glory (as light is the glory of the sun), but on the other hand, there is a glory which . . . bestows itself [externally] on those judged to be worthy. There are two types of the latter glory; the first is servile [δουλική], offered by a creature to his superior: 'A son honors his father and a servant his master' [Malachi 1:6]; but the second is the glory shared by intimates [οἰκειακή], and it is this which the Spirit fulfills." Basil of Caesarea, On the Holy Spirit, 18.46; Anderson, 73–74. Basil indicates three different levels in the knowledge of God. The Father, Son, and Spirit share a "natural" or essential knowledge. Creatures share a "servile" knowledge that is external, like the relation between a master and his servant. However, Christians share an intimate knowledge that is located in the Spirit, like the relation of a son to his father.

cept within the Spirit. Without the Spirit, humanity remains external to Jesus' flesh and is unable to perceive the full spiritual identity that dwells within him. Without the Spirit, humanity tries to see while surrounded by thick darkness. In communion with the Spirit, humanity is brought into the light that illuminates the face of Jesus revealing him to be the Christ, the Son of the living God. Thus, the Spirit is the crucial link in the divine economy that allows the baptized to know God from within his own life.[34]

GREGORY NAZIANZEN: ORATION ON THE HOLY SPIRIT

Basil's argument was certainly effective; in a clever use of rhetoric, he turned his opponents' argument from silence against them. Indeed, Basil's success is enshrined in the Constantinopolitan Creed. The amended creed of Nicaea does not explicitly label the Spirit as God nor claim that he is *homoousias* with the Father and the Son. His divinity is implied in the baptismal and doxological formula that correlates the Father, Son, and Spirit in an equality of dignity. The Spirit is the "Lord

---

[34] "If we are illumined by divine power [δυνάμεως φωτιστικῆς], and fix our eyes on the beauty of the image of the invisible God [τῷ κάλλει τῆς τοῦ Θεοῦ τοῦ ἀοράτου εἰκόνος ἐνατενίζομεν], and through the image are led up to the indescribable beauty of its source [τοῦ ἀρχετύπου], it is because we have been inseparably joined to the Spirit of knowledge [ἀχωρίστως τὸ τῆς γνώσεως Πνεῦμα]. He gives those who love the vision of truth the power which enables them to see the image, and this power is Himself [τὴν ἐποπτικὴν τῆς εἰκόνος δύναμιν ἐν ἑαυτῷ]. He does not reveal it to them from the outside [οὐκ ἔξωθεν], but leads them to knowledge in himself [ἐν ἑαυτῷ εἰσάγον πρὸς τὴν ἐπίγνωσιν], 'No one knows the Father except the Son,' and 'No one can say "Jesus is Lord" except in the Holy Spirit.' Notice that it does not say *through* [διά] the Spirit, but *in* [ἐν] the Spirit. It also says, 'God is Spirit, and those who worship Him must worship in Spirit and Truth,' and 'in Thy light do we see light,' [in] the illumination of the Holy Spirit [ἐν τῷ φωτισμῷ τοῦ Πνεύματος], 'the true light that enlightens every man that comes into the world.' He reveals the glory of the Only-Begotten in himself [ἐν ἑαυτῷ δείκνυσι τὴν δόξαν τοῦ Μονογενοῦς], and he gives true worshippers the knowledge of God in himself. The way [to] divine knowledge [ἡ ὁδὸς τῆς θεογνωσίας] ascends from one Spirit through the one Son to the one Father [ἀπο ἑνὸς Πνεύματος διὰ τοῦ ἑνὸν Υἱοῦ ἐπὶ Τὸν ἕνα Πατέρα]. Likewise, natural goodness, inherent holiness and royal dignity reaches from [ἐκ] the Father through [διά] the Only-Begotten to [ἐπι] the Spirit." Basil of Caesarea, *On the Holy Spirit,* 18.47; Anderson, 74–75. In this text, Basil certainly emphasizes the internal character of the Spirit's revelation through the repetition of ἐν ἑαυτῷ. The illumination of the baptized is within the Spirit.

and Giver of life" who "with the Father and the Son is to be worshipped and glorified." Basil's argument was effective, but it came at a cost. His focus on the Spirit's relationship to the Church left the Spirit's relationship to the Father and the Son ambiguous and open to attack. Basil's silence concerning the essential divinity of the Spirit may have been rhetorically clever, but for his friend, colleague and successor, Gregory Nazianzen, it was theologically annoying.[35] Basil's silence concerning the Spirit's essential ontology allowed his writings to be co-opted by the Eunomians, who opposed the confession of the Spirit's essential divinity. Basil's silence became a burden that Gregory, as Basil's friend, felt obligated to bear.[36]

In his Oration on the Holy Spirit (*Oration* 31),[37] Gregory recognizes that the argument concerning the Spirit's divinity has reached a new stage.[38] Gregory acknowledges the benefits gained from those who have

---

[35] In his letter to Basil, Gregory uses an incident at a *symposium* of orthodox friends to express his own disappointment with Basil's "economy" of speech. Gregory relates a conversation with a monk who recognizes the difference between Nazianzen and Basil. While Gregory speaks "openly on the Godhead of the Spirit (φανερῶς τὸ Πνεῦμα θεολογεῖς)," Basil "hints obscurely" and "merely suggests the doctrine, but does not openly speak out the truth; flooding people's ears with more policy than piety (πολιτικώτερον ἢ εὐσεβέστερον), and hiding his duplicity by the power of his eloquence (τῇ δυνάμει τοῦ λόγου τὴν διπλόην περικαλύπτων)." Gregory Nazianzen, *Epistle* 58, *NPNF*² 7:455 (*PG* 37:113–18). It seems clear that Gregory himself shares the irritation of this orthodox monk in regard to Basil's diplomatic reserve. Basil's angry reply to Gregory demonstrates that he, too, understood his friend's true sentiment.

[36] See Gregory Nazianzen, *Oration* 43.68–69. In his panegyric on St. Basil, Gregory expresses his belief that it was his part to confess boldly the Spirit's divinity whereas Basil's place as bishop demanded a more moderate tone.

[37] For the original Greek of Gregory's *Orations*, see Gregoire De Nazianze, *Discours* 27–31, Sources Chrétiennes, vol. 250 (Paris: Les Editions du Cerf, 1978). For an English translation, see St. Gregory of Nazianzus, *On God and Christ,* trans. Frederick Williams and Lionel Wickham, Popular Patristics Series, no. 23 (Crestwood, NY: St. Vladimir's Seminary Press, 2002).

[38] Concerning the historical context surrounding Gregory's *Theological Orations*, see John McGuckin, *Saint Gregory of Nazianzus* (Crestwood, NY: St. Vladimir's Seminary Press, 2001). McGuckin points out that *Oration* 31 on the Spirit builds upon *Oration* 41 on Pentecost. In his Pentecost sermon, Gregory recognizes that his boldness was not always received well. It is like "the noise of thunder to weak ears and the sun to feeble eyes and solid food to those still drinking milk." *Oration* 41, 6; *NPNF*² 7:381. Thus, Gregory sees the need to move slowly with his hearers and even forecasts a "more mature discourse" to come in the future. It seems that *Oration* 31 is the more mature discourse he had promised to deliver.

offered scriptural studies focused on the names for the Holy Spirit.[39]
Here Gregory is certainly referring to his friend, Basil among others,
who argued for the correlative relationship of the Spirit to the Father
and Son. Gregory, however, is clearly not content to practice Basil's
rhetorical restraint. For Gregory, the new stage in this controversy is to
acknowledge explicitly the essential divinity of the Spirit. "For our part,"
writes Gregory, "we have such confidence [θαρροῦμεν] in the Godhead
of the Spirit [τῇ θεότητι τοῦ Πνεύματος], that, rash though some may
find it, we shall begin our theological exposition by applying identical
expressions to the Three."[40] Gregory knows that his confidence will
bring the charge of innovation and extremism. Yet, Gregory is
undaunted and responds to this charge with what is perhaps a
conscious rejection of Basil's rhetorical silence.[41] "We shall extol the
Spirit; we shall not be afraid. If we do have fear, it will be of silence not
of preaching (ἡσυχάζοντες οὐ κηρύσσοντες)."[42]

Gregory knows that his bold claim will be nothing but a vain
assertion if he does not provide substantive theological support.
Gregory is well aware that his confident assertion of the Spirit's essential
divinity demands an answer to his opponents' strongest challenge.[43] In
what way does the Spirit derive from the Father so that it is distinct
from the Son's generation and yet ensures his essential divinity? The
Son's generation from the Father resonated with common familial ex-

---

[39] For example, see Basil, *Against Eunomius*, 3.3, in *St. Basil of Caesarea, Against Euno-mius*, 189.

[40] *Oration* 31, 3; *On God and Christ*, 118.

[41] McGuckin, *St. Gregory of Nazianzus*, 301. McGuckin shows that Gregory, in a more diplomatic way, turns Basil's treatment of the Spirit into a work of "preparatory paideia" upon which Gregory's own work will be constructed. McGuckin continues, "In this way the work of Basil is characterized as grammatikos in comparison to rhetorikos, a step-ping place on the way somewhere else. The attitude is nothing new, Gregory more or less told Basil to his face while he was still alive that his pneumatology was insufficient, and that was one of the reasons they had so seriously fallen out."

[42] *Oration* 31, 3; *On God and Christ*, 118.

[43] Cf. McGuckin, *St. Gregory of Nazianzus*, 300ff. McGuckin indicates that the op-position to Gregory's bold assertion of the Spirit's divinity included more than merely the Eunomians or Arians. It also included supporters of Nicea who "thought that the problems of the previous generation of the Church had largely been caused by the unfortunate word Homoousion and did not see why now it should be extended to the Spirit." McGuckin, *St. Gregory of Nazianzus*, 301.

perience. The Spirit's divine production did not enjoy such an advantage. Gregory's opponents mocked every attempt to explain the mystery of the Spirit's procession. Gregory characterizes his opponents' arguments this way: "The Holy Spirit must either be ingenerate or begotten. If he is ingenerate, there are two unoriginate beings. If he is begotten, we again have alternatives: either begotten from the Father or from the Son. If from the Father, there will be two sons who are brothers. . . . If begotten from the Son, our God apparently has a grandson."[44] With such mockery, Gregory's opponents challenge trinitarian defenders to distinguish the Father's production of the Spirit from his generation of the Son.

Hidden within the challenge of Gregory's opponents was the issue of anthropomorphic theology. For the Eunomians, the defenders of Nicaea were using anthropological language to describe the divine essence. The Nicene Creed's emphasis on fatherhood, begetting, and sonship appeared to impose human images upon the divine nature. Such a foreign and unworthy imposition seemed to the Eunomians to be blasphemous and idolatrous on a fundamental level. Gregory recognizes this charge and agrees that anthropomorphic language does not operate on the level of essence. For Gregory, just because we speak of the Son's generation from the Father does not necessitate "the transfer [μεταφέρειν] of our human relations [συγγενείαις] to the deity [ἐπὶ τὸ θεῖον]."[45] The divine essence is utterly different from that of created human beings. However, despite the essential chasm that separates divinity from creation, Gregory is not willing to eliminate all anthropomorphic theology. In the beginning, humanity was created in the image and likeness of God; in the last days, God became flesh and dwelt among us. For Gregory, the biblical narrative implies that the experience of being human entails a divine aspect and that God's own life bears an affinity with humanity. For Gregory, this likeness does not

---

[44] *Oration* 31, 7; *On God and Christ*, 121. The same question challenged Athanasius. See Athanasius' third letter to Serapion (*Serap.* 3.1.3). It is evident from Athanasius' discussion of the question that orthodox theologians found it especially difficult to give an adequate explanation. The difficulty lies in the need to distinguish "proceeding" from "begetting."

[45] *Oration* 31, 7; author's translation. Cf. *NPNF*² 7:320.

operate on the level of essence, but on the level of *hypostasis*.[46] Divinity
and humanity do not share an essential likeness, but their beings both
share a *hypostatic* mode of existence. In other words, both God and man
subsist as a personal fellowship capable of face-to-face interaction; both
divinity and humanity share personal modes of existence that consist in
mutual relations of generation, communion, love, self-giving, and reciprocal exchange between distinct beings.

For Gregory, the *hypostatic* mode of existence becomes a third level
of ontology.[47] The first level consists in the essence [*ousia*]; only the
Father, Son, and Spirit know each other on the level of essence. Indeed,
their knowledge of one another is so complete that it consists in a
perfect *perichoresis* and an absolute identification of attributes. The
second level of ontology consists in the external will of the Creator.

---

[46] Here Basil argues that "unbegotten" and "begotten" do not describe "what a thing is
(τὸ τί ἐστιν)", but "how it is (τὸ ὅπως ἐστιν)." To illustrate what he means, Basil refers
to Luke's genealogy of Jesus which ends with Adam being derived from God (Luke 3).
Basil concludes, "Clearly, that which is 'from no one' is 'without origin,' and that which
is 'without origin' is 'unbegotten.' Therefore, just as being 'from someone' is not the
substance when we are talking about human beings, so too when we are talking about
the God of the universe it is not possible to say that 'unbegotten' (which is equivalent to
saying 'from no one') is the substance." Basil, *Against Eunomius*, 1.15, in *St. Basil of
Caesarea, Against Eunomius*, 114. In this interesting argument, Basil implies that
humanity, in its generative relations, shares a similarity with God's *hypostatic* subsistence. It was perhaps natural for Gregory Nazianzen to extend this similarity when
arguing the Holy Spirit's direct derivation from the Father.

[47] "How shall we pass over the following point, which is no less amazing than the rest?
Father, they say, is a name either of an essence [οὐσίας] or of an action [ἐνεργείας],
thinking to bind us down on both sides. If we say that it is a name of an essence, they
will say that we agree with them that the Son is of another essence, since there is but one
essence of God, and this, according to them, is preoccupied by the Father. On the other
hand, if we say that it is the name of an action, we shall be supposed to acknowledge
plainly that the Son is created and not begotten. For where there is an agent there must
also be an effect. And they will say they wonder how that which is made can be identical
with that which made it. I should myself have been frightened with your distinction, if it
had been necessary to accept one or other of the alternatives, and not rather put both
aside, and state a third and truer one, namely, that Father is not a name either of an
essence or of an action, most clever sirs. But it is the name of the Relation [σχέσεως] in
which the Father stands to the Son, and the Son to the Father. For as with us these
names make known a genuine and intimate relation, so, in the case before us too, they
denote an identity of nature between Him that is begotten and Him that begets."
Gregory Nazianzen, *Oration* 29.16; NPNF² 7:306–307. It is interesting that in this text
Gregory connects the divine relations of Father and Son to human experience.

Creatures have an existence that is grounded in God's *ad extra* activity and, therefore, have a creaturely being that is inherently subject to time, limited by space, and susceptible to death. Having been brought forth into existence from non-being, creatures are naturally vulnerable to the threat of a return to non-being. This creaturely relationship, grounded in God's external will, provides the basis for a certain natural knowledge of God. While only the Father, Son, and Spirit know each other essentially, human beings as God's creatures can receive glimpses of what God is like. Creatures can know God in the same way that a reader receives a partial understanding of an author by considering his books. However, such a knowledge is always external to God's being and, therefore, fundamentally incomplete.

For Gregory, the Gospel of Christ and the gift of the Spirit provide a third level of ontology—the *hypostasis*. The divine essence does not exist nor has it ever existed as a solitary substance turned into itself. Rather, the divine essence has always dwelt within the *hypostases* of the Father, Son, and Spirit. The theological shift from the primacy of essence, which characterized Greek philosophy, to the primacy of *hypostasis*, is truly revolutionary; the full narrative of this shift is beyond the scope of this paper.[48] It is sufficient perhaps to consider that instead of God's life being grounded in the divine essence (*ousia*) generally, Gregory grounds it in the particular *hypostasis* of the Father.[49] Such a

---

[48] Concerning the Christian development of personhood, see John Zizioulas, *Being as Communion* (St. Vladimir's Seminary Press), 1985.

[49] "Now the name of that which is without beginning [τῷ ἀνάρχῳ] is Father, and of the beginning [τῇ ἀρχῇ] Son, and of that which is with the beginning [μετά τῆς αρχῆς], Holy Spirit; and the one nature [φύσις μία] in the three is God. But the union [ἕνωσις] is the Father, out of whom and toward whom the succeeding ones are brought forth [ἐξ οὗ καὶ πρὸς ὄν ἀνάγεται τὰ ἑξῆς]." Gregory Nazianzen, *Oration* 42.15; author's translation. Cf. *NPNF*[2] 7:390. For discussion of the significance of this shift from *ousia* to *hypostasis*, cf. T. F. Torrance, *The Trinitarian Faith* (T&T Clark, 1995), 236ff. and 313ff. Torrance sees problems in the Cappadocian perspective that shifts the focus from the language of *homoousias* to the language of *hypostasis*. In contrast, John Zizioulas defends the Cappadocian theology against Torrance's critique. See Zizioulas, *Communion & Otherness*, 123ff. The issue seems to this author to come down to the following question: what exactly is communicated from the Father to the Son in the relation of begetting or from the Father to the Spirit in the relation of procession? Torrance seems to equate "being" (τὸ εἶναι) with the *ousia* and, therefore, maintains that the Father simply communicates his essence (*ousia*) to the Son and Spirit. However, this seems inadequate since it implies that there is no difference between begetting and spirating; both rela-

revolution makes the Father truly and radically free from all necessity. The Father, Son, and Holy Spirit do not experience their subsistence as something given to them or imposed upon them from the outside. The Greek preoccupation with essence led them to a fatalism in which everything is a slave to the laws of one's own essence. Neither God nor man could ever become anything other than what their respective essences allowed. By confessing the primacy of *hypostasis*, Gregory asserted a radical freedom for the Father that even included a freedom over his own being. Thus, the Father is not limited to a monistic essence, but in an act of free love communicates his own being in the begetting of the Son and the spiration of the Spirit. Indeed, this communication is so total and so complete that it results in the Son and Spirit being *homoousias* with the Father. They do not merely share one essence, but the very same essence. The very being and life of the Father is communicated to the Son and Spirit so that an exact identification of attributes prevails among them. The Father, Son, and Spirit are not merely all omnipotent; rather, they each possess the exact same omnipotence, albeit in different ways. The Father possesses this omnipotence in the way of One who is its source and generator; the Son possesses this omnipotence in the way of One who is begotten or generated from the Father; and the Spirit possesses the very same omnipotence in the way of One who proceeds from the Father.

For Gregory, this hypostatic mode of existence not only holds the primacy in God, but also in humanity. Man began his existence as a creature grounded in the creative will, but through Christ and the Spirit he is called to be a son. By his holy incarnation, death, and resurrection, the only-begotten Son has brought humanity into his own *hypostatic* life and offered it with himself to the Father. In Baptism, Christians are united in the Spirit and incorporated into that humanity that has been *hypostatized* by the Son. The baptized share in Jesus' own sonship and have his Spirit within them crying out "Abba, Father." Thus, Christians occupy a kind of middle ground for Gregory. Only the Father, Son, and

---

tions communicate the exact same content—the single divine *ousia*. The Father does not merely beget an essence; he begets the Son. Zizioulas is correct to maintain that "being" (τὸ εἶναι) includes the *hypostasis*. Thus, the Father communicates a *hypostatic* subsistence in his begetting of the Son. For the Cappadocians, persons generate persons, not merely bare essences or essential attributes.

Spirit know each other on the level of essence; all humanity, as creatures of God, can know the Creator on the level of his external will, though now even that has been darkened by his sin and rebellion; however, the baptized know God on the level of *hypostasis*. In the fellowship of the Spirit, the Church beholds the face of Christ as the true icon of the Father.

This *hypostatic* mode of existence, however, is not a foreign reality imposed unnaturally upon humanity. For Gregory, humanity was created in the beginning to grow, multiply, fill the earth and subdue it within a *hypostatic* fellowship. Just as God's own being has its ground, not in a general divine essence, but in the *hypostasis* of the Father, so also humanity has its ground *hypostatically* in Adam. Thus, while anthropomorphic language does not work on the level of essence, for Gregory it certainly does work on the level of *hypostasis*. While God's essence cannot be described anthropomorphically in terms of gender, passion, change, or any fleshly attributes, *hypostatically* God is confessed in terms of fatherhood, sonship, and begetting. It is this line of thought that inspires Gregory to connect the mutual relations of the Father, Son, and Spirit with the *hypostatic* fellowship of the human family.

Earlier it was mentioned that the strongest challenge of the Eunomians against the divinity of the Spirit was the ambiguity of his derivation from the Father. The act of begetting easily resonated with the common human experience of fathers generating children. However, the procession of the Spirit lacked such a concrete and experiential association. Gregory must first distinguish the Spirit's derivation from the Son's generation; second, he must demonstrate that such a derivation ensures that the Spirit is *homoousias* with the Father and the Son. It is precisely here that Gregory's contemplation of mutual relations within the human family bears fruit.

> What was Adam? A creature of God [πλάσμα Θεοῦ]. What then was Eve? A fragment of the creature [τμῆμα τοῦ πλάσματος]. And what was Seth? The begotten of both [γέννημα]. Does it then seem to you that Creature and Fragment and Begotten are the same thing [ταὐτόν]? Of course it does not. But were not these persons consubstantial [Ὁμοούσια]? Of course they were. Well then, here it is an

acknowledged fact that different persons [τὰ διαφόρως ὑποστάντα] may have the same substance [τῆς αὐτῆς οὐσίας]. I say this, not that I would attribute creation or fraction or any property of body to the Godhead [let none of your contenders for a word be down upon me again], but that I may contemplate in these [ἐπὶ τούτων φεωρῶν], as on a stage [ὡς ἐπὶ σκηνῆς], things which are objects of thought alone [τὰ νοούμενα]. For it is not possible to trace out any image [εἰκαζομένων] exactly to the whole extent of the truth. But, they say, what is the meaning of all this? For is not the one an offspring, and the other a something else of the One? Did not both Eve and Seth come from the one Adam? And were they both begotten by him [γεννήματα]? No; but the one was a fragment of him, and the other was begotten by him. And yet the two were one and the same thing [ταὐτόν]; both were human beings; no one will deny that. Will you then give up your contention against the Spirit, that He must be either altogether begotten [ἢ γέννημα πάντως], or else cannot be con-substantial [μὴ ὁμοούσιον], or be God; and admit from human things [ἐκ τῶν ἀνθρωπίνων] the possibility of our position? I think it will be well for you, unless you are determined to be very quarrelsome, and to fight against what is proved to demonstration.[50]

Gregory's use of human relations as an image of the internal life of the Trinity is truly fascinating and worthy of consideration. Gregory employs this imagery immediately following his general rejection of illus-trations from "natural history" (*Oration* 31.10). Later, in *Oration* 31.31, Gregory comments on his vain attempt to find an appropriate "icon" for the "divine nature." He explicitly rejects the illustrations of water (source, spring, and river) and light (sun, beam, and light). This emphasis on the inadequacy of illustrations drawn from the created world suggests that, for Gregory, the narrative of Eve's procession from the side of Adam and the begetting of Seth operate on a higher level than examples from creation. Indeed, Gregory describes these human relations as "a tabernacle (σκηνῆς)" designed by God for "contem-plation (θεωρῶν)." Such language is very suggestive. Like the Old Testament tabernacle, human relations are sacramental signs in which humanity is given a glimpse of God's own *hypostatic* communion.

---

[50] *Oration* 31, 11; *NPNF²* 7:321.

While Gregory does not expound on the place of this human imagery in his own thought, the use of Eve's derivation from Adam as an image of the Spirit's procession does invite exploration.[51]

It is clear that Gregory does not employ the narrative of Adam, Eve, and Seth as an image of the divine essence. Nazianzen is careful to emphasize that on the level of essence God is unknowable; there is no image that can outline the "pure reality (καθαρῶς τὴν ἀλήθειαν)" of God's being. However, in the production of Eve from Adam's side and the generation of Seth, Gregory suggests that the *hypostatic* relations in which the Father, Son, and Spirit subsist are indicated. Here it may be worth considering that the relation between male and female in the human race is fundamentally different from the relation of male and female in the animals. Since the animals were created from a distance by the mere command of God, the male and female of each species possess a more independent creation. In the animals, gender is more utilitarian, providing for the external procreation of the species. However, in humanity, Eve is not created independently from Adam; she proceeds directly from his side—flesh of his flesh, bone of his bones, and, presumably, breath of his breath. The intimate way in which God forms the man from the dust and brings forth the woman out of him suggests that the relations of love in which the Father, Son, and Spirit subsist are being reflected. Adam and Eve are meant to subsist within a mutual exchange of being. Here, gender is not merely a matter of external, utilitarian difference, but an image of *hypostatic* relations consisting in love, mutual exchange, and the generation of life. The piercing of Adam's side for the formation of Eve indicates that humanity is not generated from independent individuals or a general human essence; rather, humanity traces its *arche* or source to a community of persons that subsists in mutual sacrifice and submission.

The connection between the production of Eve and the procession of the Spirit offers a twist to the *filioque* controversy. While the *filioque* clause implicitly places the Spirit third, deriving his *hypostasis* from the

---

[51] Gregory brings the familial relations of Adam, Eve, and Seth into his discussion of the Holy Trinity again in *Oration* 39.12. Here Gregory argues that "unbegotten" and "begotten" are not two separate natures. His argument refers to Adam, Seth, and Eve. Even though Adam and Seth are generated differently, they are not on that account diverse essences.

Father and the Son, Gregory's image places the Spirit second.[52] Instead
of the dual procession of the Spirit, it is the Son who derives his being
from the Father in the Spirit. Indeed, the narrative of Eve's procession
from Adam may explain Gregory Nazianzen's passing comment that
procession occupies the "middle (μέσον)" or mediating position
between being "unbegotten and begotten (ἀηεννήτου καὶ γεννητοῦ)"
(*Oration* 31.8). In this text, Gregory may have the Eunomians in mind.
The Eunomians maintained that the Father's unbegottenness and the
Son's begottenness were mutually exclusive and essentially opposed to
one another. However, against the Eunomians, Gregory maintains that
the procession of the Spirit prevents the Son's division from the Father.
A father's generation of a child can become merely a biological function
in which the child is given an external and independent existence. By
her procession from Adam's own side, Eve, in her motherhood, ensures
the permanent relation between Adam and Seth. Seth is not merely
generated from Adam, but also generated within Eve. Eve is the one in
whom Adam and Seth are permanently united as father and son. In the
same way, the Son is not merely begotten from the Father so as to be an

---

[52] Here I do not intend to suggest a change in the ordering of the Son and Spirit; rather,
I intend to point out that the Cappadocians do not seem to insist upon a certain
ordering. Indeed, the Spirit's connection to Eve seems to suggest that the derivation of
the Spirit from the Father is just as direct and intimate as the Son's begetting. Thus,
Gregory is able to speak of the Spirit as "forefunner" (προτρέχει) of the Son (*Oration*
31.29). This same expression is used by Basil of Caesarea, *On the Holy Spirit,* 19.49.
Basil, too, is resistant to any numbering of the trinitarian persons in the way of plurality.
He writes, "If we count, we do *not* add, increasing from one to many [ἀφ' ἑνὸς εἰς
πλῆθος]. We do not say, 'one, two, three,' or 'first, second, and third.' God says, 'I am
the first and I am the last.' We have never to this present day heard of a second God. We
worship God from God [Θεὸν ἐκ Θεοῦ], confessing the uniqueness of the persons [τὸ
ἰδιάζον τῶν ὑποστάσεων], while maintaining the unity of the Monarchy. We do not
divide divine knowledge [τὴν θεολογίαν] and scatter the pieces to the winds; we behold
[θεωρεῖσθαι] one Form [so to speak] united by the invariableness of the Godhead,
present in God the Father and God the Only-begotten. The Son is in the Father and the
Father in the Son; what the Father is, the Son is likewise and vice-versa—such is the
unity. As unique Persons, they are one and one; as sharing a common nature [τὸ κοινὸν
τῆς φύσεως], both are one." Basil of Caesarea, *On the Holy Spirit,* 18, 45; Anderson, 72;
emphasis original. This perspective suggests an issue that is complementary to the
filioque. If we are willing to say that the Spirit proceeds from the Father through the
Son, are we also willing to say that the Son is begotten by the Father in the Spirit? The
two questions seem to be inherent in one another. Basil and Gregory Nazianzen
emphasize the latter half of this question against those denying the Spirit's divinity.

external individual, but begotten in the Spirit who proceeds from the Father. In the Spirit, the relation between the Father and the Son is revealed to be an eternal and consubstantial fellowship; in the Spirit, the begotten Son remains internal to the Father's being and the Father internal to the Son. In other words, while the Father is the source of the Son's identity as the only begotten, the Spirit is the place in which the Son is and continues to be the only-begotten of the Father.

If the above interpretation is consistent with Gregory Nazianzen's trinitarian thought, then the relation between Eve's production and the Spirit's procession bears strong ecclesial connotations. Immediately following the familial imagery of Eve's and Seth's respective derivations from Adam, Gregory concludes this way: "For the present it will be suf-ficient for us to say just this: it is the Spirit in whom we worship [ἐν ᾧ προσκυνοῦμεν] and through whom we pray [δι' οὗ προσευχόμεθα]."[53] Here Gregory is on more familiar ground as he travels a well-worn path paved by others especially his friend Basil of Caesarea. In his work *On the Holy Spirit*, Basil expounds on the preposition "ἐν," which is often associated with the Spirit. For Basil, the Spirit is the place or fellowship or light in which man's eyes are able to perceive Jesus as the icon of the Father. For Gregory, the Spirit as the place in which prayer and worship can take place is perhaps analogous to Eve as the one in whom Adam's generation of Seth is constituted.

This same line of thought is found again in Gregory's under-standing of Mary's place in the virgin birth. In his first letter to Cledonius,[54] Gregory rejects Apollinarian Christology. At the heart of this letter is a list of anathemas that express the core of Nazianzen's Christological thought. Significantly, Gregory begins with the virgin birth.

> If anyone does not accept holy Mary as *Theotokos* is divided from the Godhead (χωρὶς τῆς θεότητος). If anyone says that he was channeled (διαδραμεῖν) through the virgin, but not in her having been formed

---

[53] Gregory of Nazianzus, *Oration* 31.12; *On God and Christ*, 125.

[54] For the original Greek of Nazianzen's letters to Cledonius, see Gregoire de Nazianze, *Lettres Theologiques,* Sources Chrétiennes, vol. 208 (Paris: Les Editions du Cerf, 1974). For an English translation, see St. Gregory of Nazianzus, *On God and Christ* (Crestwood, NY: St. Vladimir's Seminary Press, 2002), 149–72.

(ἐν αὐτῇ διαπεπλάσθαι) both divinely and humanly (divinely, on the one hand, as apart from man, humanly, on the other hand, as with the law of conception), are similarly atheist. If anyone says the man has been formed (διαπεπλάσθαι τὸν ἄνθρωπον) then God put him on (ὑποδεδυκέναι), he is condemned. This is not the birth of God (γέννησις), but a fleeing from birth. If anyone brings in two sons, one from the God and Father, the second from the mother, but not one and the same, also fall away from the sonship (υἱοθεσίας) promised to those who believe in an orthodox way.... For both are one in the mixing (συγκράσει), God humanified (ἐνανθρωπήσαντος) and man deified (θεωθέντος), or however one should label it.[55]

Gregory is clearly against any attempt to divide the divinity from the humanity of Christ. However, this truth can perhaps be pushed a little further. For Gregory, there can now be no division between the eternal generation of the Son from the Father and the generation of his flesh from the Virgin Mary.[56] For Gregory, two separate births would imply two hypostases, that is, two independent modes of existence. The virgin birth is not merely a historical miracle that initiates the human narrative of Jesus; rather, Mary must be confessed as *Theotokos* precisely because her virginal womb is the place in which the flesh, derived from the virgin's own substance, is assumed into the Father's eternal generation of the Son. Her virginal womb is the place in which the "mixing" of God and man is permanently constituted. Thus, for Gregory, Mary is

---

[55] *First Letter to Cledonius*, 101, 5; author's translation. Cf. *NPNF²* 7:439; *On God and Christ*, 156–57.

[56] See Gregory Nazianzen's second letter to Cledonius, where he writes, "Since a question is being mooted concerning the divine "inmanning [ἐνανθρωπήσεως]," or "fleshing [σαρκώσεως]," you should [expressly] declare to all, in reference to ourselves, that we treat the Son of God begotten of the Father and thereafter of the Virgin Mary as a single item [τὸν γεννηθέντα ἐκ τοῦ Πατρὸς καὶ μετὰ τοῦτο ἐκ τῆς ἁγίας Παρθένου Μαρίας εἰς ἕν], and that we do not name two sons but worship one and the same Son in undivided Godhead and honor." Gregory of Nazianzus, *Second Letter to Cledonius*, 102.2; *On God and Christ*, 167. In this text, Gregory speaks of one begetting from the Father and *afterwards* from Mary. For Gregory, the humanity of Christ does not have a birth that is separate or independent from the Son's generation from the Father. It is precisely the Son's eternal generation from the Father that is manifested in the Virgin Mary and now includes the humanity taken from her within its own reality. For Nazianzen, two births would necessarily mean two sons or two separate *hypostases*—one generated from the Father and the other from Mary. Such a separation is the error of Nestorius, which compelled him to deny that Mary is *theotokos*.

the true mother in whom God is "humanified" and man is "deified." The baptismal overtones here are certainly evident. To divide the births, for Nazianzen, is to "fall away from the sonship or adoption promised to those who believe in an orthodox way." The baptismal water is the virginal womb, sanctified by the Spirit, in which the Father and his children are permanently and eternally joined.

In his third Theological Oration, Gregory considers the relationship between the Son's eternal generation from the Father and his birth from the virgin. For Gregory, the salvation of humanity depends upon the truth that these are not two separate and independent generations, but intimately bound together in one. "What he was, he remained [διέμεινεν]; what he was not, he assumed [προσέλαβεν]."[57] The assumption of humanity into the divine person of the Son is essential to the intimate exchange between God and humanity that is the very content of salvation. If the humanity of Jesus has a birth independent and separate from his divine Sonship, then the narrative of salvation is divided into two. Thus, Gregory argues, "He was born [ἐγεννήθη], but had also been begotten [ἐγεγέννητο]; on the one hand, from the woman, yet also a virgin. This one human in character [ἀνθρώπινον]; the other one divine [θεῖον]. This one without father [ἀπάτωρ], yet the other without mother [ἀμήτωρ]. The whole is of divinity [ὅλον τοῦτο θεότητος]."[58] For Gregory, the human nature is not merely an external addition to the Son of God; the Son's generation from Mary's body is not a foreign reality that remains outside the Son so that after the incarnation he is some kind of hybrid *hypostasis*. Rather, the *hypostasis* of the Son internalizes the human nature and its generation from the woman so completely that the divine Son remains a single whole. While the human essence has been assumed, the *hypostasis* of the Son remains what it has always been—the second person of the Trinity and the only begotten of the Father.

For Gregory, Jesus' *hypostatic* identification as the second person of the Trinity is a fundamental hermeneutic for the Christian reading of Scripture. The holistic unity of the Son means that the subject of the verbs throughout the Scriptures—the lowly human actions as well as the

---

[57] *Oration* 29.19; author's translation. Cf. *On God and Christ*, 86.
[58] *Oration* 29.19; author's translation. Cf. *On God and Christ*, 86.

divine—remains one and the same Son of God. The same one "was wrapped in swaddling clothes [ἐσπαργανώθη]," but also "took off the swathing bands of the grave by his rising again [ἀποσπαργανοῦται τὰ τῆς ταφῆς ἀνιστάμενος]."[59] In light of Gregory's trinitarian understanding, it seems evident that the Holy Spirit is the link connecting his eternal generation from the Father and his birth from the virgin. In the Spirit, his generation from the Father and his birth of the woman are united into a single, "whole [ὅλον]" reality. In the fellowship of the Spirit, humanity is assumed into the Son's own *hypostatic* relation to the Father. The ecclesial consequences of this perspective are equally clear. It is in the Spirit that the baptized are born of that humanity assumed by the Son in the womb of the Virgin and, thereby, incorporated into the Father's begetting of the Son. Only in this way can the baptized be called "children of God," not merely metaphorically, but truly. God's birth of a woman and humanity's generation from the heavenly Father have become one reality in Jesus and form the foundation for the salvific character of Baptism.

Conclusion: Gregory's Legacy?

For Gregory Nazianzen, there is a profound difference between images that humanity tries to impose upon God and images that God himself speaks into existence. It is for this reason that Gregory finally rejects most illustrations for God's trinitarian nature that are drawn from the created realm. All of them fall short of the true reality because they cannot represent the true character of the *hypostatic* communication in and through which the Father, Son, and Spirit subsist. The sun, the ray, and its light constitute an example of three things inherent in one another; however, they cannot represent the fullness or wholeness of communication that takes place in the Father's begetting of his Son. The wholeness of the sun as the source is simply not present in its rays, light, or warmth. All such illustrations fall short, not only because they are infinitely separated from God on the level of essence, but also because they lack a *hypostatic* subsistence. The sun, its ray, and its light are not persons.

---

[59] *Oration* 29.19; author's translation. Cf. *On God and Christ*, 86.

Thus, the one image Gregory employs is the production of Eve and Seth from Adam. Following the example of St. Paul and many Fathers before him, Gregory seems to recognize these human relations as constituting the image that God himself has spoken into existence. Like everything else in creation, humanity falls short of truly representing God on the level of essence. Essentially, God is fundamentally unknowable. Gender cannot be imposed upon God's essence any more than the qualities of the sun can be ascribed to the divine nature. However, humanity has subsisted from the beginning within *hypostatic* relations. This *hypostatic* subsistence allows humanity to experience the mutual communication, sacrifice, community, and love that characterize the life of the Holy Trinity. From the beginning, humanity is created, not with a transcendent authoritative Word, but from within a community of love. "Let us make man . . ." (Genesis 1:26). For the Early Church Fathers, the change from "let there be" to "let us make" represents a fundamental shift in the narrative of creation. This shift is then magnified in Genesis 2, where humanity is given life within a *hypostatic* community. The procession of Eve from the side of Adam and the generation of Seth from the two who are one establish the foundation for the narrative of God's self-revelation made perfect in the blood and water flowing from the side of the Crucified.

Therefore, Gregory Nazianzen testifies to the truth that the contemplation of the Trinity moved him naturally to immerse himself in anthropology, and the contemplation of anthropology moved him back into the contemplation of the Trinity. For Gregory, the connecting link is, of course, Christology. In Jesus, the fullness of God and the fullness of humanity are forever joined in the divine *hypostasis* of the Son. Yet, this joining is not the Son's act alone; it is a joining that originates from the Father and is perfected in the Spirit. Questions concerning the Son's divinity compelled fourth-century theologians to consider the relation between fathers and sons. Questions concerning the Spirit moved Gregory into a contemplation of the woman and her unique *hypostatic* place within the narrative of redemption. The Father's generation of children through his Son must take place in the Spirit. The Spirit is the setting or fellowship that is as essential to the Father's begetting as mothers are essential to the human family.

Gregory's bold assertion linking the Spirit's procession from the Father to Eve's derivation from Adam was a natural consequence of God's creation of humanity in his own image. While the theological connection between woman and the Spirit had roots in the patristic tradition,[60] it is an aspect of his argument that is not given much prominence in his orthodox successors. Gregory, the great hero of the Spirit's consubstantial divinity, left the Council of Constantinople in profound disappointment. While many bishops tacitly supported Gregory's confession of the Spirit's divinity, most disliked the *homoousion* language and were not willing to extend its use to the Spirit. Basil's caution and reserve won the day. Indeed, the council proved even more timid than Basil, confessing the Spirit as merely "conglorified" (συνδοξαζόμενον) with the Father and the Son. As John McGuckin points out, originally this language was chosen for its ambiguity.[61] Even Arians were content to confess Jesus as worthy of "conglorification" with the Father. The majority of bishops gathered at Constantinople refused to accept Nazianzen's bold confession that the Spirit is *homoousion* with the Father and the Son. Yet, the council even resisted the language of *homotimos* ("one and the same worship"), which Basil had used to confess the equality of honor shared by the Trinity.[62]

The distaste of fourth-century bishops for the language of *homoousias* makes their caution concerning the connection of the Spirit's procession to the production of Eve from Adam's side more understandable.[63] Eve, as image of the Spirit, effectively distinguished

---

[60] See *2 Clement* 14.1–5; Methodius of Olympus, *Banquet of the Ten Virgins*, Discourse 3.8.

[61] McGuckin, *St. Gregory of Nazianzus*, 367ff.

[62] Basil, *On the Holy Spirit* 15.32, 15.72, 15.79.

[63] There are some theologians who took up the idea of Eve as image of the Spirit. Concerning the connection between Eve and the Spirit, see Pseudo-Athanasius, *Quaestiones Allae*. In answer to the question of how the Spirit proceeds, the ancient author writes, "It is not fitting for you to ask concerning this; for this also is beyond exposition. Yet, you should learn also concerning this that as the breathing [ἡ ἀναποή] of man proceeds [ἐκπορεύεται] out of the soul, so also the Holy Spirit proceeds from the Father. Also just as Eve is neither begotten nor unbegotten, but midway between them [ἀλλὰ μέσως], so also the Holy Spirit proceeds from the Father. For Adam is unbegotten, but Seth is begotten, and Eve proceeds [ἐκπορευτή]. For Eve was neither begotten, as Seth was begotten, nor unbegotten as Adam. Rather, she proceeded from the side of Adam

"procession" from "begetting" and emphasized a relation that was fundamentally *homoousias* in character. Within the family, the woman is not merely a utilitarian vessel used by the father for the generation of children. Rather, the mother truly contributes to the generation in a way that makes her consubstantial with the child.[64] The obvious consub-

---

[ἐπορεύθη ἐκ τῆς πλευρᾶς τοῦ Ἀδάμ]. Indeed, unbegotten Adam is intended to be a type [εἰς τύπον] of the unbegotten Father; and begotten Seth is intended to be a type of the begotten Son; and Eve proceeding [ἐκπορευτή] from the side of Adam is intended to be a type of the All-holy Spirit [εἰς τύπον τοῦ παναγίου Πνεύματος]. For in our forefathers the Holy Trinity was typified [ἐτυπώθη]." Author's translation (*PG* 28:785). See also John of Damascus, where he writes, "For no other generation is like [ὁμοιοῦται] to the generation of the Son of God, since no other is Son of God. For though the Holy Spirit proceedeth from the Father, yet this is not generative in character but processional. This is a different mode of existence, alike incomprehensible and unknown, just as is the generation of the Son. Wherefore all the qualities the Father has are the Son's, save the Father is unbegotten, and this exception involves no difference in essence [οὐσίας διαφοράν] nor dignity [ἀξίωμα], but only a different mode of existence [τρόπον ὑπάρξεως]. We have an analogy in Adam, who was not begotten [ἀγέννητος] (for God Himself moulded [πλάσμα] him), and Seth, who was begotten [γεννητός], for he is Adam's son, and Eve, who proceeded [ἐκπορευθεῖσα] out of Adam's side [ἐκ τῆς τοῦ Ἀδὰμ πλευρᾶς], for she was not begotten. These do not differ from each other in nature [οὐ φύσει διαφέρουσιν], for they are human beings [ἄνθρωποι]: but they differ in the mode of existence [τῷ τῆς ὑπάρξεως τρόπῳ]." *De Fide Orthodoxa* 1, 8; *NPNF*[2] 9:8, second set of numbers (*PG* 94:816–817).

[64] John Chrysostom, who may have been influenced some by Gregory Nazianzen, certainly develops the idea of the family as image of the Holy Trinity: "And thus, the father, the mother, and the child are one flesh from the essential comingling [συνουσίας συγκραθεῖσα] of the two; for also the child is born from the mixing of the seeds [μιγέντων τῶν σπερμάτων] so that the three should be one flesh [τοὺς τρεῖς εἶναι μίαν σάρκα]. Thus, therefore, we are made one flesh with Christ through essential participation [διὰ μετουσίας], and we much more that the child. Why or in what way? Because it has been thus from the beginning [ἐξ ἀρχῆς]." *On the Epistle to the Ephesians,* Homily 20; author's translation (*PG* 62:139–40). Cf. *NPNF*[1] 13:146. See also Chrysostom's comments in his homily on Paul's letter to the Colossians, where he writes: "See the mystery of marriage [Εἶδες τοῦ γάμου τὸ μυστήριον]! He makes one out of one [ἐξ ἑνὸς ἕνα], and again of the two he makes one [καὶ πάλιν τοὺς δύο τούτους ἕνα ποιήσας] thus making one [οὕτω ποιεῖ ἕνα], so that now out of one a man is born [νῦν ἐξ ἑνὸς τίκτεται ἄνθρωπος]. For the woman and the man are not two men, but one man [ἄνθρωπος εἷς].... Indeed from the formation of her body [τῆς τοῦ σώματος διαπλάσεως] one can see that they are one; for she came from his side and they are two halves [ἀπὸ τῆς πλευρᾶς γέγονε καὶ ὥσπερ ἡμίτομα δύο εἰσί]. On account of this, she is called a helper [βοηθόν] in order that he might demonstrate that they are one; for on account of this, he honors their co-habitation even before being father and mother [πατρὸς καὶ μητρὸς προτιμᾷ τὴν συνοίκησιν] to display their oneness." John Chrysostom, *On the Epistle to the Colossians,* Homily 12, author's translation (*PG* 62:387–88). Cf. *NPNF*[1] 13:318–19.

stantial emphasis made this image less attractive to the bishops at Constantinople. Basil's diplomatic caution prevailed for the moment. However, Gregory's bold theology had the last and definitive word. It is a testament to the effectiveness of Gregory's argument that the Church, almost universally, now interprets the third article of the Nicene-Constantinopolitan Creed through Nazianzen's eyes as confessing the full divinity of the Spirit.[65]

Gregory Nazianzen testifies to the early Christian conviction that theology and anthropology are inseparable. In this testimony, Gregory is an heir of the four Gospels, the prophetic and apostolic witness, and the post-apostolic preaching of the Early Church. Irenaeus, bishop of Lyons in the second century, maintained that "the glory of God is the living man."[66] Gregory works out his trinitarian thought within the anthropological framework expressed in this aphorism. For Gregory, to expound upon the hypostatic relations in which the Holy Trinity subsists is to unveil the mystery of humanity's own subsistence. The doctrine of the Trinity is not a retreat into transcendent, philosophical speculation, but an immersion in the scriptural narrative and the mystery of humanity's likeness to God. This likeness does not operate on the level of essence, as if created being has anything in common with the eternal essence of the Creator; nor does this likeness merely consist in the external activities of the moral will. Rather, for Gregory humanity's likeness to God consists in the hypostatic mode of existence. The man and the woman do not merely procreate for the preservation of the species; rather, they are created to subsist in a community of love that acts as a "tabernacle" in which God's own being is manifested. Thus, for Nazianzen, the Christian theologian is meant to contemplate God from within a certain experience of being human, and humanity is to be understood from within the mystery of the Trinity.

Gregory Nazianzen's suggestion that the mystery of the Spirit's procession is reflected in the woman's hypostatic relation to Adam is an example of his anthropological theology. For Nazianzen, the doctrine of the Trinity is nothing other than the content of Christian Baptism. The Father's begetting of the Son is the reality in which Baptism is con-

---

[65] McGuckin, *St. Gregory of Nazianzus*, 367.

[66] Irenaeus, *Adversus Haereses*, iv, 20, 7; *ANF* 1:490.

stituted because both take place in the same setting. The Spirit, in whom the Father's begetting of the Son rests, is the same Spirit who descends upon the Virgin and joins with the waters of Baptism. In the Spirit, the baptized are incorporated into that humanity that has been assumed by the Son from Mary, put to death on the cross, and raised on the third day. The Spirit's hypostatic identity as the place or fellowship in which the Father generates children is an expression of Gregory's ecclesiology. The Spirit's place within the Godhead illuminates the Church's own hypostatic subsistence as virgin, bride, and mother. Yet, the converse is also true: the meaning of motherhood informs his contemplation of the scriptural narrative and his confession of the Holy Spirit as the "Lord and giver of life."[67]

The patristic witness, therefore, comes with a warning for the Church. The failure to connect theology and anthropology promises profound consequences for the Church's confession and mission. Indeed, at the end of this essay, I find myself asking several questions that need thoughtful investigation. Has the Church's historical timidity concerning the Spirit's consubstantial divinity led to an undeveloped pneumatology, inviting the charismatic overemphasis on the Spirit as working independent of the Father and the Son? Has this timidity also shaped the Church's ecclesiology? The clericalism of the Medieval Church tended to treat the lay congregation as merely a passive receptacle of clerical grace and, therefore, as non-essential to the Gospel. Finally, has this undeveloped pneumatology also led to an undeveloped understanding of woman in the image of God? The failure to develop the rich theological place accorded to the woman in the narrative of salvation has allowed the secular, psychosocial redefinition of the woman that prevails in our time. Our age desperately needs the Church and her theologians to rediscover the connection between anthropology and theology. The breakdown of the family is not merely a sociological problem, but a theological one. The broken world is

---

[67] McGuckin, *St. Gregory of Nazianzus*, 1ff. McGuckin's exceptional biography of Gregory Nazianzen shows that Gregory's mother, Nonna, had a central place in Nazianzen's theological and personal development. It would be worth considering in what way his reverence for his mother shaped his contemplation of Mary in the narrative of Scripture, of the Church in the economy of salvation, and of the Spirit in the fellowship of the Trinity.

calling the Church to recover her own identity as the family of God, that is, as the setting in which humanity is assumed into the theological fellowship of the Father, Son, and Holy Spirit.

THE BEAUTY OF HOLINESS

Scott R. Murray[1]

Dean Wenthe finds joy in the beauty of the Lord (Ps 27:4). He finds that beauty in many places. Those who, like me, had the pleasure of attending his classes at the seminary will remember the chortling pleasure he exhibited when he contemplated the joys of hithpael verbs. He would wax eloquent about the beauty of those Hebrew words. Wenthe recognizes that beauty is a gift of the Lord—a gift often unseen, unnoticed, and unappreciated by moderns. He sees that although we have become rich in things, we westerners suffer from poverty in the things of God. He grieves the ugliness of our culture under the influence of Enlightenment philosophy and its focus on the pursuit of truth in the human mind: "Cogito ergo sum." The Enlightenment project to find certainty and truth in the human mind runs aground on the Rock, who is God. Truth is limited to thinking, to the detriment of beauty in the world, beauty that comes from God and is related to who God is.

As his career advanced, Wenthe pleaded with the church to pay homage to God's beauty. He recognized that we humans have lost wisdom in a blizzard of information, as T. S. Eliot intoned in *The Rock*, where he ponders the loss of wisdom in a sea of knowledge and the loss of knowledge in an avalanche of information.[2] Oh yes, we know, but we fail to comprehend the whole story. We are failing to see the forest for the trees.

---

[1] Research for this article was provided by Vicar Christopher Nuttleman (CTSFW '14).

[2] T. S. Eliot, *The Waste Land and Other Poems* (New York: Harcourt, Brace and Co. 1934), 81.

Perhaps spooked by the avalanche of information with which we are inundated, we moderns have been handicapped by an acceptance of less. Once we reduce truth to human thought, a mere digestion of information, then there is a risk of narcissism, ending in horrifying solipsism. Of course, no one in the Christian community is expressly advocating this descent into the loss of God's greater and larger truth and its attendant wisdom. However, even academic communities, which ought to know better, are encouraging both less knowledge and less wisdom, rejecting essential language competence by suggesting that well-trained clergy might simply be ignorant of the Greek language.[3] If we are throwing overboard the first pillar of the trivium in our education, what will become of the wisdom that should follow it? So even though we still give lip service to the idea of truth, God's truth, perhaps we find ourselves too easily capitulating to fearful ignorance in the face of the power of mere information.[4]

There are, regrettably, noisy advocates in the Church for the worst in postmodernism, championing a relativistic definition of truth: "Your truth is your truth, but it may not be mine. Truth is what is true for you." This truth is unworthy of the name. Dean Wenthe rejects wholeheartedly this fear-filled reductionism by leading us back to first principles. Hithpaels are important after all. No wonder they are such a source of joy and beauty for him. Just as the Reformation sprang from the clear waters of the return *ad fontes*—back to the sources—so in our day, if the truth is to remain with us, we must return there again, resourcing ourselves with what is needed for a fullness of truth to dwell among us. Anything less has never been acceptable to Wenthe as a leader and a scholar.

We have been satisfied with less, insofar as we have not seen truth as a whole in our culture. This is also true of the Church to the extent that the Church is suffused by the culture that surrounds it instead of its own culture. The Church is literally its own cult that begins with the

---

[3] Martin Luther warns us: "In proportion then as we value the gospel, let us zealously hold to the languages" (AE 45:359).

[4] "Contemporary education therefore tends to the elimination of meaning—except in the sense of a meaning that we impose by force upon the world." Stratford Caldecott, *Beauty for Truth's Sake* (Grand Rapids: Brazos Press, 2009), 17.

First Commandment and with worship of the Holy Trinity. This cultus distinguishes it from the culture of the world, which is a cult of an entirely different kind. Learning must be suffused with wholeness from the Holy Trinity, revealed in Jesus Christ. The whole, then, is summed up in Christ. Here is the place where the doctrine of justification functions to tie the whole self-revelation of God to the work of this one person and to relate that whole self-revelation to the world. There is unity and wholeness in him (Colossians 2:8). There can be no gestalt apart from him (Colossians 1:17). Generic God-talk will never do. Only Christological fullness will tie everything together in the divine goal of saving sinners. Here is what Lutheran thinking can offer to the whole project to resource a revival of learning that includes with truth both beauty and wisdom. Center and edges are tied together only in Christ and his saving work. This Christological-salvific unity is what is truly catholic in thinking about the relationships among truth, beauty, and wisdom.[5]

The recovery of classical forms of education in the revival of the *trivium* certainly provides an eminent beginning for the renewal of Christian learning.[6] But an unwillingness to recover the quadrivium along with the trivium risks losing the point of reviving the trivium, as Stratford Caldecott argues. The trivium was intended to lead to the quadrivium, which consisted of arithmetic, geometry, astronomy, and music. Caldecott claims that the trivium had as its goal not only the contemplation of the theological and philosophical truths of higher learning, but also the recognition of the divine gift of beauty within the gestalt and its relationship with those truths. He criticizes Dorothy Sayers's failure to point from the trivium to the quadrivium in her highly influential "The Lost Tools of Learning."[7] As Caldecott points out, "the quadrivium is essential to a liberal education in the traditional

---

[5] Such an understanding is notably missing in a contemporary Roman Catholic like Angelo Scola. See "The Primordial Relationship between God and the Human Person in Catholicism and Islam," http://www.oasiscenter.eu/node/273, (accessed May 31, 2013).

[6] The trivium is made up of grammar, rhetoric, and logic. These are the elementary tools of learning that were impressed on the learner in medieval education.

[7] Dorothy Sayers, *A Matter of Eternity: Selections From the Writings of Dorothy L. Sayers*, ed. R. K. Sprague (London and Oxford: A. R. Mowbray, 1973).

sense."[8] The quadrivium gave the student access to the relation of number over time and space. This study was to seek the relations of numerical harmony in nature and prepared the student for philosophy as metaphysics. These then equipped the mind for the higher truths of philosophy and theology. As Hugh of St. Victor (d. AD 1141) wrote about the preparatory nature of the trivium and quadrivium, "For these, one might say, constitute the best instruments, the best rudiments, by which the way is prepared for the mind's complete knowledge of philosophic truth."[9] For Hugh, as for the Greeks, philosophic truth included theology. Already with the sharp distinction between philosophy and theology posited by Aquinas in the thirteenth century and the advent of Franciscan nominalism, the universities saw a splintering of the unity of knowledge. According to Caldecott, the unity of trivium and quadrivium were only fully realized in the cathedrals, where learning was put to the service of the liturgy in wholeness of life lived under the Holy Trinity, and not in the universities. In the cathedrals "the sacred sciences of the *quadrivium* were expressed in massed stone and statuary, rose windows and labyrinths, and in the interplay between light, music, and sacramental gesture."[10]

While we are seeing a revival of the trivium in our classical schools,[11] that will not be sufficient to reassert the wholeness and unity of knowledge. The habits of mind that seek for all the gifts of the created world that God has embedded there must be cultivated in students who have been impoverished by the technological turn taken by much of western education today. As Caldecott says,

> The purpose of an education is not merely to communicate information, let alone current scientific opinion, nor to train future workers and managers. It is to teach the ability to think, discriminate, speak,

---

[8] Caldecott, *Beauty for Truth's Sake*, 23.

[9] Hugh of St. Victor, *The Didascalicon*, trans. Jerome Taylor (New York and London: Columbia University Press, 1961), 87.

[10] Caldecott, *Beauty for Truth's Sake*, 27.

[11] Memorial Lutheran School, Houston, Texas, is in the never ending process of reviving the trivium. The school is seeing growth in knowledge and improvement in test scores. Those who are interested in reviving truly liberal education, that is, education that is freeing, should see the work of the Consortium for Classical Lutheran Education (www.ccle.org).

and write, and, along with this, the ability to perceive the inner, connecting principles, the intrinsic relations, the *logoi*, of creation, which the ancient Christian Pythagorean tradition (right through the medieval period) understood in terms of number and cosmic harmony.[12]

While Lutherans might well be uncertain as to how this would look in particular instances, the search for it in a proper education will always be a part of true learning. Truth and beauty must not be separated. Theology has something to say to us about the meaning of the world. He who is the truth incarnate can also deliver to us the tools to see the beauty he has placed in the world.

The fracturing of knowledge into various unrelated disciplines has caused anxiety not only among Christian thinkers but also among secularists like Allan Bloom.[13] Caldecott argues that the unity of knowledge is beauty.[14] Unfortunately, he also posits that everything in some way or respect partakes of beauty. This is untenable, given the depravity that accrues to the world by means of the fall. What God has meant to be truly good (Genesis 1–3), and therefore beautiful, has been bent, that is, perverted from God's purposes and put at the service of what is ugly or lacking in beauty, as Augustine would have it. Beauty would be the unity of all right thought. Beauty still accrues to what is truly God's in the world, but the lack of righteousness and holiness also lacks beauty.

But perhaps this is all a non-biblical construct. What does God's Word say of the relationship between holiness and beauty? Καλός is used nearly 600 times in the Septuagint to translate טוב. This translation leads many to question the very category of beauty in the Hebrew mind.[15] Hebrew culture had no room for a Hellenized, platonic ideal of beauty. The Greek ideal of life is couched in terms of Καλός and ἀγαθός, but for the Hebrew, life (while also being conceived generally as more substantial than ideal) is of the רוח יהוה, the breath of the Lord

---

[12] Caldecott, *Beauty for Truth's Sake*, 28.

[13] Allan Bloom, *The Closing of the American Mind* (New York: Simon and Schuster, 1987).

[14] Caldecott, *Beauty for Truth's Sake*, 31.

[15] Καλός, *Theological Dictionary of the New Testament*, 10 vols., ed. G. Kittel and G. Friedrich, trans. G. W. Bromiley (Grand Rapids: Eerdmans, 1964–76), 3:544.

(Ezekiel 37, Genesis 2; see especially Genesis 7:22). We have already said that we cannot distinguish moral good from the beautiful. They exhibit an interpenetrating relationship, each embodying the other.

Καλός is commonly employed for טוב in moral situations, where 'the beautiful' equates to "the good." Just as breath is from God and Torah is from God, so beauty is from God. Something is beautiful only regarding its place in God's created order.[16] Beauty is integrated into creation under God's Law. The beautiful was often conceived of as what we might call merely the "fitting."[17] This partly explains its limited use as a concept.

For the Hebrew, beauty is not the exception, but the rule—truly, it is the Torah. Just as the Bible does not conceive of life as its own reality, unowed to God, even so it does not see beauty apart from his will and ordering. The Old Testament does indeed dwell on the beauty of things as they are placed by God in his creation. Beauty can and is corrupted into evil and ugliness—beauties become pigs (Proverbs 11:22)—when it is unhinged from the creative intent. Where this divine intention is most visible and audible is in the precinct of praise and salvation, the temple (1 Chronicles 16:29; Psalm 29:2; 96:9). Beauty and truth are deeply liturgical. The Spirit of God inspired the tabernacle artists, and what their hands made was meant to inspire in turn. A betrayal of beauty is a step toward betraying the justifying God and a breach of the First Commandment. We are to think about God and his beauty because he has revealed himself in his Word and in his world. We are not merely to feel beauty but to know it, and so we must educate and lead the educated into knowing beauty, an effort sorely lacking at all levels of education today, squirreled away in art and music departments on the edges of college curricula or in extra-curricular programs.

Our difficulty in identifying beauty and distinguishing it from its lack has led postmodernists to argue that there is no difference between the beautiful and the ugly. Present fashion fads confirm this judgment; just consider the ubiquitous piercings and tattoos. But who, given the

---

[16] See Nathan Jastram, "Man as Male and Female: Created in the Image of God," *Concordia Theological Quarterly* (January 2004): 5–96.

[17] William A. Dyrness, "Aesthetics in the Old Testament: Beauty in Context," *Journal of the Evangelical Theological Society* 28, no. 4 (December 1, 1985): 422.

choice between looking at a beautiful sunset and looking into a cesspool, will say that he would prefer to look into a cesspool? No one. Why is that? No one would argue that they are equally beautiful, even if they might be hard pressed to state precisely why. If beauty is an attribute of God, we begin to see why humans created in his image might be attracted to that which is more beautiful and not attracted to that which is less beautiful. The psalmist connects the worship experience with the experience of the beauty of God: "One thing I ask of the LORD, this is what I seek: that I may dwell in the house of the LORD all the days of my life, to gaze upon the beauty of the LORD and to seek him in his temple" (Psalm 27:4). The Hebrew word translated here as "beauty" also means pleasantness and the favor of God, and thus is not far from the meaning of grace; it is in the same semantic domain. Perhaps grace could be thought of as God's beauty in action.

When we contemplate the beauty of God, we are not thinking of mere appearance. We are not talking about skin-deep beauty. With God we are talking about beauty pure and simple: the beauty of holiness, beauty in its very essence. See how we grope when we try to speak of God's attributes! We have no experience of such things unalloyed by our creatureliness and sin. So our groping for God through the attracttion of beautiful things is either only a faint hint of his existence and character or merely a byway in which our speculation traps us and makes us subject to the creation rather than children of the Creator. These are the elemental things of the world, created for our blessedness, signs of God, but not a sure revelation of the divine character. This is why we must begin with words in the trivium and move on to beauty in the quadrivium; only then can we approach theology itself.

The aesthete worships beauty; its objects are the things of this world, many of them visible. But what makes the thing that is seen superior to the instruments of the body and mind that perceive such things? How is a beautiful sunset a clearer intimation of God's character than the eye that sees it? The eye was created by God to perceive beauty and thus has priority over the things of beauty themselves, because humans are the foremost creatures of God. Humans can partake of the beauty of holiness because they are gifted with it by the One who is himself beauty and holiness.

The perfect beauty of holiness comes to us in the person of God's Son. Even though "his appearance was so marred, beyond human semblance, and his form beyond that of the children of mankind" (Isaiah 52:14), he was the most beautiful because his beauty was placed at the service of that same mankind that thought him marred and was, in fact, the cause of it. His cross is the key that unlocks all the beauty in the world and tells us that it belongs to God. Mere prettiness is silenced by the beauty of the man born of a peasant mother, who shoulders the world's sin, offers his face to the mockers and his back to the smiters, and is nailed to the ugliest sign of beauty: the cross of Christ. Caldecott has it right when he says that the place where all important questions are answered for Christians is in the cross, although Lutherans would argue that this is true for all persons, not just for Christians (John 14:6). The hymn confronts us with this truth: "Jesus, Thy blood and righteousness / My beauty are, my glorious dress" (*LSB* 563:1). Such gory beauty! It becomes us well unto salvation. Here is the beauty of holiness. No wonder that the medieval church building was cruciform in shape; it evokes the beauty of Christ's holiness. Here is the beauty of holiness and the holiness of beauty.

JESUS: THE SECOND AND GREATER ADAM[1]

Thomas J. Egger

In countless ways, our lives are interwoven with the lives of others. Other people have shaped my personal history, impacted my daily work and well-being, and held sway over my future prospects. The ingenuity of Thomas Edison or Steve Jobs, the poet or musician who summons sublime stirrings in the heart, the broken car window and emptied glove box left by a faceless thief, the patient reminders of a mother teaching her child etiquette—every human life is profoundly affected by hundreds and even thousands of others.

This festschrift honors Dean Wenthe for the ways in which he has enriched our lives with his indefatigable and ever-cheerful labor in the cause of confessional Lutheranism. As an exegete, I have been moved by Dean's persistent summons to hear the Scriptural story of the incarnate Christ in all its sublimity, goodness, richness, and beauty—and to live in this story and in this Lord. As a father, friend, pastor, professor, and seminary president, Dean has influenced and benefitted so many.

The present essay expounds the work of two individuals who have a direct and defining impact upon *every* person in the world, every member of the human family throughout history. The first is Adam, the father of us all. The second is Jesus Christ.

In Adam we glimpse the goodness and the greatness that God intended for human creatures. Yet we only glimpse these, because Adam spoils them for all humankind, forfeiting them in the first moments of

---

[1] A version of this article appeared in *Modern Reformation* 22, no. 6 (November/December 2013): 40–45.

the world. In Christ, we behold a second and greater Adam, the restorer of human goodness and greatness. What Adam squandered in a moment, the second Adam regains for all and bestows forever. As Paul writes: "As one trespass led to condemnation for all men, so one act of righteousness leads to justification and life for all men" (Romans 5:18).

HEARING VOICES

Adam's act of disobedience and Jesus' act of obedience may at first seem like apples and oranges, or at least like apples and something else. Adam ate forbidden fruit. Jesus gave himself over to crucifixion. Some hymns and prayers connect these actions together around the theme of a tree: "On the tree of the cross you gave salvation to mankind that, whence death arose, thence life might also rise again and that he who by a tree once overcame likewise by a tree might be overcome."[2]

The Genesis narrative presents a more fundamental connection between Adam's disobedience and Christ's obedience: the theme of trusting the Word of God. In Genesis 3, the serpent speaks: "Did God really say?" and "You will not surely die." Eve listens to the serpent's voice, and she trusts the testimony of her own eyes. She eats, and so does Adam.

They hide, and God comes seeking. He calls to Adam, "Where are you?" Then he asks, "Who told you that you were naked? Have you eaten from the tree of which I commanded you not to eat?" God climactically addresses Adam: "Because you have listened to the voice of your wife, and have eaten of the tree of which I commanded you, 'You shall not eat of it,' cursed is the ground because of you." Adam abandons the clear word of God and prefers instead the voice of his wife, which, in this case, channels the voice of the ancient serpent himself. Luther writes: "All this is the old devil and the old serpent who made enthusiasts of Adam and Eve. He led them from the external Word of God to spiritualizing and to their own imaginations" (SA III 8 5).

Not so the second Adam. Jesus entrusts himself wholly to the Father's will and word. When the "old snake" tempts Jesus in the wilderness—to live by bread rather than by God's Word, to avoid the

---

[2] *Lutheran Worship* (St. Louis: Concordia, 1982), 147.

cross and to seek rule and renown in another way—Jesus recites the written, prophetic Word of God. Three times, he entrusts himself to the voice of God in Holy Scripture. "Be gone, Satan!" he says. "For it is written . . ." (Matthew 4:10).

As his Passion drew nearer, Jesus knew that he must "go as it is written of him . . . that the Scriptures of the prophets might be fulfilled" (Matthew 26:24, 56). He "must go to Jerusalem and suffer many things . . . and be killed, and on the third day be raised." With vigor and faithful-sounding rhetoric, Peter rebukes Jesus: "Far be it from you, Lord! This shall never happen to you." And Jesus replies to Peter, "Get behind me, Satan! You are not setting your mind on the things of God, but on the things of man" (Matthew 16:21–23). Precisely where Adam failed, Jesus prevails.

DEATH TO ALL, LIFE TO ALL

Adam is the first human. He stands in a unique relation to all other humans. Even Eve, the mother of us all, was taken from him. Like her, every man and woman who has come after is "flesh of his flesh, and bone of his bone." Adam's very name suggests this: the Hebrew word *adam* (אָדָם) is both his proper name as well as the generic noun meaning "human, humanity." And the Genesis narrative makes clear that Adam is the father of every nation of the world.

For this reason, when Adam disobeyed the single command of God, the devastating consequences extended not only to himself but also, through him, to the entire human lineage. When Adam defied God, he brought corruption, death, and divine judgment to all. He whom God blessed and intended to be fruitful and multiply and fill the earth with human goodness and life instead will now be fruitful and multiply and fill the earth with human wickedness and death.

Adam, however, is not the only man who stands in a direct and defining relationship to all humanity. When the Son of God came down from heaven and, incarnate by the Holy Spirit of the Virgin Mary, was made man, he shared in the same human nature as all of us. God sent him out of love for all humanity (John 3:16). But Jesus' direct relationship with mankind consists especially in this: that the Lord laid on him the iniquity of us all (Isaiah 53:6). He is the Lamb of God who takes away the sins of the world (John 1:29). He is the propitiation for the sins of the whole world (1 John 2:2). Like Adam, Jesus Christ thus stands in direct relation to every human. Adam sinned and bequeathed sin and death to all. In turn, Jesus takes upon himself the sin and death of all and bestows instead the gift of eternal life.

LIFE FROM DUST, TWICE

But this promise of eternal life—a deeply human, bodily eternal life— strains credulity within sight of the graves and cemeteries which dot the earth, with their grisly, decomposing counter-evidence. So it was that when Paul preached the resurrection of the dead, most Greeks thought it a foolish notion. Impossible. "How are the dead raised? With what kind of body do they come?" (1 Corinthians 15:35).

To Christians, who confess the resurrection of the body, Paul's reply may seem strange:

> It is sown a natural body [NRSV reads "physical body"], it is raised a spiritual body. . . . Just as we have borne the image of the man of dust [Adam], we shall also bear the image of the man of heaven [Christ]. . . . Flesh and blood cannot inherit the kingdom of God, nor does the perishable inherit the imperishable (1 Corinthians 15:44, 49–50).

Paul's logic is grounded in the Genesis account of Adam's creation: God formed Adam from the dust of the ground and then breathed into his nostrils the breath of life. But a tragic irony follows, involving Adam's name. *Adam* derives from the Hebrew word *adamah* (אֲדָמָה), meaning "earth, ground." It was God's intention that *Adam*, who was taken from the *adamah* (Genesis 2:7) should joyfully cultivate the *adamah* (2:5) and exercise dominion over all the other creatures upon the face of the *adamah*—creatures which God had also formed from the *adamah* (1:28; 2:19). Instead, because of the sin of *Adam*, God curses the *adamah* with thorns and thistles (3:17) and declares to *Adam* that he (and we) must die and return to the *adamah* (3:19).

So how can the dead be raised? What kind of bodies would they have after they have returned to dirt and dust? In answer, Paul pro-claims Jesus Christ as a second man (1 Corinthians 15:47) and as the

Last Adam (15:45). Adam forfeited his status as a truly "living being," enlivened by God's breath, but Christ comes as the "life-giving spirit" (1 Corinthians 15:45) to revive Adam and all his believing children. Yes, we expect Jesus to vivify our bodies from the dusty graves of the *adamah*—Paul argues by subtle allusion—because our God has done this before, namely, on the sixth day of creation when he gave life to "the man of dust." It is not a foolish hope. It is not impossible. The Last Adam, the man from heaven, will breathe life into lifeless dust once more, and our bodies will be raised—honorable, glorious, and imperishable.

Appearing after his resurrection, Jesus invites, "See my hands and my feet, that it is I myself. Touch me, and see. For a spirit does not have flesh and bones as you see that I have" (Luke 24:39). In the resurrection, we will be like Christ, no longer sharing the dust-destiny of Adam, but only the heavenly destiny of Christ. Yet it will still be a human, bodily, flesh-and-blood existence. *Perishable* flesh cannot inherit the kingdom of God, but the Last Adam will raise our flesh and blood *imperishable*. Luther writes,

> Then we shall have the same form and essence which he now has since his resurrection. . . . The entire body will be as pure and bright as the sun and as light as the air, and, finally, so healthy, so blissful, and filled with such heavenly, eternal joy in God that it will never hunger, thirst, grow weary, or decline.[3]

GOODNESS LOST, GOODNESS RESTORED

After his sin, Adam's true identity and nature become horribly disfigured. His sin has been wildly transformative. He is exposed in nakedness and covered in shame. He dreads the presence of God. Though Adam and Eve were created in the image of God himself, in his likeness, corrupt Adam now fathers sons "in his own likeness, after his image" (Genesis 5:3). Adam's offspring starkly display this transformation. His firstborn son, Cain, envies and slays his own brother, and Cain's descendent Lamech waxes poetic about his own exponential brutality.

---

[3] Martin Luther, "Commentary on 1 Corinthians 15," AE 28:196.

By Genesis 6, God sees that "all flesh had corrupted their way on the earth" and that the earth was "filled with violence through them."

Of all the theological implications of the biblical Adam, this is the dimension most highlighted by the Reformers. Luther describes the impact of Adam's sin upon our nature as the "Old Adam" in us who, he writes in the Large Catechism, "is born in us from Adam, irascible, spiteful, envious, unchaste, greedy, lazy, proud, yes, and unbelieving; he is beset with all vices and by nature has nothing good in him (LC IV 65–66)." The Augsburg Confession states that

> since the fall of Adam all men who are propagated according to nature are born in sin. That is to say, they are without fear of God, are without trust in God, and are concupiscent. This disease or vice of origin is truly sin, which even now damns and brings eternal death on those who are not born again through Baptism and the Holy Spirit (AC II 1–2).

Humankind, created in the image and likeness of the holy God, the God of goodness and love, has become a parody of their original selves—and a mockery of the God who created them

Enter the second Adam, who is himself "the image of the invisible God" (Colossians 1:15). Christ bears God's image both as the eternal divine Son sent by the Father and also as a true man, who in his humanity incarnates the original image of God in man and who restores this image in all who believe. C. F. W. Walther once preached:

> Christ not only wants to forgive all men their sins, but also to free them from their sins. He not only wants to declare them righteous by grace, but he also wants to make them truly righteous. He not only came to comfort and soothe their hearts, but also to cleanse and sanctify them. He came not only to reconcile them with God, but also to reunite them with God, not only to make them acceptable to God, but to make them like God. In short, he came to restore the entire lost image of God in them. He came to lead them back into the state of innocence, to make them perfectly healthy in body and soul, and thus finally to bring them to the blessed goal for which God destined them from eternity and called them into existence.[4]

---

[4] *Select Sermons of Walther*, trans. E. Myers (St. Louis: Hope Press, 1966), 23ff.

Already now, through his Word and Sacraments, Christ is restoring the image of God—Christ's own image—in those who believe. Just as Adam's trespass engendered an Adam-like train of violence, strife, and suffering, so Christ's obedient death for sinners is followed by a train of Christ-like fruit in the world: compassion, reconciliation, generosity, hospitality, justice, and above all, trust in God. Still, in this life, Christ's restoration of the image of God in us is a mere beginning. Again, Walther:

> Here Christians have only the first-fruits of Christ's harvest.... The time of full maturity comes only with eternal life. But blessed are all Christians! The time will surely come. As Christ ... restored the deaf-mute not only in part but completely, so he will also restore in the world to come the image of God in which they were originally created in all who truly believe in him. Yes, there by his grace the redeemed will shine more gloriously than they would have had they not fallen.[5]

A FORMER DOMINION AND GREATNESS—LOST

How different things once were. In the day that God created all things and declared them good, the first Adam stood as unique among God's creatures, the pinnacle and lord of all the rest.

> The divine breath of life is breathed into him alone; the command and prohibition of God is given to him alone; he has to name the animals, i.e., he is their lord (Gen. 2). He almost has divine position; the earth with all its creatures is subject to him (Ps. 8). God created him in his image ..., and gave him dominion (Gen. 1:26–28).[6]

Luther suggests that, before sin,

> [Adam's] intellect was the clearest, his memory was the best, and his will was the most straightforward—all in the most beautiful tranquility of mind, without any fear of death and without any anxiety. To these inner qualities came also those most ... superb qualities of body and of all the limbs, qualities in which he surpassed all

---

[5] *Select Sermons of Walther*, 23ff.

[6] Fritz Maass, " *'adhām*," *Theological Dictionary of the Old Testament*, 15 vols., ed. G. Johannes Botterweck and Helmer Ringgren, trans. John T. Willis (Grand Rapids: Eerdmans, 1974–2006), 1:84.

the remaining living creatures. I am fully convinced that before Adam's sin his eyes were so sharp and clear that they surpassed those of the lynx and eagle. He was stronger than the lions and the bears, whose strength is very great; and he handled them the way we handle puppies.[7]

In our fallen state and disordered world, it is difficult to comprehend or imagine the glorious, exalted creatures we were created to be. God gave Adam and Eve "dominion over the fish of the sea and over the birds of the heavens and over every living thing that moves on the earth" (Genesis 1:28). But since the Fall, everything is different. Pestered by mosquitoes and gnats, cringing before barking dogs, stalked by lions and wolves, oppressed by heat and cold, starved by drought and locust, devastated by storms and floods, drowned by raging seas, humankind restlessly scratches out its daily bread by the sweat of the brow amid thorns and thistles.

In our modern health-obsessed culture, we imagine that we at least have dominion over our own bodies; but in truth, even this little domain escapes our will and rule, invaded by pathogens, taunted by obesity, debilitated by injury, and, finally, destroyed and disintegrated by death. Ever since the day when Adam colluded with the serpent to invert the dominion of humanity over other living things, man has groaned—and all creation with him. The whole creation longs for the restoration of humanity's dominion, the greatness that Adam lost.

DOMINION AND GREATNESS REGAINED

In restoring us to the image of God, Jesus has regained not only humanity's original goodness, but also humanity's original greatness and dominion. Lutherans have not always accented this dimension of the Gospel and, at first, it may seem to run against the grain of Scripture's warnings regarding human pride: "The haughty looks of man shall be brought low, and the lofty pride of men shall be humbled, and the Lord alone shall be exalted in that day" (Isaiah 2:11). "Put not your trust in princes, in a son of man, in whom there is no salvation. When his breath departs he returns to the earth; on that very day his plans perish"

---

[7] Luther, *Commentary on Genesis*, AE 1:62.

(Psalm 146:3–4). All such passages, however, reference humanity after the Fall—a corrupt, dying, impotent, and groundlessly boastful race. As such, the Law of God reveals to us our true present standing: we are low, weak, shameful, damnable.

But from the womb of Mary has come a second Adam. This new Adam exercises true dominion over the seas, over the fish, over the fig tree, over disease, over the angels and the demons. "Who is this, then, that even wind and sea obey him?" Jesus' disciples ask (Mark 4:41). And the answer is not merely, "*This is God*, in human flesh," but also, "This is God, *in human flesh!*" A second Adam has come to restore the human dominion and greatness that Adam lost in Eden.

Jesus has promised that when he comes again at the end of this age, the present disordered creation will be rolled up like a garment, refined, purified, renewed and reconstituted—and humankind will reign. It is true that the Lord alone will be exalted on that day and that the eternal kingship will belong to God and to the Lamb forever and ever. To his anointed Son, God declares, "Ask of me, and I shall give you the nations for your inheritance, and for your possession the ends of the earth, and you shall rule them with a rod of iron" (Psalm 2:9–10a).[8]

Yet the one given this dominion is the *man* Jesus Christ, the second Adam. God will "judge the world in righteousness by a *man* whom he has appointed," Paul announces (Acts 17:31).

In Christ, God has appointed a *man* as the judge, heir, and Lord over his creation, and he will restore humankind to its former greatness and dominion as co-judges, co-heirs, and co-regents with Christ. Paul writes, "Do you not know that the saints will judge the world? . . . Do you not know that we are to judge angels?" (1 Corinthians 6:2–3). "They shall inherit the earth," Jesus says about the blessed people of his kingdom (Matthew 5:5). "If we endure we will also reign with him," Paul writes (2 Timothy 2:12), and John hears Jesus himself declaring, "The one who conquers, I will grant him to sit with me on my throne" (Revelation 3:21).

With joy we will superintend the new earth and all its creatures. "And there shall no longer be any curse" (Revelation 22:3 NASB), and

---

[8] Author's translation, relying on the Septuagint.